M000286483

Apache HTTP Server 2.4 Reference Manual 2/3

A catalogue record for this book is available from the Hong Kong Public Libraries.

Published in Hong Kong by Samurai Media Limited.

Email: info@samuraimedia.org

ISBN 978-988-8381-80-7

Background Cover Image by https://www.flickr.com/people/webtreatsetc/

Contents

Chapter 10

Apache modules

10.1 Terms Used to Describe Modules

This document describes the terms that are used to describe each Apache module (p. 1025) .

Description

A brief description of the purpose of the module.

Status

This indicates how tightly bound into the Apache Web server the module is; in other words, you may need to recompile the server in order to gain access to the module and its functionality. Possible values for this attribute are:

MPM A module with status "MPM" is a Multi-Processing Module (p. 80) . Unlike the other types of modules, Apache must have one and only one MPM in use at any time. This type of module is responsible for basic request handling and dispatching.

Base A module labeled as having "Base" status is compiled and loaded into the server by default, and is therefore normally available unless you have taken steps to remove the module from your configuration.

Extension A module with "Extension" status is not normally compiled and loaded into the server. To enable the module and its functionality, you may need to change the server build configuration files and re-compile Apache.

Experimental "Experimental" status indicates that the module is available as part of the Apache kit, but you are on your own if you try to use it. The module is being documented for completeness, and is not necessarily supported.

External Modules which are not included with the base Apache distribution ("third-party modules") may use the "External" status. We are not responsible for, nor do we support such modules.

Source File

This quite simply lists the name of the source file which contains the code for the module. This is also the name used by the <IFMODULE> directive.

Module Identifier

This is a string which identifies the module for use in the LOADMODULE directive when dynamically loading modules. In particular, it is the name of the external variable of type module in the source file.

Compatibility

If the module was not part of the original Apache version 2 distribution, the version in which it was introduced should be listed here. In addition, if the module is limited to particular platforms, the details will be listed here.

10.2 Terms Used to Describe Directives

This document describes the terms that are used to describe each Apache configuration directive (p. 1030) .

See also

- Configuration files (p. 30)

Description

A brief description of the purpose of the directive.

Syntax

This indicates the format of the directive as it would appear in a configuration file. This syntax is extremely directive-specific, and is described in detail in the directive's definition. Generally, the directive name is followed by a series of one or more space-separated arguments. If an argument contains a space, the argument must be enclosed in double quotes. Optional arguments are enclosed in square brackets. Where an argument can take on more than one possible value, the possible values are separated by vertical bars "—". Literal text is presented in the default font, while argument-types for which substitution is necessary are *emphasized.* Directives which can take a variable number of arguments will end in "..." indicating that the last argument is repeated.

Directives use a great number of different argument types. A few common ones are defined below.

URL A complete Uniform Resource Locator including a scheme, hostname, and optional pathname as in `http://www.example.com/path/to/file.html`

URL-path The part of a *url* which follows the scheme and hostname as in `/path/to/file.html`. The *url-path* represents a web-view of a resource, as opposed to a file-system view.

file-path The path to a file in the local file-system beginning with the root directory as in `/usr/local/apache/htdocs/path/to/file.html`. Unless otherwise specified, a *file-path* which does not begin with a slash will be treated as relative to the ServerRoot (p. 354) .

directory-path The path to a directory in the local file-system beginning with the root directory as in `/usr/local/apache/htdocs/path/to/`.

filename The name of a file with no accompanying path information as in `file.html`.

regex A Perl-compatible regular expression. The directive definition will specify what the *regex* is matching against.

extension In general, this is the part of the *filename* which follows the last dot. However, Apache recognizes multiple filename extensions, so if a *filename* contains more than one dot, each dot-separated part of the filename following the first dot is an *extension*. For example, the *filename* `file.html.en` contains two extensions: `.html` and `.en`. For Apache directives, you may specify *extensions* with or without the leading dot. In addition, *extensions* are not case sensitive.

MIME-type A method of describing the format of a file which consists of a major format type and a minor format type, separated by a slash as in `text/html`.

env-variable The name of an environment variable (p. 82) defined in the Apache configuration process. Note this is not necessarily the same as an operating system environment variable. See the environment variable documentation (p. 82) for more details.

Default

If the directive has a default value (*i.e.*, if you omit it from your configuration entirely, the Apache Web server will behave as though you set it to a particular value), it is described here. If there is no default value, this section should say "*None*". Note that the default listed here is not necessarily the same as the value the directive takes in the default httpd.conf distributed with the server.

Context

This indicates where in the server's configuration files the directive is legal. It's a comma-separated list of one or more of the following values:

server config This means that the directive may be used in the server configuration files (*e.g.*, `httpd.conf`), but **not** within any <VIRTUALHOST> or <DIRECTORY> containers. It is not allowed in `.htaccess` files at all.

virtual host This context means that the directive may appear inside <VIRTUALHOST> containers in the server configuration files.

directory A directive marked as being valid in this context may be used inside <DIRECTORY>, <LOCATION>, <FILES>, <IF>, and <PROXY> containers in the server configuration files, subject to the restrictions outlined in Configuration Sections (p. 33) .

.htaccess If a directive is valid in this context, it means that it can appear inside *per*-directory `.htaccess` files. It may not be processed, though depending upon the overrides currently active.

The directive is *only* allowed within the designated context; if you try to use it elsewhere, you'll get a configuration error that will either prevent the server from handling requests in that context correctly, or will keep the server from operating at all – *i.e.*, the server won't even start.

The valid locations for the directive are actually the result of a Boolean OR of all of the listed contexts. In other words, a directive that is marked as being valid in "`server config, .htaccess`" can be used in the `httpd.conf` file and in `.htaccess` files, but not within any <DIRECTORY> or <VIRTUALHOST> containers.

Override

This directive attribute indicates which configuration override must be active in order for the directive to be processed when it appears in a `.htaccess` file. If the directive's context doesn't permit it to appear in `.htaccess` files, then no context will be listed.

Overrides are activated by the ALLOWOVERRIDE directive, and apply to a particular scope (such as a directory) and all descendants, unless further modified by other ALLOWOVERRIDE directives at lower levels. The documentation for that directive also lists the possible override names available.

Status

This indicates how tightly bound into the Apache Web server the directive is; in other words, you may need to recompile the server with an enhanced set of modules in order to gain access to the directive and its functionality. Possible values for this attribute are:

Core If a directive is listed as having "Core" status, that means it is part of the innermost portions of the Apache Web server, and is always available.

MPM A directive labeled as having "MPM" status is provided by a Multi-Processing Module (p. 80) . This type of directive will be available if and only if you are using one of the MPMs listed on the Module line of the directive definition.

Base A directive labeled as having "Base" status is supported by one of the standard Apache modules which is compiled into the server by default, and is therefore normally available unless you've taken steps to remove the module from your configuration.

Extension A directive with "Extension" status is provided by one of the modules included with the Apache server kit, but the module isn't normally compiled into the server. To enable the directive and its functionality, you will need to change the server build configuration files and re-compile Apache.

Experimental "Experimental" status indicates that the directive is available as part of the Apache kit, but you're on your own if you try to use it. The directive is being documented for completeness, and is not necessarily supported. The module which provides the directive may or may not be compiled in by default; check the top of the page which describes the directive and its module to see if it remarks on the availability.

Module

This quite simply lists the name of the source module which defines the directive.

Compatibility

If the directive wasn't part of the original Apache version 2 distribution, the version in which it was introduced should be listed here. In addition, if the directive is available only on certain platforms, it will be noted here.

10.3 Apache Module core

Description:	Core Apache HTTP Server features that are always available
Status:	Core

Directives

- AcceptFilter
- AcceptPathInfo
- AccessFileName
- AddDefaultCharset
- AllowEncodedSlashes
- AllowOverride
- AllowOverrideList
- CGIMapExtension
- CGIPassAuth
- ContentDigest
- DefaultRuntimeDir
- DefaultType
- Define
- <Directory>
- <DirectoryMatch>
- DocumentRoot
- <Else>
- <ElseIf>
- EnableMMAP
- EnableSendfile
- Error
- ErrorDocument
- ErrorLog
- ErrorLogFormat
- ExtendedStatus
- FileETag
- <Files>
- <FilesMatch>
- ForceType
- GprofDir
- HostnameLookups
- <If>
- <IfDefine>
- <IfModule>
- Include

- IncludeOptional
- KeepAlive
- KeepAliveTimeout
- <Limit>
- <LimitExcept>
- LimitInternalRecursion
- LimitRequestBody
- LimitRequestFields
- LimitRequestFieldSize
- LimitRequestLine
- LimitXMLRequestBody
- <Location>
- <LocationMatch>
- LogLevel
- MaxKeepAliveRequests
- MaxRangeOverlaps
- MaxRangeReversals
- MaxRanges
- MergeTrailers
- Mutex
- NameVirtualHost
- Options
- Protocol
- Protocols
- ProtocolsHonorOrder
- RLimitCPU
- RLimitMEM
- RLimitNPROC
- ScriptInterpreterSource
- SeeRequestTail
- ServerAdmin
- ServerAlias
- ServerName
- ServerPath
- ServerRoot
- ServerSignature
- ServerTokens
- SetHandler
- SetInputFilter
- SetOutputFilter
- TimeOut

- TraceEnable
- UnDefine
- UseCanonicalName
- UseCanonicalPhysicalPort
- <VirtualHost>

AcceptFilter Directive

Description:	Configures optimizations for a Protocol's Listener Sockets
Syntax:	`AcceptFilter protocol accept_filter`
Context:	server config
Status:	Core
Module:	core

This directive enables operating system specific optimizations for a listening socket by the PROTOCOL type. The basic premise is for the kernel to not send a socket to the server process until either data is received or an entire HTTP Request is buffered. Only FreeBSD's Accept Filters[1], Linux's more primitive `TCP_DEFER_ACCEPT`, and Windows' optimized AcceptEx() are currently supported.

Using `none` for an argument will disable any accept filters for that protocol. This is useful for protocols that require a server send data first, such as `ftp:` or `nntp`:

```
AcceptFilter nntp none
```

The default protocol names are `https` for port 443 and `http` for all other ports. To specify that another protocol is being used with a listening port, add the *protocol* argument to the LISTEN directive.

The default values on FreeBSD are:

```
AcceptFilter http httpready
AcceptFilter https dataready
```

The `httpready` accept filter buffers entire HTTP requests at the kernel level. Once an entire request is received, the kernel then sends it to the server. See the

accf_http(9)[2] man page for more details. Since HTTPS requests are encrypted, only the accf_data(9)[3] filter is used.

The default values on Linux are:

```
AcceptFilter http data
AcceptFilter https data
```

Linux's `TCP_DEFER_ACCEPT` does not support buffering http requests. Any value besides `none` will enable `TCP_DEFER_ACCEPT` on that listener. For more details see the Linux

tcp(7)[4] man page.

The default values on Windows are:

```
AcceptFilter http data
AcceptFilter https data
```

[1] http://www.freebsd.org/cgi/man.cgi?query=accept_filter&sektion=9
[2] http://www.freebsd.org/cgi/man.cgi?query=accf_http&sektion=9
[3] http://www.freebsd.org/cgi/man.cgi?query=accf_data&sektion=9
[4] http://homepages.cwi.nl/~aeb/linux/man2html/man7/tcp.7.html

Window's mpm_winnt interprets the AcceptFilter to toggle the AcceptEx() API, and does not support http protocol buffering. There are two values which utilize the Windows AcceptEx() API and will recycle network sockets between connections. `data` waits until data has been transmitted as documented above, and the initial data buffer and network endpoint addresses are all retrieved from the single AcceptEx() invocation. `connect` will use the AcceptEx() API, also retrieve the network endpoint addresses, but like `none` the `connect` option does not wait for the initial data transmission.

On Windows, `none` uses accept() rather than AcceptEx() and will not recycle sockets between connections. This is useful for network adapters with broken driver support, as well as some virtual network providers such as vpn drivers, or spam, virus or spyware filters.

See also

- PROTOCOL

AcceptPathInfo Directive

Description:	Resources accept trailing pathname information
Syntax:	`AcceptPathInfo On|Off|Default`
Default:	`AcceptPathInfo Default`
Context:	server config, virtual host, directory, .htaccess
Override:	FileInfo
Status:	Core
Module:	core

This directive controls whether requests that contain trailing pathname information that follows an actual filename (or non-existent file in an existing directory) will be accepted or rejected. The trailing pathname information can be made available to scripts in the `PATH_INFO` environment variable.

For example, assume the location `/test/` points to a directory that contains only the single file `here.html`. Then requests for `/test/here.html/more` and `/test/nothere.html/more` both collect `/more` as `PATH_INFO`.

The three possible arguments for the ACCEPTPATHINFO directive are:

`Off` A request will only be accepted if it maps to a literal path that exists. Therefore a request with trailing pathname information after the true filename such as `/test/here.html/more` in the above example will return a 404 NOT FOUND error.

`On` A request will be accepted if a leading path component maps to a file that exists. The above example `/test/here.html/more` will be accepted if `/test/here.html` maps to a valid file.

`Default` The treatment of requests with trailing pathname information is determined by the handler (p. 98) responsible for the request. The core handler for normal files defaults to rejecting `PATH_INFO` requests. Handlers that serve scripts, such as cgi-script (p. 549) and isapi-handler (p. 640) , generally accept `PATH_INFO` by default.

The primary purpose of the `AcceptPathInfo` directive is to allow you to override the handler's choice of accepting or rejecting `PATH_INFO`. This override is required, for example, when you use a filter (p. 100) , such as INCLUDES (p. 624) , to generate content based on `PATH_INFO`. The core handler would usually reject the request, so you can use the following configuration to enable such a script:

```
<Files "mypaths.shtml">
  Options +Includes
  SetOutputFilter INCLUDES
  AcceptPathInfo On
</Files>
```

AccessFileName Directive

Description:	Name of the distributed configuration file
Syntax:	`AccessFileName filename [filename] ...`
Default:	`AccessFileName .htaccess`
Context:	server config, virtual host
Status:	Core
Module:	core

While processing a request, the server looks for the first existing configuration file from this list of names in every directory of the path to the document, if distributed configuration files are enabled for that directory. For example:

```
AccessFileName .acl
```

Before returning the document `/usr/local/web/index.html`, the server will read `/.acl`, `/usr/.acl`, `/usr/local/.acl` and `/usr/local/web/.acl` for directives unless they have been disabled with:

```
<Directory "/">
    AllowOverride None
</Directory>
```

See also

- ALLOWOVERRIDE
- Configuration Files (p. 30)
- .htaccess Files (p. 239)

AddDefaultCharset Directive

Description:	Default charset parameter to be added when a response content-type is `text/plain` or `text/html`
Syntax:	`AddDefaultCharset On|Off|charset`
Default:	`AddDefaultCharset Off`
Context:	server config, virtual host, directory, .htaccess
Override:	FileInfo
Status:	Core
Module:	core

This directive specifies a default value for the media type charset parameter (the name of a character encoding) to be added to a response if and only if the response's content-type is either `text/plain` or `text/html`. This should override any charset specified in the body of the response via a `META` element, though the exact behavior is often dependent on the user's client configuration. A setting of `AddDefaultCharset Off` disables this functionality. `AddDefaultCharset On` enables a default charset of `iso-8859-1`. Any other value is assumed to be the *charset* to be used, which should be one of the IANA registered charset values[5] for use in Internet media types (MIME types). For example:

```
AddDefaultCharset utf-8
```

ADDDEFAULTCHARSET should only be used when all of the text resources to which it applies are known to be in that character encoding and it is too inconvenient to label their charset individually. One such example is to add the charset parameter to resources containing generated content, such as legacy CGI scripts, that might be vulnerable to cross-site

[5] http://www.iana.org/assignments/character-sets

scripting attacks due to user-provided data being included in the output. Note, however, that a better solution is to just fix (or delete) those scripts, since setting a default charset does not protect users that have enabled the "auto-detect character encoding" feature on their browser.

See also

- ADDCHARSET

AllowEncodedSlashes Directive

Description:	Determines whether encoded path separators in URLs are allowed to be passed through
Syntax:	`AllowEncodedSlashes On|Off|NoDecode`
Default:	`AllowEncodedSlashes Off`
Context:	server config, virtual host
Status:	Core
Module:	core
Compatibility:	NoDecode option available in 2.3.12 and later.

The ALLOWENCODEDSLASHES directive allows URLs which contain encoded path separators (`%2F` for / and additionally `%5C` for \ on accordant systems) to be used in the path info.

With the default value, `Off`, such URLs are refused with a 404 (Not found) error.

With the value `On`, such URLs are accepted, and encoded slashes are decoded like all other encoded characters.

With the value `NoDecode`, such URLs are accepted, but encoded slashes are not decoded but left in their encoded state.

Turning ALLOWENCODEDSLASHES `On` is mostly useful when used in conjunction with `PATH_INFO`.

Note

If encoded slashes are needed in path info, use of `NoDecode` is strongly recommended as a security measure. Allowing slashes to be decoded could potentially allow unsafe paths.

See also

- ACCEPTPATHINFO

AllowOverride Directive

Description:	Types of directives that are allowed in `.htaccess` files
Syntax:	`AllowOverride All|None|directive-type [directive-type] ...`
Default:	`AllowOverride None (2.3.9 and later), AllowOverride All (2.3.8 and earlier)`
Context:	directory
Status:	Core
Module:	core

When the server finds an `.htaccess` file (as specified by ACCESSFILENAME), it needs to know which directives declared in that file can override earlier configuration directives.

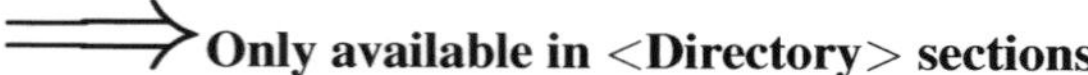

Only available in <Directory> sections

ALLOWOVERRIDE is valid only in <DIRECTORY> sections specified without regular expressions, not in <LOCATION>, <DIRECTORYMATCH> or <FILES> sections.

When this directive is set to `None` and ALLOWOVERRIDELIST is set to `None` .htaccess, files are completely ignored. In this case, the server will not even attempt to read `.htaccess` files in the filesystem.

When this directive is set to `All`, then any directive which has the .htaccess Context (p. 351) is allowed in `.htaccess` files.

The *directive-type* can be one of the following groupings of directives.

AuthConfig Allow use of the authorization directives (AUTHDBMGROUPFILE, AUTHDBMUSERFILE, AUTHGROUPFILE, AUTHNAME, AUTHTYPE, AUTHUSERFILE, REQUIRE, *etc.*).

FileInfo Allow use of the directives controlling document types (ERRORDOCUMENT, FORCETYPE, LANGUAGEPRIORITY, SETHANDLER, SETINPUTFILTER, SETOUTPUTFILTER, and MOD_MIME Add* and Remove* directives), document meta data (HEADER, REQUESTHEADER, SETENVIF, SETENVIFNOCASE, BROWSERMATCH, COOKIEEXPIRES, COOKIEDOMAIN, COOKIESTYLE, COOKIETRACKING, COOKIENAME), MOD_REWRITE directives (REWRITEENGINE, REWRITEOPTIONS, REWRITEBASE, REWRITECOND, REWRITERULE), MOD_ALIAS directives (REDIRECT, REDIRECTTEMP, REDIRECTPERMANENT, REDIRECTMATCH), and ACTION from MOD_ACTIONS.

Indexes Allow use of the directives controlling directory indexing (ADDDESCRIPTION, ADDICON, ADDICONBYENCODING, ADDICONBYTYPE, DEFAULTICON, DIRECTORYINDEX, `FancyIndexing` (p. 511) , HEADERNAME, INDEXIGNORE, INDEXOPTIONS, READMENAME, *etc.*).

Limit Allow use of the directives controlling host access (ALLOW, DENY and ORDER).

Nonfatal=[Override—Unknown—All] Allow use of AllowOverride option to treat syntax errors in .htaccess as nonfatal. Instead of causing an Internal Server Error, disallowed or unrecognised directives will be ignored and a warning logged:

- **Nonfatal=Override** treats directives forbidden by AllowOverride as nonfatal.
- **Nonfatal=Unknown** treats unknown directives as nonfatal. This covers typos and directives implemented by a module that's not present.
- **Nonfatal=All** treats both the above as nonfatal.

Note that a syntax error in a valid directive will still cause an internal server error.

Security
Nonfatal errors may have security implications for .htaccess users. For example, if AllowOverride disallows AuthConfig, users' configuration designed to restrict access to a site will be disabled.

Options[=*Option*,...] Allow use of the directives controlling specific directory features (OPTIONS and XBITHACK). An equal sign may be given followed by a comma-separated list, without spaces, of options that may be set using the OPTIONS command.

Implicit disabling of Options
Even though the list of options that may be used in .htaccess files can be limited with this directive, as long as any OPTIONS directive is allowed any other inherited option can be disabled by using the non-relative syntax. In other words, this mechanism cannot force a specific option to remain *set* while allowing any others to be set.

```
AllowOverride Options=Indexes,MultiViews
```

Example:

```
AllowOverride AuthConfig Indexes
```

In the example above, all directives that are neither in the group `AuthConfig` nor `Indexes` cause an internal server error.

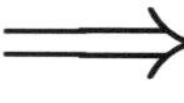

For security and performance reasons, do not set `AllowOverride` to anything other than `None` in your `<Directory "/">` block. Instead, find (or create) the `<Directory>` block that refers to the directory where you're actually planning to place a `.htaccess` file.

See also

- ACCESSFILENAME
- ALLOWOVERRIDELIST
- Configuration Files (p. 30)
- .htaccess Files (p. 239)

AllowOverrideList Directive

Description:	Individual directives that are allowed in `.htaccess` files
Syntax:	`AllowOverrideList None|directive [directive-type] ...`
Default:	`AllowOverrideList None`
Context:	directory
Status:	Core
Module:	core

When the server finds an `.htaccess` file (as specified by ACCESSFILENAME), it needs to know which directives declared in that file can override earlier configuration directives.

Only available in <Directory> sections

ALLOWOVERRIDELIST is valid only in <DIRECTORY> sections specified without regular expressions, not in <LOCATION>, <DIRECTORYMATCH> or <FILES> sections.

When this directive is set to `None` and ALLOWOVERRIDE is set to `None`, then .htaccess files are completely ignored. In this case, the server will not even attempt to read `.htaccess` files in the filesystem.

Example:

```
AllowOverride None
AllowOverrideList Redirect RedirectMatch
```

In the example above, only the `Redirect` and `RedirectMatch` directives are allowed. All others will cause an internal server error.

Example:

```
AllowOverride AuthConfig
AllowOverrideList CookieTracking CookieName
```

In the example above, ALLOWOVERRIDE grants permission to the `AuthConfig` directive grouping and ALLOWOVERRIDELIST grants permission to only two directives from the `FileInfo` directive grouping. All others will cause an internal server error.

See also

- ACCESSFILENAME
- ALLOWOVERRIDE
- Configuration Files (p. 30)
- .htaccess Files (p. 239)

CGIMapExtension Directive

Description:	Technique for locating the interpreter for CGI scripts
Syntax:	`CGIMapExtension cgi-path .extension`
Context:	directory, .htaccess
Override:	FileInfo
Status:	Core
Module:	core
Compatibility:	NetWare only

This directive is used to control how Apache httpd finds the interpreter used to run CGI scripts. For example, setting `CGIMapExtension sys:\foo.nlm .foo` will cause all CGI script files with a `.foo` extension to be passed to the FOO interpreter.

CGIPassAuth Directive

Description:	Enables passing HTTP authorization headers to scripts as CGI variables
Syntax:	`CGIPassAuth On|Off`
Default:	`CGIPassAuth Off`
Context:	directory, .htaccess
Override:	AuthConfig
Status:	Core
Module:	core
Compatibility:	Available in Apache HTTP Server 2.4.13 and later

CGIPASSAUTH allows scripts access to HTTP authorization headers such as `Authorization`, which is required for scripts that implement HTTP Basic authentication. Normally these HTTP headers are hidden from scripts. This is to disallow scripts from seeing user ids and passwords used to access the server when HTTP Basic authentication is enabled in the web server. This directive should be used when scripts are allowed to implement HTTP Basic authentication.

This directive can be used instead of the compile-time setting `SECURITY_HOLE_PASS_AUTHORIZATION` which has been available in previous versions of Apache HTTP Server.

The setting is respected by any modules which use `ap_add_common_vars()`, such as MOD_CGI, MOD_CGID, MOD_PROXY_FCGI, MOD_PROXY_SCGI, and so on. Notably, it affects modules which don't handle the request in the usual sense but still use this API; examples of this are MOD_INCLUDE and MOD_EXT_FILTER. Third-party modules that don't use `ap_add_common_vars()` may choose to respect the setting as well.

ContentDigest Directive

Description:	Enables the generation of `Content-MD5` HTTP Response headers
Syntax:	`ContentDigest On|Off`
Default:	`ContentDigest Off`
Context:	server config, virtual host, directory, .htaccess
Override:	Options
Status:	Core
Module:	core

This directive enables the generation of `Content-MD5` headers as defined in RFC1864 respectively RFC2616.

MD5 is an algorithm for computing a "message digest" (sometimes called "fingerprint") of arbitrary-length data, with a high degree of confidence that any alterations in the data will be reflected in alterations in the message digest.

The `Content-MD5` header provides an end-to-end message integrity check (MIC) of the entity-body. A proxy or client may check this header for detecting accidental modification of the entity-body in transit. Example header:

```
Content-MD5: AuLb7Dp1rqtRtxz2m9kRpA==
```

Note that this can cause performance problems on your server since the message digest is computed on every request (the values are not cached).

`Content-MD5` is only sent for documents served by the CORE, and not by any module. For example, SSI documents, output from CGI scripts, and byte range responses do not have this header.

DefaultRuntimeDir Directive

Description:	Base directory for the server run-time files
Syntax:	`DefaultRuntimeDir directory-path`
Default:	`DefaultRuntimeDir DEFAULT_REL_RUNTIMEDIR (logs/)`
Context:	server config
Status:	Core
Module:	core
Compatibility:	Available in Apache 2.4.2 and later

The DEFAULTRUNTIMEDIR directive sets the directory in which the server will create various run-time files (shared memory, locks, etc.). If set as a relative path, the full path will be relative to SERVERROOT.

Example

```
DefaultRuntimeDir scratch/
```

The default location of DEFAULTRUNTIMEDIR may be modified by changing the `DEFAULT_REL_RUNTIMEDIR` #define at build time.

Note: SERVERROOT should be specified before this directive is used. Otherwise, the default value of SERVERROOT would be used to set the base directory.

See also

- the security tips (p. 338) for information on how to properly set permissions on the SERVERROOT

DefaultType Directive

Description:	This directive has no effect other than to emit warnings if the value is not `none`. In prior versions, DefaultType would specify a default media type to assign to response content for which no other media type configuration could be found.
Syntax:	`DefaultType media-type|none`
Default:	`DefaultType none`
Context:	server config, virtual host, directory, .htaccess
Override:	FileInfo
Status:	Core
Module:	core
Compatibility:	The argument `none` is available in Apache httpd 2.2.7 and later. All other choices are DISABLED for 2.3.x and later.

This directive has been disabled. For backwards compatibility of configuration files, it may be specified with the value `none`, meaning no default media type. For example:

```
DefaultType None
```

`DefaultType None` is only available in httpd-2.2.7 and later.

Use the mime.types configuration file and the ADDTYPE to configure media type assignments via file extensions, or the FORCETYPE directive to configure the media type for specific resources. Otherwise, the server will send the response without a Content-Type header field and the recipient may attempt to guess the media type.

Define Directive

Description:	Define a variable
Syntax:	`Define parameter-name [parameter-value]`
Context:	server config, virtual host, directory
Status:	Core
Module:	core

In its one parameter form, DEFINE is equivalent to passing the `-D` argument to `httpd`. It can be used to toggle the use of <IFDEFINE> sections without needing to alter `-D` arguments in any startup scripts.

In addition to that, if the second parameter is given, a config variable is set to this value. The variable can be used in the configuration using the `${VAR}` syntax. The variable is always globally defined and not limited to the scope of the surrounding config section.

```
<IfDefine TEST>
  Define servername test.example.com
</IfDefine>
<IfDefine !TEST>
  Define servername www.example.com
  Define SSL
</IfDefine>

DocumentRoot "/var/www/${servername}/htdocs"
```

Variable names may not contain colon ":" characters, to avoid clashes with REWRITEMAP's syntax.

Directory Directive

Description:	Enclose a group of directives that apply only to the named file-system directory, sub-directories, and their contents.
Syntax:	`<Directory "directory-path"> ... </Directory>`
Context:	server config, virtual host
Status:	Core
Module:	core

<DIRECTORY> and `</Directory>` are used to enclose a group of directives that will apply only to the named directory, sub-directories of that directory, and the files within the respective directories. Any directive that is allowed in a directory context may be used. *Directory-path* is either the full path to a directory, or a wild-card string using Unix shell-style matching. In a wild-card string, `?` matches any single character, and `*` matches any sequences of characters. You may also use `[]` character ranges. None of the wildcards match a '/' character, so `<Directory "/*/public_html">` will not match `/home/user/public_html`, but `<Directory "/home/*/public_html">` will match. Example:

```
<Directory "/usr/local/httpd/htdocs">
  Options Indexes FollowSymLinks
</Directory>
```

Directory paths *may* be quoted, if you like, however, it *must* be quoted if the path contains spaces. This is because a space would otherwise indicate the end of an argument.

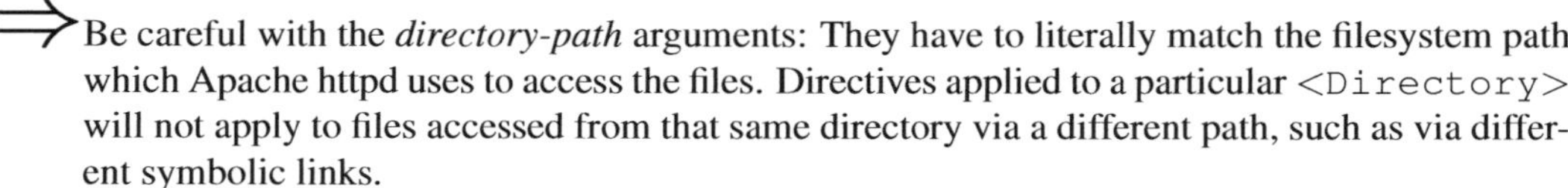

⟹ Be careful with the *directory-path* arguments: They have to literally match the filesystem path which Apache httpd uses to access the files. Directives applied to a particular <Directory> will not apply to files accessed from that same directory via a different path, such as via different symbolic links.

Regular expressions can also be used, with the addition of the ~ character. For example:

```
<Directory ~ "^/www/[0-9]{3}">

</Directory>
```

would match directories in /www/ that consisted of three numbers.

If multiple (non-regular expression) <DIRECTORY> sections match the directory (or one of its parents) containing a document, then the directives are applied in the order of shortest match first, interspersed with the directives from the .htaccess files. For example, with

```
<Directory "/">
  AllowOverride None
</Directory>

<Directory "/home">
  AllowOverride FileInfo
</Directory>
```

for access to the document /home/web/dir/doc.html the steps are:

- Apply directive AllowOverride None (disabling .htaccess files).
- Apply directive AllowOverride FileInfo (for directory /home).
- Apply any FileInfo directives in /home/.htaccess, /home/web/.htaccess and /home/web/dir/.htaccess in that order.

Regular expressions are not considered until after all of the normal sections have been applied. Then all of the regular expressions are tested in the order they appeared in the configuration file. For example, with

```
<Directory ~ "abc$">
  # ... directives here ...
</Directory>
```

the regular expression section won't be considered until after all normal <DIRECTORY>s and .htaccess files have been applied. Then the regular expression will match on /home/abc/public_html/abc and the corresponding <DIRECTORY> will be applied.

Note that the default access for <Directory "/"> is to permit all access. This means that Apache httpd will serve any file mapped from an URL. It is recommended that you change this with a block such as

```
<Directory "/">
  Require all denied
</Directory>
```

and then override this for directories you *want* accessible. See the Security Tips (p. 338) page for more details.

The directory sections occur in the `httpd.conf` file. <DIRECTORY> directives cannot nest, and cannot appear in a <LIMIT> or <LIMITEXCEPT> section.

See also

- How <Directory>, <Location> and <Files> sections work (p. 33) for an explanation of how these different sections are combined when a request is received

DirectoryMatch Directive

Description:	Enclose directives that apply to the contents of file-system directories matching a regular expression.
Syntax:	`<DirectoryMatch regex> ... </DirectoryMatch>`
Context:	server config, virtual host
Status:	Core
Module:	core

<DIRECTORYMATCH> and `</DirectoryMatch>` are used to enclose a group of directives which will apply only to the named directory (and the files within), the same as <DIRECTORY>. However, it takes as an argument a regular expression. For example:

```
<DirectoryMatch "^/www/(.+/)?[0-9]{3}/">
    # ...
</DirectoryMatch>
```

matches directories in `/www/` (or any subdirectory thereof) that consist of three numbers.

**Compatability**
Prior to 2.3.9, this directive implicitly applied to sub-directories (like <DIRECTORY>) and could not match the end of line symbol ($). In 2.3.9 and later, only directories that match the expression are affected by the enclosed directives.

**Trailing Slash**
This directive applies to requests for directories that may or may not end in a trailing slash, so expressions that are anchored to the end of line ($) must be written with care.

From 2.4.8 onwards, named groups and backreferences are captured and written to the environment with the corresponding name prefixed with "MATCH_" and in upper case. This allows elements of paths to be referenced from within expressions (p. 89) and modules like MOD_REWRITE. In order to prevent confusion, numbered (unnamed) backreferences are ignored. Use named groups instead.

```
<DirectoryMatch "^/var/www/combined/(?<sitename>[^/]+)">
    Require ldap-group cn=%{env:MATCH_SITENAME},ou=combined,o=Example
</DirectoryMatch>
```

See also

- <DIRECTORY> for a description of how regular expressions are mixed in with normal <DIRECTORY>s
- How <Directory>, <Location> and <Files> sections work (p. 33) for an explanation of how these different sections are combined when a request is received

DocumentRoot Directive

Description:	Directory that forms the main document tree visible from the web
Syntax:	`DocumentRoot directory-path`
Default:	`DocumentRoot "/usr/local/apache/htdocs"`
Context:	server config, virtual host
Status:	Core
Module:	core

This directive sets the directory from which `httpd` will serve files. Unless matched by a directive like ALIAS, the server appends the path from the requested URL to the document root to make the path to the document. Example:

```
DocumentRoot "/usr/web"
```

then an access to `http://my.example.com/index.html` refers to `/usr/web/index.html`. If the *directory-path* is not absolute then it is assumed to be relative to the SERVERROOT.

The DOCUMENTROOT should be specified without a trailing slash.

See also

- Mapping URLs to Filesystem Locations (p. 61)

Else Directive

Description:	Contains directives that apply only if the condition of a previous <IF> or <ELSEIF> section is not satisfied by a request at runtime
Syntax:	`<Else> ... </Else>`
Context:	server config, virtual host, directory, .htaccess
Override:	All
Status:	Core
Module:	core

The <ELSE> applies the enclosed directives if and only if the most recent <IF> or <ELSEIF> section in the same scope has not been applied. For example: In

```
<If "-z req('Host')">
  # ...
</If>
<Else>
  # ...
</Else>
```

The <IF> would match HTTP/1.0 requests without a *Host:* header and the <ELSE> would match requests with a *Host:* header.

See also

- <IF>
- <ELSEIF>
- How <Directory>, <Location>, <Files> sections work (p. 33) for an explanation of how these different sections are combined when a request is received. <IF>, <ELSEIF>, and <ELSE> are applied last.

ElseIf Directive

Description:	Contains directives that apply only if a condition is satisfied by a request at runtime while the condition of a previous <IF> or <ELSEIF> section is not satisfied
Syntax:	`<ElseIf expression> ... </ElseIf>`
Context:	server config, virtual host, directory, .htaccess
Override:	All
Status:	Core
Module:	core

The <ELSEIF> applies the enclosed directives if and only if both the given condition evaluates to true and the most recent <IF> or <ELSEIF> section in the same scope has not been applied. For example: In

```
<If "-R '10.1.0.0/16'">
  #...
</If>
<ElseIf "-R '10.0.0.0/8'">
  #...
</ElseIf>
<Else>
  #...
</Else>
```

The <ELSEIF> would match if the remote address of a request belongs to the subnet 10.0.0.0/8 but not to the subnet 10.1.0.0/16.

See also

- Expressions in Apache HTTP Server (p. 89) , for a complete reference and more examples.
- <IF>
- <ELSE>
- How <Directory>, <Location>, <Files> sections work (p. 33) for an explanation of how these different sections are combined when a request is received. <IF>, <ELSEIF>, and <ELSE> are applied last.

EnableMMAP Directive

Description:	Use memory-mapping to read files during delivery
Syntax:	`EnableMMAP On|Off`
Default:	`EnableMMAP On`
Context:	server config, virtual host, directory, .htaccess
Override:	FileInfo
Status:	Core
Module:	core

This directive controls whether the `httpd` may use memory-mapping if it needs to read the contents of a file during delivery. By default, when the handling of a request requires access to the data within a file – for example, when delivering a server-parsed file using MOD_INCLUDE – Apache httpd memory-maps the file if the OS supports it.

This memory-mapping sometimes yields a performance improvement. But in some environments, it is better to disable the memory-mapping to prevent operational problems:

- On some multiprocessor systems, memory-mapping can reduce the performance of the `httpd`.
- Deleting or truncating a file while `httpd` has it memory-mapped can cause `httpd` to crash with a segmentation fault.

For server configurations that are vulnerable to these problems, you should disable memory-mapping of delivered files by specifying:

```
EnableMMAP Off
```

For NFS mounted files, this feature may be disabled explicitly for the offending files by specifying:

```
<Directory "/path-to-nfs-files">
  EnableMMAP Off
</Directory>
```

EnableSendfile Directive

Description:	Use the kernel sendfile support to deliver files to the client
Syntax:	`EnableSendfile On|Off`
Default:	`EnableSendfile Off`
Context:	server config, virtual host, directory, .htaccess
Override:	FileInfo
Status:	Core
Module:	core
Compatibility:	Default changed to Off in version 2.3.9.

This directive controls whether `httpd` may use the sendfile support from the kernel to transmit file contents to the client. By default, when the handling of a request requires no access to the data within a file – for example, when delivering a static file – Apache httpd uses sendfile to deliver the file contents without ever reading the file if the OS supports it.

This sendfile mechanism avoids separate read and send operations, and buffer allocations. But on some platforms or within some filesystems, it is better to disable this feature to avoid operational problems:

- Some platforms may have broken sendfile support that the build system did not detect, especially if the binaries were built on another box and moved to such a machine with broken sendfile support.
- On Linux the use of sendfile triggers TCP-checksum offloading bugs on certain networking cards when using IPv6.
- On Linux on Itanium, `sendfile` may be unable to handle files over 2GB in size.
- With a network-mounted DOCUMENTROOT (e.g., NFS, SMB, CIFS, FUSE), the kernel may be unable to serve the network file through its own cache.

For server configurations that are not vulnerable to these problems, you may enable this feature by specifying:

```
EnableSendfile On
```

For network mounted files, this feature may be disabled explicitly for the offending files by specifying:

```
<Directory "/path-to-nfs-files">
  EnableSendfile Off
</Directory>
```

Please note that the per-directory and .htaccess configuration of ENABLESENDFILE is not supported by MOD_CACHE_DISK. Only global definition of ENABLESENDFILE is taken into account by the module.

Error Directive

Description:	Abort configuration parsing with a custom error message
Syntax:	`Error message`
Context:	server config, virtual host, directory, .htaccess
Status:	Core
Module:	core
Compatibility:	2.3.9 and later

If an error can be detected within the configuration, this directive can be used to generate a custom error message, and halt configuration parsing. The typical use is for reporting required modules which are missing from the configuration.

```
# Example
# ensure that mod_include is loaded
<IfModule !include_module>
  Error "mod_include is required by mod_foo.  Load it with LoadModule."
</IfModule>

# ensure that exactly one of SSL,NOSSL is defined
<IfDefine SSL>
<IfDefine NOSSL>
  Error "Both SSL and NOSSL are defined.  Define only one of them."
</IfDefine>
</IfDefine>
<IfDefine !SSL>
<IfDefine !NOSSL>
  Error "Either SSL or NOSSL must be defined."
</IfDefine>
</IfDefine>
```

ErrorDocument Directive

Description:	What the server will return to the client in case of an error
Syntax:	`ErrorDocument error-code document`
Context:	server config, virtual host, directory, .htaccess
Override:	FileInfo
Status:	Core
Module:	core

In the event of a problem or error, Apache httpd can be configured to do one of four things,

1. output a simple hardcoded error message
2. output a customized message
3. internally redirect to a local *URL-path* to handle the problem/error
4. redirect to an external *URL* to handle the problem/error

The first option is the default, while options 2-4 are configured using the ERRORDOCUMENT directive, which is followed by the HTTP response code and a URL or a message. Apache httpd will sometimes offer additional information regarding the problem/error.

From 2.4.13, expression syntax (p. 89) can be used inside the directive to produce dynamic strings and URLs.

URLs can begin with a slash (/) for local web-paths (relative to the DOCUMENTROOT), or be a full URL which the client can resolve. Alternatively, a message can be provided to be displayed by the browser. Note that deciding whether the parameter is an URL, a path or a message is performed before any expression is parsed. Examples:

```
ErrorDocument 500 http://foo.example.com/cgi-bin/tester
ErrorDocument 404 /cgi-bin/bad_urls.pl
ErrorDocument 401 /subscription_info.html
ErrorDocument 403 "Sorry can't allow you access today"
ErrorDocument 403 Forbidden!
ErrorDocument 403 /cgi-bin/forbidden.pl?referrer=%{escape:%{HTTP_REFERER}}
```

Additionally, the special value `default` can be used to specify Apache httpd's simple hardcoded message. While not required under normal circumstances, `default` will restore Apache httpd's simple hardcoded message for configurations that would otherwise inherit an existing ERRORDOCUMENT.

```
ErrorDocument 404 /cgi-bin/bad_urls.pl

<Directory "/web/docs">
  ErrorDocument 404 default
</Directory>
```

Note that when you specify an ERRORDOCUMENT that points to a remote URL (ie. anything with a method such as `http` in front of it), Apache HTTP Server will send a redirect to the client to tell it where to find the document, even if the document ends up being on the same server. This has several implications, the most important being that the client will not receive the original error status code, but instead will receive a redirect status code. This in turn can confuse web robots and other clients which try to determine if a URL is valid using the status code. In addition, if you use a remote URL in an `ErrorDocument 401`, the client will not know to prompt the user for a password since it will not receive the 401 status code. Therefore, **if you use an `ErrorDocument 401` directive, then it must refer to a local document.**

Microsoft Internet Explorer (MSIE) will by default ignore server-generated error messages when they are "too small" and substitute its own "friendly" error messages. The size threshold varies depending on the type of error, but in general, if you make your error document greater than 512 bytes, then MSIE will show the server-generated error rather than masking it. More information is available in Microsoft Knowledge Base article Q294807[6].

Although most error messages can be overridden, there are certain circumstances where the internal messages are used regardless of the setting of ERRORDOCUMENT. In particular, if a malformed request is detected, normal request processing will be immediately halted and the internal error message returned. This is necessary to guard against security problems caused by bad requests.

If you are using mod_proxy, you may wish to enable PROXYERROROVERRIDE so that you can provide custom error messages on behalf of your Origin servers. If you don't enable ProxyErrorOverride, Apache httpd will not generate custom error documents for proxied content.

See also

- documentation of customizable responses (p. 75)

[6]http://support.microsoft.com/default.aspx?scid=kb;en-us;Q294807

ErrorLog Directive

Description:	Location where the server will log errors
Syntax:	`ErrorLog file-path|syslog[:facility]`
Default:	`ErrorLog logs/error_log (Unix) ErrorLog logs/error.log (Windows and OS/2)`
Context:	server config, virtual host
Status:	Core
Module:	core

The ERRORLOG directive sets the name of the file to which the server will log any errors it encounters. If the *file-path* is not absolute then it is assumed to be relative to the SERVERROOT.

```
ErrorLog "/var/log/httpd/error_log"
```

If the *file-path* begins with a pipe character "|" then it is assumed to be a command to spawn to handle the error log.

```
ErrorLog "|/usr/local/bin/httpd_errors"
```

See the notes on piped logs (p. 53) for more information.

Using `syslog` instead of a filename enables logging via syslogd(8) if the system supports it. The default is to use syslog facility `local7`, but you can override this by using the `syslog:facility` syntax where *facility* can be one of the names usually documented in syslog(1). The facility is effectively global, and if it is changed in individual virtual hosts, the final facility specified affects the entire server.

```
ErrorLog syslog:user
```

Additional modules can provide their own ErrorLog providers. The syntax is similar to the `syslog` example above.

SECURITY: See the security tips (p. 338) document for details on why your security could be compromised if the directory where log files are stored is writable by anyone other than the user that starts the server.

Note
When entering a file path on non-Unix platforms, care should be taken to make sure that only forward slashes are used even though the platform may allow the use of back slashes. In general it is a good idea to always use forward slashes throughout the configuration files.

See also

- LOGLEVEL
- Apache HTTP Server Log Files (p. 53)

ErrorLogFormat Directive

Description:	Format specification for error log entries
Syntax:	`ErrorLogFormat [connection|request] format`
Context:	server config, virtual host
Status:	Core
Module:	core

ERRORLOGFORMAT allows to specify what supplementary information is logged in the error log in addition to the actual log message.

```
#Simple example
ErrorLogFormat "[%t] [%l] [pid %P] %F: %E: [client %a] %M"
```

Specifying `connection` or `request` as first parameter allows to specify additional formats, causing additional information to be logged when the first message is logged for a specific connection or request, respectively. This additional information is only logged once per connection/request. If a connection or request is processed without causing any log message, the additional information is not logged either.

It can happen that some format string items do not produce output. For example, the Referer header is only present if the log message is associated to a request and the log message happens at a time when the Referer header has already been read from the client. If no output is produced, the default behavior is to delete everything from the preceding space character to the next space character. This means the log line is implicitly divided into fields on non-whitespace to whitespace transitions. If a format string item does not produce output, the whole field is omitted. For example, if the remote address `%a` in the log format `[%t] [%l] [%a] %M` is not available, the surrounding brackets are not logged either. Space characters can be escaped with a backslash to prevent them from delimiting a field. The combination '%' (percent space) is a zero-width field delimiter that does not produce any output.

The above behavior can be changed by adding modifiers to the format string item. A - (minus) modifier causes a minus to be logged if the respective item does not produce any output. In once-per-connection/request formats, it is also possible to use the + (plus) modifier. If an item with the plus modifier does not produce any output, the whole line is omitted.

A number as modifier can be used to assign a log severity level to a format item. The item will only be logged if the severity of the log message is not higher than the specified log severity level. The number can range from 1 (alert) over 4 (warn) and 7 (debug) to 15 (trace8).

For example, here's what would happen if you added modifiers to the `%{Referer}i` token, which logs the `Referer` request header.

Modified Token	Meaning
`%-{Referer}i`	Logs a - if `Referer` is not set.
`%+{Referer}i`	Omits the entire line if `Referer` is not set.
`%4{Referer}i`	Logs the `Referer` only if the log message severity is higher than 4.

Some format string items accept additional parameters in braces.

FormatString	Description
`%%`	The percent sign
`%a`	Client IP address and port of the request
`%{c}a`	Underlying peer IP address and port of the connection (see the MOD_REMOTEIP module)
`%A`	Local IP-address and port
`%{`*name*`}e`	Request environment variable *name*
`%E`	APR/OS error status code and string
`%F`	Source file name and line number of the log call
`%{`*name*`}i`	Request header *name*
`%k`	Number of keep-alive requests on this connection
`%l`	Loglevel of the message
`%L`	Log ID of the request
`%{c}L`	Log ID of the connection
`%{C}L`	Log ID of the connection if used in connection scope, empty otherwise
`%m`	Name of the module logging the message
`%M`	The actual log message
`%{`*name*`}n`	Request note *name*
`%P`	Process ID of current process
`%T`	Thread ID of current thread
`%{g}T`	System unique thread ID of current thread (the same ID as displayed by e.g. `top`; currently Linux or

`%t`	The current time
`%{u}t`	The current time including micro-seconds
`%{cu}t`	The current time in compact ISO 8601 format, including micro-seconds
`%v`	The canonical SERVERNAME of the current server.
`%V`	The server name of the server serving the request according to the USECANONICALNAME setting.
\ (backslash space)	Non-field delimiting space
% (percent space)	Field delimiter (no output)

The log ID format `%L` produces a unique id for a connection or request. This can be used to correlate which log lines belong to the same connection or request, which request happens on which connection. A `%L` format string is also available in MOD_LOG_CONFIG to allow to correlate access log entries with error log lines. If MOD_UNIQUE_ID is loaded, its unique id will be used as log ID for requests.

```
#Example (default format for threaded MPMs)
ErrorLogFormat "[%{u}t] [%-m:%l] [pid %P:tid %T] %7F: %E: [client\ %a] %M%,\ref
```

This would result in error messages such as:

```
[Thu May 12 08:28:57.652118 2011] [core:error] [pid 8777:tid
4326490112] [client ::1:58619] File does not exist:
/usr/local/apache2/htdocs/favicon.ico
```

Notice that, as discussed above, some fields are omitted entirely because they are not defined.

```
#Example (similar to the 2.2.x format)
ErrorLogFormat "[%t] [%l] %7F: %E: [client\ %a] %M%,\referer\%{Referer}i"

#Advanced example with request/connection log IDs
ErrorLogFormat "[%{uc}t] [%-m:%-l] [R:%L] [C:%{C}L] %7F: %E: %M"
ErrorLogFormat request "[%{uc}t] [R:%L] Request %k on C:%{c}L pid:%P tid:%T"
ErrorLogFormat request "[%{uc}t] [R:%L] UA:'%+{User-Agent}i'"
ErrorLogFormat request "[%{uc}t] [R:%L] Referer:'%+{Referer}i'"
ErrorLogFormat connection "[%{uc}t] [C:%{c}L] local\ %a remote\ %A"
```

See also

- ERRORLOG
- LOGLEVEL
- Apache HTTP Server Log Files (p. 53)

ExtendedStatus Directive

Description:	Keep track of extended status information for each request
Syntax:	`ExtendedStatus On|Off`
Default:	`ExtendedStatus Off[*]`
Context:	server config
Status:	Core
Module:	core

This option tracks additional data per worker about the currently executing request and creates a utilization summary. You can see these variables during runtime by configuring MOD_STATUS. Note that other modules may rely on this scoreboard.

This setting applies to the entire server and cannot be enabled or disabled on a virtualhost-by-virtualhost basis. The collection of extended status information can slow down the server. Also note that this setting cannot be changed during a graceful restart.

⟹ Note that loading MOD_STATUS will change the default behavior to ExtendedStatus On, while other third party modules may do the same. Such modules rely on collecting detailed information about the state of all workers. The default is changed by MOD_STATUS beginning with version 2.3.6. The previous default was always Off.

FileETag Directive

Description:	File attributes used to create the ETag HTTP response header for static files
Syntax:	`FileETag component ...`
Default:	`FileETag MTime Size`
Context:	server config, virtual host, directory, .htaccess
Override:	FileInfo
Status:	Core
Module:	core
Compatibility:	The default used to be "INodeMTimeSize" in 2.3.14 and earlier.

The FILEETAG directive configures the file attributes that are used to create the `ETag` (entity tag) response header field when the document is based on a static file. (The `ETag` value is used in cache management to save network bandwidth.) The FILEETAG directive allows you to choose which of these – if any – should be used. The recognized keywords are:

INode The file's i-node number will be included in the calculation

MTime The date and time the file was last modified will be included

Size The number of bytes in the file will be included

All All available fields will be used. This is equivalent to:

```
FileETag INode MTime Size
```

None If a document is file-based, no `ETag` field will be included in the response

The `INode`, `MTime`, and `Size` keywords may be prefixed with either + or −, which allow changes to be made to the default setting inherited from a broader scope. Any keyword appearing without such a prefix immediately and completely cancels the inherited setting.

If a directory's configuration includes `FileETagINodeMTimeSize`, and a subdirectory's includes `FileETag-INode`, the setting for that subdirectory (which will be inherited by any sub-subdirectories that don't override it) will be equivalent to `FileETagMTimeSize`.

Warning
Do not change the default for directories or locations that have WebDAV enabled and use MOD_DAV_FS as a storage provider. MOD_DAV_FS uses `MTimeSize` as a fixed format for `ETag` comparisons on conditional requests. These conditional requests will break if the `ETag` format is changed via FILEETAG.

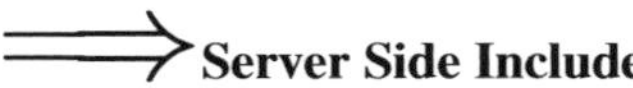**Server Side Includes**

An ETag is not generated for responses parsed by MOD_INCLUDE since the response entity can change without a change of the INode, MTime, or Size of the static file with embedded SSI directives.

Files Directive

Description:	Contains directives that apply to matched filenames
Syntax:	`<Files "filename"> ... </Files>`
Context:	server config, virtual host, directory, .htaccess
Override:	All
Status:	Core
Module:	core

The <FILES> directive limits the scope of the enclosed directives by filename. It is comparable to the <DIRECTORY> and <LOCATION> directives. It should be matched with a `</Files>` directive. The directives given within this section will be applied to any object with a basename (last component of filename) matching the specified filename. <FILES> sections are processed in the order they appear in the configuration file, after the <DIRECTORY> sections and `.htaccess` files are read, but before <LOCATION> sections. Note that <FILES> can be nested inside <DIRECTORY> sections to restrict the portion of the filesystem they apply to.

The *filename* argument should include a filename, or a wild-card string, where `?` matches any single character, and `*` matches any sequences of characters.

```
<Files "cat.html">
    # Insert stuff that applies to cat.html here
</Files>

<Files "?at.*">
    # This would apply to cat.html, bat.html, hat.php and so on.
</Files>
```

Regular expressions can also be used, with the addition of the ~ character. For example:

```
<Files ~ "\.(gif|jpe?g|png)$">
    #...
</Files>
```

would match most common Internet graphics formats. <FILESMATCH> is preferred, however.

Note that unlike <DIRECTORY> and <LOCATION> sections, <FILES> sections can be used inside `.htaccess` files. This allows users to control access to their own files, at a file-by-file level.

See also

- How <Directory>, <Location> and <Files> sections work (p. 33) for an explanation of how these different sections are combined when a request is received

FilesMatch Directive

Description:	Contains directives that apply to regular-expression matched filenames
Syntax:	`<FilesMatch regex> ... </FilesMatch>`
Context:	server config, virtual host, directory, .htaccess
Override:	All
Status:	Core
Module:	core

The <FILESMATCH> directive limits the scope of the enclosed directives by filename, just as the <FILES> directive does. However, it accepts a regular expression. For example:

```
<FilesMatch ".+\.(gif|jpe?g|png)$">
    # ...
</FilesMatch>
```

would match most common Internet graphics formats.

⟹ The .+ at the start of the regex ensures that files named .png, or .gif, for example, are not matched.

From 2.4.8 onwards, named groups and backreferences are captured and written to the environment with the corresponding name prefixed with "MATCH_" and in upper case. This allows elements of files to be referenced from within expressions (p. 89) and modules like MOD_REWRITE. In order to prevent confusion, numbered (unnamed) backreferences are ignored. Use named groups instead.

```
<FilesMatch "^(?<sitename>[^/]+)">
    require ldap-group cn=%{env:MATCH_SITENAME},ou=combined,o=Example
</FilesMatch>
```

See also

- How <Directory>, <Location> and <Files> sections work (p. 33) for an explanation of how these different sections are combined when a request is received

ForceType Directive

Description:	Forces all matching files to be served with the specified media type in the HTTP Content-Type header field
Syntax:	ForceType media-type|None
Context:	directory, .htaccess
Override:	FileInfo
Status:	Core
Module:	core

When placed into an .htaccess file or a <DIRECTORY>, or <LOCATION> or <FILES> section, this directive forces all matching files to be served with the content type identification given by *media-type*. For example, if you had a directory full of GIF files, but did not want to label them all with .gif, you might want to use:

```
ForceType image/gif
```

Note that this directive overrides other indirect media type associations defined in mime.types or via the ADDTYPE.

You can also override more general FORCETYPE settings by using the value of None:

```
# force all files to be image/gif:
<Location "/images">
  ForceType image/gif
</Location>

# but normal mime-type associations here:
<Location "/images/mixed">
  ForceType None
</Location>
```

This directive primarily overrides the content types generated for static files served out of the filesystem. For resources other than static files, where the generator of the response typically specifies a Content-Type, this directive has no effect.

**Note**

When explicit directives such as SETHANDLER or ADDHANDLER do not apply to the current request, the internal handler name normally set by those directives is set to match the content type specified by this directive. This is a historical behavior that some third-party modules (such as mod_php) may use "magic" content types used only to signal the module to take responsibility for the matching request. Configurations that rely on such "magic" types should be avoided by the use of SETHANDLER or ADDHANDLER.

GprofDir Directive

Description:	Directory to write gmon.out profiling data to.
Syntax:	`GprofDir /tmp/gprof/|/tmp/gprof/%`
Context:	server config, virtual host
Status:	Core
Module:	core

When the server has been compiled with gprof profiling support, GPROFDIR causes `gmon.out` files to be written to the specified directory when the process exits. If the argument ends with a percent symbol ('%'), subdirectories are created for each process id.

This directive currently only works with the PREFORK MPM.

HostnameLookups Directive

Description:	Enables DNS lookups on client IP addresses
Syntax:	`HostnameLookups On|Off|Double`
Default:	`HostnameLookups Off`
Context:	server config, virtual host, directory
Status:	Core
Module:	core

This directive enables DNS lookups so that host names can be logged (and passed to CGIs/SSIs in `REMOTE_HOST`). The value `Double` refers to doing double-reverse DNS lookup. That is, after a reverse lookup is performed, a forward lookup is then performed on that result. At least one of the IP addresses in the forward lookup must match the original address. (In "tcpwrappers" terminology this is called `PARANOID`.)

Regardless of the setting, when MOD_AUTHZ_HOST is used for controlling access by hostname, a double reverse lookup will be performed. This is necessary for security. Note that the result of this double-reverse isn't generally available unless you set `HostnameLookups Double`. For example, if only `HostnameLookups On` and a request is made to an object that is protected by hostname restrictions, regardless of whether the double-reverse fails or not, CGIs will still be passed the single-reverse result in `REMOTE_HOST`.

The default is `Off` in order to save the network traffic for those sites that don't truly need the reverse lookups done. It is also better for the end users because they don't have to suffer the extra latency that a lookup entails. Heavily loaded sites should leave this directive `Off`, since DNS lookups can take considerable amounts of time. The utility `logresolve`, compiled by default to the `bin` subdirectory of your installation directory, can be used to look up host names from logged IP addresses offline.

Finally, if you have hostname-based Require directives (p. 505) , a hostname lookup will be performed regardless of the setting of `HostnameLookups`.

If Directive

Description:	Contains directives that apply only if a condition is satisfied by a request at runtime
Syntax:	`<If expression> ... </If>`
Context:	server config, virtual host, directory, .htaccess
Override:	All
Status:	Core
Module:	core

The <IF> directive evaluates an expression at runtime, and applies the enclosed directives if and only if the expression evaluates to true. For example:

```
<If "-z req('Host')">
```

would match HTTP/1.0 requests without a *Host:* header. Expressions may contain various shell-like operators for string comparison (==, !=, <, ...), integer comparison (`-eq`, `-ne`, ...), and others (`-n`, `-z`, `-f`, ...). It is also possible to use regular expressions,

```
<If "%{QUERY_STRING} =~ /(delete|commit)=.*?elem/">
```

shell-like pattern matches and many other operations. These operations can be done on request headers (`req`), environment variables (`env`), and a large number of other properties. The full documentation is available in Expressions in Apache HTTP Server (p. 89) .

Only directives that support the directory context (p. 351) can be used within this configuration section.

> **!** Certain variables, such as `CONTENT_TYPE` and other response headers, are set after <If> conditions have already been evaluated, and so will not be available to use in this directive.

See also

- Expressions in Apache HTTP Server (p. 89) , for a complete reference and more examples.
- <ELSEIF>
- <ELSE>
- How <Directory>, <Location>, <Files> sections work (p. 33) for an explanation of how these different sections are combined when a request is received. <IF>, <ELSEIF>, and <ELSE> are applied last.

IfDefine Directive

Description:	Encloses directives that will be processed only if a test is true at startup
Syntax:	`<IfDefine [!]parameter-name> ... </IfDefine>`
Context:	server config, virtual host, directory, .htaccess
Override:	All
Status:	Core
Module:	core

The `<IfDefine test>...</IfDefine>` section is used to mark directives that are conditional. The directives within an <IFDEFINE> section are only processed if the *test* is true. If *test* is false, everything between the start and end markers is ignored.

The *test* in the <IFDEFINE> section directive can be one of two forms:

- *parameter-name*

- ! *parameter-name*

In the former case, the directives between the start and end markers are only processed if the parameter named *parameter-name* is defined. The second format reverses the test, and only processes the directives if *parameter-name* is **not** defined.

The *parameter-name* argument is a define as given on the `httpd` command line via `-Dparameter` at the time the server was started or by the DEFINE directive.

<IFDEFINE> sections are nest-able, which can be used to implement simple multiple-parameter tests. Example:

```
httpd -DReverseProxy -DUseCache -DMemCache ...
```

```
<IfDefine ReverseProxy>
  LoadModule proxy_module   modules/mod_proxy.so
  LoadModule proxy_http_module   modules/mod_proxy_http.so
  <IfDefine UseCache>
    LoadModule cache_module   modules/mod_cache.so
    <IfDefine MemCache>
      LoadModule mem_cache_module   modules/mod_mem_cache.so
    </IfDefine>
    <IfDefine !MemCache>
      LoadModule cache_disk_module   modules/mod_cache_disk.so
    </IfDefine>
  </IfDefine>
</IfDefine>
```

IfModule Directive

Description:	Encloses directives that are processed conditional on the presence or absence of a specific module
Syntax:	`<IfModule [!]module-file|module-identifier> ... </IfModule>`
Context:	server config, virtual host, directory, .htaccess
Override:	All
Status:	Core
Module:	core
Compatibility:	Module identifiers are available in version 2.1 and later.

The `<IfModule test>...</IfModule>` section is used to mark directives that are conditional on the presence of a specific module. The directives within an <IFMODULE> section are only processed if the *test* is true. If *test* is false, everything between the start and end markers is ignored.

The *test* in the <IFMODULE> section directive can be one of two forms:

- *module*
- !*module*

In the former case, the directives between the start and end markers are only processed if the module named *module* is included in Apache httpd – either compiled in or dynamically loaded using LOADMODULE. The second format reverses the test, and only processes the directives if *module* is **not** included.

The *module* argument can be either the module identifier or the file name of the module, at the time it was compiled. For example, `rewrite_module` is the identifier and `mod_rewrite.c` is the file name. If a module consists of several source files, use the name of the file containing the string `STANDARD20_MODULE_STUFF`.

<IFMODULE> sections are nest-able, which can be used to implement simple multiple-module tests.

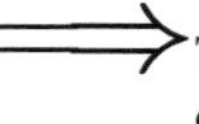This section should only be used if you need to have one configuration file that works whether or not a specific module is available. In normal operation, directives need not be placed in <IFMODULE> sections.

Include Directive

Description:	Includes other configuration files from within the server configuration files
Syntax:	`Include file-path|directory-path|wildcard`
Context:	server config, virtual host, directory
Status:	Core
Module:	core
Compatibility:	Directory wildcard matching available in 2.3.6 and later

This directive allows inclusion of other configuration files from within the server configuration files.

Shell-style (`fnmatch()`) wildcard characters can be used in the filename or directory parts of the path to include several files at once, in alphabetical order. In addition, if INCLUDE points to a directory, rather than a file, Apache httpd will read all files in that directory and any subdirectory. However, including entire directories is not recommended, because it is easy to accidentally leave temporary files in a directory that can cause `httpd` to fail. Instead, we encourage you to use the wildcard syntax shown below, to include files that match a particular pattern, such as *.conf, for example.

The INCLUDE directive will **fail with an error** if a wildcard expression does not match any file. The INCLUDEOPTIONAL directive can be used if non-matching wildcards should be ignored.

The file path specified may be an absolute path, or may be relative to the SERVERROOT directory.

Examples:

```
Include /usr/local/apache2/conf/ssl.conf
Include /usr/local/apache2/conf/vhosts/*.conf
```

Or, providing paths relative to your SERVERROOT directory:

```
Include conf/ssl.conf
Include conf/vhosts/*.conf
```

Wildcards may be included in the directory or file portion of the path. This example will fail if there is no subdirectory in conf/vhosts that contains at least one *.conf file:

```
Include conf/vhosts/*/*.conf
```

Alternatively, the following command will just be ignored in case of missing files or directories:

```
IncludeOptional conf/vhosts/*/*.conf
```

See also

- INCLUDEOPTIONAL
- `apachectl`

IncludeOptional Directive

Description:	Includes other configuration files from within the server configuration files
Syntax:	`IncludeOptional file-path|directory-path|wildcard`
Context:	server config, virtual host, directory
Status:	Core
Module:	core
Compatibility:	Available in 2.3.6 and later

This directive allows inclusion of other configuration files from within the server configuration files. It works identically to the INCLUDE directive, with the exception that if wildcards do not match any file or directory, the INCLUDEOPTIONAL directive will be silently ignored instead of causing an error.

See also

- INCLUDE
- `apachectl`

KeepAlive Directive

Description:	Enables HTTP persistent connections
Syntax:	`KeepAlive On|Off`
Default:	`KeepAlive On`
Context:	server config, virtual host
Status:	Core
Module:	core

The Keep-Alive extension to HTTP/1.0 and the persistent connection feature of HTTP/1.1 provide long-lived HTTP sessions which allow multiple requests to be sent over the same TCP connection. In some cases this has been shown to result in an almost 50% speedup in latency times for HTML documents with many images. To enable Keep-Alive connections, set `KeepAlive On`.

For HTTP/1.0 clients, Keep-Alive connections will only be used if they are specifically requested by a client. In addition, a Keep-Alive connection with an HTTP/1.0 client can only be used when the length of the content is known in advance. This implies that dynamic content such as CGI output, SSI pages, and server-generated directory listings will generally not use Keep-Alive connections to HTTP/1.0 clients. For HTTP/1.1 clients, persistent connections are the default unless otherwise specified. If the client requests it, chunked encoding will be used in order to send content of unknown length over persistent connections.

When a client uses a Keep-Alive connection, it will be counted as a single "request" for the MAXCONNECTIONSPERCHILD directive, regardless of how many requests are sent using the connection.

See also

- MAXKEEPALIVEREQUESTS

KeepAliveTimeout Directive

Description:	Amount of time the server will wait for subsequent requests on a persistent connection
Syntax:	`KeepAliveTimeout num[ms]`
Default:	`KeepAliveTimeout 5`
Context:	server config, virtual host
Status:	Core
Module:	core

The number of seconds Apache httpd will wait for a subsequent request before closing the connection. By adding a postfix of ms the timeout can be also set in milliseconds. Once a request has been received, the timeout value specified by the TIMEOUT directive applies.

Setting KEEPALIVETIMEOUT to a high value may cause performance problems in heavily loaded servers. The higher the timeout, the more server processes will be kept occupied waiting on connections with idle clients.

If KEEPALIVETIMEOUT is **not** set for a name-based virtual host, the value of the first defined virtual host best matching the local IP and port will be used.

Limit Directive

Description:	Restrict enclosed access controls to only certain HTTP methods
Syntax:	`<Limit method [method] ... > ... </Limit>`
Context:	directory, .htaccess
Override:	AuthConfig, Limit
Status:	Core
Module:	core

Access controls are normally effective for **all** access methods, and this is the usual desired behavior. **In the general case, access control directives should not be placed within a <LIMIT> section.**

The purpose of the <LIMIT> directive is to restrict the effect of the access controls to the nominated HTTP methods. For all other methods, the access restrictions that are enclosed in the <LIMIT> bracket **will have no effect**. The following example applies the access control only to the methods `POST`, `PUT`, and `DELETE`, leaving all other methods unprotected:

```
<Limit POST PUT DELETE>
  Require valid-user
</Limit>
```

The method names listed can be one or more of: `GET`, `POST`, `PUT`, `DELETE`, `CONNECT`, `OPTIONS`, `PATCH`, `PROPFIND`, `PROPPATCH`, `MKCOL`, `COPY`, `MOVE`, `LOCK`, and `UNLOCK`. **The method name is case-sensitive.** If `GET` is used, it will also restrict `HEAD` requests. The `TRACE` method cannot be limited (see TRACEENABLE).

> **!** A <LIMITEXCEPT> section should always be used in preference to a <LIMIT> section when restricting access, since a <LIMITEXCEPT> section provides protection against arbitrary methods.

The <LIMIT> and <LIMITEXCEPT> directives may be nested. In this case, each successive level of <LIMIT> or <LIMITEXCEPT> directives must further restrict the set of methods to which access controls apply.

> **!** When using <LIMIT> or <LIMITEXCEPT> directives with the REQUIRE directive, note that the first REQUIRE to succeed authorizes the request, regardless of the presence of other REQUIRE directives.

For example, given the following configuration, all users will be authorized for `POST` requests, and the `Require group editors` directive will be ignored in all cases:

```
<LimitExcept GET>
  Require valid-user
</LimitExcept>
<Limit POST>
  Require group editors
</Limit>
```

LimitExcept Directive

Description:	Restrict access controls to all HTTP methods except the named ones
Syntax:	`<LimitExcept method [method] ... > ... </LimitExcept>`
Context:	directory, .htaccess
Override:	AuthConfig, Limit
Status:	Core
Module:	core

<LIMITEXCEPT> and </LimitExcept> are used to enclose a group of access control directives which will then apply to any HTTP access method **not** listed in the arguments; i.e., it is the opposite of a <LIMIT> section and can be used to control both standard and nonstandard/unrecognized methods. See the documentation for <LIMIT> for more details.

For example:

```
<LimitExcept POST GET>
  Require valid-user
</LimitExcept>
```

LimitInternalRecursion Directive

Description:	Determine maximum number of internal redirects and nested subrequests
Syntax:	`LimitInternalRecursion number [number]`
Default:	`LimitInternalRecursion 10`
Context:	server config, virtual host
Status:	Core
Module:	core

An internal redirect happens, for example, when using the ACTION directive, which internally redirects the original request to a CGI script. A subrequest is Apache httpd's mechanism to find out what would happen for some URI if it were requested. For example, MOD_DIR uses subrequests to look for the files listed in the DIRECTORYINDEX directive.

LIMITINTERNALRECURSION prevents the server from crashing when entering an infinite loop of internal redirects or subrequests. Such loops are usually caused by misconfigurations.

The directive stores two different limits, which are evaluated on per-request basis. The first *number* is the maximum number of internal redirects that may follow each other. The second *number* determines how deeply subrequests may be nested. If you specify only one *number*, it will be assigned to both limits.

```
LimitInternalRecursion 5
```

LimitRequestBody Directive

Description:	Restricts the total size of the HTTP request body sent from the client
Syntax:	`LimitRequestBody bytes`
Default:	`LimitRequestBody 0`
Context:	server config, virtual host, directory, .htaccess
Override:	All
Status:	Core
Module:	core

This directive specifies the number of *bytes* from 0 (meaning unlimited) to 2147483647 (2GB) that are allowed in a request body. See the note below for the limited applicability to proxy requests.

The LIMITREQUESTBODY directive allows the user to set a limit on the allowed size of an HTTP request message body within the context in which the directive is given (server, per-directory, per-file or per-location). If the client request exceeds that limit, the server will return an error response instead of servicing the request. The size of a normal request message body will vary greatly depending on the nature of the resource and the methods allowed on that resource. CGI scripts typically use the message body for retrieving form information. Implementations of the PUT method will require a value at least as large as any representation that the server wishes to accept for that resource.

This directive gives the server administrator greater control over abnormal client request behavior, which may be useful for avoiding some forms of denial-of-service attacks.

If, for example, you are permitting file upload to a particular location and wish to limit the size of the uploaded file to 100K, you might use the following directive:

```
LimitRequestBody 102400
```

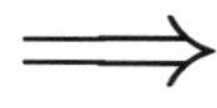

For a full description of how this directive is interpreted by proxy requests, see the MOD_PROXY documentation.

LimitRequestFields Directive

Description:	Limits the number of HTTP request header fields that will be accepted from the client
Syntax:	`LimitRequestFields number`
Default:	`LimitRequestFields 100`
Context:	server config, virtual host
Status:	Core
Module:	core

Number is an integer from 0 (meaning unlimited) to 32767. The default value is defined by the compile-time constant DEFAULT_LIMIT_REQUEST_FIELDS (100 as distributed).

The LIMITREQUESTFIELDS directive allows the server administrator to modify the limit on the number of request header fields allowed in an HTTP request. A server needs this value to be larger than the number of fields that a normal client request might include. The number of request header fields used by a client rarely exceeds 20, but this may vary among different client implementations, often depending upon the extent to which a user has configured their browser to support detailed content negotiation. Optional HTTP extensions are often expressed using request header fields.

This directive gives the server administrator greater control over abnormal client request behavior, which may be useful for avoiding some forms of denial-of-service attacks. The value should be increased if normal clients see an error response from the server that indicates too many fields were sent in the request.

For example:

```
LimitRequestFields 50
```

Warning
When name-based virtual hosting is used, the value for this directive is taken from the default (first-listed) virtual host for the local IP and port combination.

LimitRequestFieldSize Directive

Description:	Limits the size of the HTTP request header allowed from the client
Syntax:	`LimitRequestFieldSize bytes`
Default:	`LimitRequestFieldSize 8190`
Context:	server config, virtual host
Status:	Core
Module:	core

This directive specifies the number of *bytes* that will be allowed in an HTTP request header.

The LIMITREQUESTFIELDSIZE directive allows the server administrator to set the limit on the allowed size of an HTTP request header field. A server needs this value to be large enough to hold any one header field from a normal client request. The size of a normal request header field will vary greatly among different client implementations, often depending upon the extent to which a user has configured their browser to support detailed content negotiation. SPNEGO authentication headers can be up to 12392 bytes.

This directive gives the server administrator greater control over abnormal client request behavior, which may be useful for avoiding some forms of denial-of-service attacks.

For example:

```
LimitRequestFieldSize 4094
```

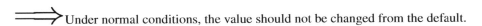

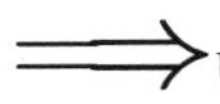Under normal conditions, the value should not be changed from the default.

Warning
When name-based virtual hosting is used, the value for this directive is taken from the default (first-listed) virtual host best matching the current IP address and port combination.

LimitRequestLine Directive

Description:	Limit the size of the HTTP request line that will be accepted from the client
Syntax:	`LimitRequestLine bytes`
Default:	`LimitRequestLine 8190`
Context:	server config, virtual host
Status:	Core
Module:	core

This directive sets the number of *bytes* that will be allowed on the HTTP request-line.

The LIMITREQUESTLINE directive allows the server administrator to set the limit on the allowed size of a client's HTTP request-line. Since the request-line consists of the HTTP method, URI, and protocol version, the LIMITREQUESTLINE directive places a restriction on the length of a request-URI allowed for a request on the server. A server needs this value to be large enough to hold any of its resource names, including any information that might be passed in the query part of a `GET` request.

This directive gives the server administrator greater control over abnormal client request behavior, which may be useful for avoiding some forms of denial-of-service attacks.

For example:

```
LimitRequestLine 4094
```

⟹ Under normal conditions, the value should not be changed from the default.

Warning
When name-based virtual hosting is used, the value for this directive is taken from the default (first-listed) virtual host best matching the current IP address and port combination.

LimitXMLRequestBody Directive

Description:	Limits the size of an XML-based request body
Syntax:	`LimitXMLRequestBody bytes`
Default:	`LimitXMLRequestBody 1000000`
Context:	server config, virtual host, directory, .htaccess
Override:	All
Status:	Core
Module:	core

Limit (in bytes) on maximum size of an XML-based request body. A value of `0` will disable any checking.

Example:

```
LimitXMLRequestBody 0
```

Location Directive

Description:	Applies the enclosed directives only to matching URLs
Syntax:	`<Location "URL-path|URL"> ... </Location>`
Context:	server config, virtual host
Status:	Core
Module:	core

The <LOCATION> directive limits the scope of the enclosed directives by URL. It is similar to the <DIRECTORY> directive, and starts a subsection which is terminated with a `</Location>` directive. <LOCATION> sections are processed in the order they appear in the configuration file, after the <DIRECTORY> sections and `.htaccess` files are read, and after the <FILES> sections.

<LOCATION> sections operate completely outside the filesystem. This has several consequences. Most importantly, <LOCATION> directives should not be used to control access to filesystem locations. Since several different URLs may map to the same filesystem location, such access controls may by circumvented.

The enclosed directives will be applied to the request if the path component of the URL meets *any* of the following criteria:

- The specified location matches exactly the path component of the URL.
- The specified location, which ends in a forward slash, is a prefix of the path component of the URL (treated as a context root).
- The specified location, with the addition of a trailing slash, is a prefix of the path component of the URL (also treated as a context root).

In the example below, where no trailing slash is used, requests to /private1, /private1/ and /private1/file.txt will have the enclosed directives applied, but /private1other would not.

```
<Location "/private1">
    # ...
</Location>
```

In the example below, where a trailing slash is used, requests to /private2/ and /private2/file.txt will have the enclosed directives applied, but /private2 and /private2other would not.

```
<Location "/private2/">
    # ...
</Location>
```

When to use <LOCATION>

> Use <LOCATION> to apply directives to content that lives outside the filesystem. For content that lives in the filesystem, use <DIRECTORY> and <FILES>. An exception is `<Location "/">`, which is an easy way to apply a configuration to the entire server.

For all origin (non-proxy) requests, the URL to be matched is a URL-path of the form `/path/`. *No scheme, hostname, port, or query string may be included.* For proxy requests, the URL to be matched is of the form `scheme://servername/path`, and you must include the prefix.

The URL may use wildcards. In a wild-card string, `?` matches any single character, and `*` matches any sequences of characters. Neither wildcard character matches a / in the URL-path.

Regular expressions can also be used, with the addition of the ~ character. For example:

```
<Location ~ "/(extra|special)/data">
    #...
</Location>
```

would match URLs that contained the substring `/extra/data` or `/special/data`. The directive <LOCATIONMATCH> behaves identical to the regex version of <LOCATION>, and is preferred, for the simple reason that ~ is hard to distinguish from - in many fonts.

The <LOCATION> functionality is especially useful when combined with the SETHANDLER directive. For example, to enable status requests but allow them only from browsers at `example.com`, you might use:

```
<Location "/status">
  SetHandler server-status
  Require host example.com
</Location>
```

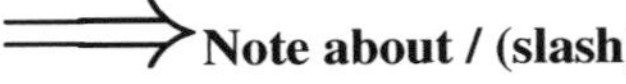**Note about / (slash)**

> The slash character has special meaning depending on where in a URL it appears. People may be used to its behavior in the filesystem where multiple adjacent slashes are frequently collapsed to a single slash (*i.e.*, `/home///foo` is the same as `/home/foo`). In URL-space this is not necessarily true. The <LOCATIONMATCH> directive and the regex version of <LOCATION> require you to explicitly specify multiple slashes if that is your intention.
> For example, `<LocationMatch "^/abc">` would match the request URL `/abc` but not the request URL `//abc`. The (non-regex) <LOCATION> directive behaves similarly when used for proxy requests. But when (non-regex) <LOCATION> is used for non-proxy requests it will implicitly match multiple slashes with a single slash. For example, if you specify `<Location "/abc/def">` and the request is to `/abc//def` then it will match.

See also

- How <Directory>, <Location> and <Files> sections work (p. 33) for an explanation of how these different sections are combined when a request is received.
- LOCATIONMATCH

LocationMatch Directive

Description:	Applies the enclosed directives only to regular-expression matching URLs
Syntax:	`<LocationMatch regex> ... </LocationMatch>`
Context:	server config, virtual host
Status:	Core
Module:	core

The <LOCATIONMATCH> directive limits the scope of the enclosed directives by URL, in an identical manner to <LOCATION>. However, it takes a regular expression as an argument instead of a simple string. For example:

```
<LocationMatch "/(extra|special)/data">
    # ...
</LocationMatch>
```

would match URLs that contained the substring `/extra/data` or `/special/data`.

⟹If the intent is that a URL **starts with** `/extra/data`, rather than merely **contains** `/extra/data`, prefix the regular expression with a ^ to require this.

```
<LocationMatch "^/(extra|special)/data">
```

From 2.4.8 onwards, named groups and backreferences are captured and written to the environment with the corresponding name prefixed with "MATCH_" and in upper case. This allows elements of URLs to be referenced from within expressions (p. 89) and modules like MOD_REWRITE. In order to prevent confusion, numbered (unnamed) backreferences are ignored. Use named groups instead.

```
<LocationMatch "^/combined/(?<sitename>[^/]+)">
    require ldap-group cn=%{env:MATCH_SITENAME},ou=combined,o=Example
</LocationMatch>
```

See also

- How <Directory>, <Location> and <Files> sections work (p. 33) for an explanation of how these different sections are combined when a request is received

LogLevel Directive

Description:	Controls the verbosity of the ErrorLog
Syntax:	`LogLevel [module:]level [module:level] ...`
Default:	`LogLevel warn`
Context:	server config, virtual host, directory
Status:	Core
Module:	core
Compatibility:	Per-module and per-directory configuration is available in Apache HTTP Server 2.3.6 and later

LOGLEVEL adjusts the verbosity of the messages recorded in the error logs (see ERRORLOG directive). The following *levels* are available, in order of decreasing significance:

Level	Description	Example
`emerg`	Emergencies - system is unusable.	"Child cannot open lock file. Exiting"
`alert`	Action must be taken immediately.	"getpwuid: couldn't determine user name from uid"
`crit`	Critical Conditions.	"socket: Failed to get a socket, exiting child"
`error`	Error conditions.	"Premature end of script headers"

warn	Warning conditions.	"child process 1234 did not exit, sending another SIGHU
notice	Normal but significant condition.	"httpd: caught SIGBUS, attempting to dump core in ..."
info	Informational.	"Server seems busy, (you may need to increase StartServ Min/MaxSpareServers)..."
debug	Debug-level messages	"Opening config file ..."
trace1	Trace messages	"proxy: FTP: control connection complete"
trace2	Trace messages	"proxy: CONNECT: sending the CONNECT request to mote proxy"
trace3	Trace messages	"openssl: Handshake: start"
trace4	Trace messages	"read from buffered SSL brigade, mode 0, 17 bytes"
trace5	Trace messages	"map lookup FAILED: map=rewritemap key=keyname"
trace6	Trace messages	"cache lookup FAILED, forcing new map lookup"
trace7	Trace messages, dumping large amounts of data	"— 0000: 02 23 44 30 13 40 ac 34 df 3d bf 9a 19 49 39 1
trace8	Trace messages, dumping large amounts of data	"— 0000: 02 23 44 30 13 40 ac 34 df 3d bf 9a 19 49 39 1

When a particular level is specified, messages from all other levels of higher significance will be reported as well. *E.g.*, when `LogLevel info` is specified, then messages with log levels of `notice` and `warn` will also be posted.

Using a level of at least `crit` is recommended.

For example:

```
LogLevel notice
```

**Note**

When logging to a regular file, messages of the level `notice` cannot be suppressed and thus are always logged. However, this doesn't apply when logging is done using `syslog`.

Specifying a level without a module name will reset the level for all modules to that level. Specifying a level with a module name will set the level for that module only. It is possible to use the module source file name, the module identifier, or the module identifier with the trailing `_module` omitted as module specification. This means the following three specifications are equivalent:

```
LogLevel info ssl:warn
LogLevel info mod_ssl.c:warn
LogLevel info ssl_module:warn
```

It is also possible to change the level per directory:

```
LogLevel info
<Directory "/usr/local/apache/htdocs/app">
  LogLevel debug
</Directory>
```

⟹ Per directory loglevel configuration only affects messages that are logged after the request has been parsed and that are associated with the request. Log messages which are associated with the connection or the server are not affected.

See also

- ErrorLog
- ErrorLogFormat
- Apache HTTP Server Log Files (p. 53)

MaxKeepAliveRequests Directive

Description:	Number of requests allowed on a persistent connection
Syntax:	`MaxKeepAliveRequests number`
Default:	`MaxKeepAliveRequests 100`
Context:	server config, virtual host
Status:	Core
Module:	core

The MAXKEEPALIVEREQUESTS directive limits the number of requests allowed per connection when KEEPALIVE is on. If it is set to `0`, unlimited requests will be allowed. We recommend that this setting be kept to a high value for maximum server performance.

For example:

```
MaxKeepAliveRequests 500
```

MaxRangeOverlaps Directive

Description:	Number of overlapping ranges (eg: `100-200,150-300`) allowed before returning the complete resource
Syntax:	`MaxRangeOverlaps default | unlimited | none | number-of-ranges`
Default:	`MaxRangeOverlaps 20`
Context:	server config, virtual host, directory
Status:	Core
Module:	core
Compatibility:	Available in Apache HTTP Server 2.3.15 and later

The MAXRANGEOVERLAPS directive limits the number of overlapping HTTP ranges the server is willing to return to the client. If more overlapping ranges than permitted are requested, the complete resource is returned instead.

default Limits the number of overlapping ranges to a compile-time default of 20.

none No overlapping Range headers are allowed.

unlimited The server does not limit the number of overlapping ranges it is willing to satisfy.

number-of-ranges A positive number representing the maximum number of overlapping ranges the server is willing to satisfy.

MaxRangeReversals Directive

Description:	Number of range reversals (eg: `100-200,50-70`) allowed before returning the complete resource
Syntax:	`MaxRangeReversals default | unlimited | none | number-of-ranges`
Default:	`MaxRangeReversals 20`
Context:	server config, virtual host, directory
Status:	Core
Module:	core
Compatibility:	Available in Apache HTTP Server 2.3.15 and later

The MAXRANGEREVERSALS directive limits the number of HTTP Range reversals the server is willing to return to the client. If more ranges reversals than permitted are requested, the complete resource is returned instead.

default Limits the number of range reversals to a compile-time default of 20.

none No Range reversals headers are allowed.

unlimited The server does not limit the number of range reversals it is willing to satisfy.

number-of-ranges A positive number representing the maximum number of range reversals the server is willing to satisfy.

MaxRanges Directive

Description:	Number of ranges allowed before returning the complete resource
Syntax:	`MaxRanges default | unlimited | none | number-of-ranges`
Default:	`MaxRanges 200`
Context:	server config, virtual host, directory
Status:	Core
Module:	core
Compatibility:	Available in Apache HTTP Server 2.3.15 and later

The MAXRANGES directive limits the number of HTTP ranges the server is willing to return to the client. If more ranges than permitted are requested, the complete resource is returned instead.

default Limits the number of ranges to a compile-time default of 200.

none Range headers are ignored.

unlimited The server does not limit the number of ranges it is willing to satisfy.

number-of-ranges A positive number representing the maximum number of ranges the server is willing to satisfy.

MergeTrailers Directive

Description:	Determines whether trailers are merged into headers
Syntax:	`MergeTrailers [on|off]`
Default:	`MergeTrailers off`
Context:	server config, virtual host
Status:	Core
Module:	core
Compatibility:	2.4.11 and later

This directive controls whether HTTP trailers are copied into the internal representation of HTTP headers. This merging occurs when the request body has been completely consumed, long after most header processing would have a chance to examine or modify request headers.

This option is provided for compatibility with releases prior to 2.4.11, where trailers were always merged.

Mutex Directive

Description:	Configures mutex mechanism and lock file directory for all or specified mutexes
Syntax:	`Mutex mechanism [default|mutex-name] ... [OmitPID]`
Default:	`Mutex default`
Context:	server config
Status:	Core
Module:	core
Compatibility:	Available in Apache HTTP Server 2.3.4 and later

The MUTEX directive sets the mechanism, and optionally the lock file location, that httpd and modules use to serialize access to resources. Specify `default` as the second argument to change the settings for all mutexes; specify a mutex name (see table below) as the second argument to override defaults only for that mutex.

The MUTEX directive is typically used in the following exceptional situations:

- change the mutex mechanism when the default mechanism selected by APR has a functional or performance problem
- change the directory used by file-based mutexes when the default directory does not support locking

Supported modules
This directive only configures mutexes which have been registered with the core server using the `ap_mutex_register()` API. All modules bundled with httpd support the MUTEX directive, but third-party modules may not. Consult the documentation of the third-party module, which must indicate the mutex name(s) which can be configured if this directive is supported.

The following mutex *mechanisms* are available:

- `default | yes` This selects the default locking implementation, as determined by APR. The default locking implementation can be displayed by running `httpd` with the `-V` option.
- `none | no` This effectively disables the mutex, and is only allowed for a mutex if the module indicates that it is a valid choice. Consult the module documentation for more information.
- `posixsem` This is a mutex variant based on a Posix semaphore.

Warning
The semaphore ownership is not recovered if a thread in the process holding the mutex segfaults, resulting in a hang of the web server.

- `sysvsem` This is a mutex variant based on a SystemV IPC semaphore.

Warning
It is possible to "leak" SysV semaphores if processes crash before the semaphore is removed.

Security
The semaphore API allows for a denial of service attack by any CGIs running under the same uid as the webserver (*i.e.*, all CGIs, unless you use something like `suexec` or `cgiwrapper`).

- `sem` This selects the "best" available semaphore implementation, choosing between Posix and SystemV IPC semaphores, in that order.
- `pthread` This is a mutex variant based on cross-process Posix thread mutexes.

Warning
On most systems, if a child process terminates abnormally while holding a mutex that uses this implementation, the server will deadlock and stop responding to requests. When this occurs, the server will require a manual restart to recover.
Solaris is a notable exception as it provides a mechanism which usually allows the mutex to be recovered after a child process terminates abnormally while holding a mutex.
If your system implements the `pthread_mutexattr_setrobust_np()` function, you may be able to use the `pthread` option safely.

- `fcntl:/path/to/mutex` This is a mutex variant where a physical (lock-)file and the `fcntl()` function are used as the mutex.

  Warning
  When multiple mutexes based on this mechanism are used within multi-threaded, multi-process environments, deadlock errors (EDEADLK) can be reported for valid mutex operations if `fcntl()` is not thread-aware, such as on Solaris.

- `flock:/path/to/mutex` This is similar to the `fcntl:/path/to/mutex` method with the exception that the `flock()` function is used to provide file locking.
- `file:/path/to/mutex` This selects the "best" available file locking implementation, choosing between `fcntl` and `flock`, in that order.

Most mechanisms are only available on selected platforms, where the underlying platform and APR support it. Mechanisms which aren't available on all platforms are *posixsem*, *sysvsem*, *sem*, *pthread*, *fcntl*, *flock*, and *file*.

With the file-based mechanisms *fcntl* and *flock*, the path, if provided, is a directory where the lock file will be created. The default directory is httpd's run-time file directory relative to ServerRoot. Always use a local disk filesystem for `/path/to/mutex` and never a directory residing on a NFS- or AFS-filesystem. The basename of the file will be the mutex type, an optional instance string provided by the module, and unless the `OmitPID` keyword is specified, the process id of the httpd parent process will be appended to make the file name unique, avoiding conflicts when multiple httpd instances share a lock file directory. For example, if the mutex name is `mpm-accept` and the lock file directory is `/var/httpd/locks`, the lock file name for the httpd instance with parent process id 12345 would be `/var/httpd/locks/mpm-accept.12345`.

Security
It is best to *avoid* putting mutex files in a world-writable directory such as `/var/tmp` because someone could create a denial of service attack and prevent the server from starting by creating a lockfile with the same name as the one the server will try to create.

The following table documents the names of mutexes used by httpd and bundled modules.

Mutex name	Module(s)	Protected resource
`mpm-accept`	PREFORK and WORKER MPMs	incoming connections, to avoid the thundering herd problem; for more information, refer to the performance tuning (p 327) documentation
`authdigest-client`	MOD_AUTH_DIGEST	client list in shared memory
`authdigest-opaque`	MOD_AUTH_DIGEST	counter in shared memory
`ldap-cache`	MOD_LDAP	LDAP result cache
`rewrite-map`	MOD_REWRITE	communication with external mapping programs, to avoid intermixed I/O from multiple requests
`ssl-cache`	MOD_SSL	SSL session cache
`ssl-stapling`	MOD_SSL	OCSP stapling response cache
`watchdog-callback`	MOD_WATCHDOG	callback function of a particular client module

The `OmitPID` keyword suppresses the addition of the httpd parent process id from the lock file name.

In the following example, the mutex mechanism for the MPM accept mutex will be changed from the compiled-in default to `fcntl`, with the associated lock file created in directory `/var/httpd/locks`. The mutex mechanism for all other mutexes will be changed from the compiled-in default to `sysvsem`.

```
Mutex sysvsem default
Mutex fcntl:/var/httpd/locks mpm-accept
```

NameVirtualHost Directive

Description:	DEPRECATED: Designates an IP address for name-virtual hosting
Syntax:	`NameVirtualHost addr[:port]`
Context:	server config
Status:	Core
Module:	core

Prior to 2.3.11, NAMEVIRTUALHOST was required to instruct the server that a particular IP address and port combination was usable as a name-based virtual host. In 2.3.11 and later, any time an IP address and port combination is used in multiple virtual hosts, name-based virtual hosting is automatically enabled for that address.

This directive currently has no effect.

See also

- Virtual Hosts documentation (p. 114)

Options Directive

Description:	Configures what features are available in a particular directory
Syntax:	`Options [+|-]option [[+|-]option] ...`
Default:	`Options FollowSymlinks`
Context:	server config, virtual host, directory, .htaccess
Override:	Options
Status:	Core
Module:	core
Compatibility:	The default was changed from All to FollowSymlinks in 2.3.11

The OPTIONS directive controls which server features are available in a particular directory.

option can be set to `None`, in which case none of the extra features are enabled, or one or more of the following:

`All` All options except for `MultiViews`.

`ExecCGI` Execution of CGI scripts using MOD_CGI is permitted.

`FollowSymLinks` The server will follow symbolic links in this directory. This is the default setting.

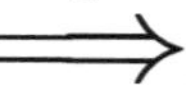

Even though the server follows the symlink it does *not* change the pathname used to match against <DIRECTORY> sections.

The `FollowSymLinks` and `SymLinksIfOwnerMatch` OPTIONS work only in <DIRECTORY> sections or `.htaccess` files.

Omitting this option should not be considered a security restriction, since symlink testing is subject to race conditions that make it circumventable.

`Includes` Server-side includes provided by MOD_INCLUDE are permitted.

`IncludesNOEXEC` Server-side includes are permitted, but the `#exec cmd` and `#exec cgi` are disabled. It is still possible to `#include virtual` CGI scripts from SCRIPTALIASed directories.

`Indexes` If a URL which maps to a directory is requested and there is no DIRECTORYINDEX (*e.g.*, `index.html`) in that directory, then MOD_AUTOINDEX will return a formatted listing of the directory.

`MultiViews` Content negotiated (p. 68) "MultiViews" are allowed using MOD_NEGOTIATION.

Note

This option gets ignored if set anywhere other than <DIRECTORY>, as MOD_NEGOTIATION needs real resources to compare against and evaluate from.

SymLinksIfOwnerMatch The server will only follow symbolic links for which the target file or directory is owned by the same user id as the link.

**Note**

The FollowSymLinks and SymLinksIfOwnerMatch OPTIONS work only in <DIRECTORY> sections or .htaccess files.

This option should not be considered a security restriction, since symlink testing is subject to race conditions that make it circumventable.

Normally, if multiple OPTIONS could apply to a directory, then the most specific one is used and others are ignored; the options are not merged. (See how sections are merged (p. 33) .) However if *all* the options on the OPTIONS directive are preceded by a + or − symbol, the options are merged. Any options preceded by a + are added to the options currently in force, and any options preceded by a − are removed from the options currently in force.

**Note**

Mixing OPTIONS with a + or − with those without is not valid syntax and will be rejected during server startup by the syntax check with an abort.

For example, without any + and − symbols:

```
<Directory "/web/docs">
  Options Indexes FollowSymLinks
</Directory>

<Directory "/web/docs/spec">
  Options Includes
</Directory>
```

then only Includes will be set for the /web/docs/spec directory. However if the second OPTIONS directive uses the + and − symbols:

```
<Directory "/web/docs">
  Options Indexes FollowSymLinks
</Directory>

<Directory "/web/docs/spec">
  Options +Includes -Indexes
</Directory>
```

then the options FollowSymLinks and Includes are set for the /web/docs/spec directory.

**Note**

Using -IncludesNOEXEC or -Includes disables server-side includes completely regardless of the previous setting.

The default in the absence of any other settings is FollowSymlinks.

Protocol Directive

Description:	Protocol for a listening socket
Syntax:	Protocol protocol
Context:	server config, virtual host
Status:	Core
Module:	core
Compatibility:	Available in Apache 2.1.5 and later. On Windows, from Apache 2.3.3 and later.

This directive specifies the protocol used for a specific listening socket. The protocol is used to determine which module should handle a request and to apply protocol specific optimizations with the ACCEPTFILTER directive.

You only need to set the protocol if you are running on non-standard ports; otherwise, `http` is assumed for port 80 and `https` for port 443.

For example, if you are running `https` on a non-standard port, specify the protocol explicitly:

```
Protocol https
```

You can also specify the protocol using the LISTEN directive.

See also

- ACCEPTFILTER
- LISTEN

Protocols Directive

Description:	Protocols available for a server/virtual host
Syntax:	`Protocols protocol ...`
Default:	`Protocols http/1.1`
Context:	server config, virtual host
Status:	Core
Module:	core
Compatibility:	Only available from Apache 2.4.17 and later.

This directive specifies the list of protocols supported for a server/virtual host. The list determines the allowed protocols a client may negotiate for this server/host.

You need to set protocols if you want to extend the available protocols for a server/host. By default, only the http/1.1 protocol (which includes the compatibility with 1.0 and 0.9 clients) is allowed.

For example, if you want to support HTTP/2 for a server with TLS, specify:

```
Protocols h2 http/1.1
```

Valid protocols are `http/1.1` for http and https connections, `h2` on https connections and `h2c` for http connections. Modules may enable more protocols.

It is safe to specify protocols that are unavailable/disabled. Such protocol names will simply be ignored.

Protocols specified in base servers are inherited for virtual hosts only if the virtual host has no own Protocols directive. Or, the other way around, Protocols directives in virtual hosts replace any such directive in the base server.

See also

- PROTOCOLSHONORORDER

ProtocolsHonorOrder Directive

Description:	Determines if order of Protocols determines precedence during negotiation
Syntax:	`ProtocolsHonorOrder On|Off`
Default:	`ProtocolsHonorOrder On`
Context:	server config, virtual host
Status:	Core
Module:	core
Compatibility:	Only available from Apache 2.4.17 and later.

This directive specifies if the server should honor the order in which the PROTOCOLS directive lists protocols.

If configured Off, the client supplied list order of protocols has precedence over the order in the server configuration.

With PROTOCOLSHONORORDER set to `on` (default), the client ordering does not matter and only the ordering in the server settings influences the outcome of the protocol negotiation.

See also

- PROTOCOLS

RLimitCPU Directive

Description:	Limits the CPU consumption of processes launched by Apache httpd children
Syntax:	`RLimitCPU seconds|max [seconds|max]`
Default:	`Unset; uses operating system defaults`
Context:	server config, virtual host, directory, .htaccess
Override:	All
Status:	Core
Module:	core

Takes 1 or 2 parameters. The first parameter sets the soft resource limit for all processes and the second parameter sets the maximum resource limit. Either parameter can be a number, or `max` to indicate to the server that the limit should be set to the maximum allowed by the operating system configuration. Raising the maximum resource limit requires that the server is running as `root` or in the initial startup phase.

This applies to processes forked from Apache httpd children servicing requests, not the Apache httpd children themselves. This includes CGI scripts and SSI exec commands, but not any processes forked from the Apache httpd parent, such as piped logs.

CPU resource limits are expressed in seconds per process.

See also

- RLIMITMEM
- RLIMITNPROC

RLimitMEM Directive

Description:	Limits the memory consumption of processes launched by Apache httpd children
Syntax:	`RLimitMEM bytes|max [bytes|max]`
Default:	`Unset; uses operating system defaults`
Context:	server config, virtual host, directory, .htaccess
Override:	All
Status:	Core
Module:	core

Takes 1 or 2 parameters. The first parameter sets the soft resource limit for all processes and the second parameter sets the maximum resource limit. Either parameter can be a number, or `max` to indicate to the server that the limit should be set to the maximum allowed by the operating system configuration. Raising the maximum resource limit requires that the server is running as `root` or in the initial startup phase.

This applies to processes forked from Apache httpd children servicing requests, not the Apache httpd children themselves. This includes CGI scripts and SSI exec commands, but not any processes forked from the Apache httpd parent, such as piped logs.

Memory resource limits are expressed in bytes per process.

See also

- RLIMITCPU
- RLIMITNPROC

RLimitNPROC Directive

Description:	Limits the number of processes that can be launched by processes launched by Apache httpd children
Syntax:	`RLimitNPROC number|max [number|max]`
Default:	`Unset; uses operating system defaults`
Context:	server config, virtual host, directory, .htaccess
Override:	All
Status:	Core
Module:	core

Takes 1 or 2 parameters. The first parameter sets the soft resource limit for all processes, and the second parameter sets the maximum resource limit. Either parameter can be a number, or `max` to indicate to the server that the limit should be set to the maximum allowed by the operating system configuration. Raising the maximum resource limit requires that the server is running as `root` or in the initial startup phase.

This applies to processes forked from Apache httpd children servicing requests, not the Apache httpd children themselves. This includes CGI scripts and SSI exec commands, but not any processes forked from the Apache httpd parent, such as piped logs.

Process limits control the number of processes per user.

**Note**

If CGI processes are **not** running under user ids other than the web server user id, this directive will limit the number of processes that the server itself can create. Evidence of this situation will be indicated by **`cannot fork`** messages in the `error_log`.

See also

- RLIMITMEM
- RLIMITCPU

ScriptInterpreterSource Directive

Description:	Technique for locating the interpreter for CGI scripts
Syntax:	`ScriptInterpreterSource Registry|Registry-Strict|Script`
Default:	`ScriptInterpreterSource Script`
Context:	server config, virtual host, directory, .htaccess
Override:	FileInfo
Status:	Core
Module:	core
Compatibility:	Win32 only.

This directive is used to control how Apache httpd finds the interpreter used to run CGI scripts. The default setting is `Script`. This causes Apache httpd to use the interpreter pointed to by the shebang line (first line, starting with `#!`) in the script. On Win32 systems this line usually looks like:

```
#!C:/Perl/bin/perl.exe
```

or, if `perl` is in the `PATH`, simply:

```
#!perl
```

Setting `ScriptInterpreterSource Registry` will cause the Windows Registry tree `HKEY_CLASSES_ROOT` to be searched using the script file extension (e.g., `.pl`) as a search key. The command defined by the registry subkey `Shell\ExecCGI\Command` or, if it does not exist, by the subkey `Shell\Open\Command` is used to open the script file. If the registry keys cannot be found, Apache httpd falls back to the behavior of the `Script` option.

Security
Be careful when using `ScriptInterpreterSource Registry` with SCRIPTALIAS'ed directories, because Apache httpd will try to execute **every** file within this directory. The `Registry` setting may cause undesired program calls on files which are typically not executed. For example, the default open command on `.htm` files on most Windows systems will execute Microsoft Internet Explorer, so any HTTP request for an `.htm` file existing within the script directory would start the browser in the background on the server. This is a good way to crash your system within a minute or so.

The option `Registry-Strict` which is new in Apache HTTP Server 2.0 does the same thing as `Registry` but uses only the subkey `Shell\ExecCGI\Command`. The `ExecCGI` key is not a common one. It must be configured manually in the windows registry and hence prevents accidental program calls on your system.

SeeRequestTail Directive

Description:	Determine if mod_status displays the first 63 characters of a request or the last 63, assuming the request itself is greater than 63 chars.
Syntax:	`SeeRequestTail On|Off`
Default:	`SeeRequestTail Off`
Context:	server config
Status:	Core
Module:	core
Compatibility:	Available in Apache httpd 2.2.7 and later.

mod_status with `ExtendedStatus On` displays the actual request being handled. For historical purposes, only 63 characters of the request are actually stored for display purposes. This directive controls whether the 1st 63 characters are stored (the previous behavior and the default) or if the last 63 characters are. This is only applicable, of course, if the length of the request is 64 characters or greater.

If Apache httpd is handling `GET/disk1/storage/apache/htdocs/images/imagestore1/food/apple` mod_status displays as follows:

Off (default)	GET/disk1/storage/apache/htdocs/images/imagestore1/food/appl
On	orage/apache/htdocs/images/imagestore1/food/apples.jpgHTTP/1

ServerAdmin Directive

Description:	Email address that the server includes in error messages sent to the client
Syntax:	`ServerAdmin email-address|URL`
Context:	server config, virtual host
Status:	Core
Module:	core

The SERVERADMIN sets the contact address that the server includes in any error messages it returns to the client. If the `httpd` doesn't recognize the supplied argument as an URL, it assumes, that it's an *email-address* and prepends it with `mailto:` in hyperlink targets. However, it's recommended to actually use an email address, since there are a lot of CGI scripts that make that assumption. If you want to use an URL, it should point to another server under your control. Otherwise users may not be able to contact you in case of errors.

It may be worth setting up a dedicated address for this, e.g.

```
ServerAdmin www-admin@foo.example.com
```

as users do not always mention that they are talking about the server!

ServerAlias Directive

Description:	Alternate names for a host used when matching requests to name-virtual hosts
Syntax:	`ServerAlias hostname [hostname] ...`
Context:	virtual host
Status:	Core
Module:	core

The SERVERALIAS directive sets the alternate names for a host, for use with name-based virtual hosts (p. 115) . The SERVERALIAS may include wildcards, if appropriate.

```
<VirtualHost *:80>
  ServerName server.example.com
  ServerAlias server server2.example.com server2
  ServerAlias *.example.com
  UseCanonicalName Off
  # ...
</VirtualHost>
```

Name-based virtual hosts for the best-matching set of <VIRTUALHOST>s are processed in the order they appear in the configuration. The first matching SERVERNAME or SERVERALIAS is used, with no different precedence for wildcards (nor for ServerName vs. ServerAlias).

The complete list of names in the VIRTUALHOST directive are treated just like a (non wildcard) SERVERALIAS.

See also

- USECANONICALNAME
- Apache HTTP Server Virtual Host documentation (p. 114)

ServerName Directive

Description:	Hostname and port that the server uses to identify itself
Syntax:	`ServerName [scheme://]fully-qualified-domain-name[:port]`
Context:	server config, virtual host
Status:	Core
Module:	core

The SERVERNAME directive sets the request scheme, hostname and port that the server uses to identify itself. This is used when creating redirection URLs.

Additionally, SERVERNAME is used (possibly in conjunction with SERVERALIAS) to uniquely identify a virtual host, when using name-based virtual hosts (p. 115) .

For example, if the name of the machine hosting the web server is `simple.example.com`, but the machine also has the DNS alias `www.example.com` and you wish the web server to be so identified, the following directive should be used:

```
ServerName www.example.com
```

The SERVERNAME directive may appear anywhere within the definition of a server. However, each appearance overrides the previous appearance (within that server).

If no SERVERNAME is specified, then the server attempts to deduce the client visible hostname by performing a reverse lookup on an IP address of the systems hostname.

If no port is specified in the SERVERNAME, then the server will use the port from the incoming request. For optimal reliability and predictability, you should specify an explicit hostname and port using the SERVERNAME directive.

If you are using name-based virtual hosts (p. 115) , the SERVERNAME inside a <VIRTUALHOST> section specifies what hostname must appear in the request's `Host:` header to match this virtual host.

Sometimes, the server runs behind a device that processes SSL, such as a reverse proxy, load balancer or SSL offload appliance. When this is the case, specify the `https://` scheme and the port number to which the clients connect in the SERVERNAME directive to make sure that the server generates the correct self-referential URLs.

See the description of the USECANONICALNAME and USECANONICALPHYSICALPORT directives for settings which determine whether self-referential URLs (e.g., by the MOD_DIR module) will refer to the specified port, or to the port number given in the client's request.

! Failure to set SERVERNAME to a name that your server can resolve to an IP address will result in a startup warning. `httpd` will then use whatever hostname it can determine, using the system's `hostname` command. This will almost never be the hostname you actually want.

```
httpd: Could not reliably determine the server's fully
qualified domain name, using rocinante.local for
ServerName
```

See also

- Issues Regarding DNS and Apache HTTP Server (p. 111)
- Apache HTTP Server virtual host documentation (p. 114)
- USECANONICALNAME
- USECANONICALPHYSICALPORT
- SERVERALIAS

ServerPath Directive

Description:	Legacy URL pathname for a name-based virtual host that is accessed by an incompatible browser
Syntax:	`ServerPath URL-path`
Context:	virtual host
Status:	Core
Module:	core

The SERVERPATH directive sets the legacy URL pathname for a host, for use with name-based virtual hosts (p. 114) .

See also

- Apache HTTP Server Virtual Host documentation (p. 114)

ServerRoot Directive

Description:	Base directory for the server installation
Syntax:	`ServerRoot directory-path`
Default:	`ServerRoot /usr/local/apache`
Context:	server config
Status:	Core
Module:	core

The SERVERROOT directive sets the directory in which the server lives. Typically it will contain the subdirectories `conf/` and `logs/`. Relative paths in other configuration directives (such as INCLUDE or LOADMODULE, for example) are taken as relative to this directory.

```
ServerRoot "/home/httpd"
```

The default location of SERVERROOT may be modified by using the `--prefix` argument to `configure` (p. 295) , and most third-party distributions of the server have a different default location from the one listed above.

See also

- the `-d` option to `httpd` (p. 25)
- the security tips (p. 338) for information on how to properly set permissions on the SERVERROOT

ServerSignature Directive

Description:	Configures the footer on server-generated documents
Syntax:	`ServerSignature On|Off|EMail`
Default:	`ServerSignature Off`
Context:	server config, virtual host, directory, .htaccess
Override:	All
Status:	Core
Module:	core

The SERVERSIGNATURE directive allows the configuration of a trailing footer line under server-generated documents (error messages, MOD_PROXY ftp directory listings, MOD_INFO output, ...). The reason why you would want to enable such a footer line is that in a chain of proxies, the user often has no possibility to tell which of the chained servers actually produced a returned error message.

The `Off` setting, which is the default, suppresses the footer line (and is therefore compatible with the behavior of Apache-1.2 and below). The `On` setting simply adds a line with the server version number and SERVERNAME of the serving virtual host, and the `EMail` setting additionally creates a "mailto:" reference to the SERVERADMIN of the referenced document.

After version 2.0.44, the details of the server version number presented are controlled by the SERVERTOKENS directive.

See also

- SERVERTOKENS

ServerTokens Directive

Description:	Configures the `Server` HTTP response header
Syntax:	`ServerTokens Major|Minor|Min[imal]|Prod[uctOnly]|OS|Full`
Default:	`ServerTokens Full`
Context:	server config
Status:	Core
Module:	core

This directive controls whether `Server` response header field which is sent back to clients includes a description of the generic OS-type of the server as well as information about compiled-in modules.

`ServerTokens Full` (or not specified) Server sends (*e.g.*): `Server: Apache/2.4.2 (Unix) PHP/4.2.2 MyMod/1.2`

`ServerTokens Prod[uctOnly]` Server sends (*e.g.*): `Server: Apache`

`ServerTokens Major` Server sends (*e.g.*): `Server: Apache/2`

`ServerTokens Minor` Server sends (*e.g.*): `Server: Apache/2.4`

`ServerTokens Min[imal]` Server sends (*e.g.*): `Server: Apache/2.4.2`

`ServerTokens OS` Server sends (*e.g.*): `Server: Apache/2.4.2 (Unix)`

This setting applies to the entire server, and cannot be enabled or disabled on a virtualhost-by-virtualhost basis.

After version 2.0.44, this directive also controls the information presented by the SERVERSIGNATURE directive.

⟹ Setting SERVERTOKENS to less than `minimal` is not recommended because it makes it more difficult to debug interoperational problems. Also note that disabling the Server: header does nothing at all to make your server more secure. The idea of "security through obscurity" is a myth and leads to a false sense of safety.

See also

- SERVERSIGNATURE

SetHandler Directive

Description:	Forces all matching files to be processed by a handler
Syntax:	`SetHandler handler-name|None`
Context:	server config, virtual host, directory, .htaccess
Override:	FileInfo
Status:	Core
Module:	core

When placed into an `.htaccess` file or a <DIRECTORY> or <LOCATION> section, this directive forces all matching files to be parsed through the handler (p. 98) given by *handler-name*. For example, if you had a directory you wanted to be parsed entirely as imagemap rule files, regardless of extension, you might put the following into an `.htaccess` file in that directory:

```
SetHandler imap-file
```

Another example: if you wanted to have the server display a status report whenever a URL of `http://servername/status` was called, you might put the following into `httpd.conf`:

```
<Location "/status">
  SetHandler server-status
</Location>
```

You could also use this directive to configure a particular handler for files with a particular file extension. For example:

```
<FilesMatch "\.php$">
    SetHandler application/x-httpd-php
</FilesMatch>
```

You can override an earlier defined SETHANDLER directive by using the value `None`.

**Note**

Because SETHANDLER overrides default handlers, normal behavior such as handling of URLs ending in a slash (/) as directories or index files is suppressed.

See also

- ADDHANDLER

SetInputFilter Directive

Description:	Sets the filters that will process client requests and POST input
Syntax:	`SetInputFilter filter[;filter...]`
Context:	server config, virtual host, directory, .htaccess
Override:	FileInfo
Status:	Core
Module:	core

The SETINPUTFILTER directive sets the filter or filters which will process client requests and POST input when they are received by the server. This is in addition to any filters defined elsewhere, including the ADDINPUTFILTER directive.

If more than one filter is specified, they must be separated by semicolons in the order in which they should process the content.

See also

- Filters (p. 100) documentation

SetOutputFilter Directive

Description:	Sets the filters that will process responses from the server
Syntax:	`SetOutputFilter filter[;filter...]`
Context:	server config, virtual host, directory, .htaccess
Override:	FileInfo
Status:	Core
Module:	core

The SETOUTPUTFILTER directive sets the filters which will process responses from the server before they are sent to the client. This is in addition to any filters defined elsewhere, including the ADDOUTPUTFILTER directive.

For example, the following configuration will process all files in the `/www/data/` directory for server-side includes.

```
<Directory "/www/data/">
  SetOutputFilter INCLUDES
</Directory>
```

If more than one filter is specified, they must be separated by semicolons in the order in which they should process the content.

See also

- Filters (p. 100) documentation

TimeOut Directive

Description:	Amount of time the server will wait for certain events before failing a request
Syntax:	`TimeOut seconds`
Default:	`TimeOut 60`
Context:	server config, virtual host
Status:	Core
Module:	core

The TIMEOUT directive defines the length of time Apache httpd will wait for I/O in various circumstances:

1. When reading data from the client, the length of time to wait for a TCP packet to arrive if the read buffer is empty.
2. When writing data to the client, the length of time to wait for an acknowledgement of a packet if the send buffer is full.
3. In MOD_CGI, the length of time to wait for output from a CGI script.
4. In MOD_EXT_FILTER, the length of time to wait for output from a filtering process.
5. In MOD_PROXY, the default timeout value if PROXYTIMEOUT is not configured.

TraceEnable Directive

Description:	Determines the behavior on `TRACE` requests
Syntax:	`TraceEnable [on|off|extended]`
Default:	`TraceEnable on`
Context:	server config, virtual host
Status:	Core
Module:	core

This directive overrides the behavior of `TRACE` for both the core server and MOD_PROXY. The default `TraceEnable on` permits `TRACE` requests per RFC 2616, which disallows any request body to accompany the request. `TraceEnable off` causes the core server and MOD_PROXY to return a `405` (Method not allowed) error to the client.

Finally, for testing and diagnostic purposes only, request bodies may be allowed using the non-compliant `TraceEnable extended` directive. The core (as an origin server) will restrict the request body to 64k (plus 8k for chunk headers if `Transfer-Encoding: chunked` is used). The core will reflect the full headers and all chunk headers with the response body. As a proxy server, the request body is not restricted to 64k.

**Note**

Despite claims to the contrary, `TRACE` is not a security vulnerability, and there is no viable reason for it to be disabled. Doing so necessarily makes your server noncompliant.

UnDefine Directive

Description:	Undefine the existence of a variable
Syntax:	`UnDefine parameter-name`
Context:	server config
Status:	Core
Module:	core

Undoes the effect of a DEFINE or of passing a `-D` argument to `httpd`.

This directive can be used to toggle the use of <IFDEFINE> sections without needing to alter `-D` arguments in any startup scripts.

While this directive is supported in virtual host context, the changes it makes are visible to any later configuration directives, beyond any enclosing virtual host.

UseCanonicalName Directive

Description:	Configures how the server determines its own name and port
Syntax:	`UseCanonicalName On|Off|DNS`
Default:	`UseCanonicalName Off`
Context:	server config, virtual host, directory
Status:	Core
Module:	core

In many situations Apache httpd must construct a *self-referential* URL – that is, a URL that refers back to the same server. With `UseCanonicalName On` Apache httpd will use the hostname and port specified in the SERVERNAME directive to construct the canonical name for the server. This name is used in all self-referential URLs, and for the values of `SERVER_NAME` and `SERVER_PORT` in CGIs.

With `UseCanonicalName Off` Apache httpd will form self-referential URLs using the hostname and port supplied by the client if any are supplied (otherwise it will use the canonical name, as defined above). These values are the same that are used to implement name-based virtual hosts (p. 115) and are available with the same clients. The CGI variables `SERVER_NAME` and `SERVER_PORT` will be constructed from the client supplied values as well.

An example where this may be useful is on an intranet server where you have users connecting to the machine using short names such as `www`. You'll notice that if the users type a shortname and a URL which is a directory, such as `http://www/splat`, *without the trailing slash*, then Apache httpd will redirect them to `http://www.example.com/splat/`. If you have authentication enabled, this will cause the user to have to authenticate twice (once for `www` and once again for `www.example.com` – see the FAQ on this subject for more information[7]). But if USECANONICALNAME is set `Off`, then Apache httpd will redirect to `http://www/splat/`.

There is a third option, `UseCanonicalName DNS`, which is intended for use with mass IP-based virtual hosting to support ancient clients that do not provide a `Host:` header. With this option, Apache httpd does a reverse DNS lookup on the server IP address that the client connected to in order to work out self-referential URLs.

Warning
If CGIs make assumptions about the values of `SERVER_NAME`, they may be broken by this option. The client is essentially free to give whatever value they want as a hostname. But if the CGI is only using `SERVER_NAME` to construct self-referential URLs, then it should be just fine.

See also

- USECANONICALPHYSICALPORT

[7] http://wiki.apache.org/httpd/FAQ#Why_does_Apache_ask_for_my_password_twice_before_serving_a_file.3F

- SERVERNAME
- LISTEN

UseCanonicalPhysicalPort Directive

Description:	Configures how the server determines its own port
Syntax:	`UseCanonicalPhysicalPort On|Off`
Default:	`UseCanonicalPhysicalPort Off`
Context:	server config, virtual host, directory
Status:	Core
Module:	core

In many situations Apache httpd must construct a *self-referential* URL – that is, a URL that refers back to the same server. With `UseCanonicalPhysicalPort On`, Apache httpd will, when constructing the canonical port for the server to honor the USECANONICALNAME directive, provide the actual physical port number being used by this request as a potential port. With `UseCanonicalPhysicalPort Off`, Apache httpd will not ever use the actual physical port number, instead relying on all configured information to construct a valid port number.

**Note**

The ordering of the lookup when the physical port is used is as follows:

`UseCanonicalName On`

1. Port provided in SERVERNAME
2. Physical port
3. Default port

`UseCanonicalName Off | DNS`

1. Parsed port from `Host:` header
2. Physical port
3. Port provided in SERVERNAME
4. Default port

With `UseCanonicalPhysicalPort Off`, the physical ports are removed from the ordering.

See also

- USECANONICALNAME
- SERVERNAME
- LISTEN

VirtualHost Directive

Description:	Contains directives that apply only to a specific hostname or IP address
Syntax:	`<VirtualHost addr[:port] [addr[:port]] ...> ... </VirtualHost>`
Context:	server config
Status:	Core
Module:	core

<VIRTUALHOST> and `</VirtualHost>` are used to enclose a group of directives that will apply only to a particular virtual host. Any directive that is allowed in a virtual host context may be used. When the server receives a request for a document on a particular virtual host, it uses the configuration directives enclosed in the <VIRTUALHOST> section. *Addr* can be any of the following, optionally followed by a colon and a port number (or *):

- The IP address of the virtual host;
- A fully qualified domain name for the IP address of the virtual host (not recommended);
- The character *, which acts as a wildcard and matches any IP address.
- The string _default_, which is an alias for *

```
<VirtualHost 10.1.2.3:80>
  ServerAdmin webmaster@host.example.com
  DocumentRoot "/www/docs/host.example.com"
  ServerName host.example.com
  ErrorLog "logs/host.example.com-error_log"
  TransferLog "logs/host.example.com-access_log"
</VirtualHost>
```

IPv6 addresses must be specified in square brackets because the optional port number could not be determined otherwise. An IPv6 example is shown below:

```
<VirtualHost [2001:db8::a00:20ff:fea7:ccea]:80>
  ServerAdmin webmaster@host.example.com
  DocumentRoot "/www/docs/host.example.com"
  ServerName host.example.com
  ErrorLog "logs/host.example.com-error_log"
  TransferLog "logs/host.example.com-access_log"
</VirtualHost>
```

Each Virtual Host must correspond to a different IP address, different port number, or a different host name for the server, in the former case the server machine must be configured to accept IP packets for multiple addresses. (If the machine does not have multiple network interfaces, then this can be accomplished with the `ifconfig alias` command – if your OS supports it).

**Note**

The use of <VIRTUALHOST> does **not** affect what addresses Apache httpd listens on. You may need to ensure that Apache httpd is listening on the correct addresses using LISTEN.

A SERVERNAME should be specified inside each <VIRTUALHOST> block. If it is absent, the SERVERNAME from the "main" server configuration will be inherited.

When a request is received, the server first maps it to the best matching <VIRTUALHOST> based on the local IP address and port combination only. Non-wildcards have a higher precedence. If no match based on IP and port occurs at all, the "main" server configuration is used.

If multiple virtual hosts contain the best matching IP address and port, the server selects from these virtual hosts the best match based on the requested hostname. If no matching name-based virtual host is found, then the first listed virtual host that matched the IP address will be used. As a consequence, the first listed virtual host for a given IP address and port combination is the default virtual host for that IP and port combination.

Security

See the security tips (p. 338) document for details on why your security could be compromised if the directory where log files are stored is writable by anyone other than the user that starts the server.

See also

- Apache HTTP Server Virtual Host documentation (p. 114)

- Issues Regarding DNS and Apache HTTP Server (p. 111)
- Setting which addresses and ports Apache HTTP Server uses (p. 78)
- How <Directory>, <Location> and <Files> sections work (p. 33) for an explanation of how these different sections are combined when a request is received

10.4 Apache Module mod_access_compat

Description:	Group authorizations based on host (name or IP address)
Status:	Extension
ModuleIdentifier:	access_compat_module
SourceFile:	mod_access_compat.c
Compatibility:	Available in Apache HTTP Server 2.3 as a compatibility module with previous versions of Apache httpd 2.x. The directives provided by this module have been deprecated by the new authz refactoring. Please see MOD_AUTHZ_HOST

Summary

The directives provided by MOD_ACCESS_COMPAT are used in <DIRECTORY>, <FILES>, and <LOCATION> sections as well as `.htaccess (p. 354)` files to control access to particular parts of the server. Access can be controlled based on the client hostname, IP address, or other characteristics of the client request, as captured in environment variables (p. 82) . The ALLOW and DENY directives are used to specify which clients are or are not allowed access to the server, while the ORDER directive sets the default access state, and configures how the ALLOW and DENY directives interact with each other.

Both host-based access restrictions and password-based authentication may be implemented simultaneously. In that case, the SATISFY directive is used to determine how the two sets of restrictions interact.

Note
The directives provided by MOD_ACCESS_COMPAT have been deprecated by the new authz refactoring. Please see MOD_AUTHZ_HOST.

In general, access restriction directives apply to all access methods (GET, PUT, POST, etc). This is the desired behavior in most cases. However, it is possible to restrict some methods, while leaving other methods unrestricted, by enclosing the directives in a <LIMIT> section.

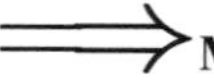

Merging of configuration sections
When any directive provided by this module is used in a new configuration section, no directives provided by this module are inherited from previous configuration sections.

Directives

- Allow
- Deny
- Order
- Satisfy

See also

- REQUIRE
- MOD_AUTHZ_HOST
- MOD_AUTHZ_CORE

Allow Directive

Description:	Controls which hosts can access an area of the server
Syntax:	`Allow from all|host|env=[!]env-variable [host|env=[!]env-variable] ...`
Context:	directory, .htaccess
Override:	Limit
Status:	Extension
Module:	mod_access_compat

The ALLOW directive affects which hosts can access an area of the server. Access can be controlled by hostname, IP address, IP address range, or by other characteristics of the client request captured in environment variables.

The first argument to this directive is always `from`. The subsequent arguments can take three different forms. If `Allow from all` is specified, then all hosts are allowed access, subject to the configuration of the DENY and ORDER directives as discussed below. To allow only particular hosts or groups of hosts to access the server, the *host* can be specified in any of the following formats:

A (partial) domain-name `Allow from example.org`
`Allow from .net example.edu`

Hosts whose names match, or end in, this string are allowed access. Only complete components are matched, so the above example will match `foo.example.org` but it will not match `fooexample.org`. This configuration will cause Apache httpd to perform a double DNS lookup on the client IP address, regardless of the setting of the HOSTNAMELOOKUPS directive. It will do a reverse DNS lookup on the IP address to find the associated hostname, and then do a forward lookup on the hostname to assure that it matches the original IP address. Only if the forward and reverse DNS are consistent and the hostname matches will access be allowed.

A full IP address `Allow from 10.1.2.3`
`Allow from 192.168.1.104 192.168.1.205`

An IP address of a host allowed access

A partial IP address `Allow from 10.1`
`Allow from 10 172.20 192.168.2`

The first 1 to 3 bytes of an IP address, for subnet restriction.

A network/netmask pair `Allow from 10.1.0.0/255.255.0.0`

A network a.b.c.d, and a netmask w.x.y.z. For more fine-grained subnet restriction.

A network/nnn CIDR specification `Allow from 10.1.0.0/16`

Similar to the previous case, except the netmask consists of nnn high-order 1 bits.

Note that the last three examples above match exactly the same set of hosts.

IPv6 addresses and IPv6 subnets can be specified as shown below:

```
Allow from 2001:db8::a00:20ff:fea7:ccea
Allow from 2001:db8::a00:20ff:fea7:ccea/10
```

The third format of the arguments to the ALLOW directive allows access to the server to be controlled based on the existence of an environment variable (p. 82). When `Allow from env=`*`env-variable`* is specified, then the request is allowed access if the environment variable *env-variable* exists. When `Allow from env=!`*`env-variable`* is specified, then the request is allowed access if the environment variable *env-variable* doesn't exist. The server provides the ability to set environment variables in a flexible way based on characteristics of the client request using the directives provided by MOD_SETENVIF. Therefore, this directive can be used to allow access based on such factors as the clients `User-Agent` (browser type), `Referer`, or other HTTP request header fields.

```
SetEnvIf User-Agent ^KnockKnock/2\.0 let_me_in
<Directory "/docroot">
    Order Deny,Allow
    Deny from all
    Allow from env=let_me_in
</Directory>
```

In this case, browsers with a user-agent string beginning with `KnockKnock/2.0` will be allowed access, and all others will be denied.

⟹ **Merging of configuration sections**
When any directive provided by this module is used in a new configuration section, no directives provided by this module are inherited from previous configuration sections.

Deny Directive

Description:	Controls which hosts are denied access to the server
Syntax:	`Deny from all|host|env=[!]env-variable [host|env=[!]env-variable] ...`
Context:	directory, .htaccess
Override:	Limit
Status:	Extension
Module:	mod_access_compat

This directive allows access to the server to be restricted based on hostname, IP address, or environment variables. The arguments for the DENY directive are identical to the arguments for the ALLOW directive.

Order Directive

Description:	Controls the default access state and the order in which ALLOW and DENY are evaluated.
Syntax:	`Order ordering`
Default:	`Order Deny,Allow`
Context:	directory, .htaccess
Override:	Limit
Status:	Extension
Module:	mod_access_compat

The ORDER directive, along with the ALLOW and DENY directives, controls a three-pass access control system. The first pass processes either all ALLOW or all DENY directives, as specified by the ORDER directive. The second pass parses the rest of the directives (DENY or ALLOW). The third pass applies to all requests which do not match either of the first two.

Note that all ALLOW and DENY directives are processed, unlike a typical firewall, where only the first match is used. The last match is effective (also unlike a typical firewall). Additionally, the order in which lines appear in the configuration files is not significant – all ALLOW lines are processed as one group, all DENY lines are considered as another, and the default state is considered by itself.

Ordering is one of:

`Allow,Deny` First, all ALLOW directives are evaluated; at least one must match, or the request is rejected. Next, all DENY directives are evaluated. If any matches, the request is rejected. Last, any requests which do not match an ALLOW or a DENY directive are denied by default.

`Deny,Allow` First, all DENY directives are evaluated; if any match, the request is denied **unless** it also matches an ALLOW directive. Any requests which do not match any ALLOW or DENY directives are permitted.

`Mutual-failure` This order has the same effect as `Order Allow,Deny` and is deprecated in its favor.

Keywords may only be separated by a comma; *no whitespace* is allowed between them.

Match	Allow,Deny result	Deny,Allow result
Match Allow only	Request allowed	Request allowed
Match Deny only	Request denied	Request denied
No match	Default to second directive: Denied	Default to second directive: Allowed
Match both Allow & Deny	Final match controls: Denied	Final match controls: Allowed

In the following example, all hosts in the example.org domain are allowed access; all other hosts are denied access.

```
Order Deny,Allow
Deny from all
Allow from example.org
```

In the next example, all hosts in the example.org domain are allowed access, except for the hosts which are in the foo.example.org subdomain, who are denied access. All hosts not in the example.org domain are denied access because the default state is to DENY access to the server.

```
Order Allow,Deny
Allow from example.org
Deny from foo.example.org
```

On the other hand, if the ORDER in the last example is changed to `Deny,Allow`, all hosts will be allowed access. This happens because, regardless of the actual ordering of the directives in the configuration file, the `Allow from example.org` will be evaluated last and will override the `Deny from foo.example.org`. All hosts not in the `example.org` domain will also be allowed access because the default state is ALLOW.

The presence of an ORDER directive can affect access to a part of the server even in the absence of accompanying ALLOW and DENY directives because of its effect on the default access state. For example,

```
<Directory "/www">
    Order Allow,Deny
</Directory>
```

will Deny all access to the `/www` directory because the default access state is set to DENY.

The ORDER directive controls the order of access directive processing only within each phase of the server's configuration processing. This implies, for example, that an ALLOW or DENY directive occurring in a <LOCATION> section will always be evaluated after an ALLOW or DENY directive occurring in a <DIRECTORY> section or `.htaccess` file, regardless of the setting of the ORDER directive. For details on the merging of configuration sections, see the documentation on How Directory, Location and Files sections work (p. 33) .

⟹ **Merging of configuration sections**
When any directive provided by this module is used in a new configuration section, no directives provided by this module are inherited from previous configuration sections.

Satisfy Directive

Description:	Interaction between host-level access control and user authentication
Syntax:	`Satisfy Any|All`
Default:	`Satisfy All`
Context:	directory, .htaccess
Override:	AuthConfig
Status:	Extension
Module:	mod_access_compat
Compatibility:	Influenced by <LIMIT> and <LIMITEXCEPT> in version 2.0.51 and later

Access policy if both ALLOW and REQUIRE used. The parameter can be either `All` or `Any`. This directive is only useful if access to a particular area is being restricted by both username/password *and* client host address. In this case the default behavior (`All`) is to require that the client passes the address access restriction *and* enters a valid username and password. With the `Any` option the client will be granted access if they either pass the host restriction or enter a valid username and password. This can be used to password restrict an area, but to let clients from particular addresses in without prompting for a password.

For example, if you wanted to let people on your network have unrestricted access to a portion of your website, but require that people outside of your network provide a password, you could use a configuration similar to the following:

```
Require valid-user
Allow from 192.168.1
Satisfy Any
```

Another frequent use of the SATISFY directive is to relax access restrictions for a subdirectory:

```
<Directory "/var/www/private">
    Require valid-user
</Directory>

<Directory "/var/www/private/public">
    Allow from all
    Satisfy Any
</Directory>
```

In the above example, authentication will be required for the `/var/www/private` directory, but will not be required for the `/var/www/private/public` directory.

Since version 2.0.51 SATISFY directives can be restricted to particular methods by <LIMIT> and <LIMITEXCEPT> sections.

**Merging of configuration sections**
When any directive provided by this module is used in a new configuration section, no directives provided by this module are inherited from previous configuration sections.

See also

- ALLOW
- REQUIRE

10.5 Apache Module mod_actions

Description:	Execute CGI scripts based on media type or request method.
Status:	Base
ModuleIdentifier:	actions_module
SourceFile:	mod_actions.c

Summary

This module has two directives. The ACTION directive lets you run CGI scripts whenever a file of a certain MIME content type is requested. The SCRIPT directive lets you run CGI scripts whenever a particular method is used in a request. This makes it much easier to execute scripts that process files.

Directives

- Action
- Script

See also

- MOD_CGI
- Dynamic Content with CGI (p. 226)
- Apache httpd's Handler Use (p. 98)

Action Directive

Description:	Activates a CGI script for a particular handler or content-type
Syntax:	`Action action-type cgi-script [virtual]`
Context:	server config, virtual host, directory, .htaccess
Override:	FileInfo
Status:	Base
Module:	mod_actions
Compatibility:	The `virtual` modifier and handler passing were introduced in Apache 2.1

This directive adds an action, which will activate *cgi-script* when *action-type* is triggered by the request. The *cgi-script* is the URL-path to a resource that has been designated as a CGI script using SCRIPTALIAS or ADDHANDLER. The *action-type* can be either a handler (p. 98) or a MIME content type. It sends the URL and file path of the requested document using the standard CGI `PATH_INFO` and `PATH_TRANSLATED` environment variables. The handler used for the particular request is passed using the `REDIRECT_HANDLER` variable.

Example: MIME type

```
# Requests for files of a particular MIME content type:
Action image/gif /cgi-bin/images.cgi
```

In this example, requests for files with a MIME content type of `image/gif` will be handled by the specified cgi script `/cgi-bin/images.cgi`.

Example: File extension

```
# Files of a particular file extension
AddHandler my-file-type .xyz
Action my-file-type "/cgi-bin/program.cgi"
```

In this example, requests for files with a file extension of `.xyz` are handled by the specified cgi script `/cgi-bin/program.cgi`.

The optional `virtual` modifier turns off the check whether the requested file really exists. This is useful, for example, if you want to use the ACTION directive in virtual locations.

```
<Location "/news">
    SetHandler news-handler
    Action news-handler "/cgi-bin/news.cgi" virtual
</Location>
```

See also

- ADDHANDLER

Script Directive

Description:	Activates a CGI script for a particular request method.
Syntax:	`Script method cgi-script`
Context:	server config, virtual host, directory
Status:	Base
Module:	mod_actions

This directive adds an action, which will activate *cgi-script* when a file is requested using the method of *method*. The *cgi-script* is the URL-path to a resource that has been designated as a CGI script using SCRIPTALIAS or ADDHANDLER. The URL and file path of the requested document is sent using the standard CGI `PATH_INFO` and `PATH_TRANSLATED` environment variables.

⟹ Any arbitrary method name may be used. **Method names are case-sensitive**, so `Script PUT` and `Script put` have two entirely different effects.

Note that the SCRIPT command defines default actions only. If a CGI script is called, or some other resource that is capable of handling the requested method internally, it will do so. Also note that SCRIPT with a method of `GET` will only be called if there are query arguments present (*e.g.*, foo.html?hi). Otherwise, the request will proceed normally.

```
# All GET requests go here
Script GET "/cgi-bin/search"

# A CGI PUT handler
Script PUT "/~bob/put.cgi"
```

10.6 Apache Module mod_alias

Description:	Provides for mapping different parts of the host filesystem in the document tree and for URL redirection
Status:	Base
ModuleIdentifier:	alias_module
SourceFile:	mod_alias.c

Summary

The directives contained in this module allow for manipulation and control of URLs as requests arrive at the server. The ALIAS and SCRIPTALIAS directives are used to map between URLs and filesystem paths. This allows for content which is not directly under the DOCUMENTROOT served as part of the web document tree. The SCRIPTALIAS directive has the additional effect of marking the target directory as containing only CGI scripts.

The REDIRECT directives are used to instruct clients to make a new request with a different URL. They are often used when a resource has moved to a new location.

MOD_ALIAS is designed to handle simple URL manipulation tasks. For more complicated tasks such as manipulating the query string, use the tools provided by MOD_REWRITE.

Directives

- Alias
- AliasMatch
- Redirect
- RedirectMatch
- RedirectPermanent
- RedirectTemp
- ScriptAlias
- ScriptAliasMatch

See also

- MOD_REWRITE
- Mapping URLs to the filesystem (p. 61)

Order of Processing

Aliases and Redirects occurring in different contexts are processed like other directives according to standard merging rules (p. 33) . But when multiple Aliases or Redirects occur in the same context (for example, in the same <VIRTUALHOST> section) they are processed in a particular order.

First, all Redirects are processed before Aliases are processed, and therefore a request that matches a REDIRECT or REDIRECTMATCH will never have Aliases applied. Second, the Aliases and Redirects are processed in the order they appear in the configuration files, with the first match taking precedence.

For this reason, when two or more of these directives apply to the same sub-path, you must list the most specific path first in order for all the directives to have an effect. For example, the following configuration will work as expected:

```
Alias "/foo/bar" "/baz"
Alias "/foo" "/gaq"
```

But if the above two directives were reversed in order, the `/foo` ALIAS would always match before the `/foo/bar` ALIAS, so the latter directive would be ignored.

Alias Directive

Description:	Maps URLs to filesystem locations
Syntax:	`Alias URL-path file-path|directory-path`
Context:	server config, virtual host
Status:	Base
Module:	mod_alias

The ALIAS directive allows documents to be stored in the local filesystem other than under the DOCUMENTROOT. URLs with a (%-decoded) path beginning with *URL-path* will be mapped to local files beginning with *directory-path*. The *URL-path* is case-sensitive, even on case-insensitive file systems.

```
Alias "/image" "/ftp/pub/image"
```

A request for `http://example.com/image/foo.gif` would cause the server to return the file `/ftp/pub/image/foo.gif`. Only complete path segments are matched, so the above alias would not match a request for `http://example.com/imagefoo.gif`. For more complex matching using regular expressions, see the ALIASMATCH directive.

Note that if you include a trailing / on the *URL-path* then the server will require a trailing / in order to expand the alias. That is, if you use

```
Alias "/icons/" "/usr/local/apache/icons/"
```

then the URL `/icons` will not be aliased, as it lacks that trailing /. Likewise, if you omit the slash on the *URL-path* then you must also omit it from the *file-path*.

Note that you may need to specify additional <DIRECTORY> sections which cover the *destination* of aliases. Aliasing occurs before <DIRECTORY> sections are checked, so only the destination of aliases are affected. (Note however <LOCATION> sections are run through once before aliases are performed, so they will apply.)

In particular, if you are creating an `Alias` to a directory outside of your DOCUMENTROOT, you may need to explicitly permit access to the target directory.

```
Alias "/image" "/ftp/pub/image"
<Directory "/ftp/pub/image">
    Require all granted
</Directory>
```

Any number slashes in the *URL-path* parameter matches any number of slashes in the requested URL-path.

AliasMatch Directive

Description:	Maps URLs to filesystem locations using regular expressions
Syntax:	`AliasMatch regex file-path|directory-path`
Context:	server config, virtual host
Status:	Base
Module:	mod_alias

This directive is equivalent to ALIAS, but makes use of regular expressions, instead of simple prefix matching. The supplied regular expression is matched against the URL-path, and if it matches, the server will substitute any parenthesized matches into the given string and use it as a filename. For example, to activate the `/icons` directory, one might use:

```
AliasMatch "^/icons(/|$)(.*)" "/usr/local/apache/icons$1$2"
```

The full range of regular expression power is available. For example, it is possible to construct an alias with case-insensitive matching of the URL-path:

```
AliasMatch "(?i)^/image(.*)" "/ftp/pub/image$1"
```

One subtle difference between ALIAS and ALIASMATCH is that ALIAS will automatically copy any additional part of the URI, past the part that matched, onto the end of the file path on the right side, while ALIASMATCH will not. This means that in almost all cases, you will want the regular expression to match the entire request URI from beginning to end, and to use substitution on the right side.

In other words, just changing ALIAS to ALIASMATCH will not have the same effect. At a minimum, you need to add ^ to the beginning of the regular expression and add `(.*)$` to the end, and add `$1` to the end of the replacement.

For example, suppose you want to replace this with AliasMatch:

```
Alias "/image/" "/ftp/pub/image/"
```

This is NOT equivalent - don't do this! This will send all requests that have /image/ anywhere in them to /ftp/pub/image/:

```
AliasMatch "/image/" "/ftp/pub/image/"
```

This is what you need to get the same effect:

```
AliasMatch "^/image/(.*)$" "/ftp/pub/image/$1"
```

Of course, there's no point in using ALIASMATCH where ALIAS would work. ALIASMATCH lets you do more complicated things. For example, you could serve different kinds of files from different directories:

```
AliasMatch "^/image/(.*)\.jpg$" "/files/jpg.images/$1.jpg"
AliasMatch "^/image/(.*)\.gif$" "/files/gif.images/$1.gif"
```

Multiple leading slashes in the requested URL are discarded by the server before directives from this module compares against the requested URL-path.

Redirect Directive

Description:	Sends an external redirect asking the client to fetch a different URL
Syntax:	`Redirect [status] URL-path URL`
Context:	server config, virtual host, directory, .htaccess
Override:	FileInfo
Status:	Base
Module:	mod_alias

The Redirect directive maps an old URL into a new one by asking the client to refetch the resource at the new location.

The old *URL-path* is a case-sensitive (%-decoded) path beginning with a slash. A relative path is not allowed.

The new *URL* may be either an absolute URL beginning with a scheme and hostname, or a URL-path beginning with a slash. In this latter case the scheme and hostname of the current server will be added.

Then any request beginning with *URL-Path* will return a redirect request to the client at the location of the target *URL*. Additional path information beyond the matched *URL-Path* will be appended to the target URL.

```
# Redirect to a URL on a different host
Redirect "/service" "http://foo2.example.com/service"

# Redirect to a URL on the same host
Redirect "/one" "/two"
```

If the client requests `http://example.com/service/foo.txt`, it will be told to access `http://foo2.example.com/service/foo.txt` instead. This includes requests with `GET` parameters, such as `http://example.com/service/foo.pl?q=23&a=42`, it will be redirected to `http://foo2.example.com/service/foo.pl?q=23&a=42`. Note that `POST`s will be discarded. Only complete path segments are matched, so the above example would not match a request for `http://example.com/servicefoo.txt`. For more complex matching using regular expressions, see the REDIRECTMATCH directive.

**Note**

Redirect directives take precedence over Alias and ScriptAlias directives, irrespective of their ordering in the configuration file.

If no *status* argument is given, the redirect will be "temporary" (HTTP status 302). This indicates to the client that the resource has moved temporarily. The *status* argument can be used to return other HTTP status codes:

permanent Returns a permanent redirect status (301) indicating that the resource has moved permanently.

temp Returns a temporary redirect status (302). This is the default.

seeother Returns a "See Other" status (303) indicating that the resource has been replaced.

gone Returns a "Gone" status (410) indicating that the resource has been permanently removed. When this status is used the *URL* argument should be omitted.

Other status codes can be returned by giving the numeric status code as the value of *status*. If the status is between 300 and 399, the *URL* argument must be present. If the status is *not* between 300 and 399, the *URL* argument must be omitted. The status must be a valid HTTP status code, known to the Apache HTTP Server (see the function `send_error_response` in http_protocol.c).

```
Redirect permanent "/one" "http://example.com/two"
Redirect 303 "/three" "http://example.com/other"
```

RedirectMatch Directive

Description:	Sends an external redirect based on a regular expression match of the current URL
Syntax:	`RedirectMatch [status] regex URL`
Context:	server config, virtual host, directory, .htaccess
Override:	FileInfo
Status:	Base
Module:	mod_alias

This directive is equivalent to REDIRECT, but makes use of regular expressions, instead of simple prefix matching. The supplied regular expression is matched against the URL-path, and if it matches, the server will substitute any parenthesized matches into the given string and use it as a filename. For example, to redirect all GIF files to like-named JPEG files on another server, one might use:

```
RedirectMatch "(.*)\.gif$" "http://other.example.com$1.jpg"
```

The considerations related to the difference between ALIAS and ALIASMATCH also apply to the difference between REDIRECT and REDIRECTMATCH. See ALIASMATCH for details.

RedirectPermanent Directive

Description:	Sends an external permanent redirect asking the client to fetch a different URL
Syntax:	`RedirectPermanent URL-path URL`
Context:	server config, virtual host, directory, .htaccess
Override:	FileInfo
Status:	Base
Module:	mod_alias

This directive makes the client know that the Redirect is permanent (status 301). Exactly equivalent to `Redirect permanent`.

RedirectTemp Directive

Description:	Sends an external temporary redirect asking the client to fetch a different URL
Syntax:	`RedirectTemp URL-path URL`
Context:	server config, virtual host, directory, .htaccess
Override:	FileInfo
Status:	Base
Module:	mod_alias

This directive makes the client know that the Redirect is only temporary (status 302). Exactly equivalent to `Redirect temp`.

ScriptAlias Directive

Description:	Maps a URL to a filesystem location and designates the target as a CGI script
Syntax:	`ScriptAlias URL-path file-path|directory-path`
Context:	server config, virtual host
Status:	Base
Module:	mod_alias

The SCRIPTALIAS directive has the same behavior as the ALIAS directive, except that in addition it marks the target directory as containing CGI scripts that will be processed by MOD_CGI's cgi-script handler. URLs with a case-sensitive (%-decoded) path beginning with *URL-path* will be mapped to scripts beginning with the second argument, which is a full pathname in the local filesystem.

```
ScriptAlias "/cgi-bin/" "/web/cgi-bin/"
```

A request for `http://example.com/cgi-bin/foo` would cause the server to run the script `/web/cgi-bin/foo`. This configuration is essentially equivalent to:

```
Alias "/cgi-bin/" "/web/cgi-bin/"
<Location "/cgi-bin" >
    SetHandler cgi-script
    Options +ExecCGI
</Location>
```

SCRIPTALIAS can also be used in conjunction with a script or handler you have. For example:

```
ScriptAlias "/cgi-bin/" "/web/cgi-handler.pl"
```

In this scenario all files requested in `/cgi-bin/` will be handled by the file you have configured, this allows you to use your own custom handler. You may want to use this as a wrapper for CGI so that you can add content, or some other bespoke action.

! It is safer to avoid placing CGI scripts under the DOCUMENTROOT in order to avoid accidentally revealing their source code if the configuration is ever changed. The SCRIPTALIAS makes this easy by mapping a URL and designating CGI scripts at the same time. If you do choose to place your CGI scripts in a directory already accessible from the web, do not use SCRIPTALIAS. Instead, use <DIRECTORY>, SETHANDLER, and OPTIONS as in:

```
<Directory "/usr/local/apache2/htdocs/cgi-bin">
    SetHandler cgi-script
    Options ExecCGI
</Directory>
```

This is necessary since multiple *URL-paths* can map to the same filesystem location, potentially bypassing the SCRIPTALIAS and revealing the source code of the CGI scripts if they are not restricted by a DIRECTORY section.

See also

- CGI Tutorial (p. 226)

ScriptAliasMatch Directive

Description:	Maps a URL to a filesystem location using a regular expression and designates the target as a CGI script
Syntax:	`ScriptAliasMatch regex file-path|directory-path`
Context:	server config, virtual host
Status:	Base
Module:	mod_alias

This directive is equivalent to SCRIPTALIAS, but makes use of regular expressions, instead of simple prefix matching. The supplied regular expression is matched against the URL-path, and if it matches, the server will substitute any parenthesized matches into the given string and use it as a filename. For example, to activate the standard `/cgi-bin`, one might use:

```
ScriptAliasMatch "^/cgi-bin(.*)" "/usr/local/apache/cgi-bin$1"
```

As for AliasMatch, the full range of regular expression power is available. For example, it is possible to construct an alias with case-insensitive matching of the URL-path:

```
ScriptAliasMatch "(?i)^/cgi-bin(.*)" "/usr/local/apache/cgi-bin$1"
```

The considerations related to the difference between ALIAS and ALIASMATCH also apply to the difference between SCRIPTALIAS and SCRIPTALIASMATCH. See ALIASMATCH for details.

10.7 Apache Module mod_allowmethods

Description:	Easily restrict what HTTP methods can be used on the server
Status:	Experimental
ModuleIdentifier:	allowmethods_module
SourceFile:	mod_allowmethods.c

Summary

This module makes it easy to restrict what HTTP methods can used on an server. The most common configuration would be:

```
<Location "/">
   AllowMethods GET POST OPTIONS
</Location>
```

Directives

- AllowMethods

AllowMethods Directive

Description:	Restrict access to the listed HTTP methods
Syntax:	`AllowMethods reset|HTTP-method [HTTP-method]...`
Default:	`AllowMethods reset`
Context:	directory
Status:	Experimental
Module:	mod_allowmethods

The HTTP-methods are case sensitive, and are generally as per RFC given in upper case. The GET and HEAD methods are treated as equivalent. The `reset` keyword can be used turn off MOD_ALLOWMETHODS in a deeper nested context:

```
<Location "/svn">
   AllowMethods reset
</Location>
```

**Caution**

The TRACE method can not be denied by this module, use TRACEENABLE instead.

MOD_ALLOWMETHODS was written to replace the rather kludgy implementation of LIMIT and LIMITEXCEPT.

10.8 Apache Module mod_asis

Description:	Sends files that contain their own HTTP headers
Status:	Base
ModuleIdentifier:	asis_module
SourceFile:	mod_asis.c

Summary

This module provides the handler `send-as-is` which causes Apache HTTP Server to send the document without adding most of the usual HTTP headers.

This can be used to send any kind of data from the server, including redirects and other special HTTP responses, without requiring a cgi-script or an nph script.

For historical reasons, this module will also process any file with the mime type `httpd/send-as-is`.

Directives This module provides no directives.

See also

- MOD_HEADERS
- MOD_CERN_META
- Apache httpd's Handler Use (p. 98)

Usage

In the server configuration file, associate files with the `send-as-is` handler *e.g.*

```
AddHandler send-as-is asis
```

The contents of any file with a `.asis` extension will then be sent by Apache httpd to the client with almost no changes. In particular, HTTP headers are derived from the file itself according to MOD_CGI rules, so an asis file must include valid headers, and may also use the CGI `Status:` header to determine the HTTP response code. The `Content-Length:` header will automatically be inserted or, if included, corrected by httpd.

Here's an example of a file whose contents are sent *as is* so as to tell the client that a file has redirected.

```
Status: 301 Now where did I leave that URL
Location: http://xyz.example.com/foo/bar.html
Content-type: text/html

<html>
<head>
<title>Lame excuses'R'us</title>
</head>
<body>
<h1>Fred's exceptionally wonderful page has moved to
<a href="http://xyz.example.com/foo/bar.html">Joe's</a> site.
</h1>
</body>
</html>
```

**Notes:**

The server always adds a `Date:` and `Server:` header to the data returned to the client, so these should not be included in the file. The server does *not* add a `Last-Modified` header; it probably should.

10.9 Apache Module mod_auth_basic

Description:	Basic HTTP authentication
Status:	Base
ModuleIdentifier:	auth_basic_module
SourceFile:	mod_auth_basic.c
Compatibility:	Available in Apache 2.1 and later

Summary

This module allows the use of HTTP Basic Authentication to restrict access by looking up users in the given providers. HTTP Digest Authentication is provided by MOD_AUTH_DIGEST. This module should usually be combined with at least one authentication module such as MOD_AUTHN_FILE and one authorization module such as MOD_AUTHZ_USER.

Directives

- AuthBasicAuthoritative
- AuthBasicFake
- AuthBasicProvider
- AuthBasicUseDigestAlgorithm

See also

- AUTHNAME
- AUTHTYPE
- REQUIRE
- Authentication howto (p. 217)

AuthBasicAuthoritative Directive

Description:	Sets whether authorization and authentication are passed to lower level modules
Syntax:	`AuthBasicAuthoritative On|Off`
Default:	`AuthBasicAuthoritative On`
Context:	directory, .htaccess
Override:	AuthConfig
Status:	Base
Module:	mod_auth_basic

Normally, each authorization module listed in AUTHBASICPROVIDER will attempt to verify the user, and if the user is not found in any provider, access will be denied. Setting the AUTHBASICAUTHORITATIVE directive explicitly to `Off` allows for both authentication and authorization to be passed on to other non-provider-based modules if there is **no userID** or **rule** matching the supplied userID. This should only be necessary when combining MOD_AUTH_BASIC with third-party modules that are not configured with the AUTHBASICPROVIDER directive. When using such modules, the order of processing is determined in the modules' source code and is not configurable.

AuthBasicFake Directive

Description:	Fake basic authentication using the given expressions for username and password
Syntax:	`AuthBasicFake off|username [password]`
Default:	`none`
Context:	directory, .htaccess
Override:	AuthConfig
Status:	Base
Module:	mod_auth_basic
Compatibility:	Apache HTTP Server 2.4.5 and later

The username and password specified are combined into an Authorization header, which is passed to the server or service behind the webserver. Both the username and password fields are interpreted using the expression parser (p. 89) , which allows both the username and password to be set based on request parameters.

If the password is not specified, the default value "password" will be used. To disable fake basic authentication for an URL space, specify "AuthBasicFake off".

In this example, we pass a fixed username and password to a backend server.

Fixed Example

```
<Location "/demo">
    AuthBasicFake demo demopass
</Location>
```

In this example, we pass the email address extracted from a client certificate, extending the functionality of the FakeBasicAuth option within the SSLOPTIONS directive. Like the FakeBasicAuth option, the password is set to the fixed string "password".

Certificate Example

```
<Location "/secure">
    AuthBasicFake "%{SSL_CLIENT_S_DN_Email}"
</Location>
```

Extending the above example, we generate a password by hashing the email address with a fixed passphrase, and passing the hash to the backend server. This can be used to gate into legacy systems that do not support client certificates.

Password Example

```
<Location "/secure">
    AuthBasicFake "%{SSL_CLIENT_S_DN_Email}" "%{sha1:passphrase-%{SSL_CLIENT_S_
</Location>
```

Exclusion Example

```
<Location "/public">
    AuthBasicFake off
</Location>
```

AuthBasicProvider Directive

Description:	Sets the authentication provider(s) for this location
Syntax:	`AuthBasicProvider provider-name [provider-name] ...`
Default:	`AuthBasicProvider file`
Context:	directory, .htaccess
Override:	AuthConfig
Status:	Base
Module:	mod_auth_basic

The AUTHBASICPROVIDER directive sets which provider is used to authenticate the users for this location. The default `file` provider is implemented by the MOD_AUTHN_FILE module. Make sure that the chosen provider module is present in the server.

Example

```
<Location "/secure">
    AuthType basic
    AuthName "private area"
    AuthBasicProvider  dbm
    AuthDBMType        SDBM
    AuthDBMUserFile    "/www/etc/dbmpasswd"
    Require            valid-user
</Location>
```

Providers are queried in order until a provider finds a match for the requested username, at which point this sole provider will attempt to check the password. A failure to verify the password does not result in control being passed on to subsequent providers.

Providers are implemented by MOD_AUTHN_DBM, MOD_AUTHN_FILE, MOD_AUTHN_DBD, MOD_AUTHNZ_LDAP and MOD_AUTHN_SOCACHE.

AuthBasicUseDigestAlgorithm Directive

Description:	Check passwords against the authentication providers as if Digest Authentication was in force instead of Basic Authentication.
Syntax:	`AuthBasicUseDigestAlgorithm MD5|Off`
Default:	`AuthBasicUseDigestAlgorithm Off`
Context:	directory, .htaccess
Override:	AuthConfig
Status:	Base
Module:	mod_auth_basic
Compatibility:	Apache HTTP Server 2.4.7 and later

Normally, when using Basic Authentication, the providers listed in AUTHBASICPROVIDER attempt to verify a user by checking their data stores for a matching username and associated password. The stored passwords are usually encrypted, but not necessarily so; each provider may choose its own storage scheme for passwords.

When using AUTHDIGESTPROVIDER and Digest Authentication, providers perform a similar check to find a matching username in their data stores. However, unlike in the Basic Authentication case, the value associated with each stored username must be an encrypted string composed from the username, realm name, and password. (See

RFC 2617, Section 3.2.2.2[8] for more details on the format used for this encrypted string.)

As a consequence of the difference in the stored values between Basic and Digest Authentication, converting from Digest Authentication to Basic Authentication generally requires that all users be assigned new passwords, as their

[8] http://tools.ietf.org/html/rfc2617#section-3.2.2.2

existing passwords cannot be recovered from the password storage scheme imposed on those providers which support Digest Authentication.

Setting the AuthBasicUseDigestAlgorithm directive to `MD5` will cause the user's Basic Authentication password to be checked using the same encrypted format as for Digest Authentication. First a string composed from the username, realm name, and password is hashed with MD5; then the username and this encrypted string are passed to the providers listed in AuthBasicProvider as if AuthType was set to `Digest` and Digest Authentication was in force.

Through the use of AuthBasicUseDigestAlgorithm a site may switch from Digest to Basic Authentication without requiring users to be assigned new passwords.

⟹ The inverse process of switching from Basic to Digest Authentication without assigning new passwords is generally not possible. Only if the Basic Authentication passwords have been stored in plain text or with a reversable encryption scheme will it be possible to recover them and generate a new data store following the Digest Authentication password storage scheme.

⟹ Only providers which support Digest Authentication will be able to authenticate users when AuthBasicUseDigestAlgorithm is set to `MD5`. Use of other providers will result in an error response and the client will be denied access.

10.10 Apache Module mod_auth_digest

Description:	User authentication using MD5 Digest Authentication
Status:	Extension
ModuleIdentifier:	auth_digest_module
SourceFile:	mod_auth_digest.c

Summary

This module implements HTTP Digest Authentication (RFC2617[9]), and provides an alternative to MOD_AUTH_BASIC where the password is not transmitted as cleartext. However, this does **not** lead to a significant security advantage over basic authentication. On the other hand, the password storage on the server is much less secure with digest authentication than with basic authentication. Therefore, using basic auth and encrypting the whole connection using MOD_SSL is a much better alternative.

Directives

- AuthDigestAlgorithm
- AuthDigestDomain
- AuthDigestNonceLifetime
- AuthDigestProvider
- AuthDigestQop
- AuthDigestShmemSize

See also

- AUTHNAME
- AUTHTYPE
- REQUIRE
- Authentication howto (p. 217)

Using Digest Authentication

To use MD5 Digest authentication, simply change the normal `AuthType Basic` and AUTHBASICPROVIDER to `AuthType Digest` and AUTHDIGESTPROVIDER, when setting up authentication, then add a AUTHDIGESTDOMAIN directive containing at least the root URI(s) for this protection space.

Appropriate user (text) files can be created using the `htdigest` tool.

Example:

```
<Location "/private/">
    AuthType Digest
    AuthName "private area"
    AuthDigestDomain "/private/" "http://mirror.my.dom/private2/"

    AuthDigestProvider file
    AuthUserFile "/web/auth/.digest_pw"
    Require valid-user
</Location>
```

[9] http://www.faqs.org/rfcs/rfc2617.html

**Note**

Digest authentication was intended to be more secure than basic authentication, but no longer fulfills that design goal. A man-in-the-middle attacker can trivially force the browser to downgrade to basic authentication. And even a passive eavesdropper can brute-force the password using today's graphics hardware, because the hashing algorithm used by digest authentication is too fast. Another problem is that the storage of the passwords on the server is insecure. The contents of a stolen htdigest file can be used directly for digest authentication. Therefore using MOD_SSL to encrypt the whole connection is strongly recommended.

MOD_AUTH_DIGEST only works properly on platforms where APR supports shared memory.

AuthDigestAlgorithm Directive

Description:	Selects the algorithm used to calculate the challenge and response hashes in digest authentication
Syntax:	`AuthDigestAlgorithm MD5|MD5-sess`
Default:	`AuthDigestAlgorithm MD5`
Context:	directory, .htaccess
Override:	AuthConfig
Status:	Extension
Module:	mod_auth_digest

The AUTHDIGESTALGORITHM directive selects the algorithm used to calculate the challenge and response hashes.

⟹ `MD5-sess` is not correctly implemented yet.

AuthDigestDomain Directive

Description:	URIs that are in the same protection space for digest authentication
Syntax:	`AuthDigestDomain URI [URI] ...`
Context:	directory, .htaccess
Override:	AuthConfig
Status:	Extension
Module:	mod_auth_digest

The AUTHDIGESTDOMAIN directive allows you to specify one or more URIs which are in the same protection space (*i.e.* use the same realm and username/password info). The specified URIs are prefixes; the client will assume that all URIs "below" these are also protected by the same username/password. The URIs may be either absolute URIs (*i.e.* including a scheme, host, port, etc.) or relative URIs.

This directive *should* always be specified and contain at least the (set of) root URI(s) for this space. Omitting to do so will cause the client to send the Authorization header for *every request* sent to this server.

The URIs specified can also point to different servers, in which case clients (which understand this) will then share username/password info across multiple servers without prompting the user each time.

AuthDigestNonceLifetime Directive

Description:	How long the server nonce is valid
Syntax:	`AuthDigestNonceLifetime seconds`
Default:	`AuthDigestNonceLifetime 300`
Context:	directory, .htaccess
Override:	AuthConfig
Status:	Extension
Module:	mod_auth_digest

The AUTHDIGESTNONCELIFETIME directive controls how long the server nonce is valid. When the client contacts the server using an expired nonce the server will send back a 401 with `stale=true`. If *seconds* is greater than 0 then it specifies the amount of time for which the nonce is valid; this should probably never be set to less than 10 seconds. If *seconds* is less than 0 then the nonce never expires.

AuthDigestProvider Directive

Description:	Sets the authentication provider(s) for this location
Syntax:	`AuthDigestProvider provider-name [provider-name] ...`
Default:	`AuthDigestProvider file`
Context:	directory, .htaccess
Override:	AuthConfig
Status:	Extension
Module:	mod_auth_digest

The AUTHDIGESTPROVIDER directive sets which provider is used to authenticate the users for this location. The default `file` provider is implemented by the MOD_AUTHN_FILE module. Make sure that the chosen provider module is present in the server.

See MOD_AUTHN_DBM, MOD_AUTHN_FILE, MOD_AUTHN_DBD and MOD_AUTHN_SOCACHE for providers.

AuthDigestQop Directive

Description:	Determines the quality-of-protection to use in digest authentication
Syntax:	`AuthDigestQop none|auth|auth-int [auth|auth-int]`
Default:	`AuthDigestQop auth`
Context:	directory, .htaccess
Override:	AuthConfig
Status:	Extension
Module:	mod_auth_digest

The AUTHDIGESTQOP directive determines the *quality-of-protection* to use. `auth` will only do authentication (username/password); `auth-int` is authentication plus integrity checking (an MD5 hash of the entity is also computed and checked); `none` will cause the module to use the old RFC-2069 digest algorithm (which does not include integrity checking). Both `auth` and `auth-int` may be specified, in which the case the browser will choose which of these to use. `none` should only be used if the browser for some reason does not like the challenge it receives otherwise.

⟹ `auth-int` is not implemented yet.

AuthDigestShmemSize Directive

Description:	The amount of shared memory to allocate for keeping track of clients
Syntax:	`AuthDigestShmemSize size`
Default:	`AuthDigestShmemSize 1000`
Context:	server config
Status:	Extension
Module:	mod_auth_digest

The AUTHDIGESTSHMEMSIZE directive defines the amount of shared memory, that will be allocated at the server startup for keeping track of clients. Note that the shared memory segment cannot be set less than the space that is necessary for tracking at least *one* client. This value is dependent on your system. If you want to find out the exact value, you may simply set AUTHDIGESTSHMEMSIZE to the value of `0` and read the error message after trying to start the server.

The *size* is normally expressed in Bytes, but you may follow the number with a `K` or an `M` to express your value as KBytes or MBytes. For example, the following directives are all equivalent:

```
AuthDigestShmemSize 1048576
AuthDigestShmemSize 1024K
AuthDigestShmemSize 1M
```

10.11 Apache Module mod_auth_form

Description:	Form authentication
Status:	Base
ModuleIdentifier:	auth_form_module
SourceFile:	mod_auth_form.c
Compatibility:	Available in Apache 2.3 and later

Summary

Warning
Form authentication depends on the MOD_SESSION modules, and these modules make use of HTTP cookies, and as such can fall victim to Cross Site Scripting attacks, or expose potentially private information to clients. Please ensure that the relevant risks have been taken into account before enabling the session functionality on your server.

This module allows the use of an HTML login form to restrict access by looking up users in the given providers. HTML forms require significantly more configuration than the alternatives, however an HTML login form can provide a much friendlier experience for end users.

HTTP basic authentication is provided by MOD_AUTH_BASIC, and HTTP digest authentication is provided by MOD_AUTH_DIGEST. This module should be combined with at least one authentication module such as MOD_AUTHN_FILE and one authorization module such as MOD_AUTHZ_USER.

Once the user has been successfully authenticated, the user's login details will be stored in a session provided by MOD_SESSION.

Directives

- AuthFormAuthoritative
- AuthFormBody
- AuthFormDisableNoStore
- AuthFormFakeBasicAuth
- AuthFormLocation
- AuthFormLoginRequiredLocation
- AuthFormLoginSuccessLocation
- AuthFormLogoutLocation
- AuthFormMethod
- AuthFormMimetype
- AuthFormPassword
- AuthFormProvider
- AuthFormSitePassphrase
- AuthFormSize
- AuthFormUsername

See also

- MOD_SESSION

- AUTHNAME
- AUTHTYPE
- REQUIRE
- Authentication howto (p. 217)

Basic Configuration

To protect a particular URL with MOD_AUTH_FORM, you need to decide where you will store your *session*, and you will need to decide what method you will use to authenticate. In this simple example, the login details will be stored in a session based on MOD_SESSION_COOKIE, and authentication will be attempted against a file using MOD_AUTHN_FILE. If authentication is unsuccessful, the user will be redirected to the form login page.

Basic example

```
AuthFormProvider file
AuthUserFile "conf/passwd"
AuthType form
AuthName realm
AuthFormLoginRequiredLocation "http://example.com/login.html"
Session On
SessionCookieName session path=/
SessionCryptoPassphrase secret
```

The directive AUTHTYPE will enable the MOD_AUTH_FORM authentication when set to the value *form*. The directives AUTHFORMPROVIDER and AUTHUSERFILE specify that usernames and passwords should be checked against the chosen file.

The directives SESSION, SESSIONCOOKIENAME and SESSIONCRYPTOPASSPHRASE create an encrypted session stored within an HTTP cookie on the browser. For more information on the different options for configuring a session, read the documentation for MOD_SESSION.

In the simple example above, a URL has been protected by MOD_AUTH_FORM, but the user has yet to be given an opportunity to enter their username and password. Options for doing so include providing a dedicated standalone login page for this purpose, or for providing the login page inline.

Standalone Login

The login form can be hosted as a standalone page, or can be provided inline on the same page.

When configuring the login as a standalone page, unsuccessful authentication attempts should be redirected to a login form created by the website for this purpose, using the AUTHFORMLOGINREQUIREDLOCATION directive. Typically this login page will contain an HTML form, asking the user to provide their usename and password.

Example login form

```
<form method="POST" action="/dologin.html">
  Username: <input type="text" name="httpd_username" value="" />
  Password: <input type="password" name="httpd_password" value="" />
  <input type="submit" name="login" value="Login" />
</form>
```

The part that does the actual login is handled by the *form-login-handler*. The action of the form should point at this handler, which is configured within Apache httpd as follows:

Form login handler example

```
<Location "/dologin.html">
    SetHandler form-login-handler
    AuthFormLoginRequiredLocation "http://example.com/login.html"
    AuthFormLoginSuccessLocation "http://example.com/success.html"
    AuthFormProvider file
    AuthUserFile "conf/passwd"
    AuthType form
    AuthName realm
    Session On
    SessionCookieName session path=/
    SessionCryptoPassphrase secret
</Location>
```

The URLs specified by the AuthFormLoginRequiredLocation directive will typically point to a page explaining to the user that their login attempt was unsuccessful, and they should try again. The AuthFormLoginSuccessLocation directive specifies the URL the user should be redirected to upon successful login.

Alternatively, the URL to redirect the user to on success can be embedded within the login form, as in the example below. As a result, the same *form-login-handler* can be reused for different areas of a website.

Example login form with location

```
<form method="POST" action="/dologin.html">
  Username: <input type="text" name="httpd_username" value="" />
  Password: <input type="password" name="httpd_password" value="" />
  <input type="submit" name="login" value="Login" />
  <input type="hidden" name="httpd_location" value="http://example.com/success.
</form>
```

Inline Login

Warning
A risk exists that under certain circumstances, the login form configured using inline login may be submitted more than once, revealing login credentials to the application running underneath. The administrator must ensure that the underlying application is properly secured to prevent abuse. If in doubt, use the standalone login configuration.

As an alternative to having a dedicated login page for a website, it is possible to configure MOD_AUTH_FORM to authenticate users inline, without being redirected to another page. This allows the state of the current page to be preserved during the login attempt. This can be useful in a situation where a time limited session is in force, and the session times out in the middle of the user request. The user can be re-authenticated in place, and they can continue where they left off.

If a non-authenticated user attempts to access a page protected by MOD_AUTH_FORM that isn't configured with a AuthFormLoginRequiredLocation directive, a *HTTP_UNAUTHORIZED* status code is returned to the browser indicating to the user that they are not authorized to view the page.

To configure inline authentication, the administrator overrides the error document returned by the *HTTP_UNAUTHORIZED* status code with a custom error document containing the login form, as follows:

Basic inline example

```
AuthFormProvider file
ErrorDocument 401 "/login.shtml"
AuthUserFile "conf/passwd"
AuthType form
AuthName realm
AuthFormLoginRequiredLocation "http://example.com/login.html"
Session On
SessionCookieName session path=/
SessionCryptoPassphrase secret
```

The error document page should contain a login form with an empty action property, as per the example below. This has the effect of submitting the form to the original protected URL, without the page having to know what that URL is.

Example inline login form

```
<form method="POST" action="">
  Username: <input type="text" name="httpd_username" value="" />
  Password: <input type="password" name="httpd_password" value="" />
  <input type="submit" name="login" value="Login" />
</form>
```

When the end user has filled in their login details, the form will make an HTTP POST request to the original password protected URL. MOD_AUTH_FORM will intercept this POST request, and if HTML fields are found present for the username and password, the user will be logged in, and the original password protected URL will be returned to the user as a GET request.

Inline Login with Body Preservation

A limitation of the inline login technique described above is that should an HTML form POST have resulted in the request to authenticate or reauthenticate, the contents of the original form posted by the browser will be lost. Depending on the function of the website, this could present significant inconvenience for the end user.

MOD_AUTH_FORM addresses this by allowing the method and body of the original request to be embedded in the login form. If authentication is successful, the original method and body will be retried by Apache httpd, preserving the state of the original request.

To enable body preservation, add three additional fields to the login form as per the example below.

Example with body preservation

```
<form method="POST" action="">
  Username: <input type="text" name="httpd_username" value="" />
  Password: <input type="password" name="httpd_password" value="" />
  <input type="submit" name="login" value="Login" />
    <input type="hidden" name="httpd_method" value="POST" />
  <input type="hidden" name="httpd_mimetype" value="application/x-www-form-urle
  <input type="hidden" name="httpd_body" value="name1=value1&name2=value2" />
</form>
```

How the method, mimetype and body of the original request are embedded within the login form will depend on the platform and technology being used within the website.

One option is to use the MOD_INCLUDE module along with the KEPTBODYSIZE directive, along with a suitable CGI script to embed the variables in the form.

Another option is to render the login form using a CGI script or other dynamic technology.

CGI example

```
AuthFormProvider file
ErrorDocument 401 "/cgi-bin/login.cgi"
...
```

Logging Out

To enable a user to log out of a particular session, configure a page to be handled by the *form-logout-handler*. Any attempt to access this URL will cause the username and password to be removed from the current session, effectively logging the user out.

By setting the AUTHFORMLOGOUTLOCATION directive, a URL can be specified that the browser will be redirected to on successful logout. This URL might explain to the user that they have been logged out, and give the user the option to log in again.

Basic logout example

```
SetHandler form-logout-handler
AuthName realm
AuthFormLogoutLocation "http://example.com/loggedout.html"
Session On
SessionCookieName session path=/
SessionCryptoPassphrase secret
```

Note that logging a user out does not delete the session; it merely removes the username and password from the session. If this results in an empty session, the net effect will be the removal of that session, but this is not guaranteed. If you want to guarantee the removal of a session, set the SESSIONMAXAGE directive to a small value, like 1 (setting the directive to zero would mean no session age limit).

Basic session expiry example

```
SetHandler form-logout-handler
AuthFormLogoutLocation "http://example.com/loggedout.html"
Session On
SessionMaxAge 1
SessionCookieName session path=/
SessionCryptoPassphrase secret
```

Usernames and Passwords

Note that form submission involves URLEncoding the form data: in this case the username and password. You should therefore pick usernames and passwords that avoid characters that are URLencoded in form submission, or you may get unexpected results.

AuthFormAuthoritative Directive

Description:	Sets whether authorization and authentication are passed to lower level modules
Syntax:	`AuthFormAuthoritative On|Off`
Default:	`AuthFormAuthoritative On`
Context:	directory, .htaccess
Override:	AuthConfig
Status:	Base
Module:	mod_auth_form

Normally, each authorization module listed in AUTHFORMPROVIDER will attempt to verify the user, and if the user is not found in any provider, access will be denied. Setting the AUTHFORMAUTHORITATIVE directive explicitly to `Off` allows for both authentication and authorization to be passed on to other non-provider-based modules if there is **no userID** or **rule** matching the supplied userID. This should only be necessary when combining MOD_AUTH_FORM with third-party modules that are not configured with the AUTHFORMPROVIDER directive. When using such modules, the order of processing is determined in the modules' source code and is not configurable.

AuthFormBody Directive

Description:	The name of a form field carrying the body of the request to attempt on successful login
Syntax:	`AuthFormBody fieldname`
Default:	`httpd_body`
Context:	directory
Status:	Base
Module:	mod_auth_form
Compatibility:	Available in Apache HTTP Server 2.3.0 and later

The AUTHFORMMETHOD directive specifies the name of an HTML field which, if present, will contain the method of the request to to submit should login be successful.

By populating the form with fields described by AUTHFORMMETHOD, AUTHFORMMIMETYPE and AUTHFORMBODY, a website can retry a request that may have been interrupted by the login screen, or by a session timeout.

AuthFormDisableNoStore Directive

Description:	Disable the CacheControl no-store header on the login page
Syntax:	`AuthFormDisableNoStore On|Off`
Default:	`AuthFormDisableNoStore Off`
Context:	directory
Status:	Base
Module:	mod_auth_form
Compatibility:	Available in Apache HTTP Server 2.3.0 and later

The AUTHFORMDISABLENOSTORE flag disables the sending of a `Cache-Control no-store` header with the error 401 page returned when the user is not yet logged in. The purpose of the header is to make it difficult for an `ecmascript` application to attempt to resubmit the login form, and reveal the username and password to the backend application. Disable at your own risk.

AuthFormFakeBasicAuth Directive

Description:	Fake a Basic Authentication header
Syntax:	`AuthFormFakeBasicAuth On|Off`
Default:	`AuthFormFakeBasicAuth Off`
Context:	directory
Status:	Base
Module:	mod_auth_form
Compatibility:	Available in Apache HTTP Server 2.3.0 and later

The AUTHFORMFAKEBASICAUTH flag determines whether a `Basic Authentication` header will be added to the request headers. This can be used to expose the username and password to an underlying application, without the underlying application having to be aware of how the login was achieved.

AuthFormLocation Directive

Description:	The name of a form field carrying a URL to redirect to on successful login
Syntax:	`AuthFormLocation fieldname`
Default:	`httpd_location`
Context:	directory
Status:	Base
Module:	mod_auth_form
Compatibility:	Available in Apache HTTP Server 2.3.0 and later

The AUTHFORMLOCATION directive specifies the name of an HTML field which, if present, will contain a URL to redirect the browser to should login be successful.

AuthFormLoginRequiredLocation Directive

Description:	The URL of the page to be redirected to should login be required
Syntax:	`AuthFormLoginRequiredLocation url`
Default:	`none`
Context:	directory
Status:	Base
Module:	mod_auth_form
Compatibility:	Available in Apache HTTP Server 2.3.0 and later. The use of the expression parser has been added in 2.4.4.

The AUTHFORMLOGINREQUIREDLOCATION directive specifies the URL to redirect to should the user not be authorised to view a page. The value is parsed using the ap_expr (p. 89) parser before being sent to the client. By default, if a user is not authorised to view a page, the HTTP response code `HTTP_UNAUTHORIZED` will be returned with the page specified by the ERRORDOCUMENT directive. This directive overrides this default.

Use this directive if you have a dedicated login page to redirect users to.

AuthFormLoginSuccessLocation Directive

Description:	The URL of the page to be redirected to should login be successful
Syntax:	`AuthFormLoginSuccessLocation url`
Default:	`none`
Context:	directory
Status:	Base
Module:	mod_auth_form
Compatibility:	Available in Apache HTTP Server 2.3.0 and later. The use of the expression parser has been added in 2.4.4.

The AUTHFORMLOGINSUCCESSLOCATION directive specifies the URL to redirect to should the user have logged in successfully. The value is parsed using the ap_expr (p. 89) parser before being sent to the client. This directive can be overridden if a form field has been defined containing another URL using the AUTHFORMLOCATION directive.

Use this directive if you have a dedicated login URL, and you have not embedded the destination page in the login form.

AuthFormLogoutLocation Directive

Description:	The URL to redirect to after a user has logged out
Syntax:	`AuthFormLogoutLocation uri`
Default:	`none`
Context:	directory
Status:	Base
Module:	mod_auth_form
Compatibility:	Available in Apache HTTP Server 2.3.0 and later. The use of the expression parser has been added in 2.4.4.

The AUTHFORMLOGOUTLOCATION directive specifies the URL of a page on the server to redirect to should the user attempt to log out. The value is parsed using the ap_expr (p. 89) parser before being sent to the client.

When a URI is accessed that is served by the handler `form-logout-handler`, the page specified by this directive will be shown to the end user. For example:

Example

```
<Location "/logout">
    SetHandler form-logout-handler
    AuthFormLogoutLocation "http://example.com/loggedout.html"
    Session on
    #...
</Location>
```

An attempt to access the URI */logout/* will result in the user being logged out, and the page */loggedout.html* will be displayed. Make sure that the page *loggedout.html* is not password protected, otherwise the page will not be displayed.

AuthFormMethod Directive

Description:	The name of a form field carrying the method of the request to attempt on successful login
Syntax:	`AuthFormMethod fieldname`
Default:	`httpd_method`
Context:	directory
Status:	Base
Module:	mod_auth_form
Compatibility:	Available in Apache HTTP Server 2.3.0 and later

The AUTHFORMMETHOD directive specifies the name of an HTML field which, if present, will contain the method of the request to to submit should login be successful.

By populating the form with fields described by AUTHFORMMETHOD, AUTHFORMMIMETYPE and AUTHFORMBODY, a website can retry a request that may have been interrupted by the login screen, or by a session timeout.

AuthFormMimetype Directive

Description:	The name of a form field carrying the mimetype of the body of the request to attempt on successful login
Syntax:	`AuthFormMimetype fieldname`
Default:	`httpd_mimetype`
Context:	directory
Status:	Base
Module:	mod_auth_form
Compatibility:	Available in Apache HTTP Server 2.3.0 and later

The AUTHFORMMETHOD directive specifies the name of an HTML field which, if present, will contain the mimetype of the request to submit should login be successful.

By populating the form with fields described by AUTHFORMMETHOD, AUTHFORMMIMETYPE and AUTHFORMBODY, a website can retry a request that may have been interrupted by the login screen, or by a session timeout.

AuthFormPassword Directive

Description:	The name of a form field carrying the login password
Syntax:	`AuthFormPassword fieldname`
Default:	`httpd_password`
Context:	directory
Status:	Base
Module:	mod_auth_form
Compatibility:	Available in Apache HTTP Server 2.3.0 and later

The AUTHFORMPASSWORD directive specifies the name of an HTML field which, if present, will contain the password to be used to log in.

AuthFormProvider Directive

Description:	Sets the authentication provider(s) for this location
Syntax:	`AuthFormProvider provider-name [provider-name] ...`
Default:	`AuthFormProvider file`
Context:	directory, .htaccess
Override:	AuthConfig
Status:	Base
Module:	mod_auth_form

The AUTHFORMPROVIDER directive sets which provider is used to authenticate the users for this location. The default `file` provider is implemented by the MOD_AUTHN_FILE module. Make sure that the chosen provider module is present in the server.

Example

```
<Location "/secure">
    AuthType form
    AuthName "private area"
    AuthFormProvider  dbm
    AuthDBMType        SDBM
    AuthDBMUserFile    "/www/etc/dbmpasswd"
    Require            valid-user
    #...
</Location>
```

Providers are implemented by MOD_AUTHN_DBM, MOD_AUTHN_FILE, MOD_AUTHN_DBD, MOD_AUTHNZ_LDAP and MOD_AUTHN_SOCACHE.

AuthFormSitePassphrase Directive

Description:	Bypass authentication checks for high traffic sites
Syntax:	`AuthFormSitePassphrase secret`
Default:	`none`
Context:	directory
Status:	Base
Module:	mod_auth_form
Compatibility:	Available in Apache HTTP Server 2.3.0 and later

The AUTHFORMSITEPASSPHRASE directive specifies a passphrase which, if present in the user session, causes Apache httpd to bypass authentication checks for the given URL. It can be used on high traffic websites to reduce the load induced on authentication infrastructure.

The passphrase can be inserted into a user session by adding this directive to the configuration for the *form-login-handler*. The *form-login-handler* itself will always run the authentication checks, regardless of whether a passphrase is specified or not.

Warning
If the session is exposed to the user through the use of MOD_SESSION_COOKIE, and the session is not protected with MOD_SESSION_CRYPTO, the passphrase is open to potential exposure through a dictionary attack. Regardless of how the session is configured, ensure that this directive is not used within URL spaces where private user data could be exposed, or sensitive transactions can be conducted. Use at own risk.

AuthFormSize Directive

Description:	The largest size of the form in bytes that will be parsed for the login details
Syntax:	`AuthFormSize size`
Default:	`8192`
Context:	directory
Status:	Base
Module:	mod_auth_form
Compatibility:	Available in Apache HTTP Server 2.3.0 and later

The AUTHFORMSIZE directive specifies the maximum size of the body of the request that will be parsed to find the login form.

If a login request arrives that exceeds this size, the whole request will be aborted with the HTTP response code `HTTP_REQUEST_TOO_LARGE`.

If you have populated the form with fields described by AUTHFORMMETHOD, AUTHFORMMIMETYPE and AUTH-FORMBODY, you probably want to set this field to a similar size as the KEPTBODYSIZE directive.

AuthFormUsername Directive

Description:	The name of a form field carrying the login username
Syntax:	`AuthFormUsername fieldname`
Default:	`httpd_username`
Context:	directory
Status:	Base
Module:	mod_auth_form
Compatibility:	Available in Apache HTTP Server 2.3.0 and later

The AUTHFORMUSERNAME directive specifies the name of an HTML field which, if present, will contain the username to be used to log in.

10.12 Apache Module mod_authn_anon

Description:	Allows "anonymous" user access to authenticated areas
Status:	Extension
ModuleIdentifier:	authn_anon_module
SourceFile:	mod_authn_anon.c
Compatibility:	Available in Apache 2.1 and later

Summary

This module provides authentication front-ends such as MOD_AUTH_BASIC to authenticate users similar to anonymous-ftp sites, *i.e.* have a 'magic' user id 'anonymous' and the email address as a password. These email addresses can be logged.

Combined with other (database) access control methods, this allows for effective user tracking and customization according to a user profile while still keeping the site open for 'unregistered' users. One advantage of using Auth-based user tracking is that, unlike magic-cookies and funny URL pre/postfixes, it is completely browser independent and it allows users to share URLs.

When using MOD_AUTH_BASIC, this module is invoked via the AUTHBASICPROVIDER directive with the `anon` value.

Directives

- Anonymous
- Anonymous_LogEmail
- Anonymous_MustGiveEmail
- Anonymous_NoUserID
- Anonymous_VerifyEmail

Example

The example below is combined with "normal" htpasswd-file based authentication and allows users in additionally as 'guests' with the following properties:

- It insists that the user enters a userID. (ANONYMOUS_NOUSERID)
- It insists that the user enters a password. (ANONYMOUS_MUSTGIVEEMAIL)
- The password entered must be a valid email address, *i.e.* contain at least one '@' and a '.'. (ANONYMOUS_VERIFYEMAIL)
- The userID must be one of `anonymous guest www test welcome` and comparison is **not** case sensitive. (ANONYMOUS)
- And the Email addresses entered in the passwd field are logged to the error log file. (ANONYMOUS_LOGEMAIL)

Example

```
<Directory "/var/www/html/private">
    AuthName "Use 'anonymous' & Email address for guest entry"
    AuthType Basic
    AuthBasicProvider file anon
    AuthUserFile "/path/to/your/.htpasswd"

    Anonymous_NoUserID off
    Anonymous_MustGiveEmail on
    Anonymous_VerifyEmail on
    Anonymous_LogEmail on
    Anonymous anonymous guest www test welcome

    Require valid-user
</Directory>
```

Anonymous Directive

Description:	Specifies userIDs that are allowed access without password verification
Syntax:	`Anonymous user [user] ...`
Context:	directory, .htaccess
Override:	AuthConfig
Status:	Extension
Module:	mod_authn_anon

A list of one or more 'magic' userIDs which are allowed access without password verification. The userIDs are space separated. It is possible to use the ' and " quotes to allow a space in a userID as well as the \escape character.

Please note that the comparison is **case-IN-sensitive**.
It's strongly recommended that the magic username '`anonymous`' is always one of the allowed userIDs.

Example:

```
Anonymous anonymous "Not Registered" "I don't know"
```

This would allow the user to enter without password verification by using the userIDs "anonymous", "AnonyMous", "Not Registered" and "I Don't Know".

As of Apache 2.1 it is possible to specify the userID as "`*`". That allows *any* supplied userID to be accepted.

Anonymous_LogEmail Directive

Description:	Sets whether the password entered will be logged in the error log
Syntax:	`Anonymous_LogEmail On|Off`
Default:	`Anonymous_LogEmail On`
Context:	directory, .htaccess
Override:	AuthConfig
Status:	Extension
Module:	mod_authn_anon

When set `On`, the default, the 'password' entered (which hopefully contains a sensible email address) is logged in the error log.

Anonymous_MustGiveEmail Directive

Description:	Specifies whether blank passwords are allowed
Syntax:	`Anonymous_MustGiveEmail On|Off`
Default:	`Anonymous_MustGiveEmail On`
Context:	directory, .htaccess
Override:	AuthConfig
Status:	Extension
Module:	mod_authn_anon

Specifies whether the user must specify an email address as the password. This prohibits blank passwords.

Anonymous_NoUserID Directive

Description:	Sets whether the userID field may be empty
Syntax:	`Anonymous_NoUserID On|Off`
Default:	`Anonymous_NoUserID Off`
Context:	directory, .htaccess
Override:	AuthConfig
Status:	Extension
Module:	mod_authn_anon

When set `On`, users can leave the userID (and perhaps the password field) empty. This can be very convenient for MS-Explorer users who can just hit return or click directly on the OK button; which seems a natural reaction.

Anonymous_VerifyEmail Directive

Description:	Sets whether to check the password field for a correctly formatted email address
Syntax:	`Anonymous_VerifyEmail On|Off`
Default:	`Anonymous_VerifyEmail Off`
Context:	directory, .htaccess
Override:	AuthConfig
Status:	Extension
Module:	mod_authn_anon

When set `On` the 'password' entered is checked for at least one '@' and a '.' to encourage users to enter valid email addresses (see the above ANONYMOUS_LOGEMAIL).

10.13 Apache Module mod_authn_core

Description:	Core Authentication
Status:	Base
ModuleIdentifier:	authn_core_module
SourceFile:	mod_authn_core.c
Compatibility:	Available in Apache 2.3 and later

Summary

This module provides core authentication capabilities to allow or deny access to portions of the web site. MOD_AUTHN_CORE provides directives that are common to all authentication providers.

Directives

- AuthName
- <AuthnProviderAlias>
- AuthType

Creating Authentication Provider Aliases

Extended authentication providers can be created within the configuration file and assigned an alias name. The alias providers can then be referenced through the directives AUTHBASICPROVIDER or AUTHDIGESTPROVIDER in the same way as a base authentication provider. Besides the ability to create and alias an extended provider, it also allows the same extended authentication provider to be reference by multiple locations.

Examples

This example checks for passwords in two different text files.

Checking multiple text password files

```
# Check here first
<AuthnProviderAlias file file1>
    AuthUserFile "/www/conf/passwords1"
</AuthnProviderAlias>

# Then check here
<AuthnProviderAlias file file2>
    AuthUserFile "/www/conf/passwords2"
</AuthnProviderAlias>

<Directory "/var/web/pages/secure">
    AuthBasicProvider file1 file2

    AuthType Basic
    AuthName "Protected Area"
    Require valid-user
</Directory>
```

The example below creates two different ldap authentication provider aliases based on the ldap provider. This allows a single authenticated location to be serviced by multiple ldap hosts:

Checking multiple LDAP servers

```
<AuthnProviderAlias ldap ldap-alias1>
    AuthLDAPBindDN cn=youruser,o=ctx
    AuthLDAPBindPassword yourpassword
    AuthLDAPURL ldap://ldap.host/o=ctx
</AuthnProviderAlias>
<AuthnProviderAlias ldap ldap-other-alias>
    AuthLDAPBindDN cn=yourotheruser,o=dev
    AuthLDAPBindPassword yourotherpassword
    AuthLDAPURL ldap://other.ldap.host/o=dev?cn
</AuthnProviderAlias>

Alias "/secure" "/webpages/secure"
<Directory "/webpages/secure">
    AuthBasicProvider ldap-other-alias  ldap-alias1

    AuthType Basic
    AuthName "LDAP Protected Place"
    Require valid-user
    # Note that Require ldap-* would not work here, since the
    # AuthnProviderAlias does not provide the config to authorization providers
    # that are implemented in the same module as the authentication provider.
</Directory>
```

AuthName Directive

Description:	Authorization realm for use in HTTP authentication
Syntax:	`AuthName auth-domain`
Context:	directory, .htaccess
Override:	AuthConfig
Status:	Base
Module:	mod_authn_core

This directive sets the name of the authorization realm for a directory. This realm is given to the client so that the user knows which username and password to send. AUTHNAME takes a single argument; if the realm name contains spaces, it must be enclosed in quotation marks. It must be accompanied by AUTHTYPE and REQUIRE directives, and directives such as AUTHUSERFILE and AUTHGROUPFILE to work.

For example:

```
AuthName "Top Secret"
```

The string provided for the `AuthName` is what will appear in the password dialog provided by most browsers.

See also

- Authentication, Authorization, and Access Control (p. 217)
- MOD_AUTHZ_CORE

AuthnProviderAlias Directive

Description:	Enclose a group of directives that represent an extension of a base authentication provider and referenced by the specified alias
Syntax:	`<AuthnProviderAlias baseProvider Alias> ... </AuthnProviderAlias>`
Context:	server config
Status:	Base
Module:	mod_authn_core

`<AuthnProviderAlias>` and `</AuthnProviderAlias>` are used to enclose a group of authentication directives that can be referenced by the alias name using one of the directives AUTHBASICPROVIDER or AUTHDIGESTPROVIDER.

⟹ This directive has no affect on authorization, even for modules that provide both authentication and authorization.

AuthType Directive

Description:	Type of user authentication
Syntax:	`AuthType None|Basic|Digest|Form`
Context:	directory, .htaccess
Override:	AuthConfig
Status:	Base
Module:	mod_authn_core

This directive selects the type of user authentication for a directory. The authentication types available are `None`, `Basic` (implemented by MOD_AUTH_BASIC), `Digest` (implemented by MOD_AUTH_DIGEST), and `Form` (implemented by MOD_AUTH_FORM).

To implement authentication, you must also use the AUTHNAME and REQUIRE directives. In addition, the server must have an authentication-provider module such as MOD_AUTHN_FILE and an authorization module such as MOD_AUTHZ_USER.

The authentication type `None` disables authentication. When authentication is enabled, it is normally inherited by each subsequent configuration section (p. 33) , unless a different authentication type is specified. If no authentication is desired for a subsection of an authenticated section, the authentication type `None` may be used; in the following example, clients may access the `/www/docs/public` directory without authenticating:

```
<Directory "/www/docs">
    AuthType Basic
    AuthName Documents
    AuthBasicProvider file
    AuthUserFile "/usr/local/apache/passwd/passwords"
    Require valid-user
</Directory>

<Directory "/www/docs/public">
    AuthType None
    Require all granted
</Directory>
```

⟹ When disabling authentication, note that clients which have already authenticated against another portion of the server's document tree will typically continue to send authentication HTTP headers or cookies with each request, regardless of whether the server actually requires authentication for every resource.

See also

- Authentication, Authorization, and Access Control (p. 217)

10.14 Apache Module mod_authn_dbd

Description:	User authentication using an SQL database
Status:	Extension
ModuleIdentifier:	authn_dbd_module
SourceFile:	mod_authn_dbd.c
Compatibility:	Available in Apache 2.1 and later

Summary

This module provides authentication front-ends such as MOD_AUTH_DIGEST and MOD_AUTH_BASIC to authenticate users by looking up users in SQL tables. Similar functionality is provided by, for example, MOD_AUTHN_FILE.

This module relies on MOD_DBD to specify the backend database driver and connection parameters, and manage the database connections.

When using MOD_AUTH_BASIC or MOD_AUTH_DIGEST, this module is invoked via the AUTHBASICPROVIDER or AUTHDIGESTPROVIDER with the `dbd` value.

Directives

- AuthDBDUserPWQuery
- AuthDBDUserRealmQuery

See also

- AUTHNAME
- AUTHTYPE
- AUTHBASICPROVIDER
- AUTHDIGESTPROVIDER
- DBDRIVER
- DBDPARAMS
- Password Formats (p. 345)

Performance and Cacheing

Some users of DBD authentication in HTTPD 2.2/2.4 have reported that it imposes a problematic load on the database. This is most likely where an HTML page contains hundreds of objects (e.g. images, scripts, etc) each of which requires authentication. Users affected (or concerned) by this kind of problem should use MOD_AUTHN_SOCACHE to cache credentials and take most of the load off the database.

Configuration Example

This simple example shows use of this module in the context of the Authentication and DBD frameworks.

```
# mod_dbd configuration
# UPDATED to include authentication cacheing
DBDriver pgsql
DBDParams "dbname=apacheauth user=apache password=xxxxxx"
```

```
DBDMin  4
DBDKeep 8
DBDMax  20
DBDExptime 300

<Directory "/usr/www/myhost/private">
  # mod_authn_core and mod_auth_basic configuration
  # for mod_authn_dbd
  AuthType Basic
  AuthName "My Server"

  # To cache credentials, put socache ahead of dbd here
  AuthBasicProvider socache dbd

  # Also required for caching: tell the cache to cache dbd lookups!
  AuthnCacheProvideFor dbd
  AuthnCacheContext my-server

  # mod_authz_core configuration
  Require valid-user

  # mod_authn_dbd SQL query to authenticate a user
  AuthDBDUserPWQuery "SELECT password FROM authn WHERE user = %s"
</Directory>
```

Exposing Login Information

If httpd was built against APR version 1.3.0 or higher, then whenever a query is made to the database server, all column values in the first row returned by the query are placed in the environment, using environment variables with the prefix "AUTHENTICATE_".

If a database query for example returned the username, full name and telephone number of a user, a CGI program will have access to this information without the need to make a second independent database query to gather this additional information.

This has the potential to dramatically simplify the coding and configuration required in some web applications.

AuthDBDUserPWQuery Directive

Description:	SQL query to look up a password for a user
Syntax:	`AuthDBDUserPWQuery query`
Context:	directory
Status:	Extension
Module:	mod_authn_dbd

The AUTHDBDUSERPWQUERY specifies an SQL query to look up a password for a specified user. The user's ID will be passed as a single string parameter when the SQL query is executed. It may be referenced within the query statement using a `%s` format specifier.

```
AuthDBDUserPWQuery "SELECT password FROM authn WHERE user = %s"
```

The first column value of the first row returned by the query statement should be a string containing the encrypted password. Subsequent rows will be ignored. If no rows are returned, the user will not be authenticated through MOD_AUTHN_DBD.

If httpd was built against APR version 1.3.0 or higher, any additional column values in the first row returned by the query statement will be stored as environment variables with names of the form `AUTHENTICATE_`*`COLUMN`*.

The encrypted password format depends on which authentication frontend (e.g. MOD_AUTH_BASIC or MOD_AUTH_DIGEST) is being used. See Password Formats (p. 345) for more information.

AuthDBDUserRealmQuery Directive

Description:	SQL query to look up a password hash for a user and realm.
Syntax:	`AuthDBDUserRealmQuery query`
Context:	directory
Status:	Extension
Module:	mod_authn_dbd

The AUTHDBDUSERREALMQUERY specifies an SQL query to look up a password for a specified user and realm in a digest authentication process. The user's ID and the realm, in that order, will be passed as string parameters when the SQL query is executed. They may be referenced within the query statement using `%s` format specifiers.

```
AuthDBDUserRealmQuery "SELECT password FROM authn WHERE user = %s AND realm = %
```

The first column value of the first row returned by the query statement should be a string containing the encrypted password. Subsequent rows will be ignored. If no rows are returned, the user will not be authenticated through MOD_AUTHN_DBD.

If httpd was built against APR version 1.3.0 or higher, any additional column values in the first row returned by the query statement will be stored as environment variables with names of the form `AUTHENTICATE_`*`COLUMN`*.

The encrypted password format depends on which authentication frontend (e.g. MOD_AUTH_BASIC or MOD_AUTH_DIGEST) is being used. See Password Formats (p. 345) for more information.

10.15 Apache Module mod_authn_dbm

Description:	User authentication using DBM files
Status:	Extension
ModuleIdentifier:	authn_dbm_module
SourceFile:	mod_authn_dbm.c
Compatibility:	Available in Apache 2.1 and later

Summary

This module provides authentication front-ends such as MOD_AUTH_DIGEST and MOD_AUTH_BASIC to authenticate users by looking up users in *dbm* password files. Similar functionality is provided by MOD_AUTHN_FILE.

When using MOD_AUTH_BASIC or MOD_AUTH_DIGEST, this module is invoked via the AUTHBASICPROVIDER or AUTHDIGESTPROVIDER with the `dbm` value.

Directives

- AuthDBMType
- AuthDBMUserFile

See also

- AUTHNAME
- AUTHTYPE
- AUTHBASICPROVIDER
- AUTHDIGESTPROVIDER
- `htpasswd`
- `htdbm`
- Password Formats (p. 345)

AuthDBMType Directive

Description:	Sets the type of database file that is used to store passwords
Syntax:	`AuthDBMType default|SDBM|GDBM|NDBM|DB`
Default:	`AuthDBMType default`
Context:	directory, .htaccess
Override:	AuthConfig
Status:	Extension
Module:	mod_authn_dbm

Sets the type of database file that is used to store the passwords. The default database type is determined at compile time. The availability of other types of database files also depends on compile-time settings (p. 20) .

It is crucial that whatever program you use to create your password files is configured to use the same type of database.

AuthDBMUserFile Directive

Description:	Sets the name of a database file containing the list of users and passwords for authentication
Syntax:	`AuthDBMUserFile file-path`
Context:	directory, .htaccess
Override:	AuthConfig
Status:	Extension
Module:	mod_authn_dbm

The AUTHDBMUSERFILE directive sets the name of a DBM file containing the list of users and passwords for user authentication. *File-path* is the absolute path to the user file.

The user file is keyed on the username. The value for a user is the encrypted password, optionally followed by a colon and arbitrary data. The colon and the data following it will be ignored by the server.

Security:
Make sure that the AUTHDBMUSERFILE is stored outside the document tree of the web-server; do *not* put it in the directory that it protects. Otherwise, clients will be able to download the AUTHDBMUSERFILE.

The encrypted password format depends on which authentication frontend (e.g. MOD_AUTH_BASIC or MOD_AUTH_DIGEST) is being used. See Password Formats (p. 345) for more information.

Important compatibility note: The implementation of `dbmopen` in the apache modules reads the string length of the hashed values from the DBM data structures, rather than relying upon the string being NULL-appended. Some applications, such as the Netscape web server, rely upon the string being NULL-appended, so if you are having trouble using DBM files interchangeably between applications this may be a part of the problem.

A perl script called `dbmmanage` is included with Apache. This program can be used to create and update DBM format password files for use with this module. Another tool for maintaining the DBM files is the included program `htdbm`.

10.16 Apache Module mod_authn_file

Description:	User authentication using text files
Status:	Base
ModuleIdentifier:	authn_file_module
SourceFile:	mod_authn_file.c
Compatibility:	Available in Apache 2.1 and later

Summary

This module provides authentication front-ends such as MOD_AUTH_DIGEST and MOD_AUTH_BASIC to authenticate users by looking up users in plain text password files. Similar functionality is provided by MOD_AUTHN_DBM.

When using MOD_AUTH_BASIC or MOD_AUTH_DIGEST, this module is invoked via the AUTHBASICPROVIDER or AUTHDIGESTPROVIDER with the `file` value.

Directives

- AuthUserFile

See also

- AUTHBASICPROVIDER
- AUTHDIGESTPROVIDER
- `htpasswd`
- `htdigest`
- Password Formats (p. 345)

AuthUserFile Directive

Description:	Sets the name of a text file containing the list of users and passwords for authentication
Syntax:	`AuthUserFile file-path`
Context:	directory, .htaccess
Override:	AuthConfig
Status:	Base
Module:	mod_authn_file

The AUTHUSERFILE directive sets the name of a textual file containing the list of users and passwords for user authentication. *File-path* is the path to the user file. If it is not absolute, it is treated as relative to the SERVERROOT.

Each line of the user file contains a username followed by a colon, followed by the encrypted password. If the same user ID is defined multiple times, MOD_AUTHN_FILE will use the first occurrence to verify the password.

The encrypted password format depends on which authentication frontend (e.g. MOD_AUTH_BASIC or MOD_AUTH_DIGEST) is being used. See Password Formats (p. 345) for more information.

For MOD_AUTH_BASIC, use the utility `htpasswd` which is installed as part of the binary distribution, or which can be found in `src/support`. See the man page (p. 312) for more details. In short:

Create a password file `Filename` with `username` as the initial ID. It will prompt for the password:

```
htpasswd -c Filename username
```

Add or modify `username2` in the password file `Filename`:

```
htpasswd Filename username2
```

Note that searching large text files is *very* inefficient; AUTHDBMUSERFILE should be used instead.

For MOD_AUTH_DIGEST, use `htdigest` instead. Note that you cannot mix user data for Digest Authentication and Basic Authentication within the same file.

Security
Make sure that the AUTHUSERFILE is stored outside the document tree of the web-server. Do **not** put it in the directory that it protects. Otherwise, clients may be able to download the AUTHUSERFILE.

10.17 Apache Module mod_authn_socache

Description:	Manages a cache of authentication credentials to relieve the load on backends
Status:	Base
ModuleIdentifier:	authn_socache_module
SourceFile:	mod_authn_socache.c
Compatibility:	Version 2.3 and later

Summary

Maintains a cache of authentication credentials, so that a new backend lookup is not required for every authenticated request.

Directives

- AuthnCacheContext
- AuthnCacheEnable
- AuthnCacheProvideFor
- AuthnCacheSOCache
- AuthnCacheTimeout

Authentication Cacheing

Some users of more heavyweight authentication such as SQL database lookups (MOD_AUTHN_DBD) have reported it putting an unacceptable load on their authentication provider. A typical case in point is where an HTML page contains hundreds of objects (images, scripts, stylesheets, media, etc), and a request to the page generates hundreds of effectively-immediate requests for authenticated additional contents.

mod_authn_socache provides a solution to this problem by maintaining a cache of authentication credentials.

Usage

The authentication cache should be used where authentication lookups impose a significant load on the server, or a backend or network. Authentication by file (MOD_AUTHN_FILE) or dbm (MOD_AUTHN_DBM) are unlikely to benefit, as these are fast and lightweight in their own right (though in some cases, such as a network-mounted file, cacheing may be worthwhile). Other providers such as SQL or LDAP based authentication are more likely to benefit, particularly where there is an observed performance issue. Amongst the standard modules, MOD_AUTHNZ_LDAP manages its own cache, so only MOD_AUTHN_DBD will usually benefit from this cache.

The basic rules to cache for a provider are:

1. Include the provider you're cacheing for in an AUTHNCACHEPROVIDEFOR directive.
2. List *socache* ahead of the provider you're cacheing for in your AUTHBASICPROVIDER or AUTHDIGEST-PROVIDER directive.

A simple usage example to accelerate MOD_AUTHN_DBD using dbm as a cache engine:

```
#AuthnCacheSOCache is optional.  If specified, it is server-wide
AuthnCacheSOCache dbm
<Directory "/usr/www/myhost/private">
```

```
    AuthType Basic
    AuthName "Cached Authentication Example"
    AuthBasicProvider socache dbd
    AuthDBDUserPWQuery "SELECT password FROM authn WHERE user = %s"
    AuthnCacheProvideFor dbd
    Require valid-user
    #Optional
    AuthnCacheContext dbd-authn-example
</Directory>
```

Cacheing with custom modules

Module developers should note that their modules must be enabled for cacheing with mod_authn_socache. A single optional API function *ap_authn_cache_store* is provided to cache credentials a provider has just looked up or generated. Usage examples are available in r957072[10], in which three authn providers are enabled for cacheing.

AuthnCacheContext Directive

Description:	Specify a context string for use in the cache key
Syntax:	`AuthnCacheContext directory|server|custom-string`
Default:	`directory`
Context:	directory
Status:	Base
Module:	mod_authn_socache

This directive specifies a string to be used along with the supplied username (and realm in the case of Digest Authentication) in constructing a cache key. This serves to disambiguate identical usernames serving different authentication areas on the server.

Two special values for this are *directory*, which uses the directory context of the request as a string, and *server* which uses the virtual host name.

The default is *directory*, which is also the most conservative setting. This is likely to be less than optimal, as it (for example) causes *$app-base*, *$app-base/images*, *$app-base/scripts* and *$app-base/media* each to have its own separate cache key. A better policy is to name the AUTHNCACHECONTEXT for the password provider: for example a *htpasswd* file or database table.

Contexts can be shared across different areas of a server, where credentials are shared. However, this has potential to become a vector for cross-site or cross-application security breaches, so this directive is not permitted in *.htaccess* contexts.

AuthnCacheEnable Directive

Description:	Enable Authn caching configured anywhere
Syntax:	`AuthnCacheEnable`
Context:	server config
Override:	None
Status:	Base
Module:	mod_authn_socache

This directive is not normally necessary: it is implied if authentication cacheing is enabled anywhere in *httpd.conf*. However, if it is not enabled anywhere in *httpd.conf* it will by default not be initialised, and is therefore not available in a *.htaccess* context. This directive ensures it is initialised so it can be used in *.htaccess*.

[10]http://svn.eu.apache.org/viewvc?view=revision&revision=957072

AuthnCacheProvideFor Directive

Description:	Specify which authn provider(s) to cache for
Syntax:	`AuthnCacheProvideFor authn-provider [...]`
Default:	`None`
Context:	directory, .htaccess
Override:	AuthConfig
Status:	Base
Module:	mod_authn_socache

This directive specifies an authentication provider or providers to cache for. Credentials found by a provider not listed in an AuthnCacheProvideFor directive will not be cached.

For example, to cache credentials found by MOD_AUTHN_DBD or by a custom provider *myprovider*, but leave those looked up by lightweight providers like file or dbm lookup alone:

```
AuthnCacheProvideFor dbd myprovider
```

AuthnCacheSOCache Directive

Description:	Select socache backend provider to use
Syntax:	`AuthnCacheSOCache provider-name[:provider-args]`
Context:	server config
Override:	None
Status:	Base
Module:	mod_authn_socache
Compatibility:	Optional provider arguments are available in Apache HTTP Server 2.4.7 and later

This is a server-wide setting to select a provider for the shared object cache (p. 104) , followed by optional arguments for that provider. Some possible values for *provider-name* are "dbm", "dc", "memcache", or "shmcb", each subject to the appropriate module being loaded. If not set, your platform's default will be used.

AuthnCacheTimeout Directive

Description:	Set a timeout for cache entries
Syntax:	`AuthnCacheTimeout timeout (seconds)`
Default:	`300 (5 minutes)`
Context:	directory, .htaccess
Override:	AuthConfig
Status:	Base
Module:	mod_authn_socache

Cacheing authentication data can be a security issue, though short-term cacheing is unlikely to be a problem. Typically a good solution is to cache credentials for as long as it takes to relieve the load on a backend, but no longer, though if changes to your users and passwords are infrequent then a longer timeout may suit you. The default 300 seconds (5 minutes) is both cautious and ample to keep the load on a backend such as dbd (SQL database queries) down.

This should not be confused with session timeout, which is an entirely separate issue. However, you may wish to check your session-management software for whether cached credentials can "accidentally" extend a session, and bear it in mind when setting your timeout.

10.18 Apache Module mod_authnz_fcgi

Description:	Allows a FastCGI authorizer application to handle Apache httpd authentication and authorization
Status:	Extension
ModuleIdentifier:	authnz_fcgi_module
SourceFile:	mod_authnz_fcgi.c
Compatibility:	Available in version 2.4.10 and later

Summary

This module allows FastCGI authorizer applications to authenticate users and authorize access to resources. It supports generic FastCGI authorizers which participate in a single phase for authentication and authorization as well as Apache httpd-specific authenticators and authorizors which participate in one or both phases.

FastCGI authorizers can authenticate using user id and password, such as for Basic authentication, or can authenticate using arbitrary mechanisms.

Directives

- AuthnzFcgiCheckAuthnProvider
- AuthnzFcgiDefineProvider

See also

- Authentication, Authorization, and Access Control (p. 217)
- MOD_AUTH_BASIC
- fcgistarter
- MOD_PROXY_FCGI

Invocation modes

The invocation modes for FastCGI authorizers supported by this module are distinguished by two characteristics, *type* and auth *mechanism*.

Type is simply authn for authentication, authz for authorization, or authnz for combined authentication and authorization.

Auth *mechanism* refers to the Apache httpd configuration mechanisms and processing phases, and can be AuthBasicProvider, Require, or check_user_id. The first two of these correspond to the directives used to enable participation in the appropriate processing phase.

Descriptions of each mode:

***Type* authn, *mechanism* AuthBasicProvider** In this mode, FCGI_ROLE is set to AUTHORIZER and FCGI_APACHE_ROLE is set to AUTHENTICATOR. The application must be defined as provider type *authn* using AUTHNZFCGIDEFINEPROVIDER and enabled with AUTHBASICPROVIDER. When invoked, the application is expected to authenticate the client using the provided user id and password. Example application:

```
#!/usr/bin/perl
use FCGI;
while (FCGI::accept >= 0) {
```

```
    die if $ENV{'FCGI_APACHE_ROLE'} ne "AUTHENTICATOR";
    die if $ENV{'FCGI_ROLE'}        ne "AUTHORIZER";
    die if !$ENV{'REMOTE_PASSWD'};
    die if !$ENV{'REMOTE_USER'};

    print STDERR "This text is written to the web server error log.\n";

    if ( ($ENV{'REMOTE_USER' } eq "foo" || $ENV{'REMOTE_USER'} eq "foo1") &
        $ENV{'REMOTE_PASSWD'} eq "bar" ) {
        print "Status: 200\n";
        print "Variable-AUTHN_1: authn_01\n";
        print "Variable-AUTHN_2: authn_02\n";
        print "\n";
    }
    else {
        print "Status: 401\n\n";
    }
}
```

Example configuration:

```
AuthnzFcgiDefineProvider authn FooAuthn fcgi://localhost:10102/
<Location "/protected/">
  AuthType Basic
  AuthName "Restricted"
  AuthBasicProvider FooAuthn
  Require ...
</Location>
```

***Type* `authz`, *mechanism* `Require`** In this mode, FCGI_ROLE is set to AUTHORIZER and FCGI_APACHE_ROLE is set to AUTHORIZER. The application must be defined as provider type *authz* using AUTHNZFCGIDEFINEPROVIDER. When invoked, the application is expected to authorize the client using the provided user id and other request data. Example application:

```
#!/usr/bin/perl
use FCGI;
while (FCGI::accept >= 0) {
    die if $ENV{'FCGI_APACHE_ROLE'} ne "AUTHORIZER";
    die if $ENV{'FCGI_ROLE'}        ne "AUTHORIZER";
    die if $ENV{'REMOTE_PASSWD'};

    print STDERR "This text is written to the web server error log.\n";

    if ($ENV{'REMOTE_USER'} eq "foo1") {
        print "Status: 200\n";
        print "Variable-AUTHZ_1: authz_01\n";
        print "Variable-AUTHZ_2: authz_02\n";
        print "\n";
    }
    else {
        print "Status: 403\n\n";
    }
}
```

Example configuration:

```
AuthnzFcgiDefineProvider authz FooAuthz fcgi://localhost:10103/
<Location "/protected/">
  AuthType ...
  AuthName ...
  AuthBasicProvider ...
  Require FooAuthz
</Location>
```

Type **authnz,** ***mechanism*** **AuthBasicProvider + Require** In this mode, which supports the web server-agnostic FastCGI AUTHORIZER protocol, FCGI_ROLE is set to AUTHORIZER and FCGI_APACHE_ROLE is not set. The application must be defined as provider type *authnz* using AUTHNZFCGIDEFINEPROVIDER. The application is expected to handle both authentication and authorization in the same invocation using the user id, password, and other request data. The invocation occurs during the Apache httpd API authentication phase. If the application returns 200 and the same provider is invoked during the authorization phase (via REQUIRE), mod_authnz_fcgi will return success for the authorization phase without invoking the application. Example application:

```
#!/usr/bin/perl
use FCGI;
while (FCGI::accept >= 0) {
    die if $ENV{'FCGI_APACHE_ROLE'};
    die if $ENV{'FCGI_ROLE'} ne "AUTHORIZER";
    die if !$ENV{'REMOTE_PASSWD'};
    die if !$ENV{'REMOTE_USER'};

    print STDERR "This text is written to the web server error log.\n";

    if ( ($ENV{'REMOTE_USER' } eq "foo" || $ENV{'REMOTE_USER'} eq "foo1") &
        $ENV{'REMOTE_PASSWD'} eq "bar" &&
        $ENV{'REQUEST_URI'} =~ m%/bar/.*%) {
        print "Status: 200\n";
        print "Variable-AUTHNZ_1: authnz_01\n";
        print "Variable-AUTHNZ_2: authnz_02\n";
        print "\n";
    }
    else {
        print "Status: 401\n\n";
    }
}
```

Example configuration:

```
AuthnzFcgiDefineProvider authnz FooAuthnz fcgi://localhost:10103/
<Location "/protected/">
  AuthType Basic
  AuthName "Restricted"
  AuthBasicProvider FooAuthnz
  Require FooAuthnz
</Location>
```

Type **authn,** ***mechanism*** **check_user_id** In this mode, FCGI_ROLE is set to AUTHORIZER and FCGI_APACHE_ROLE is set to AUTHENTICATOR. The application must be defined as provider type *authn* using AUTHNZFCGIDEFINEPROVIDER. AUTHNZFCGICHECKAUTHNPROVIDER specifies when it is called. Example application:

```
#!/usr/bin/perl
use FCGI;
while (FCGI::accept >= 0) {
    die if $ENV{'FCGI_APACHE_ROLE'} ne "AUTHENTICATOR";
    die if $ENV{'FCGI_ROLE'} ne "AUTHORIZER";

    # This authorizer assumes that the RequireBasicAuth option of
    # AuthnzFcgiCheckAuthnProvider is On:
    die if !$ENV{'REMOTE_PASSWD'};
    die if !$ENV{'REMOTE_USER'};

    print STDERR "This text is written to the web server error log.\n";

    if ( ($ENV{'REMOTE_USER' } eq "foo" || $ENV{'REMOTE_USER'} eq "foo1") &
        $ENV{'REMOTE_PASSWD'} eq "bar" ) {
        print "Status: 200\n";
        print "Variable-AUTHNZ_1: authnz_01\n";
        print "Variable-AUTHNZ_2: authnz_02\n";
        print "\n";
    }
    else {
        print "Status: 401\n\n";
        # If a response body is written here, it will be returned to
        # the client.
    }
}
```

Example configuration:

```
AuthnzFcgiDefineProvider authn FooAuthn fcgi://localhost:10103/
<Location "/protected/">
  AuthType ...
  AuthName ...
  AuthnzFcgiCheckAuthnProvider FooAuthn \
                               Authoritative On \
                               RequireBasicAuth Off \
                               UserExpr "%{reqenv:REMOTE_USER}"
  Require ...
</Location>
```

Additional examples

1. If your application supports the separate authentication and authorization roles (AUTHENTICATOR and AUTHORIZER), define separate providers as follows, even if they map to the same application:

```
AuthnzFcgiDefineProvider authn  FooAuthn  fcgi://localhost:10102/
AuthnzFcgiDefineProvider authz  FooAuthz  fcgi://localhost:10102/
```

Specify the authn provider on AUTHBASICPROVIDER and the authz provider on REQUIRE:

```
AuthType Basic
AuthName "Restricted"
AuthBasicProvider FooAuthn
Require FooAuthz
```

2. If your application supports the generic `AUTHORIZER` role (authentication and authorizer in one invocation), define a single provider as follows:

```
AuthnzFcgiDefineProvider authnz FooAuthnz fcgi://localhost:10103/
```

   Specify the authnz provider on both AUTHBASICPROVIDER and REQUIRE:

```
AuthType Basic
AuthName "Restricted"
AuthBasicProvider FooAuthnz
Require FooAuthnz
```

Limitations

The following are potential features which are not currently implemented:

Apache httpd access checker The Apache httpd API *access check* phase is a separate phase from authentication and authorization. Some other FastCGI implementations implement this phase, which is denoted by the setting of `FCGI_APACHE_ROLE` to `ACCESS_CHECKER`.

Local (Unix) sockets or pipes Only TCP sockets are currently supported.

Support for mod_authn_socache mod_authn_socache interaction should be implemented for applications which participate in Apache httpd-style authentication.

Support for digest authentication using AuthDigestProvider This is expected to be a permanent limitation as there is no authorizer flow for retrieving a hash.

Application process management This is expected to be permanently out of scope for this module. Application processes must be controlled by other means. For example, `fcgistarter` can be used to start them.

AP_AUTH_INTERNAL_PER_URI All providers are currently registered as AP_AUTH_INTERNAL_PER_CONF, which means that checks are not performed again for internal subrequests with the same access control configuration as the initial request.

Protocol data charset conversion If mod_authnz_fcgi runs in an EBCDIC compilation environment, all FastCGI protocol data is written in EBCDIC and expected to be received in EBCDIC.

Multiple requests per connection Currently the connection to the FastCGI authorizer is closed after every phase of processing. For example, if the authorizer handles separate *authn* and *authz* phases then two connections will be used.

URI Mapping URIs from clients can't be mapped, such as with the PROXYPASS used with FastCGI responders.

Logging

1. Processing errors are logged at log level `error` and higher.
2. Messages written by the application are logged at log level `warn`.
3. General messages for debugging are logged at log level `debug`.
4. Environment variables passed to the application are logged at log level `trace2`. The value of the `REMOTE_PASSWD` variable will be obscured, but **any other sensitive data will be visible in the log**.
5. All I/O between the module and the FastCGI application, including all environment variables, will be logged in printable and hex format at log level `trace5`. **All sensitive data will be visible in the log.**

LOGLEVEL can be used to configure a log level specific to mod_authnz_fcgi. For example:

```
LogLevel info authnz_fcgi:trace8
```

AuthnzFcgiCheckAuthnProvider Directive

Description:	Enables a FastCGI application to handle the check_authn authentication hook.
Syntax:	`AuthnzFcgiCheckAuthnProvider provider-name|None option ...`
Default:	`none`
Context:	directory
Status:	Extension
Module:	mod_authnz_fcgi

This directive is used to enable a FastCGI authorizer to handle a specific processing phase of authentication or authorization.

Some capabilities of FastCGI authorizers require enablement using this directive instead of AUTHBASICPROVIDER:

- Non-Basic authentication; generally, determining the user id of the client and returning it from the authorizer; see the `UserExpr` option below
- Selecting a custom response code; for a non-200 response from the authorizer, the code from the authorizer will be the status of the response
- Setting the body of a non-200 response; if the authorizer provides a response body with a non-200 response, that body will be returned to the client; up to 8192 bytes of text are supported

provider-name This is the name of a provider defined with AUTHNZFCGIDEFINEPROVIDER.

None Specify `None` to disable a provider enabled with this directive in an outer scope, such as in a parent directory.

option The following options are supported:

Authoritative On—Off (default On) This controls whether or not other modules are allowed to run when this module has a FastCGI authorizer configured and it fails the request.

DefaultUser *userid* When the authorizer returns success and `UserExpr` is configured and evaluates to an empty string (e.g., authorizer didn't return a variable), this value will be used as the user id. This is typically used when the authorizer has a concept of guest, or unauthenticated, users and guest users are mapped to some specific user id for logging and other purposes.

RequireBasicAuth On—Off (default Off) This controls whether or not Basic auth is required before passing the request to the authorizer. If required, the authorizer won't be invoked without a user id and password; 401 will be returned for a request without that.

UserExpr *expr* (no default) When Basic authentication isn't provided by the client and the authorizer determines the user, this expression, evaluated after calling the authorizer, determines the user. The expression follows ap_expr syntax (p. 89) and must resolve to a string. A typical use is to reference a `Variable-XXX` setting returned by the authorizer using an option like `UserExpr "%{reqenv:XXX}"`. If this option is specified and the user id can't be retrieved using the expression after a successful authentication, the request will be rejected with a 500 error.

AuthnzFcgiDefineProvider Directive

Description:	Defines a FastCGI application as a provider for authentication and/or authorization
Syntax:	`AuthnzFcgiDefineProvider type provider-name backend-address`
Default:	`none`
Context:	server config
Status:	Extension
Module:	mod_authnz_fcgi

This directive is used to define a FastCGI application as a provider for a particular phase of authentication or authorization.

type This must be set to *authn* for authentication, *authz* for authorization, or *authnz* for a generic FastCGI authorizer which performs both checks.

provider-name This is used to assign a name to the provider which is used in other directives such as AUTHBASICPROVIDER and REQUIRE.

backend-address This specifies the address of the application, in the form *fcgi://hostname:port/*. The application process(es) must be managed independently, such as with `fcgistarter`.

10.19 Apache Module mod_authnz_ldap

Description:	Allows an LDAP directory to be used to store the database for HTTP Basic authentication.
Status:	Extension
ModuleIdentifier:	authnz_ldap_module
SourceFile:	mod_authnz_ldap.c
Compatibility:	Available in version 2.1 and later

Summary

This module allows authentication front-ends such as MOD_AUTH_BASIC to authenticate users through an ldap directory.

MOD_AUTHNZ_LDAP supports the following features:

- Known to support the OpenLDAP SDK[11] (both 1.x and 2.x), Novell LDAP SDK[12] and the iPlanet (Netscape)[13] SDK.
- Complex authorization policies can be implemented by representing the policy with LDAP filters.
- Uses extensive caching of LDAP operations via mod_ldap (p. 649) .
- Support for LDAP over SSL (requires the Netscape SDK) or TLS (requires the OpenLDAP 2.x SDK or Novell LDAP SDK).

When using MOD_AUTH_BASIC, this module is invoked via the AUTHBASICPROVIDER directive with the `ldap` value.

Directives

- AuthLDAPAuthorizePrefix
- AuthLDAPBindAuthoritative
- AuthLDAPBindDN
- AuthLDAPBindPassword
- AuthLDAPCharsetConfig
- AuthLDAPCompareAsUser
- AuthLDAPCompareDNOnServer
- AuthLDAPDereferenceAliases
- AuthLDAPGroupAttribute
- AuthLDAPGroupAttributeIsDN
- AuthLDAPInitialBindAsUser
- AuthLDAPInitialBindPattern
- AuthLDAPMaxSubGroupDepth
- AuthLDAPRemoteUserAttribute
- AuthLDAPRemoteUserIsDN
- AuthLDAPSearchAsUser

[11] http://www.openldap.org/
[12] http://developer.novell.com/ndk/cldap.htm
[13] http://www.iplanet.com/downloads/developer/

- AuthLDAPSubGroupAttribute
- AuthLDAPSubGroupClass
- AuthLDAPUrl

See also

- MOD_LDAP
- MOD_AUTH_BASIC
- MOD_AUTHZ_USER
- MOD_AUTHZ_GROUPFILE

Contents

General caveats

This module caches authentication and authorization results based on the configuration of MOD_LDAP. Changes made to the backing LDAP server will not be immediately reflected on the HTTP Server, including but not limited to user lockouts/revocations, password changes, or changes to group memberships. Consult the directives in MOD_LDAP for details of the cache tunables.

Operation

There are two phases in granting access to a user. The first phase is authentication, in which the MOD_AUTHNZ_LDAP authentication provider verifies that the user's credentials are valid. This is also called the *search/bind* phase. The second phase is authorization, in which MOD_AUTHNZ_LDAP determines if the authenticated user is allowed access to the resource in question. This is also known as the *compare* phase.

MOD_AUTHNZ_LDAP registers both an authn_ldap authentication provider and an authz_ldap authorization handler. The authn_ldap authentication provider can be enabled through the AUTHBASICPROVIDER directive using the `ldap` value. The authz_ldap handler extends the REQUIRE directive's authorization types by adding `ldap-user`, `ldap-dn` and `ldap-group` values.

The Authentication Phase

During the authentication phase, MOD_AUTHNZ_LDAP searches for an entry in the directory that matches the username that the HTTP client passes. If a single unique match is found, then MOD_AUTHNZ_LDAP attempts to bind to the directory server using the DN of the entry plus the password provided by the HTTP client. Because it does a search, then a bind, it is often referred to as the search/bind phase. Here are the steps taken during the search/bind phase.

1. Generate a search filter by combining the attribute and filter provided in the AUTHLDAPURL directive with the username passed by the HTTP client.
2. Search the directory using the generated filter. If the search does not return exactly one entry, deny or decline access.
3. Fetch the distinguished name of the entry retrieved from the search and attempt to bind to the LDAP server using that DN and the password passed by the HTTP client. If the bind is unsuccessful, deny or decline access.

The following directives are used during the search/bind phase

AUTHLDAPURL	Specifies the LDAP server, the base DN, the attribute to use in the search, as well as extra search filter to use.
AUTHLDAPBINDDN	An optional DN to bind with during the search phase.
AUTHLDAPBINDPASSWORD	An optional password to bind with during the search phase.

The Authorization Phase

During the authorization phase, MOD_AUTHNZ_LDAP attempts to determine if the user is authorized to access the resource. Many of these checks require MOD_AUTHNZ_LDAP to do a compare operation on the LDAP server. This is why this phase is often referred to as the compare phase. MOD_AUTHNZ_LDAP accepts the following REQUIRE directives to determine if the credentials are acceptable:

- Grant access if there is a `Require ldap-user` directive, and the username in the directive matches the username passed by the client.
- Grant access if there is a `Require ldap-dn` directive, and the DN in the directive matches the DN fetched from the LDAP directory.
- Grant access if there is a `Require ldap-group` directive, and the DN fetched from the LDAP directory (or the username passed by the client) occurs in the LDAP group or, potentially, in one of its sub-groups.
- Grant access if there is a `Require ldap-attribute` directive, and the attribute fetched from the LDAP directory matches the given value.
- Grant access if there is a `Require ldap-filter` directive, and the search filter successfully finds a single user object that matches the dn of the authenticated user.

- otherwise, deny or decline access

Other REQUIRE values may also be used which may require loading additional authorization modules.

- Grant access to all successfully authenticated users if there is a `Require valid-user` directive. (requires MOD_AUTHZ_USER)
- Grant access if there is a `Require group` directive, and MOD_AUTHZ_GROUPFILE has been loaded with the AUTHGROUPFILE directive set.
- others...

MOD_AUTHNZ_LDAP uses the following directives during the compare phase:

AUTHLDAPURL	The attribute specified in the URL is used in compare operations for `Require ldap-user` operation.
AUTHLDAPCOMPAREDNONSERVER	Determines the behavior of the `Require ldap-dn` directive.
AUTHLDAPGROUPATTRIBUTE	Determines the attribute to use for comparisons in the `Requi` `ldap-group` directive.
AUTHLDAPGROUPATTRIBUTEISDN	Specifies whether to use the user DN or the username when doing comparis for the `Require ldap-group` directive.
AUTHLDAPMAXSUBGROUPDEPTH	Determines the maximum depth of sub-groups that will be evaluated du comparisons in the `Require ldap-group` directive.
AUTHLDAPSUBGROUPATTRIBUTE	Determines the attribute to use when obtaining sub-group members of the rent group during comparisons in the `Require ldap-group` directive.
AUTHLDAPSUBGROUPCLASS	Specifies the LDAP objectClass values used to identify if queried directory jects really are group objects (as opposed to user objects) during the `Requi` `ldap-group` directive's sub-group processing.

The Require Directives

Apache's REQUIRE directives are used during the authorization phase to ensure that a user is allowed to access a resource. mod_authnz_ldap extends the authorization types with `ldap-user`, `ldap-dn`, `ldap-group`, `ldap-attribute` and `ldap-filter`. Other authorization types may also be used but may require that additional authorization modules be loaded.

Since v2.4.8, expressions (p. 89) are supported within the LDAP require directives.

Require ldap-user

The `Require ldap-user` directive specifies what usernames can access the resource. Once MOD_AUTHNZ_LDAP has retrieved a unique DN from the directory, it does an LDAP compare operation using the username specified in the `Require ldap-user` to see if that username is part of the just-fetched LDAP entry. Multiple users can be granted access by putting multiple usernames on the line, separated with spaces. If a username has a space in it, then it must be surrounded with double quotes. Multiple users can also be granted access by using multiple `Require ldap-user` directives, with one user per line. For example, with a AUTHLDAPURL of `ldap://ldap/o=Example?cn` (i.e., `cn` is used for searches), the following Require directives could be used to restrict access:

```
Require ldap-user "Barbara Jenson"
Require ldap-user "Fred User"
Require ldap-user "Joe Manager"
```

Because of the way that MOD_AUTHNZ_LDAP handles this directive, Barbara Jenson could sign on as *Barbara Jenson*, *Babs Jenson* or any other `cn` that she has in her LDAP entry. Only the single `Require ldap-user` line is needed to support all values of the attribute in the user's entry.

If the uid attribute was used instead of the cn attribute in the URL above, the above three lines could be condensed to

```
Require ldap-user bjenson fuser jmanager
```

Require ldap-group

This directive specifies an LDAP group whose members are allowed access. It takes the distinguished name of the LDAP group. Note: Do not surround the group name with quotes. For example, assume that the following entry existed in the LDAP directory:

```
dn: cn=Administrators, o=Example
objectClass: groupOfUniqueNames
uniqueMember: cn=Barbara Jenson, o=Example
uniqueMember: cn=Fred User, o=Example
```

The following directive would grant access to both Fred and Barbara:

```
Require ldap-group cn=Administrators, o=Example
```

Members can also be found within sub-groups of a specified LDAP group if AuthLDAPMaxSubGroupDepth is set to a value greater than 0. For example, assume the following entries exist in the LDAP directory:

```
dn: cn=Employees, o=Example
objectClass: groupOfUniqueNames
uniqueMember: cn=Managers, o=Example
uniqueMember: cn=Administrators, o=Example
uniqueMember: cn=Users, o=Example

dn: cn=Managers, o=Example
objectClass: groupOfUniqueNames
uniqueMember: cn=Bob Ellis, o=Example
uniqueMember: cn=Tom Jackson, o=Example

dn: cn=Administrators, o=Example
objectClass: groupOfUniqueNames
uniqueMember: cn=Barbara Jenson, o=Example
uniqueMember: cn=Fred User, o=Example

dn: cn=Users, o=Example
objectClass: groupOfUniqueNames
uniqueMember: cn=Allan Jefferson, o=Example
uniqueMember: cn=Paul Tilley, o=Example
uniqueMember: cn=Temporary Employees, o=Example

dn: cn=Temporary Employees, o=Example
objectClass: groupOfUniqueNames
uniqueMember: cn=Jim Swenson, o=Example
uniqueMember: cn=Elliot Rhodes, o=Example
```

The following directives would allow access for Bob Ellis, Tom Jackson, Barbara Jenson, Fred User, Allan Jefferson, and Paul Tilley but would not allow access for Jim Swenson, or Elliot Rhodes (since they are at a sub-group depth of 2):

```
Require ldap-group cn=Employees, o=Example
AuthLDAPMaxSubGroupDepth 1
```

Behavior of this directive is modified by the AUTHLDAPGROUPATTRIBUTE, AUTHLDAPGROUPATTRIBUTEISDN, AUTHLDAPMAXSUBGROUPDEPTH, AUTHLDAPSUBGROUPATTRIBUTE, and AUTHLDAPSUBGROUPCLASS directives.

Require ldap-dn

The `Require ldap-dn` directive allows the administrator to grant access based on distinguished names. It specifies a DN that must match for access to be granted. If the distinguished name that was retrieved from the directory server matches the distinguished name in the `Require ldap-dn`, then authorization is granted. Note: do not surround the distinguished name with quotes.

The following directive would grant access to a specific DN:

```
Require ldap-dn cn=Barbara Jenson, o=Example
```

Behavior of this directive is modified by the AUTHLDAPCOMPAREDNONSERVER directive.

Require ldap-attribute

The `Require ldap-attribute` directive allows the administrator to grant access based on attributes of the authenticated user in the LDAP directory. If the attribute in the directory matches the value given in the configuration, access is granted.

The following directive would grant access to anyone with the attribute employeeType = active

```
Require ldap-attribute employeeType=active
```

Multiple attribute/value pairs can be specified on the same line separated by spaces or they can be specified in multiple `Require ldap-attribute` directives. The effect of listing multiple attribute/values pairs is an OR operation. Access will be granted if any of the listed attribute values match the value of the corresponding attribute in the user object. If the value of the attribute contains a space, only the value must be within double quotes.

The following directive would grant access to anyone with the city attribute equal to "San Jose" or status equal to "Active"

```
Require ldap-attribute city="San Jose" status=active
```

Require ldap-filter

The `Require ldap-filter` directive allows the administrator to grant access based on a complex LDAP search filter. If the dn returned by the filter search matches the authenticated user dn, access is granted.

The following directive would grant access to anyone having a cell phone and is in the marketing department

```
Require ldap-filter &(cell=*)(department=marketing)
```

The difference between the `Require ldap-filter` directive and the `Require ldap-attribute` directive is that `ldap-filter` performs a search operation on the LDAP directory using the specified search filter rather than a simple attribute comparison. If a simple attribute comparison is all that is required, the comparison operation performed by `ldap-attribute` will be faster than the search operation used by `ldap-filter` especially within a large directory.

Examples

- Grant access to anyone who exists in the LDAP directory, using their UID for searches.

```
AuthLDAPURL "ldap://ldap1.example.com:389/ou=People, o=Example?uid?sub?(obj
Require valid-user
```

- The next example is the same as above; but with the fields that have useful defaults omitted. Also, note the use of a redundant LDAP server.

```
AuthLDAPURL "ldap://ldap1.example.com ldap2.example.com/ou=People, o=Exampl
Require valid-user
```

- The next example is similar to the previous one, but it uses the common name instead of the UID. Note that this could be problematical if multiple people in the directory share the same `cn`, because a search on `cn` **must** return exactly one entry. That's why this approach is not recommended: it's a better idea to choose an attribute that is guaranteed unique in your directory, such as `uid`.

```
AuthLDAPURL "ldap://ldap.example.com/ou=People, o=Example?cn"
Require valid-user
```

- Grant access to anybody in the Administrators group. The users must authenticate using their UID.

```
AuthLDAPURL ldap://ldap.example.com/o=Example?uid
Require ldap-group cn=Administrators, o=Example
```

- Grant access to anybody in the group whose name matches the hostname of the virtual host. In this example an expression (p. 89) is used to build the filter.

```
AuthLDAPURL ldap://ldap.example.com/o=Example?uid
Require ldap-group cn=%{SERVER_NAME}, o=Example
```

- The next example assumes that everyone at Example who carries an alphanumeric pager will have an LDAP attribute of `qpagePagerID`. The example will grant access only to people (authenticated via their UID) who have alphanumeric pagers:

```
AuthLDAPURL ldap://ldap.example.com/o=Example?uid??(qpagePagerID=*)
Require valid-user
```

- The next example demonstrates the power of using filters to accomplish complicated administrative requirements. Without filters, it would have been necessary to create a new LDAP group and ensure that the group's members remain synchronized with the pager users. This becomes trivial with filters. The goal is to grant access to anyone who has a pager, plus grant access to Joe Manager, who doesn't have a pager, but does need to access the same resource:

```
AuthLDAPURL ldap://ldap.example.com/o=Example?uid??(|(qpagePagerID=*)(uid=j
Require valid-user
```

  This last may look confusing at first, so it helps to evaluate what the search filter will look like based on who connects, as shown below. If Fred User connects as `fuser`, the filter would look like

```
(&(|(qpagePagerID=*)(uid=jmanager))(uid=fuser))
```

  The above search will only succeed if *fuser* has a pager. When Joe Manager connects as *jmanager*, the filter looks like

```
(&(|(qpagePagerID=*)(uid=jmanager))(uid=jmanager))
```

  The above search will succeed whether *jmanager* has a pager or not.

Using TLS

To use TLS, see the MOD_LDAP directives LDAPTRUSTEDCLIENTCERT, LDAPTRUSTEDGLOBALCERT and LDAPTRUSTEDMODE.

An optional second parameter can be added to the AUTHLDAPURL to override the default connection type set by LDAPTRUSTEDMODE. This will allow the connection established by an *ldap://* Url to be upgraded to a secure connection on the same port.

Using SSL

To use SSL, see the MOD_LDAP directives LDAPTRUSTEDCLIENTCERT, LDAPTRUSTEDGLOBALCERT and LDAPTRUSTEDMODE.

To specify a secure LDAP server, use *ldaps://* in the AUTHLDAPURL directive, instead of *ldap://*.

Exposing Login Information

when this module performs *authentication*, ldap attributes specified in the AUTHLDAPURL directive are placed in environment variables with the prefix "AUTHENTICATE_".

when this module performs *authorization*, ldap attributes specified in the AUTHLDAPURL directive are placed in environment variables with the prefix "AUTHORIZE_".

If the attribute field contains the username, common name and telephone number of a user, a CGI program will have access to this information without the need to make a second independent LDAP query to gather this additional information.

This has the potential to dramatically simplify the coding and configuration required in some web applications.

Using Active Directory

An Active Directory installation may support multiple domains at the same time. To distinguish users between domains, an identifier called a User Principle Name (UPN) can be added to a user's entry in the directory. This UPN usually takes the form of the user's account name, followed by the domain components of the particular domain, for example *somebody@nz.example.com.*

You may wish to configure the MOD_AUTHNZ_LDAP module to authenticate users present in any of the domains making up the Active Directory forest. In this way both *somebody@nz.example.com* and *someone@au.example.com* can be authenticated using the same query at the same time.

To make this practical, Active Directory supports the concept of a Global Catalog. This Global Catalog is a read only copy of selected attributes of all the Active Directory servers within the Active Directory forest. Querying the Global Catalog allows all the domains to be queried in a single query, without the query spanning servers over potentially slow links.

If enabled, the Global Catalog is an independent directory server that runs on port 3268 (3269 for SSL). To search for a user, do a subtree search for the attribute *userPrincipalName*, with an empty search root, like so:

```
AuthLDAPBindDN apache@example.com
AuthLDAPBindPassword password
AuthLDAPURL ldap://10.0.0.1:3268/?userPrincipalName?sub
```

Users will need to enter their User Principal Name as a login, in the form *somebody@nz.example.com.*

Using Microsoft FrontPage with mod_authnz_ldap

Normally, FrontPage uses FrontPage-web-specific user/group files (i.e., the MOD_AUTHN_FILE and MOD_AUTHZ_GROUPFILE modules) to handle all authentication. Unfortunately, it is not possible to just change to LDAP authentication by adding the proper directives, because it will break the *Permissions* forms in the FrontPage client, which attempt to modify the standard text-based authorization files.

Once a FrontPage web has been created, adding LDAP authentication to it is a matter of adding the following directives to *every* `.htaccess` file that gets created in the web

```
AuthLDAPURL          "the url"
AuthGroupFile        "mygroupfile"
Require group        "mygroupfile"
```

How It Works

FrontPage restricts access to a web by adding the `Require valid-user` directive to the `.htaccess` files. The `Require valid-user` directive will succeed for any user who is valid *as far as LDAP is concerned.* This means that anybody who has an entry in the LDAP directory is considered a valid user, whereas FrontPage considers only those people in the local user file to be valid. By substituting the ldap-group with group file authorization, Apache is allowed to consult the local user file (which is managed by FrontPage) - instead of LDAP - when handling authorizing the user.

Once directives have been added as specified above, FrontPage users will be able to perform all management operations from the FrontPage client.

Caveats

- When choosing the LDAP URL, the attribute to use for authentication should be something that will also be valid for putting into a MOD_AUTHN_FILE user file. The user ID is ideal for this.
- When adding users via FrontPage, FrontPage administrators should choose usernames that already exist in the LDAP directory (for obvious reasons). Also, the password that the administrator enters into the form is ignored, since Apache will actually be authenticating against the password in the LDAP database, and not against the password in the local user file. This could cause confusion for web administrators.
- Apache must be compiled with MOD_AUTH_BASIC, MOD_AUTHN_FILE and MOD_AUTHZ_GROUPFILE in order to use FrontPage support. This is because Apache will still use the MOD_AUTHZ_GROUPFILE group file for determine the extent of a user's access to the FrontPage web.
- The directives must be put in the `.htaccess` files. Attempting to put them inside <LOCATION> or <DIRECTORY> directives won't work. This is because MOD_AUTHNZ_LDAP has to be able to grab the AUTHGROUPFILE directive that is found in FrontPage `.htaccess` files so that it knows where to look for the valid user list. If the MOD_AUTHNZ_LDAP directives aren't in the same `.htaccess` file as the FrontPage directives, then the hack won't work, because MOD_AUTHNZ_LDAP will never get a chance to process the `.htaccess` file, and won't be able to find the FrontPage-managed user file.

AuthLDAPAuthorizePrefix Directive

Description:	Specifies the prefix for environment variables set during authorization
Syntax:	`AuthLDAPAuthorizePrefix prefix`
Default:	`AuthLDAPAuthorizePrefix AUTHORIZE_`
Context:	directory, .htaccess
Override:	AuthConfig
Status:	Extension
Module:	mod_authnz_ldap
Compatibility:	Available in version 2.3.6 and later

This directive allows you to override the prefix used for environment variables set during LDAP authorization. If *AUTHENTICATE_* is specified, consumers of these environment variables see the same information whether LDAP has performed authentication, authorization, or both.

**Note**

No authorization variables are set when a user is authorized on the basis of `Require valid-user`.

AuthLDAPBindAuthoritative Directive

Description:	Determines if other authentication providers are used when a user can be mapped to a DN but the server cannot successfully bind with the user's credentials.
Syntax:	`AuthLDAPBindAuthoritativeoff|on`
Default:	`AuthLDAPBindAuthoritative on`
Context:	directory, .htaccess
Override:	AuthConfig
Status:	Extension
Module:	mod_authnz_ldap

By default, subsequent authentication providers are only queried if a user cannot be mapped to a DN, but not if the user can be mapped to a DN and their password cannot be verified with an LDAP bind. If AUTHLDAPBINDAUTHORITATIVE is set to *off*, other configured authentication modules will have a chance to validate the user if the LDAP bind (with the current user's credentials) fails for any reason.

This allows users present in both LDAP and AUTHUSERFILE to authenticate when the LDAP server is available but the user's account is locked or password is otherwise unusable.

See also

- AUTHUSERFILE
- AUTHBASICPROVIDER

AuthLDAPBindDN Directive

Description:	Optional DN to use in binding to the LDAP server
Syntax:	`AuthLDAPBindDN distinguished-name`
Context:	directory, .htaccess
Override:	AuthConfig
Status:	Extension
Module:	mod_authnz_ldap

An optional DN used to bind to the server when searching for entries. If not provided, MOD_AUTHNZ_LDAP will use an anonymous bind.

AuthLDAPBindPassword Directive

Description:	Password used in conjuction with the bind DN
Syntax:	`AuthLDAPBindPassword password`
Context:	directory, .htaccess
Override:	AuthConfig
Status:	Extension
Module:	mod_authnz_ldap
Compatibility:	*exec:* was added in 2.4.5.

A bind password to use in conjunction with the bind DN. Note that the bind password is probably sensitive data, and should be properly protected. You should only use the AUTHLDAPBINDDN and AUTHLDAPBINDPASSWORD if you absolutely need them to search the directory.

If the value begins with exec: the resulting command will be executed and the first line returned to standard output by the program will be used as the password.

```
#Password used as-is
AuthLDAPBindPassword secret

#Run /path/to/program to get my password
AuthLDAPBindPassword exec:/path/to/program

#Run /path/to/otherProgram and provide arguments
AuthLDAPBindPassword "exec:/path/to/otherProgram argument1"
```

AuthLDAPCharsetConfig Directive

Description:	Language to charset conversion configuration file
Syntax:	`AuthLDAPCharsetConfig file-path`
Context:	server config
Status:	Extension
Module:	mod_authnz_ldap

The AUTHLDAPCHARSETCONFIG directive sets the location of the language to charset conversion configuration file. *File-path* is relative to the SERVERROOT. This file specifies the list of language extensions to character sets. Most administrators use the provided `charset.conv` file, which associates common language extensions to character sets.

The file contains lines in the following format:

```
Language-Extension charset [Language-String] ...
```

The case of the extension does not matter. Blank lines, and lines beginning with a hash character (#) are ignored.

AuthLDAPCompareAsUser Directive

Description:	Use the authenticated user's credentials to perform authorization comparisons
Syntax:	`AuthLDAPCompareAsUser on|off`
Default:	`AuthLDAPCompareAsUser off`
Context:	directory, .htaccess
Override:	AuthConfig
Status:	Extension
Module:	mod_authnz_ldap
Compatibility:	Available in version 2.3.6 and later

When set, and MOD_AUTHNZ_LDAP has authenticated the user, LDAP comparisons for authorization use the queried distinguished name (DN) and HTTP basic authentication password of the authenticated user instead of the servers configured credentials.

The *ldap-attribute*, *ldap-user*, and *ldap-group* (single-level only) authorization checks use comparisons.

This directive only has effect on the comparisons performed during nested group processing when AUTHLDAPSEARCHASUSER is also enabled.

This directive should only be used when your LDAP server doesn't accept anonymous comparisons and you cannot use a dedicated AUTHLDAPBINDDN.

See also

- AUTHLDAPINITIALBINDASUSER
- AUTHLDAPSEARCHASUSER

AuthLDAPCompareDNOnServer Directive

Description:	Use the LDAP server to compare the DNs
Syntax:	`AuthLDAPCompareDNOnServer on|off`
Default:	`AuthLDAPCompareDNOnServer on`
Context:	directory, .htaccess
Override:	AuthConfig
Status:	Extension
Module:	mod_authnz_ldap

When set, MOD_AUTHNZ_LDAP will use the LDAP server to compare the DNs. This is the only foolproof way to compare DNs. MOD_AUTHNZ_LDAP will search the directory for the DN specified with the `Require dn` directive, then, retrieve the DN and compare it with the DN retrieved from the user entry. If this directive is not set, MOD_AUTHNZ_LDAP simply does a string comparison. It is possible to get false negatives with this approach, but it is much faster. Note the MOD_LDAP cache can speed up DN comparison in most situations.

AuthLDAPDereferenceAliases Directive

Description:	When will the module de-reference aliases
Syntax:	`AuthLDAPDereferenceAliases never|searching|finding|always`
Default:	`AuthLDAPDereferenceAliases always`
Context:	directory, .htaccess
Override:	AuthConfig
Status:	Extension
Module:	mod_authnz_ldap

This directive specifies when MOD_AUTHNZ_LDAP will de-reference aliases during LDAP operations. The default is `always`.

AuthLDAPGroupAttribute Directive

Description:	LDAP attributes used to identify the user members of groups.
Syntax:	`AuthLDAPGroupAttribute attribute`
Default:	`AuthLDAPGroupAttribute member uniquemember`
Context:	directory, .htaccess
Override:	AuthConfig
Status:	Extension
Module:	mod_authnz_ldap

This directive specifies which LDAP attributes are used to check for user members within groups. Multiple attributes can be used by specifying this directive multiple times. If not specified, then MOD_AUTHNZ_LDAP uses the `member` and `uniquemember` attributes.

AuthLDAPGroupAttributeIsDN Directive

Description:	Use the DN of the client username when checking for group membership
Syntax:	`AuthLDAPGroupAttributeIsDN on|off`
Default:	`AuthLDAPGroupAttributeIsDN on`
Context:	directory, .htaccess
Override:	AuthConfig
Status:	Extension
Module:	mod_authnz_ldap

When set `on`, this directive says to use the distinguished name of the client username when checking for group membership. Otherwise, the username will be used. For example, assume that the client sent the username `bjenson`, which corresponds to the LDAP DN `cn=Babs Jenson, o=Example`. If this directive is set, MOD_AUTHNZ_LDAP will check if the group has `cn=Babs Jenson, o=Example` as a member. If this directive is not set, then MOD_AUTHNZ_LDAP will check if the group has `bjenson` as a member.

AuthLDAPInitialBindAsUser Directive

Description:	Determines if the server does the initial DN lookup using the basic authentication users' own username, instead of anonymously or with hard-coded credentials for the server
Syntax:	`AuthLDAPInitialBindAsUser off|on`
Default:	`AuthLDAPInitialBindAsUser off`
Context:	directory, .htaccess
Override:	AuthConfig
Status:	Extension
Module:	mod_authnz_ldap
Compatibility:	Available in version 2.3.6 and later

By default, the server either anonymously, or with a dedicated user and password, converts the basic authentication username into an LDAP distinguished name (DN). This directive forces the server to use the verbatim username and password provided by the incoming user to perform the initial DN search.

If the verbatim username can't directly bind, but needs some cosmetic transformation, see AUTHLDAPINITIALBINDPATTERN.

This directive should only be used when your LDAP server doesn't accept anonymous searches and you cannot use a dedicated AUTHLDAPBINDDN.

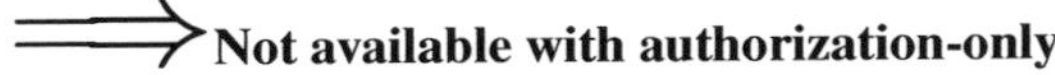

Not available with authorization-only

This directive can only be used if this module authenticates the user, and has no effect when this module is used exclusively for authorization.

See also

- AuthLDAPInitialBindPattern
- AuthLDAPBindDN
- AuthLDAPCompareAsUser
- AuthLDAPSearchAsUser

AuthLDAPInitialBindPattern Directive

Description:	Specifies the transformation of the basic authentication username to be used when binding to the LDAP server to perform a DN lookup
Syntax:	`AuthLDAPInitialBindPatternregex substitution`
Default:	`AuthLDAPInitialBindPattern (.*) $1 (remote username used verbatim)`
Context:	directory, .htaccess
Override:	AuthConfig
Status:	Extension
Module:	mod_authnz_ldap
Compatibility:	Available in version 2.3.6 and later

If AuthLDAPInitialBindAsUser is set to *ON*, the basic authentication username will be transformed according to the regular expression and substitution arguments.

The regular expression argument is compared against the current basic authentication username. The substitution argument may contain backreferences, but has no other variable interpolation.

This directive should only be used when your LDAP server doesn't accept anonymous searches and you cannot use a dedicated AuthLDAPBindDN.

```
AuthLDAPInitialBindPattern (.+) $1@example.com
```

```
AuthLDAPInitialBindPattern (.+) cn=$1,dc=example,dc=com
```

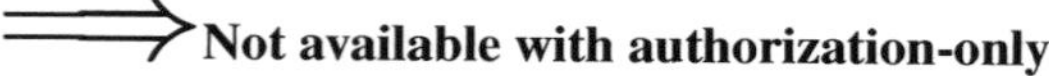

Not available with authorization-only

This directive can only be used if this module authenticates the user, and has no effect when this module is used exclusively for authorization.

debugging

The substituted DN is recorded in the environment variable *LDAP_BINDASUSER*. If the regular expression does not match the input, the verbatim username is used.

See also

- AuthLDAPInitialBindAsUser
- AuthLDAPBindDN

AuthLDAPMaxSubGroupDepth Directive

Description:	Specifies the maximum sub-group nesting depth that will be evaluated before the user search is discontinued.
Syntax:	`AuthLDAPMaxSubGroupDepth Number`
Default:	`AuthLDAPMaxSubGroupDepth 10`
Context:	directory, .htaccess
Override:	AuthConfig
Status:	Extension
Module:	mod_authnz_ldap
Compatibility:	Available in version 2.3.0 and later

When this directive is set to a non-zero value `X` combined with use of the `Require ldap-group someGroupDN` directive, the provided user credentials will be searched for as a member of the `someGroupDN` directory object or of any group member of the current group up to the maximum nesting level `X` specified by this directive.

See the `Require ldap-group` section for a more detailed example.

**Nested groups performance**
When AuthLDAPSubGroupAttribute overlaps with AuthLDAPGroupAttribute (as it does by default and as required by common LDAP schemas), uncached searching for sub-groups in large groups can be very slow. If you use large, non-nested groups, set AuthLDAPMaxSubGroupDepth to zero.

AuthLDAPRemoteUserAttribute Directive

Description:	Use the value of the attribute returned during the user query to set the REMOTE_USER environment variable
Syntax:	`AuthLDAPRemoteUserAttribute uid`
Default:	`none`
Context:	directory, .htaccess
Override:	AuthConfig
Status:	Extension
Module:	mod_authnz_ldap

If this directive is set, the value of the `REMOTE_USER` environment variable will be set to the value of the attribute specified. Make sure that this attribute is included in the list of attributes in the AuthLDAPUrl definition, otherwise this directive will have no effect. This directive, if present, takes precedence over AuthLDAPRemoteUserIsDN. This directive is useful should you want people to log into a website using an email address, but a backend application expects the username as a userid.

AuthLDAPRemoteUserIsDN Directive

Description:	Use the DN of the client username to set the REMOTE_USER environment variable
Syntax:	`AuthLDAPRemoteUserIsDN on|off`
Default:	`AuthLDAPRemoteUserIsDN off`
Context:	directory, .htaccess
Override:	AuthConfig
Status:	Extension
Module:	mod_authnz_ldap

If this directive is set to on, the value of the `REMOTE_USER` environment variable will be set to the full distinguished name of the authenticated user, rather than just the username that was passed by the client. It is turned off by default.

AuthLDAPSearchAsUser Directive

Description:	Use the authenticated user's credentials to perform authorization searches
Syntax:	`AuthLDAPSearchAsUser on|off`
Default:	`AuthLDAPSearchAsUser off`
Context:	directory, .htaccess
Override:	AuthConfig
Status:	Extension
Module:	mod_authnz_ldap
Compatibility:	Available in version 2.3.6 and later

When set, and MOD_AUTHNZ_LDAP has authenticated the user, LDAP searches for authorization use the queried distinguished name (DN) and HTTP basic authentication password of the authenticated user instead of the servers configured credentials.

The *ldap-filter* and *ldap-dn* authorization checks use searches.

This directive only has effect on the comparisons performed during nested group processing when AUTHLDAPCOMPAREASUSER is also enabled.

This directive should only be used when your LDAP server doesn't accept anonymous searches and you cannot use a dedicated AUTHLDAPBINDDN.

See also

- AUTHLDAPINITIALBINDASUSER
- AUTHLDAPCOMPAREASUSER

AuthLDAPSubGroupAttribute Directive

Description:	Specifies the attribute labels, one value per directive line, used to distinguish the members of the current group that are groups.
Syntax:	`AuthLDAPSubGroupAttribute attribute`
Default:	`AuthLDAPSubgroupAttribute member uniquemember`
Context:	directory, .htaccess
Override:	AuthConfig
Status:	Extension
Module:	mod_authnz_ldap
Compatibility:	Available in version 2.3.0 and later

An LDAP group object may contain members that are users and members that are groups (called nested or sub groups). The `AuthLDAPSubGroupAttribute` directive identifies the labels of group members and the `AuthLDAPGroupAttribute` directive identifies the labels of the user members. Multiple attributes can be used by specifying this directive multiple times. If not specified, then MOD_AUTHNZ_LDAP uses the `member` and `uniqueMember` attributes.

AuthLDAPSubGroupClass Directive

Description:	Specifies which LDAP objectClass values identify directory objects that are groups during sub-group processing.
Syntax:	`AuthLDAPSubGroupClass LdapObjectClass`
Default:	`AuthLDAPSubGroupClass groupOfNames groupOfUniqueNames`
Context:	directory, .htaccess
Override:	AuthConfig
Status:	Extension
Module:	mod_authnz_ldap
Compatibility:	Available in version 2.3.0 and later

An LDAP group object may contain members that are users and members that are groups (called nested or sub groups). The `AuthLDAPSubGroupAttribute` directive identifies the labels of members that may be sub-groups of the current group (as opposed to user members). The `AuthLDAPSubGroupClass` directive specifies the LDAP objectClass values used in verifying that these potential sub-groups are in fact group objects. Verified sub-groups can then be searched for more user or sub-group members. Multiple attributes can be used by specifying this directive multiple times. If not specified, then MOD_AUTHNZ_LDAP uses the `groupOfNames` and `groupOfUniqueNames` values.

AuthLDAPUrl Directive

Description:	URL specifying the LDAP search parameters
Syntax:	`AuthLDAPUrl url [NONE|SSL|TLS|STARTTLS]`
Context:	directory, .htaccess
Override:	AuthConfig
Status:	Extension
Module:	mod_authnz_ldap

An RFC 2255 URL which specifies the LDAP search parameters to use. The syntax of the URL is

```
ldap://host:port/basedn?attribute?scope?filter
```

If you want to specify more than one LDAP URL that Apache should try in turn, the syntax is:

```
AuthLDAPUrl "ldap://ldap1.example.com ldap2.example.com/dc=..."
```

Caveat: *If you specify multiple servers, you need to enclose the entire URL string in quotes; otherwise you will get an error:* ***"AuthLDAPURL takes one argument, URL to define LDAP connection.."*** You can of course use search parameters on each of these.

ldap For regular ldap, use the string `ldap`. For secure LDAP, use `ldaps` instead. Secure LDAP is only available if Apache was linked to an LDAP library with SSL support.

host:port The name/port of the ldap server (defaults to `localhost:389` for `ldap`, and `localhost:636` for `ldaps`). To specify multiple, redundant LDAP servers, just list all servers, separated by spaces. MOD_AUTHNZ_LDAP will try connecting to each server in turn, until it makes a successful connection. If multiple ldap servers are specified, then entire LDAP URL must be encapsulated in double quotes.

Once a connection has been made to a server, that connection remains active for the life of the `httpd` process, or until the LDAP server goes down.

If the LDAP server goes down and breaks an existing connection, MOD_AUTHNZ_LDAP will attempt to re-connect, starting with the primary server, and trying each redundant server in turn. Note that this is different than a true round-robin search.

basedn The DN of the branch of the directory where all searches should start from. At the very least, this must be the top of your directory tree, but could also specify a subtree in the directory.

attribute The attribute to search for. Although RFC 2255 allows a comma-separated list of attributes, only the first attribute will be used, no matter how many are provided. If no attributes are provided, the default is to use `uid`. It's a good idea to choose an attribute that will be unique across all entries in the subtree you will be using. All attributes listed will be put into the environment with an AUTHENTICATE_ prefix for use by other modules.

scope The scope of the search. Can be either `one` or `sub`. Note that a scope of `base` is also supported by RFC 2255, but is not supported by this module. If the scope is not provided, or if `base` scope is specified, the default is to use a scope of `sub`.

filter A valid LDAP search filter. If not provided, defaults to `(objectClass=*)`, which will search for all objects in the tree. Filters are limited to approximately 8000 characters (the definition of `MAX_STRING_LEN` in the Apache source code). This should be more than sufficient for any application. In 2.4.10 and later, The word "none" may be used to not use any filter, which may be required by some primitive LDAP servers.

When doing searches, the attribute, filter and username passed by the HTTP client are combined to create a search filter that looks like `(&(`*`filter`*`)(`*`attribute=username`*`))`.

For example, consider an URL of `ldap://ldap.example.com/o=Example?cn?sub?(posixid=*)`. When a client attempts to connect using a username of `Babs Jenson`, the resulting search filter will be `(&(posixid=*)(cn=Babs Jenson))`.

An optional parameter can be added to allow the LDAP Url to override the connection type. This parameter can be one of the following:

NONE Establish an unsecure connection on the default LDAP port. This is the same as `ldap://` on port 389.

SSL Establish a secure connection on the default secure LDAP port. This is the same as `ldaps://`

TLS — STARTTLS Establish an upgraded secure connection on the default LDAP port. This connection will be initiated on port 389 by default and then upgraded to a secure connection on the same port.

See above for examples of AUTHLDAPURL URLs.

10.20 Apache Module mod_authz_core

Description:	Core Authorization
Status:	Base
ModuleIdentifier:	authz_core_module
SourceFile:	mod_authz_core.c
Compatibility:	Available in Apache HTTPD 2.3 and later

Summary

This module provides core authorization capabilities so that authenticated users can be allowed or denied access to portions of the web site. MOD_AUTHZ_CORE provides the functionality to register various authorization providers. It is usually used in conjunction with an authentication provider module such as MOD_AUTHN_FILE and an authorization module such as MOD_AUTHZ_USER. It also allows for advanced logic to be applied to the authorization processing.

Directives

- AuthMerging
- <AuthzProviderAlias>
- AuthzSendForbiddenOnFailure
- Require
- <RequireAll>
- <RequireAny>
- <RequireNone>

Creating Authorization Provider Aliases

Extended authorization providers can be created within the configuration file and assigned an alias name. The alias providers can then be referenced through the REQUIRE directive in the same way as a base authorization provider. Besides the ability to create and alias an extended provider, it also allows the same extended authorization provider to be referenced by multiple locations.

Example

The example below creates two different ldap authorization provider aliases based on the ldap-group authorization provider. This example allows a single authorization location to check group membership within multiple ldap hosts:

```
<AuthzProviderAlias ldap-group ldap-group-alias1 cn=my-group,o=ctx>
    AuthLDAPBindDN cn=youruser,o=ctx
    AuthLDAPBindPassword yourpassword
    AuthLDAPURL ldap://ldap.host/o=ctx
</AuthzProviderAlias>

<AuthzProviderAlias ldap-group ldap-group-alias2 cn=my-other-group,o=dev>
    AuthLDAPBindDN cn=youruser,o=dev
    AuthLDAPBindPassword yourotherpassword
    AuthLDAPURL ldap://other.ldap.host/o=dev?cn
</AuthzProviderAlias>
```

```
Alias "/secure" "/webpages/secure"
<Directory "/webpages/secure">
    Require all granted

    AuthBasicProvider file

    AuthType Basic
    AuthName LDAP_Protected_Place

    #implied OR operation
    Require ldap-group-alias1
    Require ldap-group-alias2
</Directory>
```

Authorization Containers

The authorization container directives <REQUIREALL>, <REQUIREANY> and <REQUIRENONE> may be combined with each other and with the REQUIRE directive to express complex authorization logic.

The example below expresses the following authorization logic. In order to access the resource, the user must either be the `superadmin` user, or belong to both the `admins` group and the `Administrators` LDAP group and either belong to the `sales` group or have the LDAP `dept` attribute `sales`. Furthermore, in order to access the resource, the user must not belong to either the `temps` group or the LDAP group `Temporary Employees`.

```
<Directory "/www/mydocs">
    <RequireAll>
        <RequireAny>
            Require user superadmin
            <RequireAll>
                Require group admins
                Require ldap-group cn=Administrators,o=Airius
                <RequireAny>
                    Require group sales
                    Require ldap-attribute dept="sales"
                </RequireAny>
            </RequireAll>
        </RequireAny>
        <RequireNone>
            Require group temps
            Require ldap-group cn=Temporary Employees,o=Airius
        </RequireNone>
    </RequireAll>
</Directory>
```

The Require Directives

MOD_AUTHZ_CORE provides some generic authorization providers which can be used with the REQUIRE directive.

Require env

The `env` provider allows access to the server to be controlled based on the existence of an environment variable (p. 82) . When `Require env` *`env-variable`* is specified, then the request is allowed access if the environment variable *env-variable* exists. The server provides the ability to set environment variables in a flexible way based on characteristics of the client request using the directives provided by MOD_SETENVIF. Therefore, this directive can be used to allow access based on such factors as the clients User-Agent (browser type), Referer, or other HTTP request header fields.

```
SetEnvIf User-Agent ^KnockKnock/2\.0 let_me_in
<Directory "/docroot">
    Require env let_me_in
</Directory>
```

In this case, browsers with a user-agent string beginning with KnockKnock/2.0 will be allowed access, and all others will be denied.

When the server looks up a path via an internal subrequest such as looking for a DIRECTORYINDEX or generating a directory listing with MOD_AUTOINDEX, per-request environment variables are *not* inherited in the subrequest. Additionally, SETENVIF directives are not separately evaluated in the subrequest due to the API phases MOD_SETENVIF takes action in.

Require all

The all provider mimics the functionality that was previously provided by the 'Allow from all' and 'Deny from all' directives. This provider can take one of two arguments which are 'granted' or 'denied'. The following examples will grant or deny access to all requests.

```
Require all granted
```

```
Require all denied
```

Require method

The method provider allows using the HTTP method in authorization decisions. The GET and HEAD methods are treated as equivalent. The TRACE method is not available to this provider, use TRACEENABLE instead.

The following example will only allow GET, HEAD, POST, and OPTIONS requests:

```
Require method GET POST OPTIONS
```

The following example will allow GET, HEAD, POST, and OPTIONS requests without authentication, and require a valid user for all other methods:

```
<RequireAny>
    Require method GET POST OPTIONS
    Require valid-user
</RequireAny>
```

Require expr

The expr provider allows basing authorization decisions on arbitrary expressions.

```
Require expr "%{TIME_HOUR} -ge 9 && %{TIME_HOUR} -le 17"
```

```
<RequireAll>
    Require expr "!(%{QUERY_STRING} =~ /secret/)"
    Require expr "%{REQUEST_URI} in { '/example.cgi', '/other.cgi' }"
</RequireAll>

Require expr "!(%{QUERY_STRING} =~ /secret/) && %{REQUEST_URI} in { '/example.c
```

The syntax is described in the ap_expr (p. 89) documentation.

Normally, the expression is evaluated before authentication. However, if the expression returns false and references the variable `%{REMOTE_USER}`, authentication will be performed and the expression will be re-evaluated.

AuthMerging Directive

Description:	Controls the manner in which each configuration section's authorization logic is combined with that of preceding configuration sections.
Syntax:	`AuthMerging Off | And | Or`
Default:	`AuthMerging Off`
Context:	directory, .htaccess
Override:	AuthConfig
Status:	Base
Module:	mod_authz_core

When authorization is enabled, it is normally inherited by each subsequent configuration section (p. 33) , unless a different set of authorization directives is specified. This is the default action, which corresponds to an explicit setting of `AuthMerging Off`.

However, there may be circumstances in which it is desirable for a configuration section's authorization to be combined with that of its predecessor while configuration sections are being merged. Two options are available for this case, `And` and `Or`.

When a configuration section contains `AuthMerging And` or `AuthMerging Or`, its authorization logic is combined with that of the nearest predecessor (according to the overall order of configuration sections) which also contains authorization logic as if the two sections were jointly contained within a <REQUIREALL> or <REQUIREANY> directive, respectively.

⟹ The setting of AUTHMERGING is not inherited outside of the configuration section in which it appears. In the following example, only users belonging to group `alpha` may access `/www/docs`. Users belonging to either groups `alpha` or `beta` may access `/www/docs/ab`. However, the default `Off` setting of AUTHMERGING applies to the <DIRECTORY> configuration section for `/www/docs/ab/gamma`, so that section's authorization directives override those of the preceding sections. Thus only users belong to the group `gamma` may access `/www/docs/ab/gamma`.

```
<Directory "/www/docs">
    AuthType Basic
    AuthName Documents
    AuthBasicProvider file
    AuthUserFile "/usr/local/apache/passwd/passwords"
    Require group alpha
</Directory>

<Directory "/www/docs/ab">
    AuthMerging Or
    Require group beta
```

```
</Directory>

<Directory "/www/docs/ab/gamma">
    Require group gamma
</Directory>
```

AuthzProviderAlias Directive

Description:	Enclose a group of directives that represent an extension of a base authorization provider and referenced by the specified alias
Syntax:	`<AuthzProviderAlias baseProvider Alias Require-Parameters> ... </AuthzProviderAlias>`
Context:	server config
Status:	Base
Module:	mod_authz_core

<AUTHZPROVIDERALIAS> and `</AuthzProviderAlias>` are used to enclose a group of authorization directives that can be referenced by the alias name using the directive REQUIRE.

AuthzSendForbiddenOnFailure Directive

Description:	Send '403 FORBIDDEN' instead of '401 UNAUTHORIZED' if authentication succeeds but authorization fails
Syntax:	`AuthzSendForbiddenOnFailure On|Off`
Default:	`AuthzSendForbiddenOnFailure Off`
Context:	directory, .htaccess
Status:	Base
Module:	mod_authz_core
Compatibility:	Available in Apache HTTPD 2.3.11 and later

If authentication succeeds but authorization fails, Apache HTTPD will respond with an HTTP response code of '401 UNAUTHORIZED' by default. This usually causes browsers to display the password dialogue to the user again, which is not wanted in all situations. AUTHZSENDFORBIDDENONFAILURE allows to change the response code to '403 FORBIDDEN'.

> **!** **Security Warning**
> Modifying the response in case of missing authorization weakens the security of the password, because it reveals to a possible attacker, that his guessed password was right.

Require Directive

Description:	Tests whether an authenticated user is authorized by an authorization provider.
Syntax:	`Require [not] entity-name [entity-name] ...`
Context:	directory, .htaccess
Override:	AuthConfig
Status:	Base
Module:	mod_authz_core

This directive tests whether an authenticated user is authorized according to a particular authorization provider and the specified restrictions. MOD_AUTHZ_CORE provides the following generic authorization providers:

`Require all granted` Access is allowed unconditionally.

`Require all denied` Access is denied unconditionally.

`Require env` ***`env-var`*** **`[`*****`env-var`*****`] ...`** Access is allowed only if one of the given environment variables is set.

`Require method` ***`http-method`*** **`[`*****`http-method`*****`] ...`** Access is allowed only for the given HTTP methods.

`Require expr` ***`expression`*** Access is allowed if *expression* evaluates to true.

Some of the allowed syntaxes provided by MOD_AUTHZ_USER, MOD_AUTHZ_HOST, and MOD_AUTHZ_GROUPFILE are:

`Require user` ***`userid`*** **`[`*****`userid`*****`] ...`** Only the named users can access the resource.

`Require group` ***`group-name`*** **`[`*****`group-name`*****`] ...`** Only users in the named groups can access the resource.

`Require valid-user` All valid users can access the resource.

`Require ip 10 172.20 192.168.2` Clients in the specified IP address ranges can access the resource.

Other authorization modules that implement require options include MOD_AUTHNZ_LDAP, MOD_AUTHZ_DBM, MOD_AUTHZ_DBD, MOD_AUTHZ_OWNER and MOD_SSL.

In most cases, for a complete authentication and authorization configuration, REQUIRE must be accompanied by AUTHNAME, AUTHTYPE and AUTHBASICPROVIDER or AUTHDIGESTPROVIDER directives, and directives such as AUTHUSERFILE and AUTHGROUPFILE (to define users and groups) in order to work correctly. Example:

```
AuthType Basic
AuthName "Restricted Resource"
AuthBasicProvider file
AuthUserFile "/web/users"
AuthGroupFile "/web/groups"
Require group admin
```

Access controls which are applied in this way are effective for **all** methods. **This is what is normally desired.** If you wish to apply access controls only to specific methods, while leaving other methods unprotected, then place the REQUIRE statement into a <LIMIT> section.

The result of the REQUIRE directive may be negated through the use of the `not` option. As with the other negated authorization directive <REQUIRENONE>, when the REQUIRE directive is negated it can only fail or return a neutral result, and therefore may never independently authorize a request.

In the following example, all users in the `alpha` and `beta` groups are authorized, except for those who are also in the `reject` group.

```
<Directory "/www/docs">
    <RequireAll>
        Require group alpha beta
        Require not group reject
    </RequireAll>
</Directory>
```

When multiple REQUIRE directives are used in a single configuration section (p. 33) and are not contained in another authorization directive like <REQUIREALL>, they are implicitly contained within a <REQUIREANY> directive. Thus the first one to authorize a user authorizes the entire request, and subsequent REQUIRE directives are ignored.

Security Warning
Exercise caution when setting authorization directives in LOCATION sections that overlap with content served out of the filesystem. By default, these configuration sections (p. 33) overwrite authorization configuration in DIRECTORY, and FILES sections.
The AUTHMERGING directive can be used to control how authorization configuration sections are merged.

See also

- Access control howto (p. 224)
- Authorization Containers
- MOD_AUTHN_CORE
- MOD_AUTHZ_HOST

RequireAll Directive

Description:	Enclose a group of authorization directives of which none must fail and at least one must succeed for the enclosing directive to succeed.
Syntax:	`<RequireAll> ... </RequireAll>`
Context:	directory, .htaccess
Override:	AuthConfig
Status:	Base
Module:	mod_authz_core

<REQUIREALL> and `</RequireAll>` are used to enclose a group of authorization directives of which none must fail and at least one must succeed in order for the <REQUIREALL> directive to succeed.

If none of the directives contained within the <REQUIREALL> directive fails, and at least one succeeds, then the <REQUIREALL> directive succeeds. If none succeed and none fail, then it returns a neutral result. In all other cases, it fails.

See also

- Authorization Containers
- Authentication, Authorization, and Access Control (p. 217)

RequireAny Directive

Description:	Enclose a group of authorization directives of which one must succeed for the enclosing directive to succeed.
Syntax:	`<RequireAny> ... </RequireAny>`
Context:	directory, .htaccess
Override:	AuthConfig
Status:	Base
Module:	mod_authz_core

<REQUIREANY> and `</RequireAny>` are used to enclose a group of authorization directives of which one must succeed in order for the <REQUIREANY> directive to succeed.

If one or more of the directives contained within the <REQUIREANY> directive succeed, then the <REQUIREANY> directive succeeds. If none succeed and none fail, then it returns a neutral result. In all other cases, it fails.

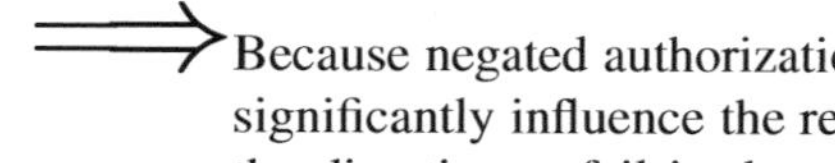

Because negated authorization directives are unable to return a successful result, they can not significantly influence the result of a <REQUIREANY> directive. (At most they could cause the directive to fail in the case where they failed and all other directives returned a neutral value.) Therefore negated authorization directives are not permitted within a <REQUIREANY> directive.

See also

- Authorization Containers
- Authentication, Authorization, and Access Control (p. 217)

RequireNone Directive

Description:	Enclose a group of authorization directives of which none must succeed for the enclosing directive to not fail.
Syntax:	`<RequireNone> ... </RequireNone>`
Context:	directory, .htaccess
Override:	AuthConfig
Status:	Base
Module:	mod_authz_core

<REQUIRENONE> and `</RequireNone>` are used to enclose a group of authorization directives of which none must succeed in order for the <REQUIRENONE> directive to not fail.

If one or more of the directives contained within the <REQUIRENONE> directive succeed, then the <REQUIRENONE> directive fails. In all other cases, it returns a neutral result. Thus as with the other negated authorization directive `Require not`, it can never independently authorize a request because it can never return a successful result. It can be used, however, to restrict the set of users who are authorized to access a resource.

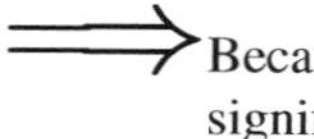

Because negated authorization directives are unable to return a successful result, they can not significantly influence the result of a <REQUIRENONE> directive. Therefore negated authorization directives are not permitted within a <REQUIRENONE> directive.

See also

- Authorization Containers
- Authentication, Authorization, and Access Control (p. 217)

10.21 Apache Module mod_authz_dbd

Description:	Group Authorization and Login using SQL
Status:	Extension
ModuleIdentifier:	authz_dbd_module
SourceFile:	mod_authz_dbd.c
Compatibility:	Available in Apache 2.4 and later

Summary

This module provides authorization capabilities so that authenticated users can be allowed or denied access to portions of the web site by group membership. Similar functionality is provided by MOD_AUTHZ_GROUPFILE and MOD_AUTHZ_DBM, with the exception that this module queries a SQL database to determine whether a user is a member of a group.

This module can also provide database-backed user login/logout capabilities. These are likely to be of most value when used in conjunction with MOD_AUTHN_DBD.

This module relies on MOD_DBD to specify the backend database driver and connection parameters, and manage the database connections.

Directives

- AuthzDBDLoginToReferer
- AuthzDBDQuery
- AuthzDBDRedirectQuery

See also

- REQUIRE
- AUTHDBDUSERPWQUERY
- DBDRIVER
- DBDPARAMS

The Require Directives

Apache's REQUIRE directives are used during the authorization phase to ensure that a user is allowed to access a resource. mod_authz_dbd extends the authorization types with `dbd-group`, `dbd-login` and `dbd-logout`.

Since v2.4.8, expressions (p. 89) are supported within the DBD require directives.

Require dbd-group

This directive specifies group membership that is required for the user to gain access.

```
Require dbd-group team
AuthzDBDQuery "SELECT group FROM authz WHERE user = %s"
```

Require dbd-login

This directive specifies a query to be run indicating the user has logged in.

```
Require dbd-login
AuthzDBDQuery "UPDATE authn SET login = 'true' WHERE user = %s"
```

Require dbd-logout

This directive specifies a query to be run indicating the user has logged out.

```
Require dbd-logout
AuthzDBDQuery "UPDATE authn SET login = 'false' WHERE user = %s"
```

Database Login

In addition to the standard authorization function of checking group membership, this module can also provide server-side user session management via database-backed login/logout capabilities. Specifically, it can update a user's session status in the database whenever the user visits designated URLs (subject of course to users supplying the necessary credentials).

This works by defining two special REQUIRE types: `Require dbd-login` and `Require dbd-logout`. For usage details, see the configuration example below.

Client Login integration

Some administrators may wish to implement client-side session management that works in concert with the server-side login/logout capabilities offered by this module, for example, by setting or unsetting an HTTP cookie or other such token when a user logs in or out.

To support such integration, MOD_AUTHZ_DBD exports an optional hook that will be run whenever a user's status is updated in the database. Other session management modules can then use the hook to implement functions that start and end client-side sessions.

Configuration example

```
# mod_dbd configuration
DBDriver pgsql
DBDParams "dbname=apacheauth user=apache pass=xxxxxx"

DBDMin  4
DBDKeep 8
DBDMax  20
DBDExptime 300

<Directory "/usr/www/my.site/team-private/">
  # mod_authn_core and mod_auth_basic configuration
  # for mod_authn_dbd
  AuthType Basic
  AuthName Team
  AuthBasicProvider dbd
```

```
  # mod_authn_dbd SQL query to authenticate a logged-in user
  AuthDBDUserPWQuery \
    "SELECT password FROM authn WHERE user = %s AND login = 'true'"

  # mod_authz_core configuration for mod_authz_dbd
  Require dbd-group team

  # mod_authz_dbd configuration
  AuthzDBDQuery "SELECT group FROM authz WHERE user = %s"

  # when a user fails to be authenticated or authorized,
  # invite them to login; this page should provide a link
  # to /team-private/login.html
  ErrorDocument 401 "/login-info.html"

  <Files "login.html">
    # don't require user to already be logged in!
    AuthDBDUserPWQuery "SELECT password FROM authn WHERE user = %s"

    # dbd-login action executes a statement to log user in
    Require dbd-login
    AuthzDBDQuery "UPDATE authn SET login = 'true' WHERE user = %s"

    # return user to referring page (if any) after
    # successful login
    AuthzDBDLoginToReferer On
  </Files>

  <Files "logout.html">
    # dbd-logout action executes a statement to log user out
    Require dbd-logout
    AuthzDBDQuery "UPDATE authn SET login = 'false' WHERE user = %s"
  </Files>
</Directory>
```

AuthzDBDLoginToReferer Directive

Description:	Determines whether to redirect the Client to the Referring page on successful login or logout if a `Referer` request header is present
Syntax:	`AuthzDBDLoginToReferer On|Off`
Default:	`AuthzDBDLoginToReferer Off`
Context:	directory
Status:	Extension
Module:	mod_authz_dbd

In conjunction with `Require dbd-login` or `Require dbd-logout`, this provides the option to redirect the client back to the Referring page (the URL in the `Referer` HTTP request header, if present). When there is no `Referer` header, `AuthzDBDLoginToReferer On` will be ignored.

AuthzDBDQuery Directive

Description:	Specify the SQL Query for the required operation
Syntax:	`AuthzDBDQuery query`
Context:	directory
Status:	Extension
Module:	mod_authz_dbd

The AUTHZDBDQUERY specifies an SQL query to run. The purpose of the query depends on the REQUIRE directive in effect.

- When used with a `Require dbd-group` directive, it specifies a query to look up groups for the current user. This is the standard functionality of other authorization modules such as MOD_AUTHZ_GROUPFILE and MOD_AUTHZ_DBM. The first column value of each row returned by the query statement should be a string containing a group name. Zero, one, or more rows may be returned.

```
Require dbd-group
AuthzDBDQuery "SELECT group FROM groups WHERE user = %s"
```

- When used with a `Require dbd-login` or `Require dbd-logout` directive, it will never deny access, but will instead execute a SQL statement designed to log the user in or out. The user must already be authenticated with MOD_AUTHN_DBD.

```
Require dbd-login
AuthzDBDQuery "UPDATE authn SET login = 'true' WHERE user = %s"
```

In all cases, the user's ID will be passed as a single string parameter when the SQL query is executed. It may be referenced within the query statement using a `%s` format specifier.

AuthzDBDRedirectQuery Directive

Description:	Specify a query to look up a login page for the user
Syntax:	`AuthzDBDRedirectQuery query`
Context:	directory
Status:	Extension
Module:	mod_authz_dbd

Specifies an optional SQL query to use after successful login (or logout) to redirect the user to a URL, which may be specific to the user. The user's ID will be passed as a single string parameter when the SQL query is executed. It may be referenced within the query statement using a `%s` format specifier.

```
AuthzDBDRedirectQuery "SELECT userpage FROM userpages WHERE user = %s"
```

The first column value of the first row returned by the query statement should be a string containing a URL to which to redirect the client. Subsequent rows will be ignored. If no rows are returned, the client will not be redirected.

Note that AUTHZDBDLOGINTOREFERER takes precedence if both are set.

10.22 Apache Module mod_authz_dbm

Description:	Group authorization using DBM files
Status:	Extension
ModuleIdentifier:	authz_dbm_module
SourceFile:	mod_authz_dbm.c
Compatibility:	Available in Apache 2.1 and later

Summary

This module provides authorization capabilities so that authenticated users can be allowed or denied access to portions of the web site by group membership. Similar functionality is provided by MOD_AUTHZ_GROUPFILE.

Directives

- AuthDBMGroupFile
- AuthzDBMType

See also

- REQUIRE

The Require Directives

Apache's REQUIRE directives are used during the authorization phase to ensure that a user is allowed to access a resource. mod_authz_dbm extends the authorization types with `dbm-group`.

Since v2.4.8, expressions (p. 89) are supported within the DBM require directives.

Require dbm-group

This directive specifies group membership that is required for the user to gain access.

```
Require dbm-group admin
```

Require dbm-file-group

When this directive is specified, the user must be a member of the group assigned to the file being accessed.

```
Require dbm-file-group
```

Example usage

Note that using mod_authz_dbm requires you to require `dbm-group` *instead of* `group`*:*

```
<Directory "/foo/bar">
  AuthType Basic
  AuthName "Secure Area"
  AuthBasicProvider dbm
```

```
  AuthDBMUserFile "site/data/users"
  AuthDBMGroupFile "site/data/users"
  Require dbm-group admin
</Directory>
```

AuthDBMGroupFile Directive

Description:	Sets the name of the database file containing the list of user groups for authorization
Syntax:	`AuthDBMGroupFile file-path`
Context:	directory, .htaccess
Override:	AuthConfig
Status:	Extension
Module:	mod_authz_dbm

The AUTHDBMGROUPFILE directive sets the name of a DBM file containing the list of user groups for user authorization. *File-path* is the absolute path to the group file.

The group file is keyed on the username. The value for a user is a comma-separated list of the groups to which the users belongs. There must be no whitespace within the value, and it must never contain any colons.

Security
Make sure that the AUTHDBMGROUPFILE is stored outside the document tree of the webserver. Do **not** put it in the directory that it protects. Otherwise, clients will be able to download the AUTHDBMGROUPFILE unless otherwise protected.

Combining Group and Password DBM files: In some cases it is easier to manage a single database which contains both the password and group details for each user. This simplifies any support programs that need to be written: they now only have to deal with writing to and locking a single DBM file. This can be accomplished by first setting the group and password files to point to the same DBM:

```
AuthDBMGroupFile "/www/userbase"
AuthDBMUserFile "/www/userbase"
```

The key for the single DBM is the username. The value consists of

```
Encrypted Password : List of Groups [ : (ignored) ]
```

The password section contains the encrypted password as before. This is followed by a colon and the comma separated list of groups. Other data may optionally be left in the DBM file after another colon; it is ignored by the authorization module. This is what www.telescope.org uses for its combined password and group database.

AuthzDBMType Directive

Description:	Sets the type of database file that is used to store list of user groups
Syntax:	`AuthzDBMType default|SDBM|GDBM|NDBM|DB`
Default:	`AuthzDBMType default`
Context:	directory, .htaccess
Override:	AuthConfig
Status:	Extension
Module:	mod_authz_dbm

Sets the type of database file that is used to store the list of user groups. The default database type is determined at compile time. The availability of other types of database files also depends on compile-time settings (p. 20) .

It is crucial that whatever program you use to create your group files is configured to use the same type of database.

10.23 Apache Module mod_authz_groupfile

Description:	Group authorization using plaintext files
Status:	Base
ModuleIdentifier:	authz_groupfile_module
SourceFile:	mod_authz_groupfile.c
Compatibility:	Available in Apache 2.1 and later

Summary

This module provides authorization capabilities so that authenticated users can be allowed or denied access to portions of the web site by group membership. Similar functionality is provided by MOD_AUTHZ_DBM.

Directives

- AuthGroupFile

See also

- REQUIRE

The Require Directives

Apache's REQUIRE directives are used during the authorization phase to ensure that a user is allowed to access a resource. mod_authz_groupfile extends the authorization types with `group` and `group-file`.

Since v2.4.8, expressions (p. 89) are supported within the groupfile require directives.

Require group

This directive specifies group membership that is required for the user to gain access.

```
Require group admin
```

Require file-group

When this directive is specified, the user must be a member of the group assigned to the file being accessed.

```
Require file-group
```

AuthGroupFile Directive

Description:	Sets the name of a text file containing the list of user groups for authorization
Syntax:	`AuthGroupFile file-path`
Context:	directory, .htaccess
Override:	AuthConfig
Status:	Base
Module:	mod_authz_groupfile

The AUTHGROUPFILE directive sets the name of a textual file containing the list of user groups for user authorization. *File-path* is the path to the group file. If it is not absolute, it is treated as relative to the SERVERROOT.

Each line of the group file contains a groupname followed by a colon, followed by the member usernames separated by spaces.

Example:
```
mygroup:  bob joe anne
```

Note that searching large text files is *very* inefficient; AUTHDBMGROUPFILE provides a much better performance.

Security
Make sure that the AUTHGROUPFILE is stored outside the document tree of the web-server; do *not* put it in the directory that it protects. Otherwise, clients may be able to download the AUTHGROUPFILE.

10.24 Apache Module mod_authz_host

Description:	Group authorizations based on host (name or IP address)
Status:	Base
ModuleIdentifier:	authz_host_module
SourceFile:	mod_authz_host.c
Compatibility:	Available in Apache 2.3 and later

Summary

The authorization providers implemented by MOD_AUTHZ_HOST are registered using the REQUIRE directive. The directive can be referenced within a <DIRECTORY>, <FILES>, or <LOCATION> section as well as `.htaccess` (p. 354) files to control access to particular parts of the server. Access can be controlled based on the client hostname or IP address.

In general, access restriction directives apply to all access methods (`GET`, `PUT`, `POST`, etc). This is the desired behavior in most cases. However, it is possible to restrict some methods, while leaving other methods unrestricted, by enclosing the directives in a <LIMIT> section.

Directives This module provides no directives.

See also

- Authentication, Authorization, and Access Control (p. 217)
- REQUIRE

The Require Directives

Apache's REQUIRE directive is used during the authorization phase to ensure that a user is allowed or denied access to a resource. mod_authz_host extends the authorization types with `ip`, `host` and `local`. Other authorization types may also be used but may require that additional authorization modules be loaded.

These authorization providers affect which hosts can access an area of the server. Access can be controlled by hostname, IP Address, or IP Address range.

Since v2.4.8, expressions (p. 89) are supported within the host require directives.

Require ip

The `ip` provider allows access to the server to be controlled based on the IP address of the remote client. When `Require ip` *`ip-address`* is specified, then the request is allowed access if the IP address matches.

A full IP address:

```
Require ip 10.1.2.3
Require ip 192.168.1.104 192.168.1.205
```

An IP address of a host allowed access

A partial IP address:

```
Require ip 10.1
Require ip 10 172.20 192.168.2
```

The first 1 to 3 bytes of an IP address, for subnet restriction.

A network/netmask pair:

```
Require ip 10.1.0.0/255.255.0.0
```

A network a.b.c.d, and a netmask w.x.y.z. For more fine-grained subnet restriction.

A network/nnn CIDR specification:

```
Require ip 10.1.0.0/16
```

Similar to the previous case, except the netmask consists of nnn high-order 1 bits.

Note that the last three examples above match exactly the same set of hosts.

IPv6 addresses and IPv6 subnets can be specified as shown below:

```
Require ip 2001:db8::a00:20ff:fea7:ccea
Require ip 2001:db8:1:1::a
Require ip 2001:db8:2:1::/64
Require ip 2001:db8:3::/48
```

Note: As the IP addresses are parsed on startup, expressions are not evaluated at request time.

Require host

The `host` provider allows access to the server to be controlled based on the host name of the remote client. When `Require host` *`host-name`* is specified, then the request is allowed access if the host name matches.

A (partial) domain-name

```
Require host example.org
Require host .net example.edu
```

Hosts whose names match, or end in, this string are allowed access. Only complete components are matched, so the above example will match `foo.example.org` but it will not match `fooexample.org`. This configuration will cause Apache to perform a double reverse DNS lookup on the client IP address, regardless of the setting of the HOSTNAMELOOKUPS directive. It will do a reverse DNS lookup on the IP address to find the associated hostname, and then do a forward lookup on the hostname to assure that it matches the original IP address. Only if the forward and reverse DNS are consistent and the hostname matches will access be allowed.

Require local

The `local` provider allows access to the server if any of the following conditions is true:

- the client address matches 127.0.0.0/8
- the client address is ::1
- both the client and the server address of the connection are the same

This allows a convenient way to match connections that originate from the local host:

```
Require local
```

Security Note

If you are proxying content to your server, you need to be aware that the client address will be the address of your proxy server, not the address of the client, and so using the `Require` directive in this context may not do what you mean. See MOD_REMOTEIP for one possible solution to this problem.

10.25 Apache Module mod_authz_owner

Description:	Authorization based on file ownership
Status:	Extension
ModuleIdentifier:	authz_owner_module
SourceFile:	mod_authz_owner.c
Compatibility:	Available in Apache 2.1 and later

Summary

This module authorizes access to files by comparing the userid used for HTTP authentication (the web userid) with the file-system owner or group of the requested file. The supplied username and password must be already properly verified by an authentication module, such as MOD_AUTH_BASIC or MOD_AUTH_DIGEST. MOD_AUTHZ_OWNER recognizes two arguments for the REQUIRE directive, `file-owner` and `file-group`, as follows:

`file-owner` The supplied web-username must match the system's name for the owner of the file being requested. That is, if the operating system says the requested file is owned by `jones`, then the username used to access it through the web must be `jones` as well.

`file-group` The name of the system group that owns the file must be present in a group database, which is provided, for example, by MOD_AUTHZ_GROUPFILE or MOD_AUTHZ_DBM, and the web-username must be a member of that group. For example, if the operating system says the requested file is owned by (system) group `accounts`, the group `accounts` must appear in the group database and the web-username used in the request must be a member of that group.

**Note**

If MOD_AUTHZ_OWNER is used in order to authorize a resource that is not actually present in the filesystem (*i.e.* a virtual resource), it will deny the access.
Particularly it will never authorize content negotiated "MultiViews" (p. 68) resources.

Directives This module provides no directives.

See also

- REQUIRE

Configuration Examples

Require file-owner

Consider a multi-user system running the Apache Web server, with each user having his or her own files in `~/public_html/private`. Assuming that there is a single AUTHDBMUSERFILE database that lists all of their web-usernames, and that these usernames match the system's usernames that actually own the files on the server, then the following stanza would allow only the user himself access to his own files. User `jones` would not be allowed to access files in `/home/smith/public_html/private` unless they were owned by `jones` instead of `smith`.

```
<Directory "/home/*/public_html/private">
    AuthType Basic
    AuthName MyPrivateFiles
    AuthBasicProvider dbm
    AuthDBMUserFile "/usr/local/apache2/etc/.htdbm-all"
    Require file-owner
</Directory>
```

Require file-group

Consider a system similar to the one described above, but with some users that share their project files in `~/public_html/project-foo`. The files are owned by the system group `foo` and there is a single AUTHDBMGROUPFILE database that contains all of the web-usernames and their group membership, *i.e.* they must be at least member of a group named `foo`. So if `jones` and `smith` are both member of the group `foo`, then both will be authorized to access the `project-foo` directories of each other.

```
<Directory "/home/*/public_html/project-foo">
    AuthType Basic
    AuthName "Project Foo Files"
    AuthBasicProvider dbm

    # combined user/group database
    AuthDBMUserFile  "/usr/local/apache2/etc/.htdbm-all"
    AuthDBMGroupFile "/usr/local/apache2/etc/.htdbm-all"

    Satisfy All
    Require file-group
</Directory>
```

10.26 Apache Module mod_authz_user

Description:	User Authorization
Status:	Base
ModuleIdentifier:	authz_user_module
SourceFile:	mod_authz_user.c
Compatibility:	Available in Apache 2.1 and later

Summary

This module provides authorization capabilities so that authenticated users can be allowed or denied access to portions of the web site. MOD_AUTHZ_USER grants access if the authenticated user is listed in a `Require user` directive. Alternatively `Require valid-user` can be used to grant access to all successfully authenticated users.

Directives This module provides no directives.

See also

- REQUIRE

The Require Directives

Apache's REQUIRE directives are used during the authorization phase to ensure that a user is allowed to access a resource. mod_authz_user extends the authorization types with `user` and `valid-user`.

Since v2.4.8, expressions (p. 89) are supported within the user require directives.

Require user

This directive specifies a list of users that are allowed to gain access.

```
Require user john paul george ringo
```

Require valid-user

When this directive is specified, any successfully authenticated user will be allowed to gain access.

```
Require valid-user
```

10.27 Apache Module mod_autoindex

Description:	Generates directory indexes, automatically, similar to the Unix `ls` command or the Win32 `dir` shell command
Status:	Base
ModuleIdentifier:	autoindex_module
SourceFile:	mod_autoindex.c

Summary

The index of a directory can come from one of two sources:

- A file located in that directory, typically called `index.html`. The DIRECTORYINDEX directive sets the name of the file or files to be used. This is controlled by MOD_DIR.
- Otherwise, a listing generated by the server. The other directives control the format of this listing. The ADDICON, ADDICONBYENCODING and ADDICONBYTYPE are used to set a list of icons to display for various file types; for each file listed, the first icon listed that matches the file is displayed. These are controlled by MOD_AUTOINDEX.

The two functions are separated so that you can completely remove (or replace) automatic index generation should you want to.

Automatic index generation is enabled with using `Options +Indexes`. See the OPTIONS directive for more details.

If the `FancyIndexing` option is given with the INDEXOPTIONS directive, the column headers are links that control the order of the display. If you select a header link, the listing will be regenerated, sorted by the values in that column. Selecting the same header repeatedly toggles between ascending and descending order. These column header links are suppressed with the INDEXOPTIONS directive's `SuppressColumnSorting` option.

Note that when the display is sorted by "Size", it's the *actual* size of the files that's used, not the displayed value - so a 1010-byte file will always be displayed before a 1011-byte file (if in ascending order) even though they both are shown as "1K".

Directives

- AddAlt
- AddAltByEncoding
- AddAltByType
- AddDescription
- AddIcon
- AddIconByEncoding
- AddIconByType
- DefaultIcon
- HeaderName
- IndexHeadInsert
- IndexIgnore
- IndexIgnoreReset
- IndexOptions
- IndexOrderDefault

- IndexStyleSheet
- ReadmeName

Autoindex Request Query Arguments

Various query string arguments are available to give the client some control over the ordering of the directory listing, as well as what files are listed. If you do not wish to give the client this control, the `IndexOptions IgnoreClient` option disables that functionality.

The column sorting headers themselves are self-referencing hyperlinks that add the sort query options shown below. Any option below may be added to any request for the directory resource.

- `C=N` sorts the directory by file name
- `C=M` sorts the directory by last-modified date, then file name
- `C=S` sorts the directory by size, then file name
- `C=D` sorts the directory by description, then file name
- `O=A` sorts the listing in Ascending Order
- `O=D` sorts the listing in Descending Order
- `F=0` formats the listing as a simple list (not FancyIndexed)
- `F=1` formats the listing as a FancyIndexed list
- `F=2` formats the listing as an HTMLTable FancyIndexed list
- `V=0` disables version sorting
- `V=1` enables version sorting
- `P=`*`pattern`* lists only files matching the given *pattern*

Note that the 'P'attern query argument is tested *after* the usual INDEXIGNORE directives are processed, and all file names are still subjected to the same criteria as any other autoindex listing. The Query Arguments parser in MOD_AUTOINDEX will stop abruptly when an unrecognized option is encountered. The Query Arguments must be well formed, according to the table above.

The simple example below, which can be clipped and saved in a header.html file, illustrates these query options. Note that the unknown `"X"` argument, for the submit button, is listed last to assure the arguments are all parsed before mod_autoindex encounters the X=Go input.

```
<form action="" method="get">
   Show me a <select name="F">
      <option value="0"> Plain list</option>
      <option value="1" selected="selected"> Fancy list</option>
      <option value="2"> Table list</option>
   </select>
   Sorted by <select name="C">
      <option value="N" selected="selected"> Name</option>
      <option value="M"> Date Modified</option>
      <option value="S"> Size</option>
      <option value="D"> Description</option>
   </select>
   <select name="O">
      <option value="A" selected="selected"> Ascending</option>
      <option value="D"> Descending</option>
   </select>
   <select name="V">
      <option value="0" selected="selected"> in Normal
      order</option>
      <option value="1"> in Version order</option>
   </select>
   Matching <input type="text" name="P" value="*" />
   <input type="submit" name="X" value="Go" />
</form>
```

AddAlt Directive

Description:	Alternate text to display for a file, instead of an icon selected by filename
Syntax:	`AddAlt string file [file] ...`
Context:	server config, virtual host, directory, .htaccess
Override:	Indexes
Status:	Base
Module:	mod_autoindex

ADDALT provides the alternate text to display for a file, instead of an icon, for `FancyIndexing`. *File* is a file extension, partial filename, wild-card expression or full filename for files to describe. If *String* contains any whitespace, you have to enclose it in quotes (" or '). This alternate text is displayed if the client is image-incapable, has image loading disabled, or fails to retrieve the icon.

```
AddAlt "PDF file" *.pdf
AddAlt Compressed *.gz *.zip *.Z
```

AddAltByEncoding Directive

Description:	Alternate text to display for a file instead of an icon selected by MIME-encoding
Syntax:	`AddAltByEncoding string MIME-encoding [MIME-encoding] ...`
Context:	server config, virtual host, directory, .htaccess
Override:	Indexes
Status:	Base
Module:	mod_autoindex

ADDALTBYENCODING provides the alternate text to display for a file, instead of an icon, for `FancyIndexing`. *MIME-encoding* is a valid content-encoding, such as `x-compress`. If *String* contains any whitespace, you have to enclose it in quotes (" or '). This alternate text is displayed if the client is image-incapable, has image loading disabled, or fails to retrieve the icon.

```
AddAltByEncoding gzip x-gzip
```

AddAltByType Directive

Description:	Alternate text to display for a file, instead of an icon selected by MIME content-type
Syntax:	`AddAltByType string MIME-type [MIME-type] ...`
Context:	server config, virtual host, directory, .htaccess
Override:	Indexes
Status:	Base
Module:	mod_autoindex

ADDALTBYTYPE sets the alternate text to display for a file, instead of an icon, for `FancyIndexing`. *MIME-type* is a valid content-type, such as `text/html`. If *String* contains any whitespace, you have to enclose it in quotes (" or '). This alternate text is displayed if the client is image-incapable, has image loading disabled, or fails to retrieve the icon.

```
AddAltByType 'plain text' text/plain
```

AddDescription Directive

Description:	Description to display for a file
Syntax:	`AddDescription string file [file] ...`
Context:	server config, virtual host, directory, .htaccess
Override:	Indexes
Status:	Base
Module:	mod_autoindex

This sets the description to display for a file, for `FancyIndexing`. *File* is a file extension, partial filename, wild-card expression or full filename for files to describe. *String* is enclosed in double quotes (").

```
AddDescription "The planet Mars" mars.gif
AddDescription "My friend Marshall" friends/mars.gif
```

The typical, default description field is 23 bytes wide. 6 more bytes are added by the `IndexOptions SuppressIcon` option, 7 bytes are added by the `IndexOptions SuppressSize` option, and 19 bytes are added by the `IndexOptions SuppressLastModified` option. Therefore, the widest default the description column is ever assigned is 55 bytes.

Since the *File* argument may be a partial file name, please remember that a too-short partial filename may match unintended files. For example, `le.html` will match the file `le.html` but will also match the file `example.html`. In the event that there may be ambiguity, use as complete a filename as you can, but keep in mind that the first match encountered will be used, and order your list of `AddDescription` directives accordingly.

See the DescriptionWidth INDEXOPTIONS keyword for details on overriding the size of this column, or allowing descriptions of unlimited length.

**Caution**

Descriptive text defined with AddDescription may contain HTML markup, such as tags and character entities. If the width of the description column should happen to truncate a tagged element (such as cutting off the end of a bolded phrase), the results may affect the rest of the directory listing.

**Arguments with path information**

Absolute paths are not currently supported and do not match anything at runtime. Arguments with relative path information, which would normally only be used in htaccess context, are implicitly prefixed with '*/' to avoid matching partial directory names.

AddIcon Directive

Description:	Icon to display for a file selected by name
Syntax:	`AddIcon icon name [name] ...`
Context:	server config, virtual host, directory, .htaccess
Override:	Indexes
Status:	Base
Module:	mod_autoindex

This sets the icon to display next to a file ending in *name* for `FancyIndexing`. *Icon* is either a (%-escaped) relative URL to the icon, a fully qualified remote URL, or of the format `(alttext, url)` where *alttext* is the text tag given for an icon for non-graphical browsers.

Name is either `^^DIRECTORY^^` for directories, `^^BLANKICON^^` for blank lines (to format the list correctly), a file extension, a wildcard expression, a partial filename or a complete filename.

`^^BLANKICON^^` is only used for formatting, and so is unnecessary if you're using `IndexOptions HTMLTable`.

```
#Examples
AddIcon (IMG,/icons/image.png) .gif .jpg .png
AddIcon /icons/dir.png ^^DIRECTORY^^
AddIcon /icons/backup.png *~
```

AddIconByType should be used in preference to AddIcon, when possible.

AddIconByEncoding Directive

Description:	Icon to display next to files selected by MIME content-encoding
Syntax:	`AddIconByEncoding icon MIME-encoding [MIME-encoding] ...`
Context:	server config, virtual host, directory, .htaccess
Override:	Indexes
Status:	Base
Module:	mod_autoindex

This sets the icon to display next to files with `FancyIndexing`. *Icon* is either a (%-escaped) relative URL to the icon, a fully qualified remote URL, or of the format `(alttext, url)` where *alttext* is the text tag given for an icon for non-graphical browsers.

MIME-encoding is a valid content-encoding, such as `x-compress`.

```
AddIconByEncoding /icons/compress.png x-compress
```

AddIconByType Directive

Description:	Icon to display next to files selected by MIME content-type
Syntax:	`AddIconByType icon MIME-type [MIME-type] ...`
Context:	server config, virtual host, directory, .htaccess
Override:	Indexes
Status:	Base
Module:	mod_autoindex

This sets the icon to display next to files of type *MIME-type* for `FancyIndexing`. *Icon* is either a (%-escaped) relative URL to the icon, a fully qualified remote URL, or of the format `(alttext,url)` where *alttext* is the text tag given for an icon for non-graphical browsers.

MIME-type is a wildcard expression matching required the mime types.

```
AddIconByType (IMG,/icons/image.png) image/*
```

DefaultIcon Directive

Description:	Icon to display for files when no specific icon is configured
Syntax:	`DefaultIcon url-path`
Context:	server config, virtual host, directory, .htaccess
Override:	Indexes
Status:	Base
Module:	mod_autoindex

The DEFAULTICON directive sets the icon to display for files when no specific icon is known, for `FancyIndexing`. *Url-path* is a (%-escaped) relative URL to the icon, or a fully qualified remote URL.

```
DefaultIcon /icon/unknown.png
```

HeaderName Directive

Description:	Name of the file that will be inserted at the top of the index listing
Syntax:	`HeaderName filename`
Context:	server config, virtual host, directory, .htaccess
Override:	Indexes
Status:	Base
Module:	mod_autoindex

The HEADERNAME directive sets the name of the file that will be inserted at the top of the index listing. *Filename* is the name of the file to include.

```
HeaderName HEADER.html
```

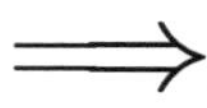
Both HeaderName and READMENAME now treat *Filename* as a URI path relative to the one used to access the directory being indexed. If *Filename* begins with a slash, it will be taken to be relative to the DOCUMENTROOT.

```
HeaderName /include/HEADER.html
```

Filename must resolve to a document with a major content type of `text/*` (*e.g.*, `text/html`, `text/plain`, etc.). This means that *filename* may refer to a CGI script if the script's actual file type (as opposed to its output) is marked as `text/html` such as with a directive like:

```
AddType text/html .cgi
```

Content negotiation (p. 68) will be performed if OPTIONS `MultiViews` is in effect. If *filename* resolves to a static `text/html` document (not a CGI script) and either one of the OPTIONS `Includes` or `IncludesNOEXEC` is enabled, the file will be processed for server-side includes (see the MOD_INCLUDE documentation).

If the file specified by HEADERNAME contains the beginnings of an HTML document (<html>, <head>, etc.) then you will probably want to set `IndexOptions +SuppressHTMLPreamble`, so that these tags are not repeated.

See also

- READMENAME

IndexHeadInsert Directive

Description:	Inserts text in the HEAD section of an index page.
Syntax:	`IndexHeadInsert "markup ..."`
Context:	server config, virtual host, directory, .htaccess
Override:	Indexes
Status:	Base
Module:	mod_autoindex

The INDEXHEADINSERT directive specifies a string to insert in the *<head>* section of the HTML generated for the index page.

```
IndexHeadInsert "<link rel=\"sitemap\" href=\"/sitemap.html\">"
```

IndexIgnore Directive

Description:	Adds to the list of files to hide when listing a directory
Syntax:	`IndexIgnore file [file] ...`
Default:	`IndexIgnore "."`
Context:	server config, virtual host, directory, .htaccess
Override:	Indexes
Status:	Base
Module:	mod_autoindex

The INDEXIGNORE directive adds to the list of files to hide when listing a directory. *File* is a shell-style wildcard expression or full filename. Multiple IndexIgnore directives add to the list, rather than replacing the list of ignored files. By default, the list contains `.` (the current directory).

```
IndexIgnore .??* *~ *# HEADER* README* RCS CVS *,v *,t
```

Regular Expressions
This directive does not currently work in configuration sections that have regular expression arguments, such as <DIRECTORYMATCH>

IndexIgnoreReset Directive

Description:	Empties the list of files to hide when listing a directory
Syntax:	`IndexIgnoreReset ON|OFF`
Context:	server config, virtual host, directory, .htaccess
Override:	Indexes
Status:	Base
Module:	mod_autoindex
Compatibility:	2.3.10 and later

The INDEXIGNORERESET directive removes any files ignored by INDEXIGNORE otherwise inherited from other configuration sections.

```
<Directory "/var/www">
    IndexIgnore *.bak .??* *~ *# HEADER* README* RCS CVS *,v *,t
</Directory>
<Directory "/var/www/backups">
    IndexIgnoreReset ON
    IndexIgnore .??* *# HEADER* README* RCS CVS *,v *,t
</Directory>
```

! Review the default configuration for a list of patterns that you might want to explicitly ignore after using this directive.

IndexOptions Directive

Description:	Various configuration settings for directory indexing
Syntax:	`IndexOptions [+|-]option [[+|-]option] ...`
Default:	`By default, no options are enabled.`
Context:	server config, virtual host, directory, .htaccess
Override:	Indexes
Status:	Base
Module:	mod_autoindex

The INDEXOPTIONS directive specifies the behavior of the directory indexing. *Option* can be one of

AddAltClass Adds an additional CSS class declaration to each row of the directory listing table when `IndexOptions HTMLTable` is in effect and an `IndexStyleSheet` is defined. Rather than the standard `even` and `odd` classes that would otherwise be applied to each row of the table, a class of `even-ALT` or `odd-ALT` where *ALT* is either the standard alt text associated with the file style (eg. *snd*, *txt*, *img*, etc) or the alt text defined by one of the various `AddAlt*` directives.

Charset=*character-set* (*Apache HTTP Server 2.0.61 and later*) The `Charset` keyword allows you to specify the character set of the generated page. The default is `UTF-8` on Windows and Mac OS X, and `ISO-8859-1` elsewhere. (It depends on whether the underlying file system uses Unicode filenames or not.)

```
IndexOptions Charset=UTF-8
```

DescriptionWidth=[*n* — *] The `DescriptionWidth` keyword allows you to specify the width of the description column in characters.

-DescriptionWidth (or unset) allows MOD_AUTOINDEX to calculate the best width.

`DescriptionWidth=n` fixes the column width to *n* bytes wide.

`DescriptionWidth=*` grows the column to the width necessary to accommodate the longest description string.

See the section on ADDDESCRIPTION for dangers inherent in truncating descriptions.

FancyIndexing This turns on fancy indexing of directories.

FoldersFirst If this option is enabled, subdirectory listings will *always* appear first, followed by normal files in the directory. The listing is basically broken into two components, the files and the subdirectories, and each is sorted separately and then displayed subdirectories-first. For instance, if the sort order is descending by name, and `FoldersFirst` is enabled, subdirectory `Zed` will be listed before subdirectory `Beta`, which will be listed before normal files `Gamma` and `Alpha`. **This option only has an effect if `FancyIndexing` is also enabled.**

HTMLTable This option with `FancyIndexing` constructs a simple table for the fancy directory listing. It is necessary for utf-8 enabled platforms or if file names or description text will alternate between left-to-right and right-to-left reading order.

IconsAreLinks This makes the icons part of the anchor for the filename, for fancy indexing.

IconHeight[=*pixels*] Presence of this option, when used with `IconWidth`, will cause the server to include `height` and `width` attributes in the `img` tag for the file icon. This allows browser to precalculate the page layout without having to wait until all the images have been loaded. If no value is given for the option, it defaults to the standard height of the icons supplied with the Apache httpd software.

This option only has an effect if `FancyIndexing` is also enabled.

IconWidth[=*pixels*] Presence of this option, when used with `IconHeight`, will cause the server to include `height` and `width` attributes in the `img` tag for the file icon. This allows browser to precalculate the page layout without having to wait until all the images have been loaded. If no value is given for the option, it defaults to the standard width of the icons supplied with the Apache httpd software.

IgnoreCase If this option is enabled, names are sorted in a case-insensitive manner. For instance, if the sort order is ascending by name, and `IgnoreCase` is enabled, file Zeta will be listed after file alfa (Note: file GAMMA will always be listed before file gamma).

IgnoreClient This option causes MOD_AUTOINDEX to ignore all query variables from the client, including sort order (implies `SuppressColumnSorting`.)

NameWidth=[*n* — *] The `NameWidth` keyword allows you to specify the width of the filename column in bytes.

`-NameWidth` (or unset) allows MOD_AUTOINDEX to calculate the best width, but only up to 20 bytes wide.

`NameWidth=n` fixes the column width to *n* bytes wide.

`NameWidth=*` grows the column to the necessary width.

ScanHTMLTitles This enables the extraction of the title from HTML documents for fancy indexing. If the file does not have a description given by ADDDESCRIPTION then httpd will read the document for the value of the `title` element. This is CPU and disk intensive.

ShowForbidden If specified, Apache httpd will show files normally hidden because the subrequest returned `HTTP_UNAUTHORIZED` or `HTTP_FORBIDDEN`

SuppressColumnSorting If specified, Apache httpd will not make the column headings in a FancyIndexed directory listing into links for sorting. The default behavior is for them to be links; selecting the column heading will sort the directory listing by the values in that column. However, query string arguments which are appended to the URL will still be honored. That behavior is controlled by `IndexOptions IgnoreClient`.

SuppressDescription This will suppress the file description in fancy indexing listings. By default, no file descriptions are defined, and so the use of this option will regain 23 characters of screen space to use for something else. See AddDescription for information about setting the file description. See also the `DescriptionWidth` index option to limit the size of the description column.

This option only has an effect if `FancyIndexing` is also enabled.

SuppressHTMLPreamble If the directory actually contains a file specified by the HeaderName directive, the module usually includes the contents of the file after a standard HTML preamble (`<html>`, `<head>`, *et cetera*). The `SuppressHTMLPreamble` option disables this behaviour, causing the module to start the display with the header file contents. The header file must contain appropriate HTML instructions in this case. If there is no header file, the preamble is generated as usual. If you also specify a ReadmeName, and if that file exists, The closing </body></html> tags are also ommitted from the output, under the assumption that you'll likely put those closing tags in that file.

SuppressIcon This will suppress the icon in fancy indexing listings. Combining both `SuppressIcon` and `SuppressRules` yields proper HTML 3.2 output, which by the final specification prohibits `img` and `hr` elements from the `pre` block (used to format FancyIndexed listings.)

SuppressLastModified This will suppress the display of the last modification date, in fancy indexing listings.

This option only has an effect if `FancyIndexing` is also enabled.

SuppressRules This will suppress the horizontal rule lines (`hr` elements) in directory listings. Combining both `SuppressIcon` and `SuppressRules` yields proper HTML 3.2 output, which by the final specification prohibits `img` and `hr` elements from the `pre` block (used to format FancyIndexed listings.)

This option only has an effect if `FancyIndexing` is also enabled.

SuppressSize This will suppress the file size in fancy indexing listings.

This option only has an effect if `FancyIndexing` is also enabled.

TrackModified This returns the `Last-Modified` and `ETag` values for the listed directory in the HTTP header. It is only valid if the operating system and file system return appropriate stat() results. Some Unix systems do so, as do OS2's JFS and Win32's NTFS volumes. OS2 and Win32 FAT volumes, for example, do not. Once this feature is enabled, the client or proxy can track changes to the list of files when they perform a `HEAD` request. Note some operating systems correctly track new and removed files, but do not track changes for sizes or dates of the files within the directory. **Changes to the size or date stamp of an existing file will not update the `Last-Modified` header on all Unix platforms.** If this is a concern, leave this option disabled.

Type=*MIME content-type* (*Apache HTTP Server 2.0.61 and later*) The `Type` keyword allows you to specify the MIME content-type of the generated page. The default is *text/html*.

```
IndexOptions Type=text/plain
```

VersionSort (*Apache HTTP Server 2.0a3 and later*) The `VersionSort` keyword causes files containing version numbers to sort in a natural way. Strings are sorted as usual, except that substrings of digits in the name and description are compared according to their numeric value.

Example:

```
foo-1.7
foo-1.7.2
foo-1.7.12
foo-1.8.2
foo-1.8.2a
foo-1.12
```

If the number starts with a zero, then it is considered to be a fraction:

```
foo-1.001
foo-1.002
foo-1.030
foo-1.04
```

XHTML (*Apache HTTP Server 2.0.49 and later*) The XHTML keyword forces MOD_AUTOINDEX to emit XHTML 1.0 code instead of HTML 3.2. **This option only has an effect if `FancyIndexing` is also enabled.**

Incremental IndexOptions Be aware of how multiple INDEXOPTIONS are handled.

- Multiple INDEXOPTIONS directives for a single directory are now merged together. The result of:

  ```
  <Directory "/foo">
      IndexOptions HTMLTable
      IndexOptions SuppressColumnsorting
  </Directory>
  ```

  will be the equivalent of

  ```
  IndexOptions HTMLTable SuppressColumnsorting
  ```

- The addition of the incremental syntax (*i.e.*, prefixing keywords with + or −).

Whenever a '+' or '-' prefixed keyword is encountered, it is applied to the current INDEXOPTIONS settings (which may have been inherited from an upper-level directory). However, whenever an unprefixed keyword is processed, it clears all inherited options and any incremental settings encountered so far. Consider the following example:

```
IndexOptions +ScanHTMLTitles -IconsAreLinks FancyIndexing
IndexOptions +SuppressSize
```

The net effect is equivalent to `IndexOptions FancyIndexing +SuppressSize`, because the unprefixed `FancyIndexing` discarded the incremental keywords before it, but allowed them to start accumulating again afterward.

To unconditionally set the INDEXOPTIONS for a particular directory, clearing the inherited settings, specify keywords without any + or − prefixes.

IndexOrderDefault Directive

Description:	Sets the default ordering of the directory index
Syntax:	`IndexOrderDefault Ascending|Descending Name|Date|Size|Description`
Default:	`IndexOrderDefault Ascending Name`
Context:	server config, virtual host, directory, .htaccess
Override:	Indexes
Status:	Base
Module:	mod_autoindex

The INDEXORDERDEFAULT directive is used in combination with the `FancyIndexing` index option. By default, fancyindexed directory listings are displayed in ascending order by filename; the INDEXORDERDEFAULT allows you to change this initial display order.

INDEXORDERDEFAULT takes two arguments. The first must be either `Ascending` or `Descending`, indicating the direction of the sort. The second argument must be one of the keywords `Name`, `Date`, `Size`, or `Description`, and identifies the primary key. The secondary key is *always* the ascending filename.

You can, if desired, prevent the client from reordering the list by also adding the `SuppressColumnSorting` index option to remove the sort link from the top of the column, along with the `IgnoreClient` index option to prevent them from manually adding sort options to the query string in order to override your ordering preferences.

IndexStyleSheet Directive

Description:	Adds a CSS stylesheet to the directory index
Syntax:	`IndexStyleSheet url-path`
Context:	server config, virtual host, directory, .htaccess
Override:	Indexes
Status:	Base
Module:	mod_autoindex

The INDEXSTYLESHEET directive sets the name of the file that will be used as the CSS for the index listing.

```
IndexStyleSheet "/css/style.css"
```

Using this directive in conjunction with `IndexOptions HTMLTable` adds a number of CSS classes to the resulting HTML. The entire table is given a CSS id of `indexlist` and the following classes are associated with the various parts of the listing:

Class	Definition
tr.indexhead	Header row of listing
th.indexcolicon and td.indexcolicon	Icon column
th.indexcolname and td.indexcolname	File name column
th.indexcollastmod and td.indexcollastmod	Last modified column
th.indexcolsize and td.indexcolsize	File size column
th.indexcoldesc and td.indexcoldesc	Description column
tr.breakrow	Horizontal rule at the bottom of the table
tr.odd and tr.even	Alternating even and odd rows

ReadmeName Directive

Description:	Name of the file that will be inserted at the end of the index listing
Syntax:	`ReadmeName filename`
Context:	server config, virtual host, directory, .htaccess
Override:	Indexes
Status:	Base
Module:	mod_autoindex

The READMENAME directive sets the name of the file that will be appended to the end of the index listing. *Filename* is the name of the file to include, and is taken to be relative to the location being indexed. If *Filename* begins with a slash, as in example 2, it will be taken to be relative to the DOCUMENTROOT.

```
# Example 1
ReadmeName FOOTER.html

# Example 2
ReadmeName /include/FOOTER.html
```

See also HEADERNAME, where this behavior is described in greater detail.

10.28 Apache Module mod_buffer

Description:	Support for request buffering
Status:	Extension
ModuleIdentifier:	buffer_module
SourceFile:	mod_buffer.c
Compatibility:	Available in Apache 2.3 and later

Summary

This module provides the ability to buffer the input and output filter stacks.

Under certain circumstances, content generators might create content in small chunks. In order to promote memory reuse, in memory chunks are always 8k in size, regardless of the size of the chunk itself. When many small chunks are generated by a request, this can create a large memory footprint while the request is being processed, and an unnecessarily large amount of data on the wire. The addition of a buffer collapses the response into the fewest chunks possible.

When httpd is used in front of an expensive content generator, buffering the response may allow the backend to complete processing and release resources sooner, depending on how the backend is designed.

The buffer filter may be added to either the input or the output filter stacks, as appropriate, using the SetInputFilter, SetOutputFilter, AddOutputFilter or AddOutputFilterByType directives.

Using buffer with mod_include

```
AddOutputFilterByType INCLUDES;BUFFER text/html
```

! The buffer filters read the request/response into RAM and then repack the request/response into the fewest memory buckets possible, at the cost of CPU time. When the request/response is already efficiently packed, buffering the request/response could cause the request/response to be slower than not using a buffer at all. These filters should be used with care, and only where necessary.

Directives

- BufferSize

See also

- Filters (p. 100)

BufferSize Directive

Description:	Maximum size in bytes to buffer by the buffer filter
Syntax:	`BufferSize integer`
Default:	`BufferSize 131072`
Context:	server config, virtual host, directory, .htaccess
Status:	Extension
Module:	mod_buffer

The BufferSize directive specifies the amount of data in bytes that will be buffered before being read from or written to each request. The default is 128 kilobytes.

10.29 Apache Module mod_cache

Description:	RFC 2616 compliant HTTP caching filter.
Status:	Extension
ModuleIdentifier:	cache_module
SourceFile:	mod_cache.c

Summary

> **!** This module should be used with care, as when the CACHEQUICKHANDLER directive is in its default value of **on**, the ALLOW and DENY directives will be circumvented. You should not enable quick handler caching for any content to which you wish to limit access by client host name, address or environment variable.

MOD_CACHE implements an RFC 2616[14] compliant **HTTP content caching filter**, with support for the caching of content negotiated responses containing the Vary header.

RFC 2616 compliant caching provides a mechanism to verify whether stale or expired content is still fresh, and can represent a significant performance boost when the origin server supports **conditional requests** by honouring the If-None-Match[15] HTTP request header. Content is only regenerated from scratch when the content has changed, and not when the cached entry expires.

As a filter, MOD_CACHE can be placed in front of content originating from any handler, including **flat files** (served from a slow disk cached on a fast disk), the output of a **CGI script** or **dynamic content generator**, or content **proxied from another server**.

In the default configuration, MOD_CACHE inserts the caching filter as far forward as possible within the filter stack, utilising the **quick handler** to bypass all per request processing when returning content to the client. In this mode of operation, MOD_CACHE may be thought of as a caching proxy server bolted to the front of the webserver, while running within the webserver itself.

When the quick handler is switched off using the CACHEQUICKHANDLER directive, it becomes possible to insert the **CACHE** filter at a point in the filter stack chosen by the administrator. This provides the opportunity to cache content before that content is personalised by the MOD_INCLUDE filter, or optionally compressed by the MOD_DEFLATE filter.

Under normal operation, MOD_CACHE will respond to and can be controlled by the Cache-Control[16] and Pragma[17] headers sent from a client in a request, or from a server within a response. Under exceptional circumstances, MOD_CACHE can be configured to override these headers and force site specific behaviour, however such behaviour will be limited to this cache only, and will not affect the operation of other caches that may exist between the client and server, and as a result is not recommended unless strictly necessary.

RFC 2616 allows for the cache to return stale data while the existing stale entry is refreshed from the origin server, and this is supported by MOD_CACHE when the CACHELOCK directive is suitably configured. Such responses will contain a Warning[18] HTTP header with a 110 response code. RFC 2616 also allows a cache to return stale data when the attempt made to refresh the stale data returns an error 500 or above, and this behaviour is supported by default by MOD_CACHE. Such responses will contain a Warning[19] HTTP header with a 111 response code.

MOD_CACHE requires the services of one or more storage management modules. The following storage management modules are included in the base Apache distribution:

---

[14] http://www.ietf.org/rfc/rfc2616.txt
[15] http://www.w3.org/Protocols/rfc2616/rfc2616-sec14.html#sec14.26
[16] http://www.w3.org/Protocols/rfc2616/rfc2616-sec14.html#sec14.9
[17] http://www.w3.org/Protocols/rfc2616/rfc2616-sec14.html#sec14.32
[18] http://www.w3.org/Protocols/rfc2616/rfc2616-sec14.html#sec14.46
[19] http://www.w3.org/Protocols/rfc2616/rfc2616-sec14.html#sec14.46

MOD_CACHE_DISK Implements a disk based storage manager. Headers and bodies are stored separately on disk, in a directory structure derived from the md5 hash of the cached URL. Multiple content negotiated responses can be stored concurrently, however the caching of partial content is not supported by this module. The `htcacheclean` tool is provided to list cached URLs, remove cached URLs, or to maintain the size of the disk cache within size and inode limits.

MOD_CACHE_SOCACHE Implements a shared object cache based storage manager. Headers and bodies are stored together beneath a single key based on the URL of the response being cached. Multiple content negotiated responses can be stored concurrently, however the caching of partial content is not supported by this module.

Further details, discussion, and examples, are provided in the Caching Guide (p. 40) .

Directives

- CacheDefaultExpire
- CacheDetailHeader
- CacheDisable
- CacheEnable
- CacheHeader
- CacheIgnoreCacheControl
- CacheIgnoreHeaders
- CacheIgnoreNoLastMod
- CacheIgnoreQueryString
- CacheIgnoreURLSessionIdentifiers
- CacheKeyBaseURL
- CacheLastModifiedFactor
- CacheLock
- CacheLockMaxAge
- CacheLockPath
- CacheMaxExpire
- CacheMinExpire
- CacheQuickHandler
- CacheStaleOnError
- CacheStoreExpired
- CacheStoreNoStore
- CacheStorePrivate

See also

- Caching Guide (p. 40)

Related Modules and Directives

Related Modules	Related Directives
MOD_CACHE_DISK	CACHEROOT
MOD_CACHE_SOCACHE	CACHEDIRLEVELS
	CACHEDIRLENGTH
	CACHEMINFILESIZE
	CACHEMAXFILESIZE
	CACHESOCACHE
	CACHESOCACHEMAXTIME
	CACHESOCACHEMINTIME
	CACHESOCACHEMAXSIZE
	CACHESOCACHEREADSIZE
	CACHESOCACHEREADTIME

Sample Configuration

Sample httpd.conf

```
#
# Sample Cache Configuration
#
LoadModule cache_module modules/mod_cache.so
<IfModule mod_cache.c>
    LoadModule cache_disk_module modules/mod_cache_disk.so
    <IfModule mod_cache_disk.c>
        CacheRoot "c:/cacheroot"
        CacheEnable disk  "/"
        CacheDirLevels 5
        CacheDirLength 3
    </IfModule>

    # When acting as a proxy, don't cache the list of security updates
    CacheDisable "http://security.update.server/update-list/"
</IfModule>
```

Avoiding the Thundering Herd

When a cached entry becomes stale, MOD_CACHE will submit a conditional request to the backend, which is expected to confirm whether the cached entry is still fresh, and send an updated entity if not.

A small but finite amount of time exists between the time the cached entity becomes stale, and the time the stale entity is fully refreshed. On a busy server, a significant number of requests might arrive during this time, and cause a **thundering herd** of requests to strike the backend suddenly and unpredictably.

To keep the thundering herd at bay, the CACHELOCK directive can be used to define a directory in which locks are created for URLs **in flight**. The lock is used as a **hint** by other requests to either suppress an attempt to cache (someone else has gone to fetch the entity), or to indicate that a stale entry is being refreshed (stale content will be returned in the mean time).

Initial caching of an entry

When an entity is cached for the first time, a lock will be created for the entity until the response has been fully cached. During the lifetime of the lock, the cache will suppress the second and subsequent attempt to cache the same entity. While this doesn't hold back the thundering herd, it does stop the cache attempting to cache the same entity multiple times simultaneously.

Refreshment of a stale entry

When an entity reaches its freshness lifetime and becomes stale, a lock will be created for the entity until the response has either been confirmed as still fresh, or replaced by the backend. During the lifetime of the lock, the second and subsequent incoming request will cause stale data to be returned, and the thundering herd is kept at bay.

Locks and Cache-Control: no-cache

Locks are used as a **hint only** to enable the cache to be more gentle on backend servers, however the lock can be overridden if necessary. If the client sends a request with a Cache-Control header forcing a reload, any lock that may be present will be ignored, and the client's request will be honored immediately and the cached entry refreshed.

As a further safety mechanism, locks have a configurable maximum age. Once this age has been reached, the lock is removed, and a new request is given the opportunity to create a new lock. This maximum age can be set using the CACHELOCKMAXAGE directive, and defaults to 5 seconds.

Example configuration

Enabling the cache lock

```
#
# Enable the cache lock
#
<IfModule mod_cache.c>
    CacheLock on
    CacheLockPath "/tmp/mod_cache-lock"
    CacheLockMaxAge 5
</IfModule>
```

Fine Control with the CACHE Filter

Under the default mode of cache operation, the cache runs as a quick handler, short circuiting the majority of server processing and offering the highest cache performance available.

In this mode, the cache **bolts onto** the front of the server, acting as if a free standing RFC 2616 caching proxy had been placed in front of the server.

While this mode offers the best performance, the administrator may find that under certain circumstances they may want to perform further processing on the request after the request is cached, such as to inject personalisation into the cached page, or to apply authorisation restrictions to the content. Under these circumstances, an administrator is often forced to place independent reverse proxy servers either behind or in front of the caching server to achieve this.

To solve this problem the CACHEQUICKHANDLER directive can be set to **off**, and the server will process all phases normally handled by a non-cached request, including the **authentication and authorisation** phases.

In addition, the administrator may optionally specify the **precise point within the filter chain** where caching is to take place by adding the **CACHE** filter to the output filter chain.

For example, to cache content before applying compression to the response, place the **CACHE** filter before the **DEFLATE** filter as in the example below:

```
# Cache content before optional compression
CacheQuickHandler off
AddOutputFilterByType CACHE;DEFLATE text/plain
```

Another option is to have content cached before personalisation is applied by MOD_INCLUDE (or another content processing filter). In this example templates containing tags understood by MOD_INCLUDE are cached before being parsed:

```
# Cache content before mod_include and mod_deflate
CacheQuickHandler off
AddOutputFilterByType CACHE;INCLUDES;DEFLATE text/html
```

You may place the **CACHE** filter anywhere you wish within the filter chain. In this example, content is cached after being parsed by MOD_INCLUDE, but before being processed by MOD_DEFLATE:

```
# Cache content between mod_include and mod_deflate
CacheQuickHandler off
AddOutputFilterByType INCLUDES;CACHE;DEFLATE text/html
```

Warning:
If the location of the **CACHE** filter in the filter chain is changed for any reason, you may need to **flush your cache** to ensure that your data served remains consistent. MOD_CACHE is not in a position to enforce this for you.

Cache Status and Logging

Once MOD_CACHE has made a decision as to whether or not an entity is to be served from cache, the detailed reason for the decision is written to the subprocess environment within the request under the **cache-status** key. This reason can be logged by the LOGFORMAT directive as follows:

```
LogFormat "%{cache-status}e ..."
```

Based on the caching decision made, the reason is also written to the subprocess environment under one the following four keys, as appropriate:

cache-hit The response was served from cache.

cache-revalidate The response was stale and was successfully revalidated, then served from cache.

cache-miss The response was served from the upstream server.

cache-invalidate The cached entity was invalidated by a request method other than GET or HEAD.

This makes it possible to support conditional logging of cached requests as per the following example:

```
CustomLog "cached-requests.log" common env=cache-hit
CustomLog "uncached-requests.log" common env=cache-miss
CustomLog "revalidated-requests.log" common env=cache-revalidate
CustomLog "invalidated-requests.log" common env=cache-invalidate
```

For module authors, a hook called *cache_status* is available, allowing modules to respond to the caching outcomes above in customised ways.

CacheDefaultExpire Directive

Description:	The default duration to cache a document when no expiry date is specified.
Syntax:	`CacheDefaultExpire seconds`
Default:	`CacheDefaultExpire 3600 (one hour)`
Context:	server config, virtual host, directory, .htaccess
Status:	Extension
Module:	mod_cache

The CACHEDEFAULTEXPIRE directive specifies a default time, in seconds, to cache a document if neither an expiry date nor last-modified date are provided with the document. The value specified with the CACHEMAXEXPIRE directive does *not* override this setting.

```
CacheDefaultExpire 86400
```

CacheDetailHeader Directive

Description:	Add an X-Cache-Detail header to the response.
Syntax:	`CacheDetailHeader on|off`
Default:	`CacheDetailHeader off`
Context:	server config, virtual host, directory, .htaccess
Status:	Extension
Module:	mod_cache
Compatibility:	Available in Apache 2.3.9 and later

When the CACHEDETAILHEADER directive is switched on, an **X-Cache-Detail** header will be added to the response containing the detailed reason for a particular caching decision.

It can be useful during development of cached RESTful services to have additional information about the caching decision written to the response headers, so as to confirm whether `Cache-Control` and other headers have been correctly used by the service and client.

If the normal handler is used, this directive may appear within a <DIRECTORY> or <LOCATION> directive. If the quick handler is used, this directive must appear within a server or virtual host context, otherwise the setting will be ignored.

```
# Enable the X-Cache-Detail header
CacheDetailHeader on
```

```
X-Cache-Detail:  "conditional cache hit:  entity refreshed" from
localhost
```

CacheDisable Directive

Description:	Disable caching of specified URLs
Syntax:	`CacheDisable url-string | on`
Context:	server config, virtual host, directory, .htaccess
Status:	Extension
Module:	mod_cache

The CACHEDISABLE directive instructs MOD_CACHE to *not* cache urls at or below *url-string*.

Example

```
CacheDisable "/local_files"
```

If used in a <LOCATION> directive, the path needs to be specified below the Location, or if the word "on" is used, caching for the whole location will be disabled.

Example

```
<Location "/foo">
    CacheDisable on
</Location>
```

The `no-cache` environment variable can be set to disable caching on a finer grained set of resources in versions 2.2.12 and later.

See also

- Environment Variables in Apache (p. 82)

CacheEnable Directive

Description:	Enable caching of specified URLs using a specified storage manager
Syntax:	`CacheEnable cache_type [url-string]`
Context:	server config, virtual host, directory
Status:	Extension
Module:	mod_cache
Compatibility:	A url-string of '/' applied to forward proxy content in 2.2 and earlier.

The CACHEENABLE directive instructs MOD_CACHE to cache urls at or below *url-string*. The cache storage manager is specified with the *cache_type* argument. The CACHEENABLE directive can alternatively be placed inside either <LOCATION> or <LOCATIONMATCH> sections to indicate the content is cacheable. *cache_type* `disk` instructs MOD_CACHE to use the disk based storage manager implemented by MOD_CACHE_DISK. *cache_type* `socache` instructs MOD_CACHE to use the shared object cache based storage manager implemented by MOD_CACHE_SOCACHE.

In the event that the URL space overlaps between different CACHEENABLE directives (as in the example below), each possible storage manager will be run until the first one that actually processes the request. The order in which the storage managers are run is determined by the order of the CACHEENABLE directives in the configuration file. CACHEENABLE directives within <LOCATION> or <LOCATIONMATCH> sections are processed before globally defined CACHEENABLE directives.

When acting as a forward proxy server, *url-string* must minimally begin with a protocol for which caching should be enabled.

```
# Cache content (normal handler only)
CacheQuickHandler off
<Location "/foo">
    CacheEnable disk
</Location>

# Cache regex (normal handler only)
CacheQuickHandler off
<LocationMatch "foo$">
    CacheEnable disk
</LocationMatch>
```

```
# Cache all but forward proxy url's (normal or quick handler)
CacheEnable  disk  /

# Cache FTP-proxied url's (normal or quick handler)
CacheEnable  disk  ftp://

# Cache forward proxy content from www.example.org (normal or quick handler)
CacheEnable  disk  http://www.example.org/
```

A hostname starting with a "*" matches all hostnames with that suffix. A hostname starting with "." matches all hostnames containing the domain components that follow.

```
# Match www.example.org, and fooexample.org
CacheEnable  disk  "http://*example.org/"
# Match www.example.org, but not fooexample.org
CacheEnable  disk  "http://.example.org/"
```

The no-cache environment variable can be set to disable caching on a finer grained set of resources in versions 2.2.12 and later.

See also

- Environment Variables in Apache (p. 82)

CacheHeader Directive

Description:	Add an X-Cache header to the response.
Syntax:	CacheHeader on|off
Default:	CacheHeader off
Context:	server config, virtual host, directory, .htaccess
Status:	Extension
Module:	mod_cache
Compatibility:	Available in Apache 2.3.9 and later

When the CACHEHEADER directive is switched on, an **X-Cache** header will be added to the response with the cache status of this response. If the normal handler is used, this directive may appear within a <DIRECTORY> or <LOCATION> directive. If the quick handler is used, this directive must appear within a server or virtual host context, otherwise the setting will be ignored.

HIT The entity was fresh, and was served from cache.

REVALIDATE The entity was stale, was successfully revalidated and was served from cache.

MISS The entity was fetched from the upstream server and was not served from cache.

```
# Enable the X-Cache header
CacheHeader on
```

```
X-Cache: HIT from localhost
```

CacheIgnoreCacheControl Directive

Description:	Ignore request to not serve cached content to client
Syntax:	`CacheIgnoreCacheControl On|Off`
Default:	`CacheIgnoreCacheControl Off`
Context:	server config, virtual host
Status:	Extension
Module:	mod_cache

Ordinarily, requests containing a Cache-Control: no-cache or Pragma: no-cache header value will not be served from the cache. The CACHEIGNORECACHECONTROL directive allows this behavior to be overridden. CACHEIGNORECACHECONTROL ON tells the server to attempt to serve the resource from the cache even if the request contains no-cache header values. Resources requiring authorization will *never* be cached.

```
CacheIgnoreCacheControl On
```

 **Warning:**
This directive will allow serving from the cache even if the client has requested that the document not be served from the cache. This might result in stale content being served.

See also

- CACHESTOREPRIVATE
- CACHESTORENOSTORE

CacheIgnoreHeaders Directive

Description:	Do not store the given HTTP header(s) in the cache.
Syntax:	`CacheIgnoreHeaders header-string [header-string] ...`
Default:	`CacheIgnoreHeaders None`
Context:	server config, virtual host
Status:	Extension
Module:	mod_cache

According to RFC 2616, hop-by-hop HTTP headers are not stored in the cache. The following HTTP headers are hop-by-hop headers and thus do not get stored in the cache in *any* case regardless of the setting of CACHEIGNOREHEADERS:

- `Connection`
- `Keep-Alive`
- `Proxy-Authenticate`
- `Proxy-Authorization`
- `TE`
- `Trailers`
- `Transfer-Encoding`
- `Upgrade`

CACHEIGNOREHEADERS specifies additional HTTP headers that should not to be stored in the cache. For example, it makes sense in some cases to prevent cookies from being stored in the cache.

CACHEIGNOREHEADERS takes a space separated list of HTTP headers that should not be stored in the cache. If only hop-by-hop headers not should be stored in the cache (the RFC 2616 compliant behaviour), CACHEIGNOREHEADERS can be set to `None`.

Example 1

```
CacheIgnoreHeaders Set-Cookie
```

Example 2

```
CacheIgnoreHeaders None
```

! **Warning:**
If headers like `Expires` which are needed for proper cache management are not stored due to a CACHEIGNOREHEADERS setting, the behaviour of mod_cache is undefined.

CacheIgnoreNoLastMod Directive

Description:	Ignore the fact that a response has no Last Modified header.
Syntax:	`CacheIgnoreNoLastMod On|Off`
Default:	`CacheIgnoreNoLastMod Off`
Context:	server config, virtual host, directory, .htaccess
Status:	Extension
Module:	mod_cache

Ordinarily, documents without a last-modified date are not cached. Under some circumstances the last-modified date is removed (during MOD_INCLUDE processing for example) or not provided at all. The CACHEIGNORENOLASTMOD directive provides a way to specify that documents without last-modified dates should be considered for caching, even without a last-modified date. If neither a last-modified date nor an expiry date are provided with the document then the value specified by the CACHEDEFAULTEXPIRE directive will be used to generate an expiration date.

```
CacheIgnoreNoLastMod On
```

CacheIgnoreQueryString Directive

Description:	Ignore query string when caching
Syntax:	`CacheIgnoreQueryString On|Off`
Default:	`CacheIgnoreQueryString Off`
Context:	server config, virtual host
Status:	Extension
Module:	mod_cache

Ordinarily, requests with query string parameters are cached separately for each unique query string. This is according to RFC 2616/13.9 done only if an expiration time is specified. The CACHEIGNOREQUERYSTRING directive tells the cache to cache requests even if no expiration time is specified, and to reply with a cached reply even if the query string differs. From a caching point of view the request is treated as if having no query string when this directive is enabled.

```
CacheIgnoreQueryString On
```

CacheIgnoreURLSessionIdentifiers Directive

Description:	Ignore defined session identifiers encoded in the URL when caching
Syntax:	`CacheIgnoreURLSessionIdentifiers identifier [identifier] ...`
Default:	`CacheIgnoreURLSessionIdentifiers None`
Context:	server config, virtual host
Status:	Extension
Module:	mod_cache

Sometimes applications encode the session identifier into the URL like in the following Examples:

- `/someapplication/image.gif;jsessionid=123456789`
- `/someapplication/image.gif?PHPSESSIONID=12345678`

This causes cachable resources to be stored separately for each session, which is often not desired. CACHEIGNOREURLSESSIONIDENTIFIERS lets define a list of identifiers that are removed from the key that is used to identify an entity in the cache, such that cachable resources are not stored separately for each session.

`CacheIgnoreURLSessionIdentifiers None` clears the list of ignored identifiers. Otherwise, each identifier is added to the list.

Example 1

```
CacheIgnoreURLSessionIdentifiers jsessionid
```

Example 2

```
CacheIgnoreURLSessionIdentifiers None
```

CacheKeyBaseURL Directive

Description:	Override the base URL of reverse proxied cache keys.
Syntax:	`CacheKeyBaseURL URL`
Default:	`CacheKeyBaseURL http://example.com`
Context:	server config, virtual host
Status:	Extension
Module:	mod_cache
Compatibility:	Available in Apache 2.3.9 and later

When the CACHEKEYBASEURL directive is specified, the URL provided will be used as the base URL to calculate the URL of the cache keys in the reverse proxy configuration. When not specified, the scheme, hostname and port of the current virtual host is used to construct the cache key. When a cluster of machines is present, and all cached entries should be cached beneath the same cache key, a new base URL can be specified with this directive.

```
# Override the base URL of the cache key.
CacheKeyBaseURL "http://www.example.com/"
```

! Take care when setting this directive. If two separate virtual hosts are accidentally given the same base URL, entries from one virtual host will be served to the other.

CacheLastModifiedFactor Directive

Description:	The factor used to compute an expiry date based on the LastModified date.
Syntax:	`CacheLastModifiedFactor float`
Default:	`CacheLastModifiedFactor 0.1`
Context:	server config, virtual host, directory, .htaccess
Status:	Extension
Module:	mod_cache

In the event that a document does not provide an expiry date but does provide a last-modified date, an expiry date can be calculated based on the time since the document was last modified. The CACHELASTMODIFIEDFACTOR directive specifies a *factor* to be used in the generation of this expiry date according to the following formula:

```
expiry-period = time-since-last-modified-date * factor expiry-date =
current-date + expiry-period
```

For example, if the document was last modified 10 hours ago, and *factor* is 0.1 then the expiry-period will be set to 10*0.1 = 1 hour. If the current time was 3:00pm then the computed expiry-date would be 3:00pm + 1hour = 4:00pm.

If the expiry-period would be longer than that set by CACHEMAXEXPIRE, then the latter takes precedence.

```
CacheLastModifiedFactor 0.5
```

CacheLock Directive

Description:	Enable the thundering herd lock.
Syntax:	`CacheLock on|off`
Default:	`CacheLock off`
Context:	server config, virtual host
Status:	Extension
Module:	mod_cache
Compatibility:	Available in Apache 2.2.15 and later

The CACHELOCK directive enables the thundering herd lock for the given URL space.

In a minimal configuration the following directive is all that is needed to enable the thundering herd lock in the default system temp directory.

```
# Enable cache lock
CacheLock on
```

CacheLockMaxAge Directive

Description:	Set the maximum possible age of a cache lock.
Syntax:	`CacheLockMaxAge integer`
Default:	`CacheLockMaxAge 5`
Context:	server config, virtual host
Status:	Extension
Module:	mod_cache

The CACHELOCKMAXAGE directive specifies the maximum age of any cache lock.

A lock older than this value in seconds will be ignored, and the next incoming request will be given the opportunity to re-establish the lock. This mechanism prevents a slow client taking an excessively long time to refresh an entity.

CacheLockPath Directive

Description:	Set the lock path directory.
Syntax:	`CacheLockPath directory`
Default:	`CacheLockPath /tmp/mod_cache-lock`
Context:	server config, virtual host
Status:	Extension
Module:	mod_cache

The CACHELOCKPATH directive allows you to specify the directory in which the locks are created. By default, the system's temporary folder is used. Locks consist of empty files that only exist for stale URLs in flight, so is significantly less resource intensive than the traditional disk cache.

CacheMaxExpire Directive

Description:	The maximum time in seconds to cache a document
Syntax:	`CacheMaxExpire seconds`
Default:	`CacheMaxExpire 86400 (one day)`
Context:	server config, virtual host, directory, .htaccess
Status:	Extension
Module:	mod_cache

The CACHEMAXEXPIRE directive specifies the maximum number of seconds for which cachable HTTP documents will be retained without checking the origin server. Thus, documents will be out of date at most this number of seconds. This maximum value is enforced even if an expiry date was supplied with the document.

```
CacheMaxExpire 604800
```

CacheMinExpire Directive

Description:	The minimum time in seconds to cache a document
Syntax:	`CacheMinExpire seconds`
Default:	`CacheMinExpire 0`
Context:	server config, virtual host, directory, .htaccess
Status:	Extension
Module:	mod_cache

The CACHEMINEXPIRE directive specifies the minimum number of seconds for which cachable HTTP documents will be retained without checking the origin server. This is only used if no valid expire time was supplied with the document.

```
CacheMinExpire 3600
```

CacheQuickHandler Directive

Description:	Run the cache from the quick handler.
Syntax:	`CacheQuickHandler on|off`
Default:	`CacheQuickHandler on`
Context:	server config, virtual host
Status:	Extension
Module:	mod_cache
Compatibility:	Apache HTTP Server 2.3.3 and later

The CACHEQUICKHANDLER directive controls the phase in which the cache is handled.

In the default enabled configuration, the cache operates within the quick handler phase. This phase short circuits the majority of server processing, and represents the most performant mode of operation for a typical server. The cache **bolts onto** the front of the server, and the majority of server processing is avoided.

When disabled, the cache operates as a normal handler, and is subject to the full set of phases when handling a server request. While this mode is slower than the default, it allows the cache to be used in cases where full processing is required, such as when content is subject to authorisation.

```
# Run cache as a normal handler
CacheQuickHandler off
```

It is also possible, when the quick handler is disabled, for the administrator to choose the precise location within the filter chain where caching is to be performed, by adding the **CACHE** filter to the chain.

```
# Cache content before mod_include and mod_deflate
CacheQuickHandler off
AddOutputFilterByType CACHE;INCLUDES;DEFLATE text/html
```

If the CACHE filter is specified more than once, the last instance will apply.

CacheStaleOnError Directive

Description:	Serve stale content in place of 5xx responses.
Syntax:	`CacheStaleOnError on|off`
Default:	`CacheStaleOnError on`
Context:	server config, virtual host, directory, .htaccess
Status:	Extension
Module:	mod_cache
Compatibility:	Available in Apache 2.3.9 and later

When the CACHESTALEONERROR directive is switched on, and when stale data is available in the cache, the cache will respond to 5xx responses from the backend by returning the stale data instead of the 5xx response. While the Cache-Control headers sent by clients will be respected, and the raw 5xx responses returned to the client on request, the 5xx response so returned to the client will not invalidate the content in the cache.

```
# Serve stale data on error.
CacheStaleOnError on
```

CacheStoreExpired Directive

Description:	Attempt to cache responses that the server reports as expired
Syntax:	`CacheStoreExpired On|Off`
Default:	`CacheStoreExpired Off`
Context:	server config, virtual host, directory, .htaccess
Status:	Extension
Module:	mod_cache

Since httpd 2.2.4, responses which have already expired are not stored in the cache. The CACHESTOREEXPIRED directive allows this behavior to be overridden. CACHESTOREEXPIRED On tells the server to attempt to cache the resource if it is stale. Subsequent requests would trigger an If-Modified-Since request of the origin server, and the response may be fulfilled from cache if the backend resource has not changed.

```
CacheStoreExpired On
```

CacheStoreNoStore Directive

Description:	Attempt to cache requests or responses that have been marked as no-store.
Syntax:	`CacheStoreNoStore On|Off`
Default:	`CacheStoreNoStore Off`
Context:	server config, virtual host, directory, .htaccess
Status:	Extension
Module:	mod_cache

Ordinarily, requests or responses with Cache-Control: no-store header values will not be stored in the cache. The CACHESTORENOSTORE directive allows this behavior to be overridden. CACHESTORENOSTORE On tells the server to attempt to cache the resource even if it contains no-store header values. Resources requiring authorization will *never* be cached.

```
CacheStoreNoStore On
```

Warning:
As described in RFC 2616, the no-store directive is intended to "prevent the inadvertent release or retention of sensitive information (for example, on backup tapes)." Enabling this option could store sensitive information in the cache. You are hereby warned.

See also

- CACHEIGNORECACHECONTROL
- CACHESTOREPRIVATE

CacheStorePrivate Directive

Description:	Attempt to cache responses that the server has marked as private
Syntax:	`CacheStorePrivate On|Off`
Default:	`CacheStorePrivate Off`
Context:	server config, virtual host, directory, .htaccess
Status:	Extension
Module:	mod_cache

Ordinarily, responses with Cache-Control: private header values will not be stored in the cache. The CACHESTOREPRIVATE directive allows this behavior to be overridden. CACHESTOREPRIVATE On tells the server to attempt to cache the resource even if it contains private header values. Resources requiring authorization will *never* be cached.

```
CacheStorePrivate On
```

Warning:
This directive will allow caching even if the upstream server has requested that the resource not be cached. This directive is only ideal for a 'private' cache.

See also

- CACHEIGNORECACHECONTROL
- CACHESTORENOSTORE

10.30 Apache Module mod_cache_disk

Description:	Disk based storage module for the HTTP caching filter.
Status:	Extension
ModuleIdentifier:	cache_disk_module
SourceFile:	mod_cache_disk.c

Summary

MOD_CACHE_DISK implements a disk based storage manager for MOD_CACHE.

The headers and bodies of cached responses are stored separately on disk, in a directory structure derived from the md5 hash of the cached URL.

Multiple content negotiated responses can be stored concurrently, however the caching of partial content is not yet supported by this module.

Atomic cache updates to both header and body files are achieved without the need for locking by storing the device and inode numbers of the body file within the header file. This has the side effect that cache entries manually moved into the cache will be ignored.

The `htcacheclean` tool is provided to list cached URLs, remove cached URLs, or to maintain the size of the disk cache within size and/or inode limits. The tool can be run on demand, or can be daemonized to offer continuous monitoring of directory sizes.

**Note:**

MOD_CACHE_DISK requires the services of MOD_CACHE, which must be loaded before mod_cache_disk.

**Note:**

MOD_CACHE_DISK uses the sendfile feature to serve files from the cache when supported by the platform, and when enabled with ENABLESENDFILE. However, per-directory and .htaccess configuration of ENABLESENDFILE are ignored by MOD_CACHE_DISK as the corresponding settings are not available to the module when a request is being served from the cache.

Directives

- CacheDirLength
- CacheDirLevels
- CacheMaxFileSize
- CacheMinFileSize
- CacheReadSize
- CacheReadTime
- CacheRoot

See also

- MOD_CACHE
- MOD_CACHE_SOCACHE
- Caching Guide (p. 40)

CacheDirLength Directive

Description:	The number of characters in subdirectory names
Syntax:	`CacheDirLength length`
Default:	`CacheDirLength 2`
Context:	server config, virtual host
Status:	Extension
Module:	mod_cache_disk

The CACHEDIRLENGTH directive sets the number of characters for each subdirectory name in the cache hierarchy. It can be used in conjunction with CACHEDIRLEVELS to determine the approximate structure of your cache hierarchy.

A high value for CACHEDIRLENGTH combined with a low value for CACHEDIRLEVELS will result in a relatively flat hierarchy, with a large number of subdirectories at each level.

⟹ The result of CACHEDIRLEVELS* CACHEDIRLENGTH must not be higher than 20.

CacheDirLevels Directive

Description:	The number of levels of subdirectories in the cache.
Syntax:	`CacheDirLevels levels`
Default:	`CacheDirLevels 2`
Context:	server config, virtual host
Status:	Extension
Module:	mod_cache_disk

The CACHEDIRLEVELS directive sets the number of subdirectory levels in the cache. Cached data will be saved this many directory levels below the CACHEROOT directory.

A high value for CACHEDIRLEVELS combined with a low value for CACHEDIRLENGTH will result in a relatively deep hierarchy, with a small number of subdirectories at each level.

⟹ The result of CACHEDIRLEVELS* CACHEDIRLENGTH must not be higher than 20.

CacheMaxFileSize Directive

Description:	The maximum size (in bytes) of a document to be placed in the cache
Syntax:	`CacheMaxFileSize bytes`
Default:	`CacheMaxFileSize 1000000`
Context:	server config, virtual host, directory, .htaccess
Status:	Extension
Module:	mod_cache_disk

The CACHEMAXFILESIZE directive sets the maximum size, in bytes, for a document to be considered for storage in the cache.

```
CacheMaxFileSize 64000
```

CacheMinFileSize Directive

Description:	The minimum size (in bytes) of a document to be placed in the cache
Syntax:	`CacheMinFileSize bytes`
Default:	`CacheMinFileSize 1`
Context:	server config, virtual host, directory, .htaccess
Status:	Extension
Module:	mod_cache_disk

The CACHEMINFILESIZE directive sets the minimum size, in bytes, for a document to be considered for storage in the cache.

```
CacheMinFileSize 64
```

CacheReadSize Directive

Description:	The minimum size (in bytes) of the document to read and be cached before sending the data downstream
Syntax:	`CacheReadSize bytes`
Default:	`CacheReadSize 0`
Context:	server config, virtual host, directory, .htaccess
Status:	Extension
Module:	mod_cache_disk

The CACHEREADSIZE directive sets the minimum amount of data, in bytes, to be read from the backend before the data is sent to the client. The default of zero causes all data read of any size to be passed downstream to the client immediately as it arrives. Setting this to a higher value causes the disk cache to buffer at least this amount before sending the result to the client. This can improve performance when caching content from a reverse proxy.

This directive only takes effect when the data is being saved to the cache, as opposed to data being served from the cache.

```
CacheReadSize 102400
```

CacheReadTime Directive

Description:	The minimum time (in milliseconds) that should elapse while reading before data is sent downstream
Syntax:	`CacheReadTime milliseconds`
Default:	`CacheReadTime 0`
Context:	server config, virtual host, directory, .htaccess
Status:	Extension
Module:	mod_cache_disk

The CACHEREADTIME directive sets the minimum amount of elapsed time that should pass before making an attempt to send data downstream to the client. During the time period, data will be buffered before sending the result to the client. This can improve performance when caching content from a reverse proxy.

The default of zero disables this option.

This directive only takes effect when the data is being saved to the cache, as opposed to data being served from the cache. It is recommended that this option be used alongside the CACHEREADSIZE directive to ensure that the server does not buffer excessively should data arrive faster than expected.

```
CacheReadTime 1000
```

CacheRoot Directive

Description:	The directory root under which cache files are stored
Syntax:	`CacheRoot directory`
Context:	server config, virtual host
Status:	Extension
Module:	mod_cache_disk

The CACHEROOT directive defines the name of the directory on the disk to contain cache files. If the MOD_CACHE_DISK module has been loaded or compiled in to the Apache server, this directive *must* be defined. Failing to provide a value for CACHEROOT will result in a configuration file processing error. The CACHEDIRLEVELS and CACHEDIRLENGTH directives define the structure of the directories under the specified root directory.

```
CacheRoot c:/cacheroot
```

10.31 Apache Module mod_cache_socache

Description:	Shared object cache (socache) based storage module for the HTTP caching filter.
Status:	Extension
ModuleIdentifier:	cache_socache_module
SourceFile:	mod_cache_socache.c

Summary

MOD_CACHE_SOCACHE implements a shared object cache (socache) based storage manager for MOD_CACHE.

The headers and bodies of cached responses are combined, and stored underneath a single key in the shared object cache. A number of implementations (p. 104) of shared object caches are available to choose from.

Multiple content negotiated responses can be stored concurrently, however the caching of partial content is not yet supported by this module.

```
# Turn on caching
CacheSocache shmcb
CacheSocacheMaxSize 102400
<Location /foo>
    CacheEnable socache
</Location>

# Fall back to the disk cache
CacheSocache shmcb
CacheSocacheMaxSize 102400
<Location /foo>
    CacheEnable socache
    CacheEnable disk
</Location>
```

**Note:**

MOD_CACHE_SOCACHE requires the services of MOD_CACHE, which must be loaded before mod_cache_socache.

Directives

- CacheSocache
- CacheSocacheMaxSize
- CacheSocacheMaxTime
- CacheSocacheMinTime
- CacheSocacheReadSize
- CacheSocacheReadTime

See also

- MOD_CACHE
- MOD_CACHE_DISK
- Caching Guide (p. 40)

CacheSocache Directive

Description:	The shared object cache implementation to use
Syntax:	`CacheSocache type[:args]`
Context:	server config, virtual host
Status:	Extension
Module:	mod_cache_socache
Compatibility:	Available in Apache 2.4.5 and later

The CACHESOCACHE directive defines the name of the shared object cache implementation to use, followed by optional arguments for that implementation. A number of implementations (p. 104) of shared object caches are available to choose from.

```
CacheSocache shmcb
```

CacheSocacheMaxSize Directive

Description:	The maximum size (in bytes) of an entry to be placed in the cache
Syntax:	`CacheSocacheMaxSize bytes`
Default:	`CacheSocacheMaxSize 102400`
Context:	server config, virtual host, directory, .htaccess
Status:	Extension
Module:	mod_cache_socache
Compatibility:	Available in Apache 2.4.5 and later

The CACHESOCACHEMAXSIZE directive sets the maximum size, in bytes, for the combined headers and body of a document to be considered for storage in the cache. The larger the headers that are stored alongside the body, the smaller the body may be.

The MOD_CACHE_SOCACHE module will only attempt to cache responses that have an explicit content length, or that are small enough to be written in one pass. This is done to allow the MOD_CACHE_DISK module to have an opportunity to cache responses larger than those cacheable within MOD_CACHE_SOCACHE.

```
CacheSocacheMaxSize 102400
```

CacheSocacheMaxTime Directive

Description:	The maximum time (in seconds) for a document to be placed in the cache
Syntax:	`CacheSocacheMaxTime seconds`
Default:	`CacheSocacheMaxTime 86400`
Context:	server config, virtual host, directory, .htaccess
Status:	Extension
Module:	mod_cache_socache
Compatibility:	Available in Apache 2.4.5 and later

The CACHESOCACHEMAXTIME directive sets the maximum freshness lifetime, in seconds, for a document to be stored in the cache. This value overrides the freshness lifetime defined for the document by the HTTP protocol.

```
CacheSocacheMaxTime 86400
```

CacheSocacheMinTime Directive

Description:	The minimum time (in seconds) for a document to be placed in the cache
Syntax:	`CacheSocacheMinTime seconds`
Default:	`CacheSocacheMinTime 600`
Context:	server config, virtual host, directory, .htaccess
Status:	Extension
Module:	mod_cache_socache
Compatibility:	Available in Apache 2.4.5 and later

The CACHESOCACHEMINTIME directive sets the amount of seconds beyond the freshness lifetime of the response that the response should be cached for in the shared object cache. If a response is only stored for its freshness lifetime, there will be no opportunity to revalidate the response to make it fresh again.

```
CacheSocacheMinTime 600
```

CacheSocacheReadSize Directive

Description:	The minimum size (in bytes) of the document to read and be cached before sending the data downstream
Syntax:	`CacheSocacheReadSize bytes`
Default:	`CacheSocacheReadSize 0`
Context:	server config, virtual host, directory, .htaccess
Status:	Extension
Module:	mod_cache_socache
Compatibility:	Available in Apache 2.4.5 and later

The CACHESOCACHEREADSIZE directive sets the minimum amount of data, in bytes, to be read from the backend before the data is sent to the client. The default of zero causes all data read of any size to be passed downstream to the client immediately as it arrives. Setting this to a higher value causes the disk cache to buffer at least this amount before sending the result to the client. This can improve performance when caching content from a slow reverse proxy.

This directive only takes effect when the data is being saved to the cache, as opposed to data being served from the cache.

```
CacheReadSize 102400
```

CacheSocacheReadTime Directive

Description:	The minimum time (in milliseconds) that should elapse while reading before data is sent downstream
Syntax:	`CacheSocacheReadTime milliseconds`
Default:	`CacheSocacheReadTime 0`
Context:	server config, virtual host, directory, .htaccess
Status:	Extension
Module:	mod_cache_socache
Compatibility:	Available in Apache 2.4.5 and later

The CACHESOCACHEREADTIME directive sets the minimum amount of elapsed time that should pass before making an attempt to send data downstream to the client. During the time period, data will be buffered before sending the result to the client. This can improve performance when caching content from a reverse proxy.

The default of zero disables this option.

This directive only takes effect when the data is being saved to the cache, as opposed to data being served from the cache. It is recommended that this option be used alongside the CACHESOCACHEREADSIZE directive to ensure that the server does not buffer excessively should data arrive faster than expected.

```
CacheSocacheReadTime 1000
```

10.32 Apache Module mod_cern_meta

Description:	CERN httpd metafile semantics
Status:	Extension
ModuleIdentifier:	cern_meta_module
SourceFile:	mod_cern_meta.c

Summary

Emulate the CERN HTTPD Meta file semantics. Meta files are HTTP headers that can be output in addition to the normal range of headers for each file accessed. They appear rather like the Apache .asis files, and are able to provide a crude way of influencing the Expires: header, as well as providing other curiosities. There are many ways to manage meta information, this one was chosen because there is already a large number of CERN users who can exploit this module.

More information on the CERN metafile semantics[20] is available.

Directives

- MetaDir
- MetaFiles
- MetaSuffix

See also

- MOD_HEADERS
- MOD_ASIS

MetaDir Directive

Description:	Name of the directory to find CERN-style meta information files
Syntax:	`MetaDir directory`
Default:	`MetaDir .web`
Context:	server config, virtual host, directory, .htaccess
Override:	Indexes
Status:	Extension
Module:	mod_cern_meta

Specifies the name of the directory in which Apache can find meta information files. The directory is usually a 'hidden' subdirectory of the directory that contains the file being accessed. Set to "." to look in the same directory as the file:

```
MetaDir .
```

Or, to set it to a subdirectory of the directory containing the files:

```
MetaDir .meta
```

[20] http://www.w3.org/pub/WWW/Daemon/User/Config/General.html#MetaDir

MetaFiles Directive

Description:	Activates CERN meta-file processing
Syntax:	`MetaFiles on|off`
Default:	`MetaFiles off`
Context:	server config, virtual host, directory, .htaccess
Override:	Indexes
Status:	Extension
Module:	mod_cern_meta

Turns on/off Meta file processing on a per-directory basis.

MetaSuffix Directive

Description:	File name suffix for the file containing CERN-style meta information
Syntax:	`MetaSuffix suffix`
Default:	`MetaSuffix .meta`
Context:	server config, virtual host, directory, .htaccess
Override:	Indexes
Status:	Extension
Module:	mod_cern_meta

Specifies the file name suffix for the file containing the meta information. For example, the default values for the two directives will cause a request to `DOCUMENT_ROOT/somedir/index.html` to look in `DOCUMENT_ROOT/somedir/.web/index.html.meta` and will use its contents to generate additional MIME header information.

Example:

```
MetaSuffix .meta
```

10.33 Apache Module mod_cgi

Description:	Execution of CGI scripts
Status:	Base
ModuleIdentifier:	cgi_module
SourceFile:	mod_cgi.c

Summary

Any file that has the handler `cgi-script` will be treated as a CGI script, and run by the server, with its output being returned to the client. Files acquire this handler either by having a name containing an extension defined by the ADDHANDLER directive, or by being in a SCRIPTALIAS directory.

For an introduction to using CGI scripts with Apache, see our tutorial on Dynamic Content With CGI (p. 226) .

When using a multi-threaded MPM under unix, the module MOD_CGID should be used in place of this module. At the user level, the two modules are essentially identical.

For backward-compatibility, the cgi-script handler will also be activated for any file with the mime-type `application/x-httpd-cgi`. The use of the magic mime-type is deprecated.

Directives

- ScriptLog
- ScriptLogBuffer
- ScriptLogLength

See also

- ACCEPTPATHINFO
- OPTIONS ExecCGI
- SCRIPTALIAS
- ADDHANDLER
- Running CGI programs under different user IDs (p. 105)
- CGI Specification[21]

CGI Environment variables

The server will set the CGI environment variables as described in the CGI specification[22], with the following provisions:

PATH_INFO This will not be available if the ACCEPTPATHINFO directive is explicitly set to `off`. The default behavior, if ACCEPTPATHINFO is not given, is that MOD_CGI will accept path info (trailing `/more/path/info` following the script filename in the URI), while the core server will return a 404 NOT FOUND error for requests with additional path info. Omitting the ACCEPTPATHINFO directive has the same effect as setting it `On` for MOD_CGI requests.

REMOTE_HOST This will only be set if HOSTNAMELOOKUPS is set to `on` (it is off by default), and if a reverse DNS lookup of the accessing host's address indeed finds a host name.

[21] http://www.ietf.org/rfc/rfc3875
[22] http://www.ietf.org/rfc/rfc3875

REMOTE_IDENT This will only be set if IDENTITYCHECK is set to `on` and the accessing host supports the ident protocol. Note that the contents of this variable cannot be relied upon because it can easily be faked, and if there is a proxy between the client and the server, it is usually totally useless.

REMOTE_USER This will only be set if the CGI script is subject to authentication.

CGI Debugging

Debugging CGI scripts has traditionally been difficult, mainly because it has not been possible to study the output (standard output and error) for scripts which are failing to run properly. These directives provide more detailed logging of errors when they occur.

CGI Logfile Format

When configured, the CGI error log logs any CGI which does not execute properly. Each CGI script which fails to operate causes several lines of information to be logged. The first two lines are always of the format:

```
%% [time] request-line
%% HTTP-status CGI-script-filename
```

If the error is that CGI script cannot be run, the log file will contain an extra two lines:

```
%%error
error-message
```

Alternatively, if the error is the result of the script returning incorrect header information (often due to a bug in the script), the following information is logged:

```
%request
All HTTP request headers received
POST or PUT entity (if any)
%response
All headers output by the CGI script
%stdout
CGI standard output
%stderr
CGI standard error
```

(The %stdout and %stderr parts may be missing if the script did not output anything on standard output or standard error).

ScriptLog Directive

Description:	Location of the CGI script error logfile
Syntax:	`ScriptLog file-path`
Context:	server config, virtual host
Status:	Base
Module:	MOD_CGI, MOD_CGID

The SCRIPTLOG directive sets the CGI script error logfile. If no SCRIPTLOG is given, no error log is created. If given, any CGI errors are logged into the filename given as argument. If this is a relative file or path it is taken relative to the SERVERROOT.

Example

```
ScriptLog logs/cgi_log
```

This log will be opened as the user the child processes run as, *i.e.* the user specified in the main USER directive. This means that either the directory the script log is in needs to be writable by that user or the file needs to be manually created and set to be writable by that user. If you place the script log in your main logs directory, do **NOT** change the directory permissions to make it writable by the user the child processes run as.

Note that script logging is meant to be a debugging feature when writing CGI scripts, and is not meant to be activated continuously on running servers. It is not optimized for speed or efficiency, and may have security problems if used in a manner other than that for which it was designed.

ScriptLogBuffer Directive

Description:	Maximum amount of PUT or POST requests that will be recorded in the scriptlog
Syntax:	`ScriptLogBuffer bytes`
Default:	`ScriptLogBuffer 1024`
Context:	server config, virtual host
Status:	Base
Module:	MOD_CGI, MOD_CGID

The size of any PUT or POST entity body that is logged to the file is limited, to prevent the log file growing too big too quickly if large bodies are being received. By default, up to 1024 bytes are logged, but this can be changed with this directive.

ScriptLogLength Directive

Description:	Size limit of the CGI script logfile
Syntax:	`ScriptLogLength bytes`
Default:	`ScriptLogLength 10385760`
Context:	server config, virtual host
Status:	Base
Module:	MOD_CGI, MOD_CGID

SCRIPTLOGLENGTH can be used to limit the size of the CGI script logfile. Since the logfile logs a lot of information per CGI error (all request headers, all script output) it can grow to be a big file. To prevent problems due to unbounded growth, this directive can be used to set an maximum file-size for the CGI logfile. If the file exceeds this size, no more information will be written to it.

10.34 Apache Module mod_cgid

Description:	Execution of CGI scripts using an external CGI daemon
Status:	Base
ModuleIdentifier:	cgid_module
SourceFile:	mod_cgid.c
Compatibility:	Unix threaded MPMs only

Summary

Except for the optimizations and the additional SCRIPTSOCK directive noted below, MOD_CGID behaves similarly to MOD_CGI. **See the MOD_CGI summary for additional details about Apache and CGI.**

On certain unix operating systems, forking a process from a multi-threaded server is a very expensive operation because the new process will replicate all the threads of the parent process. In order to avoid incurring this expense on each CGI invocation, MOD_CGID creates an external daemon that is responsible for forking child processes to run CGI scripts. The main server communicates with this daemon using a unix domain socket.

This module is used by default instead of MOD_CGI whenever a multi-threaded MPM is selected during the compilation process. At the user level, this module is identical in configuration and operation to MOD_CGI. The only exception is the additional directive `ScriptSock` which gives the name of the socket to use for communication with the cgi daemon.

Directives

- CGIDScriptTimeout
- ScriptLog (p. 550)
- ScriptLogBuffer (p. 551)
- ScriptLogLength (p. 551)
- ScriptSock

See also

- MOD_CGI
- Running CGI programs under different user IDs (p. 105)

CGIDScriptTimeout Directive

Description:	The length of time to wait for more output from the CGI program
Syntax:	`CGIDScriptTimeout time[s|ms]`
Default:	`value of TIMEOUT directive when unset`
Context:	server config, virtual host, directory, .htaccess
Status:	Base
Module:	mod_cgid
Compatibility:	CGIDScriptTimeout defaults to zero in releases 2.4 and earlier

This directive limits the length of time to wait for more output from the CGI program. If the time is exceeded, the request and CGI are terminated.

Example

```
CGIDScriptTimeout 20
```

ScriptSock Directive

Description:	The filename prefix of the socket to use for communication with the cgi daemon
Syntax:	`ScriptSock file-path`
Default:	`ScriptSock cgisock`
Context:	server config
Status:	Base
Module:	mod_cgid

This directive sets the filename prefix of the socket to use for communication with the CGI daemon, an extension corresponding to the process ID of the server will be appended. The socket will be opened using the permissions of the user who starts Apache (usually root). To maintain the security of communications with CGI scripts, it is important that no other user has permission to write in the directory where the socket is located.

If *file-path* is not an absolute path, the location specified will be relative to the value of DEFAULTRUNTIMEDIR.

Example

```
ScriptSock /var/run/cgid.sock
```

10.35 Apache Module mod_charset_lite

Description:	Specify character set translation or recoding
Status:	Extension
ModuleIdentifier:	charset_lite_module
SourceFile:	mod_charset_lite.c

Summary

MOD_CHARSET_LITE allows the server to change the character set of responses before sending them to the client. In an EBCDIC environment, Apache always translates HTTP protocol content (e.g. response headers) from the code page of the Apache process locale to ISO-8859-1, but not the body of responses. In any environment, MOD_CHARSET_LITE can be used to specify that response bodies should be translated. For example, if files are stored in EBCDIC, then MOD_CHARSET_LITE can translate them to ISO-8859-1 before sending them to the client.

This module provides a small subset of configuration mechanisms implemented by Russian Apache and its associated `mod_charset`.

Directives

- CharsetDefault
- CharsetOptions
- CharsetSourceEnc

Common Problems

Invalid character set names

The character set name parameters of CHARSETSOURCEENC and CHARSETDEFAULT must be acceptable to the translation mechanism used by APR on the system where MOD_CHARSET_LITE is deployed. These character set names are not standardized and are usually not the same as the corresponding values used in http headers. Currently, APR can only use iconv(3), so you can easily test your character set names using the iconv(1) program, as follows:

```
iconv -f charsetsourceenc-value -t charsetdefault-value
```

Mismatch between character set of content and translation rules

If the translation rules don't make sense for the content, translation can fail in various ways, including:

- The translation mechanism may return a bad return code, and the connection will be aborted.
- The translation mechanism may silently place special characters (e.g., question marks) in the output buffer when it cannot translate the input buffer.

CharsetDefault Directive

Description:	Charset to translate into
Syntax:	`CharsetDefault charset`
Context:	server config, virtual host, directory, .htaccess
Override:	FileInfo
Status:	Extension
Module:	mod_charset_lite

The CHARSETDEFAULT directive specifies the charset that content in the associated container should be translated to.

The value of the *charset* argument must be accepted as a valid character set name by the character set support in APR. Generally, this means that it must be supported by iconv.

Example

```
<Directory "/export/home/trawick/apacheinst/htdocs/convert">
    CharsetSourceEnc  UTF-16BE
    CharsetDefault    ISO-8859-1
</Directory>
```

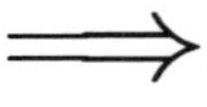

Specifying the same charset for both CHARSETSOURCEENC and CHARSETDEFAULT disables translation. The charset need not match the charset of the response, but it must be a valid charset on the system.

CharsetOptions Directive

Description:	Configures charset translation behavior
Syntax:	`CharsetOptions option [option] ...`
Default:	`CharsetOptions ImplicitAdd`
Context:	server config, virtual host, directory, .htaccess
Override:	FileInfo
Status:	Extension
Module:	mod_charset_lite

The CHARSETOPTIONS directive configures certain behaviors of MOD_CHARSET_LITE. *Option* can be one of

`ImplicitAdd | NoImplicitAdd` The `ImplicitAdd` keyword specifies that MOD_CHARSET_LITE should implicitly insert its filter when the configuration specifies that the character set of content should be translated. If the filter chain is explicitly configured using the ADDOUTPUTFILTER directive, `NoImplicitAdd` should be specified so that MOD_CHARSET_LITE doesn't add its filter.

`TranslateAllMimeTypes | NoTranslateAllMimeTypes` Normally, MOD_CHARSET_LITE will only perform translation on a small subset of possible mimetypes. When the `TranslateAllMimeTypes` keyword is specified for a given configuration section, translation is performed without regard for mimetype.

CharsetSourceEnc Directive

Description:	Source charset of files
Syntax:	`CharsetSourceEnc charset`
Context:	server config, virtual host, directory, .htaccess
Override:	FileInfo
Status:	Extension
Module:	mod_charset_lite

The CHARSETSOURCEENC directive specifies the source charset of files in the associated container.

The value of the *charset* argument must be accepted as a valid character set name by the character set support in APR. Generally, this means that it must be supported by iconv.

Example

```
<Directory "/export/home/trawick/apacheinst/htdocs/convert">
    CharsetSourceEnc  UTF-16BE
    CharsetDefault    ISO-8859-1
</Directory>
```

The character set names in this example work with the iconv translation support in Solaris 8.

⟹ Specifying the same charset for both CHARSETSOURCEENC and CHARSETDEFAULT disables translation. The charset need not match the charset of the response, but it must be a valid charset on the system.

10.36 Apache Module mod_data

Description:	Convert response body into an RFC2397 data URL
Status:	Extension
ModuleIdentifier:	data_module
SourceFile:	mod_data.c
Compatibility:	Available in Apache 2.3 and later

Summary

This module provides the ability to convert a response into an RFC2397 data URL[23].

Data URLs can be embedded inline within web pages using something like the MOD_INCLUDE module, to remove the need for clients to make separate connections to fetch what may potentially be many small images. Data URLs may also be included into pages generated by scripting languages such as PHP.

An example of a data URL


```
data:image/gif;base64,R0lGODdhMAAwAPAAAAAAAP///ywAAAAAMAAw
AAAC8IyPqcvt3wCcDkiLc7C0qwyGHhSWpjQu5yqmCYsapyuvUUlvONmOZtfzgFz
ByTB10QgxOR0TqBQejhRNzOfkVJ+5YiUqrXF5Y5lKh/DeuNcP5yLWGsEbtLiOSp
a/TPg7JpJHxyendzWTBfX0cxOnKPjgBzi4diinWGdkF8kjdfnycQZXZeYGejmJl
ZeGl9i2icVqaNVailT6F5iJ90m6mvuTS4OK05M0vDk0Q4XUtwvKOzrcd3iq9uis
F81M1OIcR7lEewwcLp7tuNNkM3uNna3F2JQFo97Vriy/Xl4/f1cf5VWzXyym7PH
hhx4dbgYKAAA7
```


The filter takes no parameters, and can be added to the filter stack using the SETOUTPUTFILTER directive, or any of the directives supported by the MOD_FILTER module.

Configuring the filter

```
<Location "/data/images">
    SetOutputFilter DATA
</Location>
```

Directives This module provides no directives.

See also

- Filters (p. 100)

[23]http://tools.ietf.org/html/rfc2397

10.37 Apache Module mod_dav

Description:	Distributed Authoring and Versioning (WebDAV[24]) functionality
Status:	Extension
ModuleIdentifier:	dav_module
SourceFile:	mod_dav.c

Summary

This module provides class 1 and class 2 WebDAV[25] ('Web-based Distributed Authoring and Versioning') functionality for Apache. This extension to the HTTP protocol allows creating, moving, copying, and deleting resources and collections on a remote web server.

Directives

- Dav
- DavDepthInfinity
- DavMinTimeout

See also

- DAVLOCKDB
- LIMITXMLREQUESTBODY
- WebDAV Resources[26]

Enabling WebDAV

To enable MOD_DAV, add the following to a container in your `httpd.conf` file:

```
Dav On
```

This enables the DAV file system provider, which is implemented by the MOD_DAV_FS module. Therefore, that module must be compiled into the server or loaded at runtime using the LOADMODULE directive.

In addition, a location for the DAV lock database must be specified in the global section of your `httpd.conf` file using the DAVLOCKDB directive:

```
DavLockDB /usr/local/apache2/var/DavLock
```

The directory containing the lock database file must be writable by the USER and GROUP under which Apache is running.

You may wish to add a <LIMIT> clause inside the <LOCATION> directive to limit access to DAV-enabled locations. If you want to set the maximum amount of bytes that a DAV client can send at one request, you have to use the LIMITXMLREQUESTBODY directive. The "normal" LIMITREQUESTBODY directive has no effect on DAV requests.

[25] http://www.webdav.org
[26] http://www.webdav.org

Full Example

```
DavLockDB "/usr/local/apache2/var/DavLock"

<Directory "/usr/local/apache2/htdocs/foo">
    Require all granted
    Dav On

    AuthType Basic
    AuthName DAV
    AuthUserFile "user.passwd"

    <LimitExcept GET POST OPTIONS>
        Require user admin
    </LimitExcept>
</Directory>
```

Security Issues

Since DAV access methods allow remote clients to manipulate files on the server, you must take particular care to assure that your server is secure before enabling MOD_DAV.

Any location on the server where DAV is enabled should be protected by authentication. The use of HTTP Basic Authentication is not recommended. You should use at least HTTP Digest Authentication, which is provided by the MOD_AUTH_DIGEST module. Nearly all WebDAV clients support this authentication method. An alternative is Basic Authentication over an SSL (p. 182) enabled connection.

In order for MOD_DAV to manage files, it must be able to write to the directories and files under its control using the USER and GROUP under which Apache is running. New files created will also be owned by this USER and GROUP. For this reason, it is important to control access to this account. The DAV repository is considered private to Apache; modifying files outside of Apache (for example using FTP or filesystem-level tools) should not be allowed.

MOD_DAV may be subject to various kinds of denial-of-service attacks. The LIMITXMLREQUESTBODY directive can be used to limit the amount of memory consumed in parsing large DAV requests. The DAVDEPTHINFINITY directive can be used to prevent PROPFIND requests on a very large repository from consuming large amounts of memory. Another possible denial-of-service attack involves a client simply filling up all available disk space with many large files. There is no direct way to prevent this in Apache, so you should avoid giving DAV access to untrusted users.

Complex Configurations

One common request is to use MOD_DAV to manipulate dynamic files (PHP scripts, CGI scripts, etc). This is difficult because a GET request will always run the script, rather than downloading its contents. One way to avoid this is to map two different URLs to the content, one of which will run the script, and one of which will allow it to be downloaded and manipulated with DAV.

```
Alias "/phparea" "/home/gstein/php_files"
Alias "/php-source" "/home/gstein/php_files"
<Location "/php-source">
    Dav On
    ForceType text/plain
</Location>
```

With this setup, `http://example.com/phparea` can be used to access the output of the PHP scripts, and `http://example.com/php-source` can be used with a DAV client to manipulate them.

Dav Directive

Description:	Enable WebDAV HTTP methods
Syntax:	`Dav On|Off|provider-name`
Default:	`Dav Off`
Context:	directory
Status:	Extension
Module:	mod_dav

Use the DAV directive to enable the WebDAV HTTP methods for the given container:

```
<Location "/foo">
    Dav On
</Location>
```

The value `On` is actually an alias for the default provider `filesystem` which is served by the MOD_DAV_FS module. Note, that once you have DAV enabled for some location, it *cannot* be disabled for sublocations. For a complete configuration example have a look at the section above.

! Do not enable WebDAV until you have secured your server. Otherwise everyone will be able to distribute files on your system.

DavDepthInfinity Directive

Description:	Allow PROPFIND, Depth: Infinity requests
Syntax:	`DavDepthInfinity on|off`
Default:	`DavDepthInfinity off`
Context:	server config, virtual host, directory
Status:	Extension
Module:	mod_dav

Use the DAVDEPTHINFINITY directive to allow the processing of `PROPFIND` requests containing the header 'Depth: Infinity'. Because this type of request could constitute a denial-of-service attack, by default it is not allowed.

DavMinTimeout Directive

Description:	Minimum amount of time the server holds a lock on a DAV resource
Syntax:	`DavMinTimeout seconds`
Default:	`DavMinTimeout 0`
Context:	server config, virtual host, directory
Status:	Extension
Module:	mod_dav

When a client requests a DAV resource lock, it can also specify a time when the lock will be automatically removed by the server. This value is only a request, and the server can ignore it or inform the client of an arbitrary value.

Use the DAVMINTIMEOUT directive to specify, in seconds, the minimum lock timeout to return to a client. Microsoft Web Folders defaults to a timeout of 120 seconds; the DAVMINTIMEOUT can override this to a higher value (like 600 seconds) to reduce the chance of the client losing the lock due to network latency.

Example

```
<Location "/MSWord">
    DavMinTimeout 600
</Location>
```

10.38 Apache Module mod_dav_fs

Description:	Filesystem provider for MOD_DAV
Status:	Extension
ModuleIdentifier:	dav_fs_module
SourceFile:	mod_dav_fs.c

Summary

This module *requires* the service of MOD_DAV. It acts as a support module for MOD_DAV and provides access to resources located in the server's file system. The formal name of this provider is `filesystem`. MOD_DAV backend providers will be invoked by using the DAV directive:

Example

```
Dav filesystem
```

Since `filesystem` is the default provider for MOD_DAV, you may simply use the value `On` instead.

Directives

- DavLockDB

See also

- MOD_DAV

DavLockDB Directive

Description:	Location of the DAV lock database
Syntax:	`DavLockDB file-path`
Context:	server config, virtual host
Status:	Extension
Module:	mod_dav_fs

Use the DAVLOCKDB directive to specify the full path to the lock database, excluding an extension. If the path is not absolute, it will be taken relative to SERVERROOT. The implementation of MOD_DAV_FS uses a SDBM database to track user locks.

Example

```
DavLockDB "var/DavLock"
```

The directory containing the lock database file must be writable by the USER and GROUP under which Apache is running. For security reasons, you should create a directory for this purpose rather than changing the permissions on an existing directory. In the above example, Apache will create files in the `var/` directory under the SERVERROOT with the base filename `DavLock` and extension name chosen by the server.

10.39 Apache Module mod_dav_lock

Description:	Generic locking module for MOD_DAV
Status:	Extension
ModuleIdentifier:	dav_lock_module
SourceFile:	mod_dav_lock.c
Compatibility:	Available in version 2.1 and later

Summary

This module implements a generic locking API which can be used by any backend provider of MOD_DAV. It *requires* at least the service of MOD_DAV. But without a backend provider which makes use of it, it's useless and should not be loaded into the server. A sample backend module which actually utilizes MOD_DAV_LOCK is mod_dav_svn[27], the subversion provider module.

Note that MOD_DAV_FS does *not* need this generic locking module, because it uses its own more specialized version.

In order to make MOD_DAV_LOCK functional, you just have to specify the location of the lock database using the DAVGENERICLOCKDB directive described below.

**Developer's Note**

In order to retrieve the pointer to the locking provider function, you have to use the `ap_lookup_provider` API with the arguments `dav-lock`, `generic`, and `0`.

Directives

- DavGenericLockDB

See also

- MOD_DAV

DavGenericLockDB Directive

Description:	Location of the DAV lock database
Syntax:	`DavGenericLockDB file-path`
Context:	server config, virtual host, directory
Status:	Extension
Module:	mod_dav_lock

Use the DAVGENERICLOCKDB directive to specify the full path to the lock database, excluding an extension. If the path is not absolute, it will be interpreted relative to SERVERROOT. The implementation of MOD_DAV_LOCK uses a SDBM database to track user locks.

Example

```
DavGenericLockDB var/DavLock
```

The directory containing the lock database file must be writable by the USER and GROUP under which Apache is running. For security reasons, you should create a directory for this purpose rather than changing the permissions on an existing directory. In the above example, Apache will create files in the `var/` directory under the SERVERROOT with the base filename `DavLock` and an extension added by the server.

[27] http://subversion.apache.org/

10.40 Apache Module mod_dbd

Description:	Manages SQL database connections
Status:	Extension
ModuleIdentifier:	dbd_module
SourceFile:	mod_dbd.c
Compatibility:	Version 2.1 and later

Summary

MOD_DBD manages SQL database connections using APR. It provides database connections on request to modules requiring SQL database functions, and takes care of managing databases with optimal efficiency and scalability for both threaded and non-threaded MPMs. For details, see the APR[28] website and this overview of the Apache DBD Framework[29] by its original developer.

Directives

- DBDExptime
- DBDInitSQL
- DBDKeep
- DBDMax
- DBDMin
- DBDParams
- DBDPersist
- DBDPrepareSQL
- DBDriver

See also

- Password Formats (p. 345)

Connection Pooling

This module manages database connections, in a manner optimised for the platform. On non-threaded platforms, it provides a persistent connection in the manner of classic LAMP (Linux, Apache, Mysql, Perl/PHP/Python). On threaded platform, it provides an altogether more scalable and efficient *connection pool*, as described in this article at ApacheTutor[30]. Note that MOD_DBD supersedes the modules presented in that article.

Apache DBD API

MOD_DBD exports five functions for other modules to use. The API is as follows:

```
typedef struct {
    apr_dbd_t *handle;
    apr_dbd_driver_t *driver;
```

[28] http://apr.apache.org/
[29] http://people.apache.org/~niq/dbd.html
[30] http://www.apachetutor.org/dev/reslist

```
    apr_hash_t *prepared;
} ap_dbd_t;

/* Export functions to access the database */

/* acquire a connection that MUST be explicitly closed.
 * Returns NULL on error
 */
AP_DECLARE(ap_dbd_t*) ap_dbd_open(apr_pool_t*, server_rec*);

/* release a connection acquired with ap_dbd_open */
AP_DECLARE(void) ap_dbd_close(server_rec*, ap_dbd_t*);

/* acquire a connection that will have the lifetime of a request
 * and MUST NOT be explicitly closed.  Return NULL on error.
 * This is the preferred function for most applications.
 */
AP_DECLARE(ap_dbd_t*) ap_dbd_acquire(request_rec*);

/* acquire a connection that will have the lifetime of a connection
 * and MUST NOT be explicitly closed.  Return NULL on error.
 */
AP_DECLARE(ap_dbd_t*) ap_dbd_cacquire(conn_rec*);

/* Prepare a statement for use by a client module */
AP_DECLARE(void) ap_dbd_prepare(server_rec*, const char*, const char*);

/* Also export them as optional functions for modules that prefer it */
APR_DECLARE_OPTIONAL_FN(ap_dbd_t*, ap_dbd_open, (apr_pool_t*, server_rec*));
APR_DECLARE_OPTIONAL_FN(void, ap_dbd_close, (server_rec*, ap_dbd_t*));
APR_DECLARE_OPTIONAL_FN(ap_dbd_t*, ap_dbd_acquire, (request_rec*));
APR_DECLARE_OPTIONAL_FN(ap_dbd_t*, ap_dbd_cacquire, (conn_rec*));
APR_DECLARE_OPTIONAL_FN(void, ap_dbd_prepare, (server_rec*, const char*, const
```

SQL Prepared Statements

MOD_DBD supports SQL prepared statements on behalf of modules that may wish to use them. Each prepared statement must be assigned a name (label), and they are stored in a hash: the `prepared` field of an `ap_dbd_t`. Hash entries are of type `apr_dbd_prepared_t` and can be used in any of the apr_dbd prepared statement SQL query or select commands.

It is up to dbd user modules to use the prepared statements and document what statements can be specified in httpd.conf, or to provide their own directives and use `ap_dbd_prepare`.

Caveat
When using prepared statements with a MySQL database, it is preferred to set `reconnect` to 0 in the connection string as to avoid errors that arise from the MySQL client reconnecting without properly resetting the prepared statements. If set to 1, any broken connections will be attempted fixed, but as mod_dbd is not informed, the prepared statements will be invalidated.

SECURITY WARNING

Any web/database application needs to secure itself against SQL injection attacks. In most cases, Apache DBD is safe, because applications use prepared statements, and untrusted inputs are only ever used as data. Of course, if you use it via third-party modules, you should ascertain what precautions they may require.

However, the *FreeTDS* driver is inherently **unsafe**. The underlying library doesn't support prepared statements, so the driver emulates them, and the untrusted input is merged into the SQL statement.

It can be made safe by *untainting* all inputs: a process inspired by Perl's taint checking. Each input is matched against a regexp, and only the match is used, according to the Perl idiom:

```
$untrusted =~ /([a-z]+)/;
$trusted = $1;
```

To use this, the untainting regexps must be included in the prepared statements configured. The regexp follows immediately after the % in the prepared statement, and is enclosed in curly brackets {}. For example, if your application expects alphanumeric input, you can use:

```
"SELECT foo FROM bar WHERE input = %s"
```

with other drivers, and suffer nothing worse than a failed query. But with FreeTDS you'd need:

```
"SELECT foo FROM bar WHERE input = %{([A-Za-z0-9]+)}s"
```

Now anything that doesn't match the regexp's $1 match is discarded, so the statement is safe.

An alternative to this may be the third-party ODBC driver, which offers the security of genuine prepared statements.

DBDExptime Directive

Description:	Keepalive time for idle connections
Syntax:	`DBDExptime time-in-seconds`
Default:	`DBDExptime 300`
Context:	server config, virtual host
Status:	Extension
Module:	mod_dbd

Set the time to keep idle connections alive when the number of connections specified in DBDKeep has been exceeded (threaded platforms only).

DBDInitSQL Directive

Description:	Execute an SQL statement after connecting to a database
Syntax:	`DBDInitSQL "SQL statement"`
Context:	server config, virtual host
Status:	Extension
Module:	mod_dbd

Modules, that wish it, can have one or more SQL statements executed when a connection to a database is created. Example usage could be initializing certain values or adding a log entry when a new connection is made to the database.

DBDKeep Directive

Description:	Maximum sustained number of connections
Syntax:	`DBDKeep number`
Default:	`DBDKeep 2`
Context:	server config, virtual host
Status:	Extension
Module:	mod_dbd

Set the maximum number of connections per process to be sustained, other than for handling peak demand (threaded platforms only).

DBDMax Directive

Description:	Maximum number of connections
Syntax:	`DBDMax number`
Default:	`DBDMax 10`
Context:	server config, virtual host
Status:	Extension
Module:	mod_dbd

Set the hard maximum number of connections per process (threaded platforms only).

DBDMin Directive

Description:	Minimum number of connections
Syntax:	`DBDMin number`
Default:	`DBDMin 1`
Context:	server config, virtual host
Status:	Extension
Module:	mod_dbd

Set the minimum number of connections per process (threaded platforms only).

DBDParams Directive

Description:	Parameters for database connection
Syntax:	`DBDParams param1=value1[,param2=value2]`
Context:	server config, virtual host
Status:	Extension
Module:	mod_dbd

As required by the underlying driver. Typically this will be used to pass whatever cannot be defaulted amongst username, password, database name, hostname and port number for connection.

Connection string parameters for current drivers include:

FreeTDS (for MSSQL and SyBase) username, password, appname, dbname, host, charset, lang, server

MySQL host, port, user, pass, dbname, sock, flags, fldsz, group, reconnect

Oracle user, pass, dbname, server

PostgreSQL The connection string is passed straight through to `PQconnectdb`

SQLite2 The connection string is split on a colon, and `part1:part2` is used as `sqlite_open(part1, atoi(part2), NULL)`

SQLite3 The connection string is passed straight through to `sqlite3_open`

ODBC datasource, user, password, connect, ctimeout, stimeout, access, txmode, bufsize

DBDPersist Directive

Description:	Whether to use persistent connections
Syntax:	`DBDPersist On|Off`
Context:	server config, virtual host
Status:	Extension
Module:	mod_dbd

If set to Off, persistent and pooled connections are disabled. A new database connection is opened when requested by a client, and closed immediately on release. This option is for debugging and low-usage servers.

The default is to enable a pool of persistent connections (or a single LAMP-style persistent connection in the case of a non-threaded server), and should almost always be used in operation.

Prior to version 2.2.2, this directive accepted only the values `0` and `1` instead of `Off` and `On`, respectively.

DBDPrepareSQL Directive

Description:	Define an SQL prepared statement
Syntax:	`DBDPrepareSQL "SQL statement" label`
Context:	server config, virtual host
Status:	Extension
Module:	mod_dbd

For modules such as authentication that repeatedly use a single SQL statement, optimum performance is achieved by preparing the statement at startup rather than every time it is used. This directive prepares an SQL statement and assigns it a label.

DBDriver Directive

Description:	Specify an SQL driver
Syntax:	`DBDriver name`
Context:	server config, virtual host
Status:	Extension
Module:	mod_dbd

Selects an apr_dbd driver by name. The driver must be installed on your system (on most systems, it will be a shared object or dll). For example, `DBDriver mysql` will select the MySQL driver in apr_dbd_mysql.so.

10.41 Apache Module mod_deflate

Description:	Compress content before it is delivered to the client
Status:	Extension
ModuleIdentifier:	deflate_module
SourceFile:	mod_deflate.c

Summary

The MOD_DEFLATE module provides the DEFLATE output filter that allows output from your server to be compressed before being sent to the client over the network.

Directives

- DeflateBufferSize
- DeflateCompressionLevel
- DeflateFilterNote
- DeflateInflateLimitRequestBody
- DeflateInflateRatioBurst
- DeflateInflateRatioLimit
- DeflateMemLevel
- DeflateWindowSize

See also

- Filters (p. 100)

Sample Configurations

Compression and TLS
Some web applications are vulnerable to an information disclosure attack when a TLS connection carries deflate compressed data. For more information, review the details of the "BREACH" family of attacks.

This is a simple configuration that compresses common text-based content types.

Compress only a few types

```
AddOutputFilterByType DEFLATE text/html text/plain text/xml text/css text/javas
```

Enabling Compression

Compression and TLS
Some web applications are vulnerable to an information disclosure attack when a TLS connection carries deflate compressed data. For more information, review the details of the "BREACH" family of attacks.

Output Compression

Compression is implemented by the DEFLATE filter (p. 100) . The following directive will enable compression for documents in the container where it is placed:

```
SetOutputFilter DEFLATE
SetEnvIfNoCase Request_URI "\.(?:gif|jpe?g|png)$" no-gzip
```

If you want to restrict the compression to particular MIME types in general, you may use the ADDOUTPUTFILTER-BYTYPE directive. Here is an example of enabling compression only for the html files of the Apache documentation:

```
<Directory "/your-server-root/manual">
    AddOutputFilterByType DEFLATE text/html
</Directory>
```

**Note**

The DEFLATE filter is always inserted after RESOURCE filters like PHP or SSI. It never touches internal subrequests.

**Note**

There is an environment variable force-gzip, set via SETENV, which will ignore the accept-encoding setting of your browser and will send compressed output.

Output Decompression

The MOD_DEFLATE module also provides a filter for inflating/uncompressing a gzip compressed response body. In order to activate this feature you have to insert the INFLATE filter into the output filter chain using SETOUTPUTFILTER or ADDOUTPUTFILTER, for example:

```
<Location "/dav-area">
    ProxyPass "http://example.com/"
    SetOutputFilter INFLATE
</Location>
```

This Example will uncompress gzip'ed output from example.com, so other filters can do further processing with it.

Input Decompression

The MOD_DEFLATE module also provides a filter for decompressing a gzip compressed request body . In order to activate this feature you have to insert the DEFLATE filter into the input filter chain using SETINPUTFILTER or ADDINPUTFILTER, for example:

```
<Location "/dav-area">
    SetInputFilter DEFLATE
</Location>
```

Now if a request contains a `Content-Encoding: gzip` header, the body will be automatically decompressed. Few browsers have the ability to gzip request bodies. However, some special applications actually do support request compression, for instance some WebDAV[31] clients.

[31] http://www.webdav.org

Note on Content-Length
If you evaluate the request body yourself, *don't trust the* `Content-Length` *header!* The Content-Length header reflects the length of the incoming data from the client and *not* the byte count of the decompressed data stream.

Dealing with proxy servers

The MOD_DEFLATE module sends a `Vary: Accept-Encoding` HTTP response header to alert proxies that a cached response should be sent only to clients that send the appropriate `Accept-Encoding` request header. This prevents compressed content from being sent to a client that will not understand it.

If you use some special exclusions dependent on, for example, the `User-Agent` header, you must manually configure an addition to the `Vary` header to alert proxies of the additional restrictions. For example, in a typical configuration where the addition of the `DEFLATE` filter depends on the `User-Agent`, you should add:

```
Header append Vary User-Agent
```

If your decision about compression depends on other information than request headers (*e.g.* HTTP version), you have to set the `Vary` header to the value `*`. This prevents compliant proxies from caching entirely.

Example

```
Header set Vary *
```

Serving pre-compressed content

Since MOD_DEFLATE re-compresses content each time a request is made, some performance benefit can be derived by pre-compressing the content and telling mod_deflate to serve them without re-compressing them. This may be accomplished using a configuration like the following:

```
<IfModule mod_headers.c>
    # Serve gzip compressed CSS files if they exist
    # and the client accepts gzip.
    RewriteCond "%{HTTP:Accept-encoding}" "gzip"
    RewriteCond "%{REQUEST_FILENAME}\.gz" -s
    RewriteRule "^(.*)\.css" "$1\.css\.gz" [QSA]

    # Serve gzip compressed JS files if they exist
    # and the client accepts gzip.
    RewriteCond "%{HTTP:Accept-encoding}" "gzip"
    RewriteCond "%{REQUEST_FILENAME}\.gz" -s
    RewriteRule "^(.*)\.js" "$1\.js\.gz" [QSA]


    # Serve correct content types, and prevent mod_deflate double gzip.
    RewriteRule "\.css\.gz$" "-" [T=text/css,E=no-gzip:1]
    RewriteRule "\.js\.gz$" "-" [T=text/javascript,E=no-gzip:1]


    <FilesMatch "(\.js\.gz|\.css\.gz)$">
```

```
        # Serve correct encoding type.
        Header append Content-Encoding gzip

        # Force proxies to cache gzipped &
        # non-gzipped css/js files separately.
        Header append Vary Accept-Encoding
    </FilesMatch>
</IfModule>
```

DeflateBufferSize Directive

Description:	Fragment size to be compressed at one time by zlib
Syntax:	`DeflateBufferSize value`
Default:	`DeflateBufferSize 8096`
Context:	server config, virtual host
Status:	Extension
Module:	mod_deflate

The DEFLATEBUFFERSIZE directive specifies the size in bytes of the fragments that zlib should compress at one time.

DeflateCompressionLevel Directive

Description:	How much compression do we apply to the output
Syntax:	`DeflateCompressionLevel value`
Default:	`Zlib's default`
Context:	server config, virtual host
Status:	Extension
Module:	mod_deflate

The DEFLATECOMPRESSIONLEVEL directive specifies what level of compression should be used, the higher the value, the better the compression, but the more CPU time is required to achieve this.

The value must between 1 (less compression) and 9 (more compression).

DeflateFilterNote Directive

Description:	Places the compression ratio in a note for logging
Syntax:	`DeflateFilterNote [type] notename`
Context:	server config, virtual host
Status:	Extension
Module:	mod_deflate

The DEFLATEFILTERNOTE directive specifies that a note about compression ratios should be attached to the request. The name of the note is the value specified for the directive. You can use that note for statistical purposes by adding the value to your access log (p. 53) .

Example

```
DeflateFilterNote ratio

LogFormat '"%r" %b (%{ratio}n) "%{User-agent}i"' deflate
CustomLog "logs/deflate_log" deflate
```

If you want to extract more accurate values from your logs, you can use the *type* argument to specify the type of data left as a note for logging. *type* can be one of:

Input Store the byte count of the filter's input stream in the note.

Output Store the byte count of the filter's output stream in the note.

Ratio Store the compression ratio (`output/input * 100`) in the note. This is the default, if the *type* argument is omitted.

Thus you may log it this way:

Accurate Logging

```
DeflateFilterNote Input instream
DeflateFilterNote Output outstream
DeflateFilterNote Ratio ratio

LogFormat '"%r" %{outstream}n/%{instream}n (%{ratio}n%%)' deflate
CustomLog "logs/deflate_log" deflate
```

See also

- MOD_LOG_CONFIG

DeflateInflateLimitRequestBody Directive

Description:	Maximum size of inflated request bodies
Syntax:	`DeflateInflateLimitRequestBodyvalue`
Default:	`None, but LimitRequestBody applies after deflation`
Context:	server config, virtual host, directory, .htaccess
Status:	Extension
Module:	mod_deflate
Compatibility:	2.4.10 and later

The DEFLATEINFLATELIMITREQUESTBODY directive specifies the maximum size of an inflated request body. If it is unset, LIMITREQUESTBODY is applied to the inflated body.

DeflateInflateRatioBurst Directive

Description:	Maximum number of times the inflation ratio for request bodies can be crossed
Syntax:	`DeflateInflateRatioBurst value`
Default:	`3`
Context:	server config, virtual host, directory, .htaccess
Status:	Extension
Module:	mod_deflate
Compatibility:	2.4.10 and later

The DEFLATEINFLATERATIOBURST directive specifies the maximum number of times the DEFLATEINFLATERATIOLIMIT can be crossed before terminating the request.

DeflateInflateRatioLimit Directive

Description:	Maximum inflation ratio for request bodies
Syntax:	`DeflateInflateRatioLimit value`
Default:	`200`
Context:	server config, virtual host, directory, .htaccess
Status:	Extension
Module:	mod_deflate
Compatibility:	2.4.10 and later

The DEFLATEINFLATERATIOLIMIT directive specifies the maximum ratio of deflated to inflated size of an inflated request body. This ratio is checked as the body is streamed in, and if crossed more than DEFLATEINFLATERATIOBURST times, the request will be terminated.

DeflateMemLevel Directive

Description:	How much memory should be used by zlib for compression
Syntax:	`DeflateMemLevel value`
Default:	`DeflateMemLevel 9`
Context:	server config, virtual host
Status:	Extension
Module:	mod_deflate

The DEFLATEMEMLEVEL directive specifies how much memory should be used by zlib for compression (a value between 1 and 9).

DeflateWindowSize Directive

Description:	Zlib compression window size
Syntax:	`DeflateWindowSize value`
Default:	`DeflateWindowSize 15`
Context:	server config, virtual host
Status:	Extension
Module:	mod_deflate

The DEFLATEWINDOWSIZE directive specifies the zlib compression window size (a value between 1 and 15). Generally, the higher the window size, the higher can the compression ratio be expected.

10.42 Apache Module mod_dialup

Description:	Send static content at a bandwidth rate limit, defined by the various old modem standards
Status:	Experimental
ModuleIdentifier:	dialup_module
SourceFile:	mod_dialup.c

Summary

It is a module that sends static content at a bandwidth rate limit, defined by the various old modem standards. So, you can browse your site with a 56k V.92 modem, by adding something like this:

```
<Location "/mysite">
    ModemStandard "V.92"
</Location>
```

Previously to do bandwidth rate limiting modules would have to block an entire thread, for each client, and insert sleeps to slow the bandwidth down. Using the new suspend feature, a handler can get callback N milliseconds in the future, and it will be invoked by the Event MPM on a different thread, once the timer hits. From there the handler can continue to send data to the client.

Directives

- ModemStandard

ModemStandard Directive

Description:	Modem standard to simulate
Syntax:	`ModemStandard V.21|V.26bis|V.32|V.92`
Context:	directory
Status:	Experimental
Module:	mod_dialup

Specify what modem standard you wish to simulate.

```
<Location "/mysite">
    ModemStandard "V.26bis"
</Location>
```

10.43 Apache Module mod_dir

Description:	Provides for "trailing slash" redirects and serving directory index files
Status:	Base
ModuleIdentifier:	dir_module
SourceFile:	mod_dir.c

Summary

The index of a directory can come from one of two sources:

- A file written by the user, typically called `index.html`. The DIRECTORYINDEX directive sets the name of this file. This is controlled by MOD_DIR.
- Otherwise, a listing generated by the server. This is provided by MOD_AUTOINDEX.

The two functions are separated so that you can completely remove (or replace) automatic index generation should you want to.

A "trailing slash" redirect is issued when the server receives a request for a URL `http://servername/foo/dirname` where `dirname` is a directory. Directories require a trailing slash, so MOD_DIR issues a redirect to `http://servername/foo/dirname/`.

Directives

- DirectoryCheckHandler
- DirectoryIndex
- DirectoryIndexRedirect
- DirectorySlash
- FallbackResource

DirectoryCheckHandler Directive

Description:	Toggle how this module responds when another handler is configured
Syntax:	`DirectoryCheckHandler On|Off`
Default:	`DirectoryCheckHandler Off`
Context:	server config, virtual host, directory, .htaccess
Override:	Indexes
Status:	Base
Module:	mod_dir
Compatibility:	Available in 2.4.8 and later. Releases prior to 2.4 implicitly act as if "DirectoryCheckHandler ON" was specified.

The DIRECTORYCHECKHANDLER directive determines whether MOD_DIR should check for directory indexes or add trailing slashes when some other handler has been configured for the current URL. Handlers can be set by directives such as SETHANDLER or by other modules, such as MOD_REWRITE during per-directory substitutions.

In releases prior to 2.4, this module did not take any action if any other handler was configured for a URL. This allows directory indexes to be served even when a SETHANDLER directive is specified for an entire directory, but it can also result in some conflicts with modules such as MOD_REWRITE.

DirectoryIndex Directive

Description:	List of resources to look for when the client requests a directory
Syntax:	`DirectoryIndex disabled	local-url [local-url] ...`
Default:	`DirectoryIndex index.html`
Context:	server config, virtual host, directory, .htaccess
Override:	Indexes
Status:	Base
Module:	mod_dir

The DIRECTORYINDEX directive sets the list of resources to look for, when the client requests an index of the directory by specifying a / at the end of the directory name. *Local-url* is the (%-encoded) URL of a document on the server relative to the requested directory; it is usually the name of a file in the directory. Several URLs may be given, in which case the server will return the first one that it finds. If none of the resources exist and the `Indexes` option is set, the server will generate its own listing of the directory.

Example

```
DirectoryIndex index.html
```

then a request for `http://example.com/docs/` would return `http://example.com/docs/index.html` if it exists, or would list the directory if it did not.

Note that the documents do not need to be relative to the directory;

```
DirectoryIndex index.html index.txt  /cgi-bin/index.pl
```

would cause the CGI script `/cgi-bin/index.pl` to be executed if neither `index.html` or `index.txt` existed in a directory.

A single argument of "disabled" prevents MOD_DIR from searching for an index. An argument of "disabled" will be interpreted literally if it has any arguments before or after it, even if they are "disabled" as well.

Note: Multiple DIRECTORYINDEX directives within the *same context* (p. 33) will add to the list of resources to look for rather than replace:

```
# Example A: Set index.html as an index page, then add index.php to that list a
<Directory "/foo">
    DirectoryIndex index.html
    DirectoryIndex index.php
</Directory>

# Example B: This is identical to example A, except it's done with a single dir
<Directory "/foo">
    DirectoryIndex index.html index.php
</Directory>

# Example C: To replace the list, you must explicitly reset it first:
# In this example, only index.php will remain as an index resource.
<Directory "/foo">
    DirectoryIndex index.html
    DirectoryIndex disabled
    DirectoryIndex index.php
</Directory>
```

DirectoryIndexRedirect Directive

Description:	Configures an external redirect for directory indexes.
Syntax:	`DirectoryIndexRedirect on | off | permanent | temp | seeother | 3xx-code`
Default:	`DirectoryIndexRedirect off`
Context:	server config, virtual host, directory, .htaccess
Override:	Indexes
Status:	Base
Module:	mod_dir
Compatibility:	Available in version 2.3.14 and later

By default, the DIRECTORYINDEX is selected and returned transparently to the client. DIRECTORYINDEXREDIRECT causes an external redirect to instead be issued.

The argument can be:

- `on`: issues a 302 redirection to the index resource.
- `off`: does not issue a redirection. This is the legacy behaviour of mod_dir.
- `permanent`: issues a 301 (permanent) redirection to the index resource.
- `temp`: this has the same effect as `on`
- `seeother`: issues a 303 redirection (also known as "See Other") to the index resource.
- *3xx-code*: issues a redirection marked by the chosen 3xx code.

Example

```
DirectoryIndexRedirect on
```

A request for `http://example.com/docs/` would return a temporary redirect to `http://example.com/docs/index.html` if it exists.

DirectorySlash Directive

Description:	Toggle trailing slash redirects on or off
Syntax:	`DirectorySlash On|Off`
Default:	`DirectorySlash On`
Context:	server config, virtual host, directory, .htaccess
Override:	Indexes
Status:	Base
Module:	mod_dir

The DIRECTORYSLASH directive determines whether MOD_DIR should fixup URLs pointing to a directory or not.

Typically if a user requests a resource without a trailing slash, which points to a directory, MOD_DIR redirects him to the same resource, but *with* trailing slash for some good reasons:

- The user is finally requesting the canonical URL of the resource
- MOD_AUTOINDEX works correctly. Since it doesn't emit the path in the link, it would point to the wrong path.
- DIRECTORYINDEX will be evaluated *only* for directories requested with trailing slash.
- Relative URL references inside html pages will work correctly.

If you don't want this effect *and* the reasons above don't apply to you, you can turn off the redirect as shown below. However, be aware that there are possible security implications to doing this.

```
# see security warning below!
<Location "/some/path">
    DirectorySlash Off
    SetHandler some-handler
</Location>
```

Security Warning
Turning off the trailing slash redirect may result in an information disclosure. Consider a situation where MOD_AUTOINDEX is active (`Options +Indexes`) and DIRECTORYINDEX is set to a valid resource (say, `index.html`) and there's no other special handler defined for that URL. In this case a request with a trailing slash would show the `index.html` file. **But a request without trailing slash would list the directory contents**.

Also note that some browsers may erroneously change POST requests into GET (thus discarding POST data) when a redirect is issued.

FallbackResource Directive

Description:	Define a default URL for requests that don't map to a file
Syntax:	`FallbackResource disabled | local-url`
Default:	`disabled - httpd will return 404 (Not Found)`
Context:	server config, virtual host, directory, .htaccess
Override:	Indexes
Status:	Base
Module:	mod_dir
Compatibility:	The `disabled` argument is available in version 2.4.4 and later

Use this to set a handler for any URL that doesn't map to anything in your filesystem, and would otherwise return HTTP 404 (Not Found). For example

```
FallbackResource /not-404.php
```

will cause requests for non-existent files to be handled by `not-404.php`, while requests for files that exist are unaffected.

It is frequently desirable to have a single file or resource handle all requests to a particular directory, except those requests that correspond to an existing file or script. This is often referred to as a 'front controller.'

In earlier versions of httpd, this effect typically required MOD_REWRITE, and the use of the `-f` and `-d` tests for file and directory existence. This now requires only one line of configuration.

```
FallbackResource /index.php
```

Existing files, such as images, css files, and so on, will be served normally.

Use the `disabled` argument to disable that feature if inheritance from a parent directory is not desired.

In a sub-URI, such as *http://example.com/blog/* this *sub-URI* has to be supplied as *local-url*:

```
<Directory "/web/example.com/htdocs/blog">
    FallbackResource /blog/index.php
```

```
</Directory>
<Directory "/web/example.com/htdocs/blog/images">
    FallbackResource disabled
</Directory>
```

10.44 Apache Module mod_dumpio

Description:	Dumps all I/O to error log as desired.
Status:	Extension
ModuleIdentifier:	dumpio_module
SourceFile:	mod_dumpio.c

Summary

`mod_dumpio` allows for the logging of all input received by Apache and/or all output sent by Apache to be logged (dumped) to the error.log file.

The data logging is done right after SSL decoding (for input) and right before SSL encoding (for output). As can be expected, this can produce extreme volumes of data, and should only be used when debugging problems.

Directives

- DumpIOInput
- DumpIOOutput

Enabling dumpio Support

To enable the module, it should be compiled and loaded in to your running Apache configuration. Logging can then be enabled or disabled separately for input and output via the below directives. Additionally, MOD_DUMPIO needs to be configured to LOGLEVEL `trace7`:

```
LogLevel dumpio:trace7
```

DumpIOInput Directive

Description:	Dump all input data to the error log
Syntax:	`DumpIOInput On|Off`
Default:	`DumpIOInput Off`
Context:	server config
Status:	Extension
Module:	mod_dumpio
Compatibility:	DumpIOInput is only available in Apache 2.1.3 and later.

Enable dumping of all input.

Example

```
DumpIOInput On
```

DumpIOOutput Directive

Description:	Dump all output data to the error log
Syntax:	`DumpIOOutput On|Off`
Default:	`DumpIOOutput Off`
Context:	server config
Status:	Extension
Module:	mod_dumpio
Compatibility:	DumpIOOutput is only available in Apache 2.1.3 and later.

Enable dumping of all output.

Example

```
DumpIOOutput On
```

10.45 Apache Module mod_echo

Description:	A simple echo server to illustrate protocol modules
Status:	Experimental
ModuleIdentifier:	echo_module
SourceFile:	mod_echo.c

Summary

This module provides an example protocol module to illustrate the concept. It provides a simple echo server. Telnet to it and type stuff, and it will echo it.

Directives

- ProtocolEcho

ProtocolEcho Directive

Description:	Turn the echo server on or off
Syntax:	`ProtocolEcho On|Off`
Default:	`ProtocolEcho Off`
Context:	server config, virtual host
Status:	Experimental
Module:	mod_echo

The PROTOCOLECHO directive enables or disables the echo server.

Example

```
ProtocolEcho On
```

10.46 Apache Module mod_env

Description:	Modifies the environment which is passed to CGI scripts and SSI pages
Status:	Base
ModuleIdentifier:	env_module
SourceFile:	mod_env.c

Summary

This module allows for control of internal environment variables that are used by various Apache HTTP Server modules. These variables are also provided to CGI scripts as native system environment variables, and available for use in SSI pages. Environment variables may be passed from the shell which invoked the `httpd` process. Alternatively, environment variables may be set or unset within the configuration process.

Directives

- PassEnv
- SetEnv
- UnsetEnv

See also

- Environment Variables (p. 82)
- SETENVIF

PassEnv Directive

Description:	Passes environment variables from the shell
Syntax:	`PassEnv env-variable [env-variable] ...`
Context:	server config, virtual host, directory, .htaccess
Override:	FileInfo
Status:	Base
Module:	mod_env

Specifies one or more native system environment variables to make available as internal environment variables, which are available to Apache HTTP Server modules as well as propagated to CGI scripts and SSI pages. Values come from the native OS environment of the shell which invoked the `httpd` process.

Example

```
PassEnv LD_LIBRARY_PATH
```

SetEnv Directive

Description:	Sets environment variables
Syntax:	`SetEnv env-variable [value]`
Context:	server config, virtual host, directory, .htaccess
Override:	FileInfo
Status:	Base
Module:	mod_env

Sets an internal environment variable, which is then available to Apache HTTP Server modules, and passed on to CGI scripts and SSI pages.

Example

```
SetEnv SPECIAL_PATH /foo/bin
```

If you omit the *value* argument, the variable is set to an empty string.

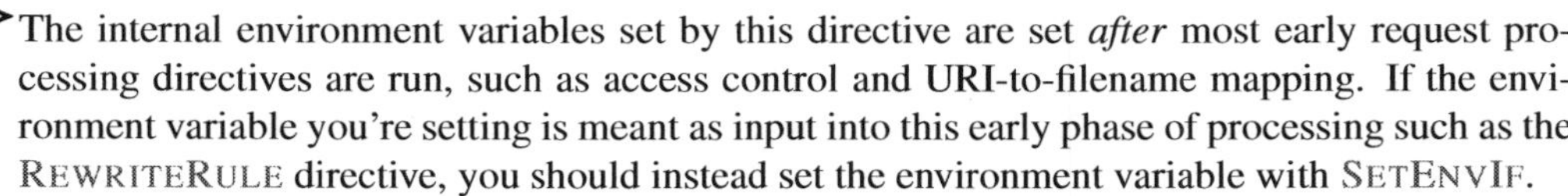

⟹ The internal environment variables set by this directive are set *after* most early request processing directives are run, such as access control and URI-to-filename mapping. If the environment variable you're setting is meant as input into this early phase of processing such as the REWRITERULE directive, you should instead set the environment variable with SETENVIF.

See also

- Environment Variables (p. 82)

UnsetEnv Directive

Description:	Removes variables from the environment
Syntax:	`UnsetEnv env-variable [env-variable] ...`
Context:	server config, virtual host, directory, .htaccess
Override:	FileInfo
Status:	Base
Module:	mod_env

Removes one or more internal environment variables from those passed on to CGI scripts and SSI pages.

Example

```
UnsetEnv LD_LIBRARY_PATH
```

10.47 Apache Module mod_example_hooks

Description:	Illustrates the Apache module API
Status:	Experimental
ModuleIdentifier:	example_hooks_module
SourceFile:	mod_example_hooks.c

Summary

The files in the `modules/examples` directory under the Apache distribution directory tree are provided as an example to those that wish to write modules that use the Apache API.

The main file is `mod_example_hooks.c`, which illustrates all the different callback mechanisms and call syntaxes. By no means does an add-on module need to include routines for all of the callbacks - quite the contrary!

The example module is an actual working module. If you link it into your server, enable the "example-hooks-handler" handler for a location, and then browse to that location, you will see a display of some of the tracing the example module did as the various callbacks were made.

Directives

- Example

Compiling the example_hooks module

To include the example_hooks module in your server, follow the steps below:

1. Run `configure` with `--enable-example-hooks` option.
2. Make the server (run "`make`").

To add another module of your own:

1. `cp modules/examples/mod_example_hooks.c modules/new_module/`*`mod_myexample.c`*
2. Modify the file.
3. Create `modules/new_module/config.m4`.
   (a) Add `APACHE_MODPATH_INIT(new_module)`.
   (b) Copy APACHE_MODULE line with "example_hooks" from `modules/examples/config.m4`.
   (c) Replace the first argument "example_hooks" with *myexample*.
   (d) Replace the second argument with brief description of your module. It will be used in `configure --help`.
   (e) If your module needs additional C compiler flags, linker flags or libraries, add them to CFLAGS, LDFLAGS and LIBS accordingly. See other `config.m4` files in modules directory for examples.
   (f) Add `APACHE_MODPATH_FINISH`.
4. Create `module/new_module/Makefile.in`. If your module doesn't need special build instructions, all you need to have in that file is `include $(top_srcdir)/build/special.mk`.
5. Run ./buildconf from the top-level directory.
6. Build the server with –enable-myexample

Using the mod_example_hooks Module

To activate the example_hooks module, include a block similar to the following in your `httpd.conf` file:

```
<Location "/example-hooks-info">
   SetHandler example-hooks-handler
</Location>
```

As an alternative, you can put the following into a `.htaccess` (p. 354) file and then request the file "test.example" from that location:

```
AddHandler example-hooks-handler ".example"
```

After reloading/restarting your server, you should be able to browse to this location and see the brief display mentioned earlier.

Example Directive

Description:	Demonstration directive to illustrate the Apache module API
Syntax:	`Example`
Context:	server config, virtual host, directory, .htaccess
Status:	Experimental
Module:	mod_example_hooks

The EXAMPLE directive just sets a demonstration flag which the example module's content handler displays. It takes no arguments. If you browse to an URL to which the example-hooks content-handler applies, you will get a display of the routines within the module and how and in what order they were called to service the document request. The effect of this directive one can observe under the point "`Example directive declared here:  YES/NO`".

10.48 Apache Module mod_expires

Description:	Generation of Expires and Cache-Control HTTP headers according to user-specified criteria
Status:	Extension
ModuleIdentifier:	expires_module
SourceFile:	mod_expires.c

Summary

This module controls the setting of the Expires HTTP header and the max-age directive of the Cache-Control HTTP header in server responses. The expiration date can set to be relative to either the time the source file was last modified, or to the time of the client access.

These HTTP headers are an instruction to the client about the document's validity and persistence. If cached, the document may be fetched from the cache rather than from the source until this time has passed. After that, the cache copy is considered "expired" and invalid, and a new copy must be obtained from the source.

To modify Cache-Control directives other than max-age (see RFC 2616 section 14.9[32]), you can use the HEADER directive.

When the Expires header is already part of the response generated by the server, for example when generated by a CGI script or proxied from an origin server, this module does not change or add an Expires or Cache-Control header.

Directives

- ExpiresActive
- ExpiresByType
- ExpiresDefault

Alternate Interval Syntax

The EXPIRESDEFAULT and EXPIRESBYTYPE directives can also be defined in a more readable syntax of the form:

```
ExpiresDefault "base  [plus num type] [num type] ..."
ExpiresByType type/encoding "base  [plus num type] [num type] ..."
```

where *base* is one of:

- access
- now (equivalent to 'access')
- modification

The plus keyword is optional. *num* should be an integer value [acceptable to atoi()], and *type* is one of:

- years
- months
- weeks

[32] http://www.w3.org/Protocols/rfc2616/rfc2616-sec14.html#sec14.9

- days
- hours
- minutes
- seconds

For example, any of the following directives can be used to make documents expire 1 month after being accessed, by default:

```
ExpiresDefault "access plus 1 month"
ExpiresDefault "access plus 4 weeks"
ExpiresDefault "access plus 30 days"
```

The expiry time can be fine-tuned by adding several '*num type*' clauses:

```
ExpiresByType text/html "access plus 1 month 15 days 2 hours"
ExpiresByType image/gif "modification plus 5 hours 3 minutes"
```

Note that if you use a modification date based setting, the Expires header will **not** be added to content that does not come from a file on disk. This is due to the fact that there is no modification time for such content.

ExpiresActive Directive

Description:	Enables generation of `Expires` headers
Syntax:	`ExpiresActive On|Off`
Default:	`ExpiresActive Off`
Context:	server config, virtual host, directory, .htaccess
Override:	Indexes
Status:	Extension
Module:	mod_expires

This directive enables or disables the generation of the `Expires` and `Cache-Control` headers for the document realm in question. (That is, if found in an `.htaccess` file, for instance, it applies only to documents generated from that directory.) If set to `Off`, the headers will not be generated for any document in the realm (unless overridden at a lower level, such as an `.htaccess` file overriding a server config file). If set to `On`, the headers will be added to served documents according to the criteria defined by the EXPIRESBYTYPE and EXPIRESDEFAULT directives (*q.v.*).

Note that this directive does not guarantee that an `Expires` or `Cache-Control` header will be generated. If the criteria aren't met, no header will be sent, and the effect will be as though this directive wasn't even specified.

ExpiresByType Directive

Description:	Value of the `Expires` header configured by MIME type
Syntax:	`ExpiresByType MIME-type <code>seconds`
Context:	server config, virtual host, directory, .htaccess
Override:	Indexes
Status:	Extension
Module:	mod_expires

This directive defines the value of the `Expires` header and the `max-age` directive of the `Cache-Control` header generated for documents of the specified type (*e.g.*, `text/html`). The second argument sets the number of seconds that will be added to a base time to construct the expiration date. The `Cache-Control: max-age` is calculated by subtracting the request time from the expiration date and expressing the result in seconds.

The base time is either the last modification time of the file, or the time of the client's access to the document. Which should be used is specified by the <*code*> field; M means that the file's last modification time should be used as the base time, and A means the client's access time should be used.

The difference in effect is subtle. If M is used, all current copies of the document in all caches will expire at the same time, which can be good for something like a weekly notice that's always found at the same URL. If A is used, the date of expiration is different for each client; this can be good for image files that don't change very often, particularly for a set of related documents that all refer to the same images (*i.e.*, the images will be accessed repeatedly within a relatively short timespan).

Example:

```
# enable expirations
ExpiresActive On
# expire GIF images after a month in the client's cache
ExpiresByType image/gif A2592000
# HTML documents are good for a week from the
# time they were changed
ExpiresByType text/html M604800
```

Note that this directive only has effect if `ExpiresActive On` has been specified. It overrides, for the specified MIME type *only*, any expiration date set by the EXPIRESDEFAULT directive.

You can also specify the expiration time calculation using an alternate syntax, described earlier in this document.

ExpiresDefault Directive

Description:	Default algorithm for calculating expiration time
Syntax:	`ExpiresDefault <code>seconds`
Context:	server config, virtual host, directory, .htaccess
Override:	Indexes
Status:	Extension
Module:	mod_expires

This directive sets the default algorithm for calculating the expiration time for all documents in the affected realm. It can be overridden on a type-by-type basis by the EXPIRESBYTYPE directive. See the description of that directive for details about the syntax of the argument, and the alternate syntax description as well.

10.49 Apache Module mod_ext_filter

Description:	Pass the response body through an external program before delivery to the client
Status:	Extension
ModuleIdentifier:	ext_filter_module
SourceFile:	mod_ext_filter.c

Summary

MOD_EXT_FILTER presents a simple and familiar programming model for filters (p. 100) . With this module, a program which reads from stdin and writes to stdout (i.e., a Unix-style filter command) can be a filter for Apache. This filtering mechanism is much slower than using a filter which is specially written for the Apache API and runs inside of the Apache server process, but it does have the following benefits:

- the programming model is much simpler
- any programming/scripting language can be used, provided that it allows the program to read from standard input and write to standard output
- existing programs can be used unmodified as Apache filters

Even when the performance characteristics are not suitable for production use, MOD_EXT_FILTER can be used as a prototype environment for filters.

Directives

- ExtFilterDefine
- ExtFilterOptions

See also

- Filters (p. 100)

Examples

Generating HTML from some other type of response

```
# mod_ext_filter directive to define a filter
# to HTML-ize text/c files using the external
# program /usr/bin/enscript, with the type of
# the result set to text/html
ExtFilterDefine c-to-html mode=output \
    intype=text/c outtype=text/html \
    cmd="/usr/bin/enscript --color -W html -Ec -o - -"

<Directory "/export/home/trawick/apacheinst/htdocs/c">
    # core directive to cause the new filter to
    # be run on output
    SetOutputFilter c-to-html

    # mod_mime directive to set the type of .c
    # files to text/c
    AddType text/c .c
</Directory>
```

Implementing a content encoding filter

Note: this gzip example is just for the purposes of illustration. Please refer to MOD_DEFLATE for a practical implementation.

```
# mod_ext_filter directive to define the external filter
ExtFilterDefine gzip mode=output cmd=/bin/gzip

<Location "/gzipped">

    # core directive to cause the gzip filter to be
    # run on output
    SetOutputFilter gzip

    # mod_headers directive to add
    # "Content-Encoding: gzip" header field
    Header set Content-Encoding gzip
</Location>
```

Slowing down the server

```
# mod_ext_filter directive to define a filter
# which runs everything through cat; cat doesn't
# modify anything; it just introduces extra pathlength
# and consumes more resources
ExtFilterDefine slowdown mode=output cmd=/bin/cat \
    preservescontentlength

<Location "/">
    # core directive to cause the slowdown filter to
    # be run several times on output
    #
    SetOutputFilter slowdown;slowdown;slowdown
</Location>
```

Using sed to replace text in the response

```
# mod_ext_filter directive to define a filter which
# replaces text in the response
#
ExtFilterDefine fixtext mode=output intype=text/html \
    cmd="/bin/sed s/verdana/arial/g"

<Location "/">
    # core directive to cause the fixtext filter to
    # be run on output
    SetOutputFilter fixtext
</Location>
```

⟹ You can do the same thing using MOD_SUBSTITUTE without invoking an external process.

Tracing another filter

```
# Trace the data read and written by mod_deflate
# for a particular client (IP 192.168.1.31)
# experiencing compression problems.
# This filter will trace what goes into mod_deflate.
ExtFilterDefine tracebefore \
    cmd="/bin/tracefilter.pl /tmp/tracebefore" \
    EnableEnv=trace_this_client

# This filter will trace what goes after mod_deflate.
# Note that without the ftype parameter, the default
# filter type of AP_FTYPE_RESOURCE would cause the
# filter to be placed *before* mod_deflate in the filter
# chain.  Giving it a numeric value slightly higher than
# AP_FTYPE_CONTENT_SET will ensure that it is placed
# after mod_deflate.
ExtFilterDefine traceafter \
    cmd="/bin/tracefilter.pl /tmp/traceafter" \
    EnableEnv=trace_this_client ftype=21

<Directory "/usr/local/docs">
    SetEnvIf Remote_Addr 192.168.1.31 trace_this_client
    SetOutputFilter tracebefore;deflate;traceafter
</Directory>
```

Here is the filter which traces the data:

```
#!/usr/local/bin/perl -w
use strict;

open(SAVE, ">$ARGV[0]")
    or die "can't open $ARGV[0]: $?";

while (<STDIN>) {
    print SAVE $_;
    print $_;
}

close(SAVE);
```

ExtFilterDefine Directive

Description:	Define an external filter
Syntax:	`ExtFilterDefine filtername parameters`
Context:	server config
Status:	Extension
Module:	mod_ext_filter

The EXTFILTERDEFINE directive defines the characteristics of an external filter, including the program to run and its arguments.

filtername specifies the name of the filter being defined. This name can then be used in SETOUTPUTFILTER directives. It must be unique among all registered filters. *At the present time, no error is reported by the register-filter API, so a problem with duplicate names isn't reported to the user.*

Subsequent parameters can appear in any order and define the external command to run and certain other characteristics. The only required parameter is `cmd=`. These parameters are:

`cmd=cmdline` The `cmd=` keyword allows you to specify the external command to run. If there are arguments after the program name, the command line should be surrounded in quotation marks (*e.g.*, `cmd="/bin/mypgm arg1 arg2"`.) Normal shell quoting is not necessary since the program is run directly, bypassing the shell. Program arguments are blank-delimited. A backslash can be used to escape blanks which should be part of a program argument. Any backslashes which are part of the argument must be escaped with backslash themselves. In addition to the standard CGI environment variables, DOCUMENT_URI, DOCUMENT_PATH_INFO, and QUERY_STRING_UNESCAPED will also be set for the program.

`mode=mode` Use `mode=output` (the default) for filters which process the response. Use `mode=input` for filters which process the request. `mode=input` is available in Apache 2.1 and later.

`intype=imt` This parameter specifies the internet media type (*i.e.*, MIME type) of documents which should be filtered. By default, all documents are filtered. If `intype=` is specified, the filter will be disabled for documents of other types.

`outtype=imt` This parameter specifies the internet media type (*i.e.*, MIME type) of filtered documents. It is useful when the filter changes the internet media type as part of the filtering operation. By default, the internet media type is unchanged.

`PreservesContentLength` The `PreservesContentLength` keyword specifies that the filter preserves the content length. This is not the default, as most filters change the content length. In the event that the filter doesn't modify the length, this keyword should be specified.

`ftype=filtertype` This parameter specifies the numeric value for filter type that the filter should be registered as. The default value, AP_FTYPE_RESOURCE, is sufficient in most cases. If the filter needs to operate at a different point in the filter chain than resource filters, then this parameter will be necessary. See the AP_FTYPE_foo definitions in util_filter.h for appropriate values.

`disableenv=env` This parameter specifies the name of an environment variable which, if set, will disable the filter.

`enableenv=env` This parameter specifies the name of an environment variable which must be set, or the filter will be disabled.

ExtFilterOptions Directive

Description:	Configure MOD_EXT_FILTER options
Syntax:	`ExtFilterOptions option [option] ...`
Default:	`ExtFilterOptions NoLogStderr`
Context:	directory
Status:	Extension
Module:	mod_ext_filter

The EXTFILTEROPTIONS directive specifies special processing options for MOD_EXT_FILTER. *Option* can be one of

`LogStderr | NoLogStderr` The `LogStderr` keyword specifies that messages written to standard error by the external filter program will be saved in the Apache error log. `NoLogStderr` disables this feature.

`Onfail=[abort|remove]` Determines how to proceed if the external filter program cannot be started. With `abort` (the default value) the request will be aborted. With `remove`, the filter is removed and the request continues without it.

```
ExtFilterOptions LogStderr
```

Messages written to the filter's standard error will be stored in the Apache error log.

10.50 Apache Module mod_file_cache

Description:	Caches a static list of files in memory
Status:	Experimental
ModuleIdentifier:	file_cache_module
SourceFile:	mod_file_cache.c

Summary

! This module should be used with care. You can easily create a broken site using MOD_FILE_CACHE, so read this document carefully.

Caching frequently requested files that change very infrequently is a technique for reducing server load. MOD_FILE_CACHE provides two techniques for caching frequently requested *static* files. Through configuration directives, you can direct MOD_FILE_CACHE to either open then `mmap()` a file, or to pre-open a file and save the file's open *file handle*. Both techniques reduce server load when processing requests for these files by doing part of the work (specifically, the file I/O) for serving the file when the server is started rather than during each request.

Notice: You cannot use this for speeding up CGI programs or other files which are served by special content handlers. It can only be used for regular files which are usually served by the Apache core content handler.

This module is an extension of and borrows heavily from the `mod_mmap_static` module in Apache 1.3.

Directives

- CacheFile
- MMapFile

Using mod_file_cache

MOD_FILE_CACHE caches a list of statically configured files via MMAPFILE or CACHEFILE directives in the main server configuration.

Not all platforms support both directives. You will receive an error message in the server error log if you attempt to use an unsupported directive. If given an unsupported directive, the server will start but the file will not be cached. On platforms that support both directives, you should experiment with both to see which works best for you.

MMapFile Directive

The MMAPFILE directive of MOD_FILE_CACHE maps a list of statically configured files into memory through the system call `mmap()`. This system call is available on most modern Unix derivatives, but not on all. There are sometimes system-specific limits on the size and number of files that can be `mmap()`ed, experimentation is probably the easiest way to find out.

This `mmap()`ing is done once at server start or restart, only. So whenever one of the mapped files changes on the filesystem you *have* to restart the server (see the Stopping and Restarting (p. 27) documentation). To reiterate that point: if the files are modified *in place* without restarting the server you may end up serving requests that are completely bogus. You should update files by unlinking the old copy and putting a new copy in place. Most tools such as `rdist` and `mv` do this. The reason why this modules doesn't take care of changes to the files is that this check would need an extra `stat()` every time which is a waste and against the intent of I/O reduction.

CacheFile Directive

The CACHEFILE directive of MOD_FILE_CACHE opens an active *handle* or *file descriptor* to the file (or files) listed in the configuration directive and places these open file handles in the cache. When the file is requested, the server retrieves the handle from the cache and passes it to the `sendfile()` (or `TransmitFile()` on Windows), socket API.

This file handle caching is done once at server start or restart, only. So whenever one of the cached files changes on the filesystem you *have* to restart the server (see the Stopping and Restarting (p. 27) documentation). To reiterate that point: if the files are modified *in place* without restarting the server you may end up serving requests that are completely bogus. You should update files by unlinking the old copy and putting a new copy in place. Most tools such as `rdist` and `mv` do this.

**Note**

Don't bother asking for a directive which recursively caches all the files in a directory. Try this instead... See the INCLUDE directive, and consider this command:

```
find /www/htdocs -type f -print \
| sed -e 's/.*/mmapfile &/' > /www/conf/mmap.conf
```

CacheFile Directive

Description:	Cache a list of file handles at startup time
Syntax:	`CacheFile file-path [file-path] ...`
Context:	server config
Status:	Experimental
Module:	mod_file_cache

The CACHEFILE directive opens handles to one or more files (given as whitespace separated arguments) and places these handles into the cache at server startup time. Handles to cached files are automatically closed on a server shutdown. When the files have changed on the filesystem, the server should be restarted to re-cache them.

Be careful with the *file-path* arguments: They have to literally match the filesystem path Apache's URL-to-filename translation handlers create. We cannot compare inodes or other stuff to match paths through symbolic links *etc.* because that again would cost extra `stat()` system calls which is not acceptable. This module may or may not work with filenames rewritten by MOD_ALIAS or MOD_REWRITE.

Example

```
CacheFile /usr/local/apache/htdocs/index.html
```

MMapFile Directive

Description:	Map a list of files into memory at startup time
Syntax:	`MMapFile file-path [file-path] ...`
Context:	server config
Status:	Experimental
Module:	mod_file_cache

The MMAPFILE directive maps one or more files (given as whitespace separated arguments) into memory at server startup time. They are automatically unmapped on a server shutdown. When the files have changed on the filesystem at least a `HUP` or `USR1` signal should be send to the server to re-`mmap()` them.

Be careful with the *file-path* arguments: They have to literally match the filesystem path Apache's URL-to-filename translation handlers create. We cannot compare inodes or other stuff to match paths through symbolic links *etc.* because that again would cost extra `stat()` system calls which is not acceptable. This module may or may not work with filenames rewritten by MOD_ALIAS or MOD_REWRITE.

Example

```
MMapFile /usr/local/apache/htdocs/index.html
```

10.51 Apache Module mod_filter

Description:	Context-sensitive smart filter configuration module
Status:	Base
ModuleIdentifier:	filter_module
SourceFile:	mod_filter.c
Compatibility:	Version 2.1 and later

Summary

This module enables smart, context-sensitive configuration of output content filters. For example, apache can be configured to process different content-types through different filters, even when the content-type is not known in advance (e.g. in a proxy).

MOD_FILTER works by introducing indirection into the filter chain. Instead of inserting filters in the chain, we insert a filter harness which in turn dispatches conditionally to a filter provider. Any content filter may be used as a provider to MOD_FILTER; no change to existing filter modules is required (although it may be possible to simplify them).

Directives

- AddOutputFilterByType
- FilterChain
- FilterDeclare
- FilterProtocol
- FilterProvider
- FilterTrace

Smart Filtering

In the traditional filtering model, filters are inserted unconditionally using ADDOUTPUTFILTER and family. Each filter then needs to determine whether to run, and there is little flexibility available for server admins to allow the chain to be configured dynamically.

MOD_FILTER by contrast gives server administrators a great deal of flexibility in configuring the filter chain. In fact, filters can be inserted based on complex boolean expressions (p. 89) This generalises the limited flexibility offered by ADDOUTPUTFILTERBYTYPE.

Filter Declarations, Providers and Chains

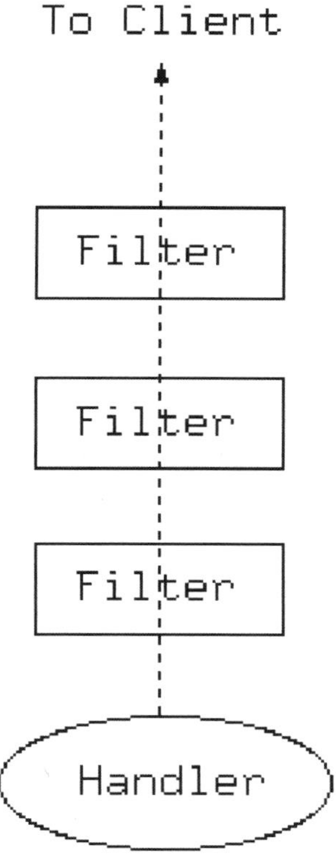

Figure 1: The traditional filter model

In the traditional model, output filters are a simple chain from the content generator (handler) to the client. This works well provided the filter chain can be correctly configured, but presents problems when the filters need to be configured dynamically based on the outcome of the handler.

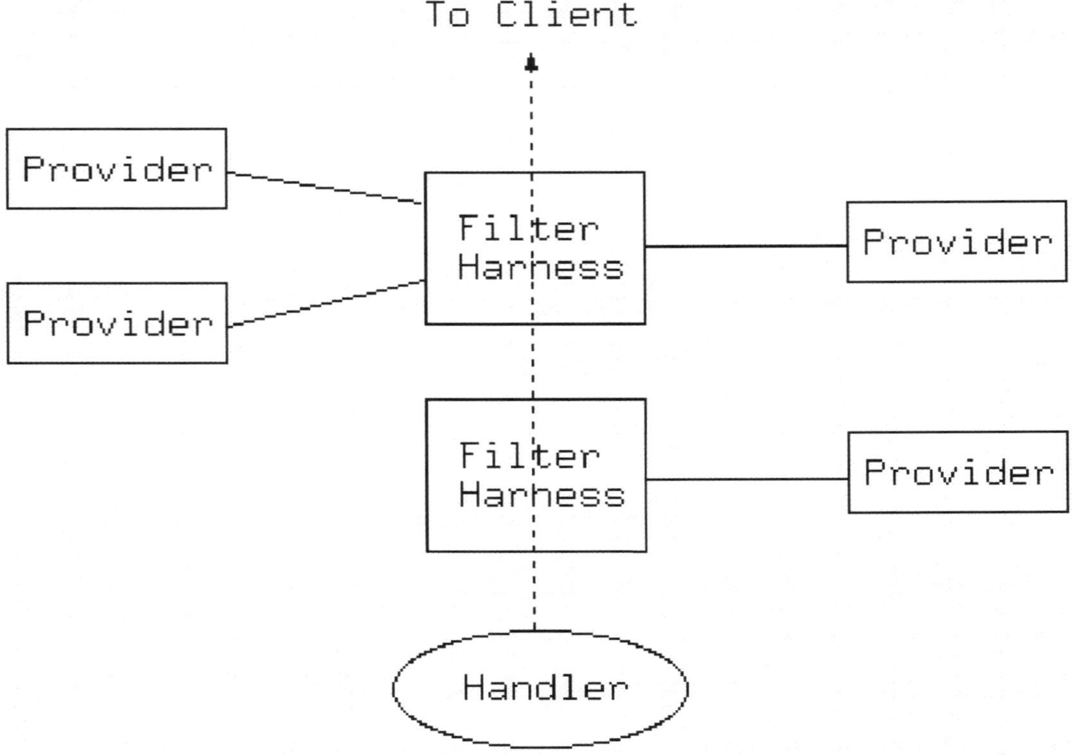

Figure 2: The MOD_FILTER model

MOD_FILTER works by introducing indirection into the filter chain. Instead of inserting filters in the chain, we insert a filter harness which in turn dispatches conditionally to a filter provider. Any content filter may be used as a provider to MOD_FILTER; no change to existing filter modules is required (although it may be possible to simplify them). There can be multiple providers for one filter, but no more than one provider will run for any single request.

A filter chain comprises any number of instances of the filter harness, each of which may have any number of providers. A special case is that of a single provider with unconditional dispatch: this is equivalent to inserting the provider filter directly into the chain.

Configuring the Chain

There are three stages to configuring a filter chain with MOD_FILTER. For details of the directives, see below.

Declare Filters The FILTERDECLARE directive declares a filter, assigning it a name and filter type. Required only if the filter is not the default type AP_FTYPE_RESOURCE.

Register Providers The FILTERPROVIDER directive registers a provider with a filter. The filter may have been declared with FILTERDECLARE; if not, FilterProvider will implicitly declare it with the default type AP_FTYPE_RESOURCE. The provider must have been registered with `ap_register_output_filter` by some module. The final argument to FILTERPROVIDER is an expression: the provider will be selected to run for a request if and only if the expression evaluates to true. The expression may evaluate HTTP request or response headers, environment variables, or the Handler used by this request. Unlike earlier versions, mod_filter now supports complex expressions involving multiple criteria with AND / OR logic (&& / ——) and brackets. The details of the expression syntax are described in the ap_expr documentation (p. 89) .

Configure the Chain The above directives build components of a smart filter chain, but do not configure it to run. The FILTERCHAIN directive builds a filter chain from smart filters declared, offering the flexibility to insert filters at the beginning or end of the chain, remove a filter, or clear the chain.

Filtering and Response Status

mod_filter normally only runs filters on responses with HTTP status 200 (OK). If you want to filter documents with other response statuses, you can set the *filter-errordocs* environment variable, and it will work on all responses regardless of status. To refine this further, you can use expression conditions with FILTERPROVIDER.

Upgrading from Apache HTTP Server 2.2 Configuration

The FILTERPROVIDER directive has changed from httpd 2.2: the *match* and *dispatch* arguments are replaced with a single but more versatile *expression*. In general, you can convert a match/dispatch pair to the two sides of an expression, using something like:

```
"dispatch = 'match'"
```

The Request headers, Response headers and Environment variables are now interpreted from syntax *%{req:foo}*, *%{resp:foo}* and *%{env:foo}* respectively. The variables *%{HANDLER}* and *%{CONTENT_TYPE}* are also supported.

Note that the match no longer support substring matches. They can be replaced by regular expression matches.

Examples

Server side Includes (SSI) A simple case of replacing ADDOUTPUTFILTERBYTYPE

```
FilterDeclare SSI
FilterProvider SSI INCLUDES "%{CONTENT_TYPE} =~ m|^text/html|"
FilterChain SSI
```

Server side Includes (SSI) The same as the above but dispatching on handler (classic SSI behaviour; .shtml files get processed).

```
FilterProvider SSI INCLUDES "%{HANDLER} = 'server-parsed'"
FilterChain SSI
```

Emulating mod_gzip with mod_deflate Insert INFLATE filter only if "gzip" is NOT in the Accept-Encoding header. This filter runs with ftype CONTENT_SET.

```
FilterDeclare gzip CONTENT_SET
FilterProvider gzip inflate "%{req:Accept-Encoding} !~ /gzip/"
FilterChain gzip
```

Image Downsampling Suppose we want to downsample all web images, and have filters for GIF, JPEG and PNG.

```
FilterProvider unpack jpeg_unpack "%{CONTENT_TYPE} = 'image/jpeg'"
FilterProvider unpack gif_unpack "%{CONTENT_TYPE} = 'image/gif'"
FilterProvider unpack png_unpack "%{CONTENT_TYPE} = 'image/png'"
```

```
FilterProvider downsample downsample_filter "%{CONTENT_TYPE} = m|^image/(jp
FilterProtocol downsample "change=yes"

FilterProvider repack jpeg_pack "%{CONTENT_TYPE} = 'image/jpeg'"
FilterProvider repack gif_pack "%{CONTENT_TYPE} = 'image/gif'"
FilterProvider repack png_pack "%{CONTENT_TYPE} = 'image/png'"
<Location "/image-filter">
    FilterChain unpack downsample repack
</Location>
```

Protocol Handling

Historically, each filter is responsible for ensuring that whatever changes it makes are correctly represented in the HTTP response headers, and that it does not run when it would make an illegal change. This imposes a burden on filter authors to re-implement some common functionality in every filter:

- Many filters will change the content, invalidating existing content tags, checksums, hashes, and lengths.
- Filters that require an entire, unbroken response in input need to ensure they don't get byteranges from a backend.
- Filters that transform output in a filter need to ensure they don't violate a `Cache-Control: no-transform` header from the backend.
- Filters may make responses uncacheable.

MOD_FILTER aims to offer generic handling of these details of filter implementation, reducing the complexity required of content filter modules. This is work-in-progress; the FILTERPROTOCOL implements some of this functionality for back-compatibility with Apache 2.0 modules. For httpd 2.1 and later, the `ap_register_output_filter_protocol` and `ap_filter_protocol` API enables filter modules to declare their own behaviour.

At the same time, MOD_FILTER should not interfere with a filter that wants to handle all aspects of the protocol. By default (i.e. in the absence of any FILTERPROTOCOL directives), MOD_FILTER will leave the headers untouched.

At the time of writing, this feature is largely untested, as modules in common use are designed to work with 2.0. Modules using it should test it carefully.

AddOutputFilterByType Directive

Description:	assigns an output filter to a particular media-type
Syntax:	`AddOutputFilterByType filter[;filter...] media-type [media-type] ...`
Context:	server config, virtual host, directory, .htaccess
Override:	FileInfo
Status:	Base
Module:	mod_filter
Compatibility:	Had severe limitations before being moved to MOD_FILTER in version 2.3.7

This directive activates a particular output filter (p. 100) for a request depending on the response media-type.

The following example uses the `DEFLATE` filter, which is provided by MOD_DEFLATE. It will compress all output (either static or dynamic) which is labeled as `text/html` or `text/plain` before it is sent to the client.

```
AddOutputFilterByType DEFLATE text/html text/plain
```

If you want the content to be processed by more than one filter, their names have to be separated by semicolons. It's also possible to use one ADDOUTPUTFILTERBYTYPE directive for each of these filters.

The configuration below causes all script output labeled as `text/html` to be processed at first by the `INCLUDES` filter and then by the `DEFLATE` filter.

```
<Location "/cgi-bin/">
    Options Includes
    AddOutputFilterByType INCLUDES;DEFLATE text/html
</Location>
```

See also

- ADDOUTPUTFILTER
- SETOUTPUTFILTER
- filters (p. 100)

FilterChain Directive

Description:	Configure the filter chain
Syntax:	`FilterChain [+=-@!]filter-name ...`
Context:	server config, virtual host, directory, .htaccess
Override:	Options
Status:	Base
Module:	mod_filter

This configures an actual filter chain, from declared filters. FILTERCHAIN takes any number of arguments, each optionally preceded with a single-character control that determines what to do:

`+filter-name` Add *filter-name* to the end of the filter chain

`@filter-name` Insert *filter-name* at the start of the filter chain

`-filter-name` Remove *filter-name* from the filter chain

`=filter-name` Empty the filter chain and insert *filter-name*

! Empty the filter chain

`filter-name` Equivalent to `+filter-name`

FilterDeclare Directive

Description:	Declare a smart filter
Syntax:	`FilterDeclare filter-name [type]`
Context:	server config, virtual host, directory, .htaccess
Override:	Options
Status:	Base
Module:	mod_filter

This directive declares an output filter together with a header or environment variable that will determine runtime configuration. The first argument is a *filter-name* for use in FILTERPROVIDER, FILTERCHAIN and FILTERPROTOCOL directives.

The final (optional) argument is the type of filter, and takes values of `ap_filter_type` - namely `RESOURCE` (the default), `CONTENT_SET`, `PROTOCOL`, `TRANSCODE`, `CONNECTION` or `NETWORK`.

FilterProtocol Directive

Description:	Deal with correct HTTP protocol handling
Syntax:	`FilterProtocol filter-name [provider-name] proto-flags`
Context:	server config, virtual host, directory, .htaccess
Override:	Options
Status:	Base
Module:	mod_filter

This directs MOD_FILTER to deal with ensuring the filter doesn't run when it shouldn't, and that the HTTP response headers are correctly set taking into account the effects of the filter.

There are two forms of this directive. With three arguments, it applies specifically to a *filter-name* and a *provider-name* for that filter. With two arguments it applies to a *filter-name* whenever the filter runs *any* provider.

Flags specified with this directive are merged with the flags that underlying providers may have registerd with MOD_FILTER. For example, a filter may internally specify the equivalent of `change=yes`, but a particular configuration of the module can override with `change=no`.

proto-flags is one or more of

`change=yes|no` Specifies whether the filter changes the content, including possibly the content length. The "no" argument is supported in 2.4.7 and later.

`change=1:1` The filter changes the content, but will not change the content length

`byteranges=no` The filter cannot work on byteranges and requires complete input

`proxy=no` The filter should not run in a proxy context

`proxy=transform` The filter transforms the response in a manner incompatible with the HTTP `Cache-Control: no-transform` header.

`cache=no` The filter renders the output uncacheable (eg by introducing randomised content changes)

FilterProvider Directive

Description:	Register a content filter
Syntax:	`FilterProvider filter-name provider-name expression`
Context:	server config, virtual host, directory, .htaccess
Override:	Options
Status:	Base
Module:	mod_filter

This directive registers a *provider* for the smart filter. The provider will be called if and only if the *expression* declared evaluates to true when the harness is first called.

provider-name must have been registered by loading a module that registers the name with `ap_register_output_filter`.

expression is an ap_expr (p. 89) .

See also

- Expressions in Apache HTTP Server (p. 89) , for a complete reference and examples.
- MOD_INCLUDE

FilterTrace Directive

Description:	Get debug/diagnostic information from MOD_FILTER
Syntax:	`FilterTrace filter-name level`
Context:	server config, virtual host, directory
Status:	Base
Module:	mod_filter

This directive generates debug information from MOD_FILTER. It is designed to help test and debug providers (filter modules), although it may also help with MOD_FILTER itself.

The debug output depends on the *level* set:

0 (default) No debug information is generated.

1 MOD_FILTER will record buckets and brigades passing through the filter to the error log, before the provider has processed them. This is similar to the information generated by mod_diagnostics[33].

2 (not yet implemented) Will dump the full data passing through to a tempfile before the provider. **For single-user debug only**; this will not support concurrent hits.

[33]http://apache.webthing.com/mod_diagnostics/

10.52 Apache Module mod_headers

Description:	Customization of HTTP request and response headers
Status:	Extension
ModuleIdentifier:	headers_module
SourceFile:	mod_headers.c

Summary

This module provides directives to control and modify HTTP request and response headers. Headers can be merged, replaced or removed.

Directives

- Header
- RequestHeader

Order of Processing

The directives provided by MOD_HEADERS can occur almost anywhere within the server configuration, and can be limited in scope by enclosing them in configuration sections (p. 33) .

Order of processing is important and is affected both by the order in the configuration file and by placement in configuration sections (p. 33) . These two directives have a different effect if reversed:

```
RequestHeader append MirrorID "mirror 12"
RequestHeader unset MirrorID
```

This way round, the `MirrorID` header is not set. If reversed, the MirrorID header is set to "mirror 12".

Early and Late Processing

MOD_HEADERS can be applied either early or late in the request. The normal mode is late, when *Request* Headers are set immediately before running the content generator and *Response* Headers just as the response is sent down the wire. Always use Late mode in an operational server.

Early mode is designed as a test/debugging aid for developers. Directives defined using the `early` keyword are set right at the beginning of processing the request. This means they can be used to simulate different requests and set up test cases, but it also means that headers may be changed at any time by other modules before generating a Response.

Because early directives are processed before the request path's configuration is traversed, early headers can only be set in a main server or virtual host context. Early directives cannot depend on a request path, so they will fail in contexts such as <DIRECTORY> or <LOCATION>.

Examples

1. Copy all request headers that begin with "TS" to the response headers:

   ```
   Header echo ^TS
   ```

2. Add a header, `MyHeader`, to the response including a timestamp for when the request was received and how long it took to begin serving the request. This header can be used by the client to intuit load on the server or in isolating bottlenecks between the client and the server.

   ```
   Header set MyHeader "%D %t"
   ```

   results in this header being added to the response:

   ```
   MyHeader: D=3775428 t=991424704447256
   ```

3. Say hello to Joe

   ```
   Header set MyHeader "Hello Joe. It took %D microseconds for Apache to serve
   ```

   results in this header being added to the response:

   ```
   MyHeader: Hello Joe. It took D=3775428 microseconds for Apache to
   serve this request.
   ```

4. Conditionally send `MyHeader` on the response if and only if header `MyRequestHeader` is present on the request. This is useful for constructing headers in response to some client stimulus. Note that this example requires the services of the MOD_SETENVIF module.

   ```
   SetEnvIf MyRequestHeader myvalue HAVE_MyRequestHeader
   Header set MyHeader "%D %t mytext" env=HAVE_MyRequestHeader
   ```

   If the header `MyRequestHeader: myvalue` is present on the HTTP request, the response will contain the following header:

   ```
   MyHeader: D=3775428 t=991424704447256 mytext
   ```

5. Enable DAV to work with Apache running HTTP through SSL hardware (problem description[34]) by replacing *https:* with *http:* in the *Destination* header:

   ```
   RequestHeader edit Destination ^https: http: early
   ```

6. Set the same header value under multiple nonexclusive conditions, but do not duplicate the value in the final header. If all of the following conditions applied to a request (i.e., if the `CGI`, `NO_CACHE` and `NO_STORE` environment variables all existed for the request):

   ```
   Header merge Cache-Control no-cache env=CGI
   Header merge Cache-Control no-cache env=NO_CACHE
   Header merge Cache-Control no-store env=NO_STORE
   ```

   then the response would contain the following header:

   ```
   Cache-Control: no-cache, no-store
   ```

[34] http://svn.haxx.se/users/archive-2006-03/0549.shtml

If `append` was used instead of `merge`, then the response would contain the following header:

```
Cache-Control: no-cache, no-cache, no-store
```

7. Set a test cookie if and only if the client didn't send us a cookie

```
Header set Set-Cookie testcookie "expr=-z %{req:Cookie}"
```

8. Append a Caching header for responses with a HTTP status code of 200

```
Header append Cache-Control s-maxage=600 "expr=%{REQUEST_STATUS} == 200"
```

Header Directive

Description:	Configure HTTP response headers
Syntax:	`Header [condition] add|append|echo|edit|edit*|merge|set|setifempty header [[expr=]value [replacement] [early|env=[!]varname|expr=expre`
Context:	server config, virtual host, directory, .htaccess
Override:	FileInfo
Status:	Extension
Module:	mod_headers
Compatibility:	SetIfEmpty available in 2.4.7 and later, expr=value available in 2.4.10 and later

This directive can replace, merge or remove HTTP response headers. The header is modified just after the content handler and output filters are run, allowing outgoing headers to be modified.

The optional *condition* argument determines which internal table of responses headers this directive will operate against. Despite the name, the default value of `onsuccess` does *not* limit an *action* to responses with a 2xx status code. Headers set under this condition are still used when, for example, a request is *successfully* proxied or generated by CGI, even when they have generated a failing status code.

When your action is a function of an existing header, you may need to specify a condition of `always`, depending on which internal table the original header was set in. The table that corresponds to `always` is used for locally generated error responses as well as successful responses. Note also that repeating this directive with both conditions makes sense in some scenarios because `always` is not a superset of `onsuccess` with respect to existing headers:

- You're adding a header to a locally generated non-success (non-2xx) response, such as a redirect, in which case only the table corresponding to `always` is used in the ultimate response.
- You're modifying or removing a header generated by a CGI script, in which case the CGI scripts are in the table corresponding to `always` and not in the default table.
- You're modifying or removing a header generated by some piece of the server but that header is not being found by the default `onsuccess` condition.

Separately from the *condition* parameter described above, you can limit an action based on HTTP status codes for e.g. proxied or CGI requests. See the example that uses %{REQUEST_STATUS} in the section above.

The action it performs is determined by the first argument (second argument if a *condition* is specified). This can be one of the following values:

add The response header is added to the existing set of headers, even if this header already exists. This can result in two (or more) headers having the same name. This can lead to unforeseen consequences, and in general `set`, `append` or `merge` should be used instead.

append The response header is appended to any existing header of the same name. When a new value is merged onto an existing header it is separated from the existing header with a comma. This is the HTTP standard way of giving a header multiple values.

echo Request headers with this name are echoed back in the response headers. *header* may be a regular expression. *value* must be omitted.

edit

edit* If this response header exists, its value is transformed according to a regular expression search-and-replace. The *value* argument is a regular expression, and the *replacement* is a replacement string, which may contain backreferences or format specifiers. The `edit` form will match and replace exactly once in a header value, whereas the `edit*` form will replace *every* instance of the search pattern if it appears more than once.

merge The response header is appended to any existing header of the same name, unless the value to be appended already appears in the header's comma-delimited list of values. When a new value is merged onto an existing header it is separated from the existing header with a comma. This is the HTTP standard way of giving a header multiple values. Values are compared in a case sensitive manner, and after all format specifiers have been processed. Values in double quotes are considered different from otherwise identical unquoted values.

set The response header is set, replacing any previous header with this name. The *value* may be a format string.

setifempty The request header is set, but only if there is no previous header with this name.
Available in 2.4.7 and later.

unset The response header of this name is removed, if it exists. If there are multiple headers of the same name, all will be removed. *value* must be omitted.

note The value of the named response *header* is copied into an internal note whose name is given by *value*. This is useful if a header sent by a CGI or proxied resource is configured to be unset but should also be logged.
Available in 2.4.7 and later.

This argument is followed by a *header* name, which can include the final colon, but it is not required. Case is ignored for `set`, `append`, `merge`, `add`, `unset` and `edit`. The *header* name for `echo` is case sensitive and may be a regular expression.

For `set`, `append`, `merge` and `add` a *value* is specified as the next argument. If *value* contains spaces, it should be surrounded by double quotes. *value* may be a character string, a string containing MOD_HEADERS specific format specifiers (and character literals), or an ap_expr (p. 89) expression prefixed with *expr=*

The following format specifiers are supported in *value*:

Format	Description
`%%`	The percent sign
`%t`	The time the request was received in Universal Coordinated Time since the epoch (Jan. 1, 19 measured in microseconds. The value is preceded by `t=`.
`%D`	The time from when the request was received to the time the headers are sent on the wire. Thi a measure of the duration of the request. The value is preceded by `D=`. The value is measure microseconds.
`%l`	The current load averages of the actual server itself. It is designed to expose the values obtai by `getloadavg()` and this represents the current load average, the 5 minute average, and the minute average. The value is preceded by `l=` with each average separated by `/`. Available in 2.4.4 and later.
`%i`	The current idle percentage of httpd (0 to 100) based on available processes and threads. The va is preceded by `i=`. Available in 2.4.4 and later.
`%b`	The current busy percentage of httpd (0 to 100) based on available processes and threads. ' value is preceded by `b=`. Available in 2.4.4 and later.
`%{VARNAME}e`	The contents of the environment variable (p. 82) `VARNAME`.
`%{VARNAME}s`	The contents of the SSL environment variable (p. 853) `VARNAME`, if MOD_SSL is enabled.

**Note**

The `%s` format specifier is only available in Apache 2.1 and later; it can be used instead of `%e` to avoid the overhead of enabling `SSLOptions +StdEnvVars`. If `SSLOptions +StdEnvVars` must be enabled anyway for some other reason, `%e` will be more efficient than `%s`.

Note on expression values

When the value parameter uses the ap_expr (p. 89) parser, some expression syntax will differ from examples that evaluate *boolean* expressions such as <If>:

- The starting point of the grammar is 'string' rather than 'expr'.
- Function calls use the %{funcname:arg} syntax rather than funcname(arg).
- Multi-argument functions are not currently accessible from this starting point
- Quote the entire parameter, such as

```
Header set foo-checksum "expr=%{md5:foo}"
```

For `edit` there is both a *value* argument which is a regular expression, and an additional *replacement* string. As of version 2.4.7 the replacement string may also contain format specifiers.

The HEADER directive may be followed by an additional argument, which may be any of:

`early` Specifies early processing.

`env=[!]varname` The directive is applied if and only if the environment variable (p. 82) `varname` exists. A `!` in front of `varname` reverses the test, so the directive applies only if `varname` is unset.

`expr=expression` The directive is applied if and only if *expression* evaluates to true. Details of expression syntax and evaluation are documented in the ap_expr (p. 89) documentation.

Except in early mode, the HEADER directives are processed just before the response is sent to the network. This means that it is possible to set and/or override most headers, except for some headers added by the HTTP header filter. Prior to 2.2.12, it was not possible to change the Content-Type header with this directive.

RequestHeader Directive

Description:	Configure HTTP request headers
Syntax:	`RequestHeader add|append|edit|edit*|merge|set|setifempty|unset header [[expr=]value [replacement] [early|env=[!]varname|expr=expre`
Context:	server config, virtual host, directory, .htaccess
Override:	FileInfo
Status:	Extension
Module:	mod_headers
Compatibility:	SetIfEmpty available in 2.4.7 and later, expr=value available in 2.4.10 and later

This directive can replace, merge, change or remove HTTP request headers. The header is modified just before the content handler is run, allowing incoming headers to be modified. The action it performs is determined by the first argument. This can be one of the following values:

`add` The request header is added to the existing set of headers, even if this header already exists. This can result in two (or more) headers having the same name. This can lead to unforeseen consequences, and in general `set`, `append` or `merge` should be used instead.

append The request header is appended to any existing header of the same name. When a new value is merged onto an existing header it is separated from the existing header with a comma. This is the HTTP standard way of giving a header multiple values.

edit

edit* If this request header exists, its value is transformed according to a regular expression search-and-replace. The *value* argument is a regular expression, and the *replacement* is a replacement string, which may contain backreferences or format specifiers. The `edit` form will match and replace exactly once in a header value, whereas the `edit*` form will replace *every* instance of the search pattern if it appears more than once.

merge The request header is appended to any existing header of the same name, unless the value to be appended already appears in the existing header's comma-delimited list of values. When a new value is merged onto an existing header it is separated from the existing header with a comma. This is the HTTP standard way of giving a header multiple values. Values are compared in a case sensitive manner, and after all format specifiers have been processed. Values in double quotes are considered different from otherwise identical unquoted values.

set The request header is set, replacing any previous header with this name

setifempty The request header is set, but only if there is no previous header with this name. Available in 2.4.7 and later.

unset The request header of this name is removed, if it exists. If there are multiple headers of the same name, all will be removed. *value* must be omitted.

This argument is followed by a header name, which can include the final colon, but it is not required. Case is ignored. For `set`, `append`, `merge` and `add` a *value* is given as the third argument. If a *value* contains spaces, it should be surrounded by double quotes. For `unset`, no *value* should be given. *value* may be a character string, a string containing format specifiers or a combination of both. The supported format specifiers are the same as for the HEADER, please have a look there for details. For `edit` both a *value* and a *replacement* are required, and are a regular expression and a replacement string respectively.

The REQUESTHEADER directive may be followed by an additional argument, which may be any of:

early Specifies early processing.

env=[!]*varname* The directive is applied if and only if the environment variable (p. 82) `varname` exists. A `!` in front of `varname` reverses the test, so the directive applies only if `varname` is unset.

expr=*expression* The directive is applied if and only if *expression* evaluates to true. Details of expression syntax and evaluation are documented in the ap_expr (p. 89) documentation.

Except in early mode, the REQUESTHEADER directive is processed just before the request is run by its handler in the fixup phase. This should allow headers generated by the browser, or by Apache input filters to be overridden or modified.

10.53 Apache Module mod_heartbeat

Description:	Sends messages with server status to frontend proxy
Status:	Experimental
ModuleIdentifier:	heartbeat_module
SourceFile:	mod_heartbeat
Compatibility:	Available in Apache 2.3 and later

Summary

MOD_HEARTBEAT sends multicast messages to a MOD_HEARTMONITOR listener that advertises the servers current connection count. Usually, MOD_HEARTMONITOR will be running on a proxy server with MOD_LBMETHOD_HEARTBEAT loaded, which allows PROXYPASS to use the "heartbeat" *lbmethod* inside of PROXYPASS.

MOD_HEARTBEAT itself is loaded on the origin server(s) that serve requests through the proxy server(s).

To use MOD_HEARTBEAT, MOD_STATUS and MOD_WATCHDOG must be either a static modules or, if a dynamic module, must be loaded before MOD_HEARTBEAT.

Directives

- HeartbeatAddress

Consuming mod_heartbeat Output

Every 1 second, this module generates a single multicast UDP packet, containing the number of busy and idle workers. The packet is a simple ASCII format, similar to GET query parameters in HTTP.

An Example Packet

```
v=1&ready=75&busy=0
```

Consumers should handle new variables besides busy and ready, separated by '&', being added in the future.

HeartbeatAddress Directive

Description:	Multicast address for heartbeat packets
Syntax:	`HeartbeatAddress addr:port`
Default:	`disabled`
Context:	server config
Status:	Experimental
Module:	mod_heartbeat

The HEARTBEATADDRESS directive specifies the multicast address to which MOD_HEARTBEAT will send status information. This address will usually correspond to a configured HEARTBEATLISTEN on a frontend proxy system.

```
HeartbeatAddress 239.0.0.1:27999
```

10.54 Apache Module mod_heartmonitor

Description:	Centralized monitor for mod_heartbeat origin servers
Status:	Experimental
ModuleIdentifier:	heartmonitor_module
SourceFile:	mod_heartmonitor.c
Compatibility:	Available in Apache 2.3 and later

Summary

MOD_HEARTMONITOR listens for server status messages generated by MOD_HEARTBEAT enabled origin servers and makes their status available to MOD_LBMETHOD_HEARTBEAT. This allows PROXYPASS to use the "heartbeat" *lb-method* inside of PROXYPASS.

This module uses the services of MOD_SLOTMEM_SHM when available instead of flat-file storage. No configuration is required to use MOD_SLOTMEM_SHM.

! To use MOD_HEARTMONITOR, MOD_STATUS and MOD_WATCHDOG must be either a static modules or, if a dynamic module, it must be loaded before MOD_HEARTMONITOR.

Directives

- HeartbeatListen
- HeartbeatMaxServers
- HeartbeatStorage

HeartbeatListen Directive

Description:	multicast address to listen for incoming heartbeat requests
Syntax:	`HeartbeatListenaddr:port`
Default:	`disabled`
Context:	server config
Status:	Experimental
Module:	mod_heartmonitor

The HEARTBEATLISTEN directive specifies the multicast address on which the server will listen for status information from MOD_HEARTBEAT-enabled servers. This address will usually correspond to a configured HEARTBEATADDRESS on an origin server.

```
HeartbeatListen 239.0.0.1:27999
```

This module is inactive until this directive is used.

HeartbeatMaxServers Directive

Description:	Specifies the maximum number of servers that will be sending heartbeat requests to this server
Syntax:	`HeartbeatMaxServers number-of-servers`
Default:	`HeartbeatMaxServers 10`
Context:	server config
Status:	Experimental
Module:	mod_heartmonitor

The HEARTBEATMAXSERVERS directive specifies the maximum number of servers that will be sending requests to this monitor server. It is used to control the size of the shared memory allocated to store the heartbeat info when MOD_SLOTMEM_SHM is in use.

HeartbeatStorage Directive

Description:	Path to store heartbeat data
Syntax:	`HeartbeatStorage file-path`
Default:	`HeartbeatStorage logs/hb.dat`
Context:	server config
Status:	Experimental
Module:	mod_heartmonitor

The HEARTBEATSTORAGE directive specifies the path to store heartbeat data. This flat-file is used only when MOD_SLOTMEM_SHM is not loaded.

10.55 Apache Module mod_http2

Description:	Support for the HTTP/2 transport layer
Status:	Extension
ModuleIdentifier:	h2_module
SourceFile:	mod_http2.c

Summary

This module provides HTTP/2 (RFC 7540) support for the Apache HTTP Server.

This module relies on libnghttp2[35] to provide the core http/2 engine.

Warning
This module is experimental. Its behaviors, directives, and defaults are subject to more change from release to release relative to other standard modules. Users are encouraged to consult the "CHANGES" file for potential updates.

Directives

- H2Direct
- H2MaxSessionStreams
- H2MaxWorkerIdleSeconds
- H2MaxWorkers
- H2MinWorkers
- H2SerializeHeaders
- H2SessionExtraFiles
- H2StreamMaxMemSize
- H2WindowSize

H2Direct Directive

Description:	H2 Direct Protocol Switch
Syntax:	`H2Direct on|off`
Default:	`H2Direct on (for non TLS)`
Context:	server config, virtual host
Status:	Extension
Module:	mod_http2

This directive toggles the usage of the HTTP/2 Direct Mode. This should be used inside a <VIRTUALHOST> section to enable direct HTTP/2 communication for that virtual host. Direct communication means that if the first bytes received by the server on a connection match the HTTP/2 preamble, the HTTP/2 protocol is switched to immediately without further negotiation. This mode falls outside the RFC 7540 but has become widely implemented as it is very convenient for development and testing. By default the direct HTTP/2 mode is enabled.

Example

```
H2Direct on
```

[35]http://nghttp2.org/

H2MaxSessionStreams Directive

Description:	Maximum number of active streams per HTTP/2 session.
Syntax:	`H2MaxSessionStreams n`
Default:	`H2MaxSessionStreams 100`
Context:	server config, virtual host
Status:	Extension
Module:	mod_http2

This directive sets the maximum number of active streams per HTTP/2 session (e.g. connection) that the server allows. A stream is active if it is not `idle` or `closed` according to RFC 7540.

Example

```
H2MaxSessionStreams 20
```

H2MaxWorkerIdleSeconds Directive

Description:	Maximum number of seconds h2 workers remain idle until shut down.
Syntax:	`H2MaxWorkerIdleSeconds n`
Default:	`H2MaxWorkerIdleSeconds 600`
Context:	server config
Status:	Extension
Module:	mod_http2

This directive sets the maximum number of seconds a h2 worker may idle until it shuts itself down. This only happens while the number of h2 workers exceeds `H2MinWorkers`.

Example

```
H2MaxWorkerIdleSeconds 20
```

H2MaxWorkers Directive

Description:	Maximum number of worker threads to use per child process.
Syntax:	`H2MaxWorkers n`
Context:	server config
Status:	Extension
Module:	mod_http2

This directive sets the maximum number of worker threads to spawn per child process for HTTP/2 processing. If this directive is not used, `mod_http2` will chose a value suitable for the `mpm` module loaded.

Example

```
H2MaxWorkers 20
```

H2MinWorkers Directive

Description:	Minimal number of worker threads to use per child process.
Syntax:	`H2MinWorkers n`
Context:	server config
Status:	Extension
Module:	mod_http2

This directive sets the minimum number of worker threads to spawn per child process for HTTP/2 processing. If this directive is not used, `mod_http2` will chose a value suitable for the `mpm` module loaded.

Example

```
H2MinWorkers 10
```

H2SerializeHeaders Directive

Description:	Serialize Request/Resoonse Processing Switch
Syntax:	`H2SerializeHeaders on|off`
Default:	`H2SerializeHeaders off`
Context:	server config, virtual host
Status:	Extension
Module:	mod_http2

This directive toggles if HTTP/2 requests shall be serialized in HTTP/1.1 format for processing by `httpd` core or if received binary data shall be passed into the `request_recs` directly.

Serialization will lower performance, but gives more backward compatibility in case custom filters/hooks need it.

Example

```
H2SerializeHeaders on
```

H2SessionExtraFiles Directive

Description:	Number of Extra File Handles
Syntax:	`H2SessionExtraFiles n`
Default:	`H2SessionExtraFiles 5`
Context:	server config, virtual host
Status:	Extension
Module:	mod_http2

This directive sets maximum number of *extra* file handles a HTTP/2 session is allowed to use. A file handle is counted as *extra* when it is transfered from a h2 worker thread to the main HTTP/2 connection handling. This commonly happens when serving static files.

Depending on the processing model configured on the server, the number of connections times number of active streams may exceed the number of file handles for the process. On the other hand, converting every file into memory bytes early results in too many buffer writes. This option helps to mitigate that.

The number of file handles used by a server process is then in the order of:

```
(h2_connections * extra_files) + (h2_max_worker)
```

Example

```
H2SessionExtraFiles 10
```

H2StreamMaxMemSize Directive

Description:	Maximum amount of output data buffered per stream.
Syntax:	`H2StreamMaxMemSize bytes`
Default:	`H2StreamMaxMemSize 65536`
Context:	server config, virtual host
Status:	Extension
Module:	mod_http2

This directive sets the maximum number of outgoing data bytes buffered in memory for an active streams. This memory is not allocated per stream as such. Allocations are counted against this limit when they are about to be done. Stream processing freezes when the limit has been reached and will only continue when buffered data has been sent out to the client.

Example

```
H2StreamMaxMemSize 128000
```

H2WindowSize Directive

Description:	Size of Stream Window for upstream data.
Syntax:	`H2WindowSize bytes`
Default:	`H2WindowSize 65536`
Context:	server config, virtual host
Status:	Extension
Module:	mod_http2

This directive sets the size of the window that is used for flow control from client to server and limits the amount of data the server has to buffer. The client will stop sending on a stream once the limit has been reached until the server announces more available space (as it has processed some of the data).

This limit affects only request bodies, not its meta data such as headers. Also, it has no effect on response bodies as the window size for those are managed by the clients.

Example

```
H2WindowSize 128000
```

10.56 Apache Module mod_ident

Description:	RFC 1413 ident lookups
Status:	Extension
ModuleIdentifier:	ident_module
SourceFile:	mod_ident.c
Compatibility:	Available in Apache 2.1 and later

Summary

This module queries an RFC 1413[36] compatible daemon on a remote host to look up the owner of a connection.

Directives

- IdentityCheck
- IdentityCheckTimeout

See also

- MOD_LOG_CONFIG

IdentityCheck Directive

Description:	Enables logging of the RFC 1413 identity of the remote user
Syntax:	`IdentityCheck On|Off`
Default:	`IdentityCheck Off`
Context:	server config, virtual host, directory
Status:	Extension
Module:	mod_ident
Compatibility:	Moved out of core in Apache 2.1

This directive enables RFC 1413[37]-compliant logging of the remote user name for each connection, where the client machine runs identd or something similar. This information is logged in the access log using the `%...l` format string (p. 661) .

⟹The information should not be trusted in any way except for rudimentary usage tracking.

Note that this can cause serious latency problems accessing your server since every request requires one of these lookups to be performed. When firewalls or proxy servers are involved, each lookup might possibly fail and add a latency duration as defined by the IDENTITYCHECKTIMEOUT directive to each hit. So in general this is not very useful on public servers accessible from the Internet.

IdentityCheckTimeout Directive

Description:	Determines the timeout duration for ident requests
Syntax:	`IdentityCheckTimeout seconds`
Default:	`IdentityCheckTimeout 30`
Context:	server config, virtual host, directory
Status:	Extension
Module:	mod_ident

[36] http://www.ietf.org/rfc/rfc1413.txt
[37] http://www.ietf.org/rfc/rfc1413.txt

This directive specifies the timeout duration of an ident request. The default value of 30 seconds is recommended by RFC 1413[38], mainly because of possible network latency. However, you may want to adjust the timeout value according to your local network speed.

[38]http://www.ietf.org/rfc/rfc1413.txt

10.57 Apache Module mod_imagemap

Description:	Server-side imagemap processing
Status:	Base
ModuleIdentifier:	imagemap_module
SourceFile:	mod_imagemap.c

Summary

This module processes `.map` files, thereby replacing the functionality of the `imagemap` CGI program. Any directory or document type configured to use the handler `imap-file` (using either AddHandler or SetHandler) will be processed by this module.

The following directive will activate files ending with `.map` as imagemap files:

```
AddHandler imap-file map
```

Note that the following is still supported:

```
AddType application/x-httpd-imap map
```

However, we are trying to phase out "magic MIME types" so we are deprecating this method.

Directives

- ImapBase
- ImapDefault
- ImapMenu

New Features

The imagemap module adds some new features that were not possible with previously distributed imagemap programs.

- URL references relative to the Referer: information.
- Default <`base`> assignment through a new map directive `base`.
- No need for `imagemap.conf` file.
- Point references.
- Configurable generation of imagemap menus.

Imagemap File

The lines in the imagemap files can have one of several formats:

```
directive value [x,y ...]
directive value "Menu text" [x,y ...]
directive value x,y ...   "Menu text"
```

The directive is one of `base`, `default`, `poly`, `circle`, `rect`, or `point`. The value is an absolute or relative URL, or one of the special values listed below. The coordinates are `x,y` pairs separated by whitespace. The quoted text is used as the text of the link if a imagemap menu is generated. Lines beginning with '#' are comments.

Imagemap File Directives

There are six directives allowed in the imagemap file. The directives can come in any order, but are processed in the order they are found in the imagemap file.

`base` Directive Has the effect of `<base href="value">` . The non-absolute URLs of the map-file are taken relative to this value. The `base` directive overrides IMAPBASE as set in a `.htaccess` file or in the server configuration files. In the absence of an IMAPBASE configuration directive, `base` defaults to `http://server_name/`.

`base_uri` is synonymous with `base`. Note that a trailing slash on the URL is significant.

`default` Directive The action taken if the coordinates given do not fit any of the `poly`, `circle` or `rect` directives, and there are no `point` directives. Defaults to `nocontent` in the absence of an IMAPDEFAULT configuration setting, causing a status code of `204 No Content` to be returned. The client should keep the same page displayed.

`poly` Directive Takes three to one-hundred points, and is obeyed if the user selected coordinates fall within the polygon defined by these points.

`circle` Takes the center coordinates of a circle and a point on the circle. Is obeyed if the user selected point is with the circle.

`rect` Directive Takes the coordinates of two opposing corners of a rectangle. Obeyed if the point selected is within this rectangle.

`point` Directive Takes a single point. The point directive closest to the user selected point is obeyed if no other directives are satisfied. Note that `default` will not be followed if a `point` directive is present and valid coordinates are given.

Values

The values for each of the directives can be any of the following:

a URL The URL can be relative or absolute URL. Relative URLs can contain '..' syntax and will be resolved relative to the `base` value.

`base` itself will not be resolved according to the current value. A statement `base mailto:` will work properly, though.

`map` Equivalent to the URL of the imagemap file itself. No coordinates are sent with this, so a menu will be generated unless IMAPMENU is set to `none`.

`menu` Synonymous with `map`.

`referer` Equivalent to the URL of the referring document. Defaults to `http://servername/` if no `Referer:` header was present.

`nocontent` Sends a status code of `204 No Content`, telling the client to keep the same page displayed. Valid for all but `base`.

`error` Fails with a `500 Server Error`. Valid for all but `base`, but sort of silly for anything but `default`.

Coordinates

`0,0 200,200` A coordinate consists of an x and a y value separated by a comma. The coordinates are separated from each other by whitespace. To accommodate the way Lynx handles imagemaps, should a user select the coordinate `0,0`, it is as if no coordinate had been selected.

Quoted Text

"*Menu Text*" After the value or after the coordinates, the line optionally may contain text within double quotes. This string is used as the text for the link if a menu is generated:

```
<a href="http://example.com/">Menu text</a>
```

If no quoted text is present, the name of the link will be used as the text:

```
<a href="http://example.com/">http://example.com</a>
```

If you want to use double quotes within this text, you have to write them as `"`.

Example Mapfile

```
#Comments are printed in a 'formatted' or 'semiformatted' menu.
#And can contain html tags.  <hr>
base referer
poly map "Could I have a menu, please?" 0,0 0,10 10,10 10,0
rect ..  0,0 77,27 "the directory of the referer"
circle http://www.inetnebr.example.com/lincoln/feedback/ 195,0 305,27
rect another_file "in same directory as referer" 306,0 419,27
point http://www.zyzzyva.example.com/ 100,100
point http://www.tripod.example.com/ 200,200
rect mailto:nate@tripod.example.com 100,150 200,0 "Bugs?"
```

Referencing your mapfile

HTML example

```
<a href="/maps/imagemap1.map">
   <img ismap src="/images/imagemap1.gif">
</a>
```

XHTML example

```
<a href="/maps/imagemap1.map">
   <img ismap="ismap" src="/images/imagemap1.gif" />
</a>
```

ImapBase Directive

Description:	Default `base` for imagemap files
Syntax:	`ImapBase map|referer|URL`
Default:	`ImapBase http://servername/`
Context:	server config, virtual host, directory, .htaccess
Override:	Indexes
Status:	Base
Module:	mod_imagemap

The IMAPBASE directive sets the default `base` used in the imagemap files. Its value is overridden by a `base` directive within the imagemap file. If not present, the `base` defaults to `http://servername/`.

See also

- USECANONICALNAME

ImapDefault Directive

Description:	Default action when an imagemap is called with coordinates that are not explicitly mapped
Syntax:	`ImapDefault error|nocontent|map|referer|URL`
Default:	`ImapDefault nocontent`
Context:	server config, virtual host, directory, .htaccess
Override:	Indexes
Status:	Base
Module:	mod_imagemap

The IMAPDEFAULT directive sets the default `default` used in the imagemap files. Its value is overridden by a `default` directive within the imagemap file. If not present, the `default` action is `nocontent`, which means that a `204 No Content` is sent to the client. In this case, the client should continue to display the original page.

ImapMenu Directive

Description:	Action if no coordinates are given when calling an imagemap
Syntax:	`ImapMenu none|formatted|semiformatted|unformatted`
Default:	`ImapMenu formatted`
Context:	server config, virtual host, directory, .htaccess
Override:	Indexes
Status:	Base
Module:	mod_imagemap

The IMAPMENU directive determines the action taken if an imagemap file is called without valid coordinates.

`none` If ImapMenu is `none`, no menu is generated, and the `default` action is performed.

`formatted` A `formatted` menu is the simplest menu. Comments in the imagemap file are ignored. A level one header is printed, then an hrule, then the links each on a separate line. The menu has a consistent, plain look close to that of a directory listing.

`semiformatted` In the `semiformatted` menu, comments are printed where they occur in the imagemap file. Blank lines are turned into HTML breaks. No header or hrule is printed, but otherwise the menu is the same as a `formatted` menu.

`unformatted` Comments are printed, blank lines are ignored. Nothing is printed that does not appear in the imagemap file. All breaks and headers must be included as comments in the imagemap file. This gives you the most flexibility over the appearance of your menus, but requires you to treat your map files as HTML instead of plaintext.

10.58 Apache Module mod_include

Description:	Server-parsed html documents (Server Side Includes)
Status:	Base
ModuleIdentifier:	include_module
SourceFile:	mod_include.c

Summary

This module provides a filter which will process files before they are sent to the client. The processing is controlled by specially formatted SGML comments, referred to as *elements*. These elements allow conditional text, the inclusion of other files or programs, as well as the setting and printing of environment variables.

Directives

- SSIEndTag
- SSIErrorMsg
- SSIETag
- SSILastModified
- SSILegacyExprParser
- SSIStartTag
- SSITimeFormat
- SSIUndefinedEcho
- XBitHack

See also

- OPTIONS
- ACCEPTPATHINFO
- Filters (p. 100)
- SSI Tutorial (p. 233)

Enabling Server-Side Includes

Server Side Includes are implemented by the `INCLUDES` filter (p. 100) . If documents containing server-side include directives are given the extension .shtml, the following directives will make Apache parse them and assign the resulting document the mime type of `text/html`:

```
AddType text/html .shtml
AddOutputFilter INCLUDES .shtml
```

The following directive must be given for the directories containing the shtml files (typically in a <DIRECTORY> section, but this directive is also valid in `.htaccess` files if ALLOWOVERRIDE `Options` is set):

```
Options +Includes
```

For backwards compatibility, the `server-parsed` handler (p. 98) also activates the INCLUDES filter. As well, Apache will activate the INCLUDES filter for any document with mime type `text/x-server-parsed-html` or `text/x-server-parsed-html3` (and the resulting output will have the mime type `text/html`).

For more information, see our Tutorial on Server Side Includes (p. 233) .

PATH_INFO with Server Side Includes

Files processed for server-side includes no longer accept requests with `PATH_INFO` (trailing pathname information) by default. You can use the ACCEPTPATHINFO directive to configure the server to accept requests with `PATH_INFO`.

Available Elements

The document is parsed as an HTML document, with special commands embedded as SGML comments. A command has the syntax:

```
<!--#element attribute=value attribute=value ...  -->
```

The value will often be enclosed in double quotes, but single quotes (') and backticks (`) are also possible. Many commands only allow a single attribute-value pair. Note that the comment terminator (-->) should be preceded by whitespace to ensure that it isn't considered part of an SSI token. Note that the leading `<!--#` is *one* token and may not contain any whitespaces.

The allowed elements are listed in the following table:

Element	Description
`config`	configure output formats
`echo`	print variables
`exec`	execute external programs
`fsize`	print size of a file
`flastmod`	print last modification time of a file
`include`	include a file
`printenv`	print all available variables
`set`	set a value of a variable

SSI elements may be defined by modules other than MOD_INCLUDE. In fact, the `exec` element is provided by MOD_CGI, and will only be available if this module is loaded.

The config Element

This command controls various aspects of the parsing. The valid attributes are:

`echomsg` (***Apache 2.1 and later***) The value is a message that is sent back to the client if the `echo` element attempts to echo an undefined variable. This overrides any SSIUNDEFINEDECHO directives.

```
<!--#config echomsg="[Value Undefined]" -->
```

`errmsg` The value is a message that is sent back to the client if an error occurs while parsing the document. This overrides any SSIERRORMSG directives.

```
<!--#config errmsg="[Oops, something broke.]" -->
```

`sizefmt` The value sets the format to be used when displaying the size of a file. Valid values are `bytes` for a count in bytes, or `abbrev` for a count in Kb or Mb as appropriate, for example a size of 1024 bytes will be printed as "1K".

```
<!--#config sizefmt="abbrev" -->
```

`timefmt` The value is a string to be used by the `strftime(3)` library routine when printing dates.

```
<!--#config timefmt=""%R, %B %d, %Y"" -->
```

The echo Element

This command prints one of the include variables defined below. If the variable is unset, the result is determined by the SSIUNDEFINEDECHO directive. Any dates printed are subject to the currently configured `timefmt`.

Attributes:

`var` The value is the name of the variable to print.

`decoding` Specifies whether Apache should strip an encoding from the variable before processing the variable further. The default is `none`, where no decoding will be done. If set to `url`, then URL decoding (also known as %-encoding; this is appropriate for use within URLs in links, etc.) will be performed. If set to `urlencoded`, application/x-www-form-urlencoded compatible encoding (found in query strings) will be stripped. If set to `base64`, base64 will be decoded, and if set to `entity`, HTML entity encoding will be stripped. Decoding is done prior to any further encoding on the variable. Multiple encodings can be stripped by specifying more than one comma separated encoding. The decoding setting will remain in effect until the next decoding attribute is encountered, or the element ends.

The `decoding` attribute must *precede* the corresponding `var` attribute to be effective.

`encoding` Specifies how Apache should encode special characters contained in the variable before outputting them. If set to `none`, no encoding will be done. If set to `url`, then URL encoding (also known as %-encoding; this is appropriate for use within URLs in links, etc.) will be performed. If set to `urlencoded`, application/x-www-form-urlencoded compatible encoding will be performed instead, and should be used with query strings. If set to `base64`, base64 encoding will be performed. At the start of an `echo` element, the default is set to `entity`, resulting in entity encoding (which is appropriate in the context of a block-level HTML element, *e.g.* a paragraph of text). This can be changed by adding an `encoding` attribute, which will remain in effect until the next `encoding` attribute is encountered or the element ends, whichever comes first.

The `encoding` attribute must *precede* the corresponding `var` attribute to be effective.

! In order to avoid cross-site scripting issues, you should *always* encode user supplied data.

Example

```
<!--#echo encoding="entity" var="QUERY_STRING" -->
```

The exec Element

The `exec` command executes a given shell command or CGI script. It requires MOD_CGI to be present in the server. If OPTIONS `IncludesNOEXEC` is set, this command is completely disabled. The valid attributes are:

cgi The value specifies a (%-encoded) URL-path to the CGI script. If the path does not begin with a slash (/), then it is taken to be relative to the current document. The document referenced by this path is invoked as a CGI script, even if the server would not normally recognize it as such. However, the directory containing the script must be enabled for CGI scripts (with SCRIPTALIAS or OPTIONS ExecCGI).

The CGI script is given the `PATH_INFO` and query string (`QUERY_STRING`) of the original request from the client; these *cannot* be specified in the URL path. The include variables will be available to the script in addition to the standard CGI (p. 549) environment.

Example

```
<!--#exec cgi="/cgi-bin/example.cgi" -->
```

If the script returns a `Location:` header instead of output, then this will be translated into an HTML anchor.

The `include virtual` element should be used in preference to `exec cgi`. In particular, if you need to pass additional arguments to a CGI program, using the query string, this cannot be done with `exec cgi`, but can be done with `include virtual`, as shown here:

```
<!--#include virtual="/cgi-bin/example.cgi?argument=value" -->
```

cmd The server will execute the given string using `/bin/sh`. The include variables are available to the command, in addition to the usual set of CGI variables.

The use of `#include virtual` is almost always prefered to using either `#exec cgi` or `#exec cmd`. The former (`#include virtual`) uses the standard Apache sub-request mechanism to include files or scripts. It is much better tested and maintained.

In addition, on some platforms, like Win32, and on unix when using suexec (p. 105) , you cannot pass arguments to a command in an `exec` directive, or otherwise include spaces in the command. Thus, while the following will work under a non-suexec configuration on unix, it will not produce the desired result under Win32, or when running suexec:

```
<!--#exec cmd="perl /path/to/perlscript arg1 arg2" -->
```

The fsize Element

This command prints the size of the specified file, subject to the `sizefmt` format specification. Attributes:

file The value is a path relative to the directory containing the current document being parsed.

```
This file is <!--#fsize file="mod_include.html" --> bytes.
```

The value of `file` cannot start with a slash (/), nor can it contain `../` so as to refer to a file above the current directory or outside of the document root. Attempting to so will result in the error message: `The given path was above the root path.`

virtual The value is a (%-encoded) URL-path. If it does not begin with a slash (/) then it is taken to be relative to the current document. Note, that this does *not* print the size of any CGI output, but the size of the CGI script itself.

```
This file is <!--#fsize virtual="/docs/mod/mod_include.html" -->
bytes.
```

Note that in many cases these two are exactly the same thing. However, the `file` attribute doesn't respect URL-space aliases.

The flastmod Element

This command prints the last modification date of the specified file, subject to the `timefmt` format specification. The attributes are the same as for the `fsize` command.

The include Element

This command inserts the text of another document or file into the parsed file. Any included file is subject to the usual access control. If the directory containing the parsed file has Options (p. 354) `IncludesNOEXEC` set, then only documents with a text MIME-type (`text/plain`, `text/html` etc.) will be included. Otherwise CGI scripts are invoked as normal using the complete URL given in the command, including any query string.

An attribute defines the location of the document, and may appear more than once in an include element; an inclusion is done for each attribute given to the include command in turn. The valid attributes are:

file The value is a path relative to the directory containing the current document being parsed. It cannot contain `../`, nor can it be an absolute path. Therefore, you cannot include files that are outside of the document root, or above the current document in the directory structure. The `virtual` attribute should always be used in preference to this one.

virtual The value is a (%-encoded) URL-path. The URL cannot contain a scheme or hostname, only a path and an optional query string. If it does not begin with a slash (/) then it is taken to be relative to the current document.

A URL is constructed from the attribute, and the output the server would return if the URL were accessed by the client is included in the parsed output. Thus included files can be nested.

If the specified URL is a CGI program, the program will be executed and its output inserted in place of the directive in the parsed file. You may include a query string in a CGI url:

```
<!--#include virtual="/cgi-bin/example.cgi?argument=value" -->
```

`include virtual` should be used in preference to `exec cgi` to include the output of CGI programs into an HTML document.

If the KeptBodySize directive is correctly configured and valid for this included file, attempts to POST requests to the enclosing HTML document will be passed through to subrequests as POST requests as well. Without the directive, all subrequests are processed as GET requests.

onerror The value is a (%-encoded) URL-path which is shown should a previous attempt to include a file or virtual attribute failed. To be effective, this attribute must be specified after the file or virtual attributes being covered. If the attempt to include the onerror path fails, or if onerror is not specified, the default error message will be included.

```
# Simple example
<!--#include virtual="/not-exist.html" onerror="/error.html" -->
```

```
# Dedicated onerror paths
<!--#include virtual="/path-a.html" onerror="/error-a.html"
virtual="/path-b.html" onerror="/error-b.html" -->
```

The printenv Element

This prints out a plain text listing of all existing variables and their values. Special characters are entity encoded (see the `echo` element for details) before being output. There are no attributes.

Example
```
<pre> <!--#printenv --> </pre>
```

The set Element

This sets the value of a variable. Attributes:

`var` The name of the variable to set.

`value` The value to give a variable.

`decoding` Specifies whether Apache should strip an encoding from the variable before processing the variable further. The default is `none`, where no decoding will be done. If set to `url`, `urlencoded`, `base64` or `entity`, URL decoding, application/x-www-form-urlencoded decoding, base64 decoding or HTML entity decoding will be performed respectively. More than one decoding can be specified by separating with commas. The decoding setting will remain in effect until the next decoding attribute is encountered, or the element ends. The `decoding` attribute must *precede* the corresponding `var` attribute to be effective.

`encoding` Specifies how Apache should encode special characters contained in the variable before setting them. The default is `none`, where no encoding will be done. If set to `url`, `urlencoding`, `base64` or `entity`, URL encoding, application/x-www-form-urlencoded encoding, base64 encoding or HTML entity encoding will be performed respectively. More than one encoding can be specified by separating with commas. The encoding setting will remain in effect until the next encoding attribute is encountered, or the element ends. The `encoding` attribute must *precede* the corresponding `var` attribute to be effective. Encodings are applied after all decodings have been stripped.

Example
```
<!--#set var="category" value="help" -->
```

Include Variables

In addition to the variables in the standard CGI environment, these are available for the `echo` command, for `if` and `elif`, and to any program invoked by the document.

`DATE_GMT` The current date in Greenwich Mean Time.

`DATE_LOCAL` The current date in the local time zone.

`DOCUMENT_NAME` The filename (excluding directories) of the document requested by the user.

`DOCUMENT_URI` The (%-decoded) URL path of the document requested by the user. Note that in the case of nested include files, this is *not* the URL for the current document. Note also that if the URL is modified internally (e.g. by an ALIAS or DIRECTORYINDEX), the modified URL is shown.

`LAST_MODIFIED` The last modification date of the document requested by the user.

`QUERY_STRING_UNESCAPED` If a query string is present, this variable contains the (%-decoded) query string, which is *escaped* for shell usage (special characters like `&` etc. are preceded by backslashes).

Variable Substitution

Variable substitution is done within quoted strings in most cases where they may reasonably occur as an argument to an SSI directive. This includes the `config`, `exec`, `flastmod`, `fsize`, `include`, `echo`, and `set` directives. If SSILEGACYEXPRPARSER is set to `on`, substitution also occurs in the arguments to conditional operators. You can insert a literal dollar sign into the string using backslash quoting:

```
<!--#set var="cur" value="\$test" -->
```

If a variable reference needs to be substituted in the middle of a character sequence that might otherwise be considered a valid identifier in its own right, it can be disambiguated by enclosing the reference in braces, *a la* shell substitution:

```
<!--#set var="Zed" value="${REMOTE_HOST}_${REQUEST_METHOD}" -->
```

This will result in the `Zed` variable being set to `"X_Y"` if `REMOTE_HOST` is `"X"` and `REQUEST_METHOD` is `"Y"`.

Flow Control Elements

The basic flow control elements are:

```
<!--#if expr="test_condition" -->
<!--#elif expr="test_condition" -->
<!--#else -->
<!--#endif -->
```

The `if` element works like an if statement in a programming language. The test condition is evaluated and if the result is true, then the text until the next `elif`, `else` or `endif` element is included in the output stream.

The `elif` or `else` statements are used to put text into the output stream if the original *test_condition* was false. These elements are optional.

The `endif` element ends the `if` element and is required.

test_condition is a boolean expression which follows the ap_expr (p. 89) syntax. The syntax can be changed to be compatible with Apache HTTPD 2.2.x using SSILEGACYEXPRPARSER.

The SSI variables set with the `var` element are exported into the request environment and can be accessed with the `reqenv` function. As a short-cut, the function name `v` is also available inside MOD_INCLUDE.

The below example will print "from local net" if client IP address belongs to the 10.0.0.0/8 subnet.

```
<!--#if expr='-R "10.0.0.0/8"' -->
   from local net
<!--#else -->
   from somewhere else
<!--#endif -->
```

The below example will print "foo is bar" if the variable `foo` is set to the value "bar".

```
<!--#if expr='v("foo") = "bar"' -->
   foo is bar
<!--#endif -->
```

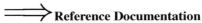

**Reference Documentation**
See also: Expressions in Apache HTTP Server (p. 89) , for a complete reference and examples.
The *restricted* functions are not available inside MOD_INCLUDE

Legacy expression syntax

This section describes the syntax of the `#if expr` element if SSILEGACYEXPRPARSER is set to `on`.

`string` true if *string* is not empty

`-A string` true if the URL represented by the string is accessible by configuration, false otherwise. This is useful where content on a page is to be hidden from users who are not authorized to view the URL, such as a link to that URL. Note that the URL is only tested for whether access would be granted, not whether the URL exists.

Example
```
<!--#if expr="-A /private" -->
   Click <a href="/private">here</a> to access private information.
<!--#endif -->
```

`string1 = string2string1 == string2string1 != string2` Compare *string1* with *string2*. If *string2* has the form `/string2/` then it is treated as a regular expression. Regular expressions are implemented by the PCRE[39] engine and have the same syntax as those in perl 5[40]. Note that == is just an alias for = and behaves exactly the same way.

If you are matching positive (= or ==), you can capture grouped parts of the regular expression. The captured parts are stored in the special variables `$1` .. `$9`. The whole string matched by the regular expression is stored in the special variable `$0`

Example
```
<!--#if expr="$QUERY_STRING = /^sid=([a-zA-Z0-9]+)/" -->
   <!--#set var="session" value="$1" -->
<!--#endif -->
```

`string1 < string2string1 <= string2string1 > string2string1 >= string2` Compare *string1* with *string2*. Note, that strings are compared *literally* (using `strcmp(3)`). Therefore the string "100" is less than "20".

`( test_condition )` true if *test_condition* is true

`! test_condition` true if *test_condition* is false

`test_condition1 && test_condition2` true if both *test_condition1* and *test_condition2* are true

`test_condition1 || test_condition2` true if either *test_condition1* or *test_condition2* is true

"=" and "!=" bind more tightly than "&&" and "||". "!" binds most tightly. Thus, the following are equivalent:

```
<!--#if expr="$a = test1 && $b = test2" -->
<!--#if expr="($a = test1) && ($b = test2)" -->
```

[39]http://www.pcre.org
[40]http://www.perl.com

The boolean operators `&&` and `||` share the same priority. So if you want to bind such an operator more tightly, you should use parentheses.

Anything that's not recognized as a variable or an operator is treated as a string. Strings can also be quoted: `'string'`. Unquoted strings can't contain whitespace (blanks and tabs) because it is used to separate tokens such as variables. If multiple strings are found in a row, they are concatenated using blanks. So,

```
string1string2 results in string1string2
and
'string1string2' results in string1string2.
```

Optimization of Boolean Expressions

If the expressions become more complex and slow down processing significantly, you can try to optimize them according to the evaluation rules:

- Expressions are evaluated from left to right
- Binary boolean operators (`&&` and `||`) are short circuited wherever possible. In conclusion with the rule above that means, MOD_INCLUDE evaluates at first the left expression. If the left result is sufficient to determine the end result, processing stops here. Otherwise it evaluates the right side and computes the end result from both left and right results.
- Short circuit evaluation is turned off as long as there are regular expressions to deal with. These must be evaluated to fill in the backreference variables (`$1` .. `$9`).

If you want to look how a particular expression is handled, you can recompile MOD_INCLUDE using the `-DDEBUG_INCLUDE` compiler option. This inserts for every parsed expression tokenizer information, the parse tree and how it is evaluated into the output sent to the client.

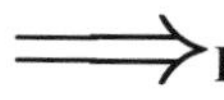**Escaping slashes in regex strings**

All slashes which are not intended to act as delimiters in your regex must be escaped. This is regardless of their meaning to the regex engine.

SSIEndTag Directive

Description:	String that ends an include element
Syntax:	`SSIEndTag tag`
Default:	`SSIEndTag "-->"`
Context:	server config, virtual host
Status:	Base
Module:	mod_include

This directive changes the string that MOD_INCLUDE looks for to mark the end of an include element.

```
SSIEndTag "%>"
```

See also

- SSISTARTTAG

SSIErrorMsg Directive

Description:	Error message displayed when there is an SSI error
Syntax:	`SSIErrorMsg message`
Default:	`SSIErrorMsg "[an error occurred while processing this directive]"`
Context:	server config, virtual host, directory, .htaccess
Override:	All
Status:	Base
Module:	mod_include

The SSIERRORMSG directive changes the error message displayed when MOD_INCLUDE encounters an error. For production servers you may consider changing the default error message to `"<!-- Error -->"` so that the message is not presented to the user.

This directive has the same effect as the `<!--#config errmsg=`*`message`*` -->` element.

```
SSIErrorMsg "<!-- Error -->"
```

SSIETag Directive

Description:	Controls whether ETags are generated by the server.
Syntax:	`SSIETag on|off`
Default:	`SSIETag off`
Context:	directory, .htaccess
Status:	Base
Module:	mod_include
Compatibility:	Available in version 2.2.15 and later.

Under normal circumstances, a file filtered by MOD_INCLUDE may contain elements that are either dynamically generated, or that may have changed independently of the original file. As a result, by default the server is asked not to generate an `ETag` header for the response by adding `no-etag` to the request notes.

The SSIETAG directive suppresses this behaviour, and allows the server to generate an `ETag` header. This can be used to enable caching of the output. Note that a backend server or dynamic content generator may generate an ETag of its own, ignoring `no-etag`, and this ETag will be passed by MOD_INCLUDE regardless of the value of this setting. SSIETAG can take on the following values:

`off` `no-etag` will be added to the request notes, and the server is asked not to generate an ETag. Where a server ignores the value of `no-etag` and generates an ETag anyway, the ETag will be respected.

`on` Existing ETags will be respected, and ETags generated by the server will be passed on in the response.

SSILastModified Directive

Description:	Controls whether `Last-Modified` headers are generated by the server.
Syntax:	`SSILastModified on|off`
Default:	`SSILastModified off`
Context:	directory, .htaccess
Status:	Base
Module:	mod_include
Compatibility:	Available in version 2.2.15 and later.

Under normal circumstances, a file filtered by MOD_INCLUDE may contain elements that are either dynamically generated, or that may have changed independently of the original file. As a result, by default the `Last-Modified` header is stripped from the response.

The SSILastModified directive overrides this behaviour, and allows the `Last-Modified` header to be respected if already present, or set if the header is not already present. This can be used to enable caching of the output. SSILastModified can take on the following values:

`off` The `Last-Modified` header will be stripped from responses, unless the XBitHack directive is set to `full` as described below.

`on` The `Last-Modified` header will be respected if already present in a response, and added to the response if the response is a file and the header is missing. The SSILastModified directive takes precedence over XBitHack.

SSILegacyExprParser Directive

Description:	Enable compatibility mode for conditional expressions.
Syntax:	`SSILegacyExprParser on|off`
Default:	`SSILegacyExprParser off`
Context:	directory, .htaccess
Status:	Base
Module:	mod_include
Compatibility:	Available in version 2.3.13 and later.

As of version 2.3.13, MOD_INCLUDE has switched to the new ap_expr (p. 89) syntax for conditional expressions in `#if` flow control elements. This directive allows to switch to the old syntax which is compatible with Apache HTTPD version 2.2.x and earlier.

SSIStartTag Directive

Description:	String that starts an include element
Syntax:	`SSIStartTag tag`
Default:	`SSIStartTag "<!--#"`
Context:	server config, virtual host
Status:	Base
Module:	mod_include

This directive changes the string that MOD_INCLUDE looks for to mark an include element to process.

You may want to use this option if you have 2 servers parsing the output of a file each processing different commands (possibly at different times).

```
SSIStartTag "<%"
SSIEndTag   "%>"
```

The example given above, which also specifies a matching SSIEndTag, will allow you to use SSI directives as shown in the example below:

SSI directives with alternate start and end tags

```
<%printenv %>
```

See also

- SSIEndTag

SSITimeFormat Directive

Description:	Configures the format in which date strings are displayed
Syntax:	`SSITimeFormat formatstring`
Default:	`SSITimeFormat "%A, %d-%b-%Y %H:%M:%S %Z"`
Context:	server config, virtual host, directory, .htaccess
Override:	All
Status:	Base
Module:	mod_include

This directive changes the format in which date strings are displayed when echoing `DATE` environment variables. The *formatstring* is as in `strftime(3)` from the C standard library.

This directive has the same effect as the `<!--#config timefmt=formatstring -->` element.

```
SSITimeFormat "%R, %B %d, %Y"
```

The above directive would cause times to be displayed in the format "22:26, June 14, 2002".

SSIUndefinedEcho Directive

Description:	String displayed when an unset variable is echoed
Syntax:	`SSIUndefinedEcho string`
Default:	`SSIUndefinedEcho "(none)"`
Context:	server config, virtual host, directory, .htaccess
Override:	All
Status:	Base
Module:	mod_include

This directive changes the string that MOD_INCLUDE displays when a variable is not set and "echoed".

```
SSIUndefinedEcho "<!-- undef -->"
```

XBitHack Directive

Description:	Parse SSI directives in files with the execute bit set
Syntax:	`XBitHack on|off|full`
Default:	`XBitHack off`
Context:	server config, virtual host, directory, .htaccess
Override:	Options
Status:	Base
Module:	mod_include

The XBITHACK directive controls the parsing of ordinary html documents. This directive only affects files associated with the MIME-type `text/html`. XBITHACK can take on the following values:

`off` No special treatment of executable files.

`on` Any `text/html` file that has the user-execute bit set will be treated as a server-parsed html document.

`full` As for `on` but also test the group-execute bit. If it is set, then set the `Last-modified` date of the returned file to be the last modified time of the file. If it is not set, then no last-modified date is sent. Setting this bit allows clients and proxies to cache the result of the request.

**Note**

You would not want to use the full option, unless you assure the group-execute bit is unset for every SSI script which might `#include` a CGI or otherwise produces different output on each hit (or could potentially change on subsequent requests).

The SSILASTMODIFIED directive takes precedence over the XBITHACK directive when SSILASTMODIFIED is set to `on`.

10.59 Apache Module mod_info

Description:	Provides a comprehensive overview of the server configuration
Status:	Extension
ModuleIdentifier:	info_module
SourceFile:	mod_info.c

Summary

To configure MOD_INFO, add the following to your `httpd.conf` file.

```
<Location "/server-info">
    SetHandler server-info
</Location>
```

You may wish to use MOD_AUTHZ_HOST inside the <LOCATION> directive to limit access to your server configuration information:

```
<Location "/server-info">
    SetHandler server-info
    Require host example.com
</Location>
```

Once configured, the server information is obtained by accessing `http://your.host.example.com/server-info`

Directives

- AddModuleInfo

Security Issues

Once MOD_INFO is loaded into the server, its handler capability is available in *all* configuration files, including per-directory files (*e.g.*, `.htaccess`). This may have security-related ramifications for your site.

In particular, this module can leak sensitive information from the configuration directives of other Apache modules such as system paths, usernames/passwords, database names, etc. Therefore, this module should **only** be used in a controlled environment and always with caution.

You will probably want to use MOD_AUTHZ_HOST to limit access to your server configuration information.

Access control

```
<Location "/server-info">
    SetHandler server-info
    # Allow access from server itself
    Require ip 127.0.0.1

    # Additionally, allow access from local workstation
    Require ip 192.168.1.17
</Location>
```

Selecting the information shown

By default, the server information includes a list of all enabled modules, and for each module, a description of the directives understood by that module, the hooks implemented by that module, and the relevant directives from the current configuration.

Other views of the configuration information are available by appending a query to the `server-info` request. For example, `http://your.host.example.com/server-info?config` will show all configuration directives.

`?<module-name>` Only information relevant to the named module

`?config` Just the configuration directives, not sorted by module

`?hooks` Only the list of Hooks each module is attached to

`?list` Only a simple list of enabled modules

`?server` Only the basic server information

Dumping the configuration on startup

If the config define `-DDUMP_CONFIG` is set, MOD_INFO will dump the pre-parsed configuration to `stdout` during server startup. Pre-parsed means that directives like <IFDEFINE> and <IFMODULE> are evaluated and environment varialbles are replaced. However it does not represent the final state of the configuration. In particular, it does not represent the merging or overriding that may happen for repeated directives.

This is roughly equivalent to the `?config` query.

Known Limitations

MOD_INFO provides its information by reading the parsed configuration, rather than reading the original configuration file. There are a few limitations as a result of the way the parsed configuration tree is created:

- Directives which are executed immediately rather than being stored in the parsed configuration are not listed. These include SERVERROOT, LOADMODULE, and LOADFILE.
- Directives which control the configuration file itself, such as INCLUDE, <IFMODULE> and <IFDEFINE> are not listed, but the included configuration directives are.
- Comments are not listed. (This may be considered a feature.)
- Configuration directives from `.htaccess` files are not listed (since they do not form part of the permanent server configuration).
- Container directives such as <DIRECTORY> are listed normally, but MOD_INFO cannot figure out the line number for the closing </DIRECTORY>.
- Directives generated by third party modules such as mod_perl[41] might not be listed.

[41] http://perl.apache.org

AddModuleInfo Directive

Description:	Adds additional information to the module information displayed by the server-info handler
Syntax:	`AddModuleInfo module-name string`
Context:	server config, virtual host
Status:	Extension
Module:	mod_info

This allows the content of *string* to be shown as HTML interpreted, **Additional Information** for the module *module-name*. Example:

```
AddModuleInfo mod_deflate.c 'See <a \
    href="http://httpd.apache.org/docs/2.4/mod/mod_deflate.html">\
    http://httpd.apache.org/docs/2.4/mod/mod_deflate.html</a>'
```

10.60 Apache Module mod_isapi

Description:	ISAPI Extensions within Apache for Windows
Status:	Base
ModuleIdentifier:	isapi_module
SourceFile:	mod_isapi.c
Compatibility:	Win32 only

Summary

This module implements the Internet Server extension API. It allows Internet Server extensions (*e.g.* ISAPI .dll modules) to be served by Apache for Windows, subject to the noted restrictions.

ISAPI extension modules (.dll files) are written by third parties. The Apache Group does not author these modules, so we provide no support for them. Please contact the ISAPI's author directly if you are experiencing problems running their ISAPI extension. **Please *do not* post such problems to Apache's lists or bug reporting pages.**

Directives

- ISAPIAppendLogToErrors
- ISAPIAppendLogToQuery
- ISAPICacheFile
- ISAPIFakeAsync
- ISAPILogNotSupported
- ISAPIReadAheadBuffer

Usage

In the server configuration file, use the ADDHANDLER directive to associate ISAPI files with the `isapi-handler` handler, and map it to them with their file extensions. To enable any .dll file to be processed as an ISAPI extension, edit the httpd.conf file and add the following line:

```
AddHandler isapi-handler .dll
```

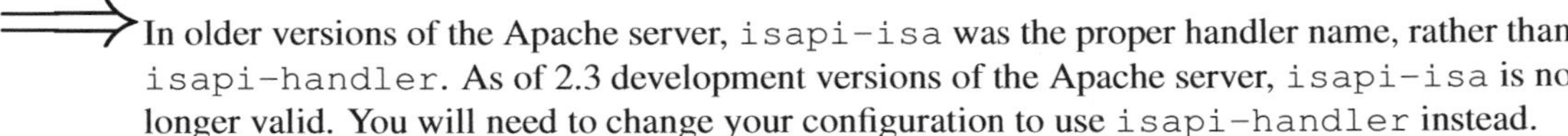

⟹ In older versions of the Apache server, `isapi-isa` was the proper handler name, rather than `isapi-handler`. As of 2.3 development versions of the Apache server, `isapi-isa` is no longer valid. You will need to change your configuration to use `isapi-handler` instead.

There is no capability within the Apache server to leave a requested module loaded. However, you may preload and keep a specific module loaded by using the following syntax in your httpd.conf:

```
ISAPICacheFile c:/WebWork/Scripts/ISAPI/mytest.dll
```

Whether or not you have preloaded an ISAPI extension, all ISAPI extensions are governed by the same permissions and restrictions as CGI scripts. That is, OPTIONS `ExecCGI` must be set for the directory that contains the ISAPI .dll file.

Review the Additional Notes and the Programmer's Journal for additional details and clarification of the specific ISAPI support offered by MOD_ISAPI.

Additional Notes

Apache's ISAPI implementation conforms to all of the ISAPI 2.0 specification, except for some "Microsoft-specific" extensions dealing with asynchronous I/O. Apache's I/O model does not allow asynchronous reading and writing in a manner that the ISAPI could access. If an ISA tries to access unsupported features, including async I/O, a message is placed in the error log to help with debugging. Since these messages can become a flood, the directive `ISAPILogNotSupported Off` exists to quiet this noise.

Some servers, like Microsoft IIS, load the ISAPI extension into the server and keep it loaded until memory usage is too high, or unless configuration options are specified. Apache currently loads and unloads the ISAPI extension each time it is requested, unless the ISAPICACHEFILE directive is specified. This is inefficient, but Apache's memory model makes this the most effective method. Many ISAPI modules are subtly incompatible with the Apache server, and unloading these modules helps to ensure the stability of the server.

Also, remember that while Apache supports ISAPI Extensions, it **does not support ISAPI Filters**. Support for filters may be added at a later date, but no support is planned at this time.

Programmer's Journal

If you are programming Apache 2.0 MOD_ISAPI modules, you must limit your calls to `ServerSupportFunction` to the following directives:

HSE_REQ_SEND_URL_REDIRECT_RESP Redirect the user to another location.
This must be a fully qualified URL (*e.g.* `http://server/location`).

HSE_REQ_SEND_URL Redirect the user to another location.
This cannot be a fully qualified URL, you are not allowed to pass the protocol or a server name (*e.g.* simply `/location`).
This redirection is handled by the server, not the browser.

Warning
In their recent documentation, Microsoft appears to have abandoned the distinction between the two `HSE_REQ_SEND_URL` functions. Apache continues to treat them as two distinct functions with different requirements and behaviors.

HSE_REQ_SEND_RESPONSE_HEADER Apache accepts a response body following the header if it follows the blank line (two consecutive newlines) in the headers string argument. This body cannot contain NULLs, since the headers argument is NULL terminated.

HSE_REQ_DONE_WITH_SESSION Apache considers this a no-op, since the session will be finished when the ISAPI returns from processing.

HSE_REQ_MAP_URL_TO_PATH Apache will translate a virtual name to a physical name.

HSE_APPEND_LOG_PARAMETER This logged message may be captured in any of the following logs:

- in the `\"%{isapi-parameter}n\"` component in a CUSTOMLOG directive
- in the `%q` log component with the ISAPIAPPENDLOGTOQUERY `On` directive
- in the error log with the ISAPIAPPENDLOGTOERRORS `On` directive

The first option, the `%{isapi-parameter}n` component, is always available and preferred.

HSE_REQ_IS_KEEP_CONN Will return the negotiated Keep-Alive status.

HSE_REQ_SEND_RESPONSE_HEADER_EX Will behave as documented, although the `fKeepConn` flag is ignored.

HSE_REQ_IS_CONNECTED Will report false if the request has been aborted.

Apache returns FALSE to any unsupported call to ServerSupportFunction, and sets the GetLastError value to ERROR_INVALID_PARAMETER.

ReadClient retrieves the request body exceeding the initial buffer (defined by ISAPIREADAHEADBUFFER). Based on the ISAPIREADAHEADBUFFER setting (number of bytes to buffer prior to calling the ISAPI handler) shorter requests are sent complete to the extension when it is invoked. If the request is longer, the ISAPI extension must use ReadClient to retrieve the remaining request body.

WriteClient is supported, but only with the HSE_IO_SYNC flag or no option flag (value of 0). Any other WriteClient request will be rejected with a return value of FALSE, and a GetLastError value of ERROR_INVALID_PARAMETER.

GetServerVariable is supported, although extended server variables do not exist (as defined by other servers.) All the usual Apache CGI environment variables are available from GetServerVariable, as well as the ALL_HTTP and ALL_RAW values.

Since httpd 2.0, MOD_ISAPI supports additional features introduced in later versions of the ISAPI specification, as well as limited emulation of async I/O and the TransmitFile semantics. Apache httpd also supports preloading ISAPI .dlls for performance.

ISAPIAppendLogToErrors Directive

Description:	Record HSE_APPEND_LOG_PARAMETER requests from ISAPI extensions to the error log
Syntax:	ISAPIAppendLogToErrors on|off
Default:	ISAPIAppendLogToErrors off
Context:	server config, virtual host, directory, .htaccess
Override:	FileInfo
Status:	Base
Module:	mod_isapi

Record HSE_APPEND_LOG_PARAMETER requests from ISAPI extensions to the server error log.

ISAPIAppendLogToQuery Directive

Description:	Record HSE_APPEND_LOG_PARAMETER requests from ISAPI extensions to the query field
Syntax:	ISAPIAppendLogToQuery on|off
Default:	ISAPIAppendLogToQuery on
Context:	server config, virtual host, directory, .htaccess
Override:	FileInfo
Status:	Base
Module:	mod_isapi

Record HSE_APPEND_LOG_PARAMETER requests from ISAPI extensions to the query field (appended to the CUSTOMLOG %q component).

ISAPICacheFile Directive

Description:	ISAPI .dll files to be loaded at startup
Syntax:	ISAPICacheFile file-path [file-path] ...
Context:	server config, virtual host
Status:	Base
Module:	mod_isapi

Specifies a space-separated list of file names to be loaded when the Apache server is launched, and remain loaded until the server is shut down. This directive may be repeated for every ISAPI .dll file desired. The full path name of each file should be specified. If the path name is not absolute, it will be treated relative to SERVERROOT.

ISAPIFakeAsync Directive

Description:	Fake asynchronous support for ISAPI callbacks
Syntax:	`ISAPIFakeAsync on|off`
Default:	`ISAPIFakeAsync off`
Context:	server config, virtual host, directory, .htaccess
Override:	FileInfo
Status:	Base
Module:	mod_isapi

While set to on, asynchronous support for ISAPI callbacks is simulated.

ISAPILogNotSupported Directive

Description:	Log unsupported feature requests from ISAPI extensions
Syntax:	`ISAPILogNotSupported on|off`
Default:	`ISAPILogNotSupported off`
Context:	server config, virtual host, directory, .htaccess
Override:	FileInfo
Status:	Base
Module:	mod_isapi

Logs all requests for unsupported features from ISAPI extensions in the server error log. This may help administrators to track down problems. Once set to on and all desired ISAPI modules are functioning, it should be set back to off.

ISAPIReadAheadBuffer Directive

Description:	Size of the Read Ahead Buffer sent to ISAPI extensions
Syntax:	`ISAPIReadAheadBuffer size`
Default:	`ISAPIReadAheadBuffer 49152`
Context:	server config, virtual host, directory, .htaccess
Override:	FileInfo
Status:	Base
Module:	mod_isapi

Defines the maximum size of the Read Ahead Buffer sent to ISAPI extensions when they are initially invoked. All remaining data must be retrieved using the `ReadClient` callback; some ISAPI extensions may not support the `ReadClient` function. Refer questions to the ISAPI extension's author.

10.61 Apache Module mod_lbmethod_bybusyness

Description:	Pending Request Counting load balancer scheduler algorithm for MOD_PROXY_BALANCER
Status:	Extension
ModuleIdentifier:	lbmethod_bybusyness_module
SourceFile:	mod_lbmethod_bybusyness.c
Compatibility:	Split off from MOD_PROXY_BALANCER in 2.3

Summary

This module does not provide any configuration directives of its own. It requires the services of MOD_PROXY_BALANCER, and provides the `bybusyness` load balancing method.

Directives This module provides no directives.

See also

- MOD_PROXY
- MOD_PROXY_BALANCER

Pending Request Counting Algorithm

Enabled via `lbmethod=bybusyness`, this scheduler keeps track of how many requests each worker is currently assigned at present. A new request is automatically assigned to the worker with the lowest number of active requests. This is useful in the case of workers that queue incoming requests independently of Apache, to ensure that queue length stays even and a request is always given to the worker most likely to service it the fastest and reduce latency.

In the case of multiple least-busy workers, the statistics (and weightings) used by the Request Counting method are used to break the tie. Over time, the distribution of work will come to resemble that characteristic of `byrequests` (as implemented by MOD_LBMETHOD_BYREQUESTS).

10.62 Apache Module mod_lbmethod_byrequests

Description:	Request Counting load balancer scheduler algorithm for MOD_PROXY_BALANCER
Status:	Extension
ModuleIdentifier:	lbmethod_byrequests_module
SourceFile:	mod_lbmethod_byrequests.c
Compatibility:	Split off from MOD_PROXY_BALANCER in 2.3

Summary

This module does not provide any configuration directives of its own. It requires the services of MOD_PROXY_BALANCER, and provides the `byrequests` load balancing method..

Directives This module provides no directives.

See also

- MOD_PROXY
- MOD_PROXY_BALANCER

Request Counting Algorithm

Enabled via `lbmethod=byrequests`, the idea behind this scheduler is that we distribute the requests among the various workers to ensure that each gets their configured share of the number of requests. It works as follows:

lbfactor is *how much we expect this worker to work*, or *the workers' work quota*. This is a normalized value representing their "share" of the amount of work to be done.

lbstatus is *how urgent this worker has to work to fulfill its quota of work*.

The *worker* is a member of the load balancer, usually a remote host serving one of the supported protocols.

We distribute each worker's work quota to the worker, and then look which of them needs to work most urgently (biggest lbstatus). This worker is then selected for work, and its lbstatus reduced by the total work quota we distributed to all workers. Thus the sum of all lbstatus does not change(*) and we distribute the requests as desired.

If some workers are disabled, the others will still be scheduled correctly.

```
for each worker in workers
    worker lbstatus += worker lbfactor
    total factor    += worker lbfactor
    if worker lbstatus > candidate lbstatus
        candidate = worker

candidate lbstatus -= total factor
```

If a balancer is configured as follows:

worker	**a**	**b**	**c**	**d**
lbfactor	25	25	25	25
lbstatus	0	0	0	0

And *b* gets disabled, the following schedule is produced:

worker	**a**
lbstatus	*-5(*
lbstatus	-2:
lbstatus	0
(repeat)	

That is it schedules: *a c d a c d a c d* ... Please note that:

worker	**a**	**b**	**c**	**d**
lbfactor	25	25	25	25

Has the exact same behavior as:

worker	**a**	**b**	**c**	**d**
lbfactor	1	1	1	1

This is because all values of *lbfactor* are normalized with respect to the others. For:

worker	**a**	**b**	**c**
lbfactor	1	4	1

worker *b* will, on average, get 4 times the requests that *a* and *c* will.

The following asymmetric configuration works as one would expect:

worker	**a**
lbfactor	70
lbstatus	*-3(*
lbstatus	40
lbstatus	*10*
lbstatus	*-2(*
lbstatus	*-5(*
lbstatus	20
lbstatus	*-1(*
lbstatus	*-4(*
lbstatus	30
lbstatus	*0*
(repeat)	

That is after 10 schedules, the schedule repeats and 7 *a* are selected with 3 *b* interspersed.

10.63 Apache Module mod_lbmethod_bytraffic

Description:	Weighted Traffic Counting load balancer scheduler algorithm for MOD_PROXY_BALANCER
Status:	Extension
ModuleIdentifier:	lbmethod_bytraffic_module
SourceFile:	mod_lbmethod_bytraffic.c
Compatibility:	Split off from MOD_PROXY_BALANCER in 2.3

Summary

This module does not provide any configuration directives of its own. It requires the services of MOD_PROXY_BALANCER, and provides the `bytraffic` load balancing method..

Directives This module provides no directives.

See also

- MOD_PROXY
- MOD_PROXY_BALANCER

Weighted Traffic Counting Algorithm

Enabled via `lbmethod=bytraffic`, the idea behind this scheduler is very similar to the Request Counting method, with the following changes:

lbfactor is *how much traffic, in bytes, we want this worker to handle.* This is also a normalized value representing their "share" of the amount of work to be done, but instead of simply counting the number of requests, we take into account the amount of traffic this worker has either seen or produced.

If a balancer is configured as follows:

worker	**a**	**b**	**c**
lbfactor	1	2	1

Then we mean that we want *b* to process twice the amount of bytes than *a* or *c* should. It does not necessarily mean that *b* would handle twice as many requests, but it would process twice the I/O. Thus, the size of the request and response are applied to the weighting and selection algorithm.

Note: input and output bytes are weighted the same.

10.64 Apache Module mod_lbmethod_heartbeat

Description:	Heartbeat Traffic Counting load balancer scheduler algorithm for MOD_PROXY_BALANCER
Status:	Experimental
ModuleIdentifier:	lbmethod_heartbeat_module
SourceFile:	mod_lbmethod_heartbeat.c
Compatibility:	Available in version 2.3 and later

Summary

lbmethod=heartbeat uses the services of MOD_HEARTMONITOR to balance between origin servers that are providing heartbeat info via the MOD_HEARTBEAT module.

This modules load balancing algorithm favors servers with more ready (idle) capacity over time, but does not select the server with the most ready capacity every time. Servers that have 0 active clients are penalized, with the assumption that they are not fully initialized.

Directives

- HeartbeatStorage

See also

- MOD_PROXY
- MOD_PROXY_BALANCER
- MOD_HEARTBEAT
- MOD_HEARTMONITOR

HeartbeatStorage Directive

Description:	Path to read heartbeat data
Syntax:	`HeartbeatStorage file-path`
Default:	`HeartbeatStorage logs/hb.dat`
Context:	server config
Status:	Experimental
Module:	mod_lbmethod_heartbeat

The HEARTBEATSTORAGE directive specifies the path to read heartbeat data. This flat-file is used only when MOD_SLOTMEM_SHM is not loaded.

10.65 Apache Module mod_ldap

Description:	LDAP connection pooling and result caching services for use by other LDAP modules
Status:	Extension
ModuleIdentifier:	ldap_module
SourceFile:	util_ldap.c

Summary

This module was created to improve the performance of websites relying on backend connections to LDAP servers. In addition to the functions provided by the standard LDAP libraries, this module adds an LDAP connection pool and an LDAP shared memory cache.

To enable this module, LDAP support must be compiled into apr-util. This is achieved by adding the `--with-ldap` flag to the `configure` script when building Apache.

SSL/TLS support is dependent on which LDAP toolkit has been linked to APR. As of this writing, APR-util supports: OpenLDAP SDK[42] (2.x or later), Novell LDAP SDK[43], Mozilla LDAP SDK[44], native Solaris LDAP SDK (Mozilla based) or the native Microsoft LDAP SDK. See the APR[45] website for details.

Directives

- LDAPCacheEntries
- LDAPCacheTTL
- LDAPConnectionPoolTTL
- LDAPConnectionTimeout
- LDAPLibraryDebug
- LDAPOpCacheEntries
- LDAPOpCacheTTL
- LDAPReferralHopLimit
- LDAPReferrals
- LDAPRetries
- LDAPRetryDelay
- LDAPSharedCacheFile
- LDAPSharedCacheSize
- LDAPTimeout
- LDAPTrustedClientCert
- LDAPTrustedGlobalCert
- LDAPTrustedMode
- LDAPVerifyServerCert

[42] http://www.openldap.org/
[43] http://developer.novell.com/ndk/cldap.htm
[44] https://wiki.mozilla.org/LDAP_C_SDK
[45] http://apr.apache.org

Example Configuration

The following is an example configuration that uses MOD_LDAP to increase the performance of HTTP Basic authentication provided by MOD_AUTHNZ_LDAP.

```
# Enable the LDAP connection pool and shared
# memory cache. Enable the LDAP cache status
# handler. Requires that mod_ldap and mod_authnz_ldap
# be loaded. Change the "yourdomain.example.com" to
# match your domain.

LDAPSharedCacheSize 500000
LDAPCacheEntries 1024
LDAPCacheTTL 600
LDAPOpCacheEntries 1024
LDAPOpCacheTTL 600

<Location "/ldap-status">
    SetHandler ldap-status

    Require host yourdomain.example.com

    Satisfy any
    AuthType Basic
    AuthName "LDAP Protected"
    AuthBasicProvider ldap
    AuthLDAPURL "ldap://127.0.0.1/dc=example,dc=com?uid?one"
    Require valid-user
</Location>
```

LDAP Connection Pool

LDAP connections are pooled from request to request. This allows the LDAP server to remain connected and bound ready for the next request, without the need to unbind/connect/rebind. The performance advantages are similar to the effect of HTTP keepalives.

On a busy server it is possible that many requests will try and access the same LDAP server connection simultaneously. Where an LDAP connection is in use, Apache will create a new connection alongside the original one. This ensures that the connection pool does not become a bottleneck.

There is no need to manually enable connection pooling in the Apache configuration. Any module using this module for access to LDAP services will share the connection pool.

LDAP connections can keep track of the ldap client credentials used when binding to an LDAP server. These credentials can be provided to LDAP servers that do not allow anonymous binds during referral chasing. To control this feature, see the LDAPREFERRALS and LDAPREFERRALHOPLIMIT directives. By default, this feature is enabled.

LDAP Cache

For improved performance, MOD_LDAP uses an aggressive caching strategy to minimize the number of times that the LDAP server must be contacted. Caching can easily double or triple the throughput of Apache when it is serving pages protected with mod_authnz_ldap. In addition, the load on the LDAP server will be significantly decreased.

MOD_LDAP supports two types of LDAP caching during the search/bind phase with a *search/bind cache* and during the compare phase with two *operation caches*. Each LDAP URL that is used by the server has its own set of these three caches.

The Search/Bind Cache

The process of doing a search and then a bind is the most time-consuming aspect of LDAP operation, especially if the directory is large. The search/bind cache is used to cache all searches that resulted in successful binds. Negative results (*i.e.*, unsuccessful searches, or searches that did not result in a successful bind) are not cached. The rationale behind this decision is that connections with invalid credentials are only a tiny percentage of the total number of connections, so by not caching invalid credentials, the size of the cache is reduced.

MOD_LDAP stores the username, the DN retrieved, the password used to bind, and the time of the bind in the cache. Whenever a new connection is initiated with the same username, MOD_LDAP compares the password of the new connection with the password in the cache. If the passwords match, and if the cached entry is not too old, MOD_LDAP bypasses the search/bind phase.

The search and bind cache is controlled with the LDAPCACHEENTRIES and LDAPCACHETTL directives.

Operation Caches

During attribute and distinguished name comparison functions, MOD_LDAP uses two operation caches to cache the compare operations. The first compare cache is used to cache the results of compares done to test for LDAP group membership. The second compare cache is used to cache the results of comparisons done between distinguished names.

Note that, when group membership is being checked, any sub-group comparison results are cached to speed future sub-group comparisons.

The behavior of both of these caches is controlled with the LDAPOPCACHEENTRIES and LDAPOPCACHETTL directives.

Monitoring the Cache

MOD_LDAP has a content handler that allows administrators to monitor the cache performance. The name of the content handler is `ldap-status`, so the following directives could be used to access the MOD_LDAP cache information:

```
<Location "/server/cache-info">
    SetHandler ldap-status
</Location>
```

By fetching the URL `http://servername/cache-info`, the administrator can get a status report of every cache that is used by MOD_LDAP cache. Note that if Apache does not support shared memory, then each `httpd` instance has its own cache, so reloading the URL will result in different information each time, depending on which `httpd` instance processes the request.

Using SSL/TLS

The ability to create an SSL and TLS connections to an LDAP server is defined by the directives LDAPTRUSTEDGLOBALCERT, LDAPTRUSTEDCLIENTCERT and LDAPTRUSTEDMODE. These directives specify the CA and optional client certificates to be used, as well as the type of encryption to be used on the connection (none, SSL or TLS/STARTTLS).

```
# Establish an SSL LDAP connection on port 636. Requires that
# mod_ldap and mod_authnz_ldap be loaded. Change the
# "yourdomain.example.com" to match your domain.

LDAPTrustedGlobalCert CA_DER "/certs/certfile.der"

<Location "/ldap-status">
    SetHandler ldap-status

    Require host yourdomain.example.com

    Satisfy any
    AuthType Basic
    AuthName "LDAP Protected"
    AuthBasicProvider ldap
    AuthLDAPURL "ldaps://127.0.0.1/dc=example,dc=com?uid?one"
    Require valid-user
</Location>

# Establish a TLS LDAP connection on port 389. Requires that
# mod_ldap and mod_authnz_ldap be loaded. Change the
# "yourdomain.example.com" to match your domain.

LDAPTrustedGlobalCert CA_DER "/certs/certfile.der:

<Location "/ldap-status">
    SetHandler ldap-status

    Require host yourdomain.example.com

    Satisfy any
    AuthType Basic
    AuthName "LDAP Protected"
    AuthBasicProvider ldap
    AuthLDAPURL "ldap://127.0.0.1/dc=example,dc=com?uid?one" TLS
    Require valid-user
</Location>
```

SSL/TLS Certificates

The different LDAP SDKs have widely different methods of setting and handling both CA and client side certificates.

If you intend to use SSL or TLS, read this section CAREFULLY so as to understand the differences between configurations on the different LDAP toolkits supported.

Netscape/Mozilla/iPlanet SDK

CA certificates are specified within a file called cert7.db. The SDK will not talk to any LDAP server whose certificate was not signed by a CA specified in this file. If client certificates are required, an optional key3.db file may be specified with an optional password. The secmod file can be specified if required. These files are in the same format as used by the Netscape Communicator or Mozilla web browsers. The easiest way to obtain these files is to grab them from your browser installation.

Client certificates are specified per connection using the LDAPTrustedClientCert directive by referring to the certificate "nickname". An optional password may be specified to unlock the certificate's private key.

The SDK supports SSL only. An attempt to use STARTTLS will cause an error when an attempt is made to contact the LDAP server at runtime.

```
# Specify a Netscape CA certificate file
LDAPTrustedGlobalCert CA_CERT7_DB "/certs/cert7.db"
# Specify an optional key3.db file for client certificate support
LDAPTrustedGlobalCert CERT_KEY3_DB "/certs/key3.db"
# Specify the secmod file if required
LDAPTrustedGlobalCert CA_SECMOD "/certs/secmod"
<Location "/ldap-status">
    SetHandler ldap-status

    Require host yourdomain.example.com

    Satisfy any
    AuthType Basic
    AuthName "LDAP Protected"
    AuthBasicProvider ldap
    LDAPTrustedClientCert CERT_NICKNAME <nickname> [password]
    AuthLDAPURL "ldaps://127.0.0.1/dc=example,dc=com?uid?one"
    Require valid-user
</Location>
```

Novell SDK

One or more CA certificates must be specified for the Novell SDK to work correctly. These certificates can be specified as binary DER or Base64 (PEM) encoded files.

Note: Client certificates are specified globally rather than per connection, and so must be specified with the LDAPTrustedGlobalCert directive as below. Trying to set client certificates via the LDAPTrustedClientCert directive will cause an error to be logged when an attempt is made to connect to the LDAP server..

The SDK supports both SSL and STARTTLS, set using the LDAPTrustedMode parameter. If an ldaps:// URL is specified, SSL mode is forced, override this directive.

```
# Specify two CA certificate files
LDAPTrustedGlobalCert CA_DER "/certs/cacert1.der"
LDAPTrustedGlobalCert CA_BASE64 "/certs/cacert2.pem"
# Specify a client certificate file and key
LDAPTrustedGlobalCert CERT_BASE64 "/certs/cert1.pem"
LDAPTrustedGlobalCert KEY_BASE64 "/certs/key1.pem" [password]
# Do not use this directive, as it will throw an error
#LDAPTrustedClientCert CERT_BASE64 "/certs/cert1.pem"
```

OpenLDAP SDK

One or more CA certificates must be specified for the OpenLDAP SDK to work correctly. These certificates can be specified as binary DER or Base64 (PEM) encoded files.

Both CA and client certificates may be specified globally (LDAPTrustedGlobalCert) or per-connection (LDAPTrustedClientCert). When any settings are specified per-connection, the global settings are superceded.

The documentation for the SDK claims to support both SSL and STARTTLS, however STARTTLS does not seem to work on all versions of the SDK. The SSL/TLS mode can be set using the LDAPTrustedMode parameter. If an ldaps:// URL is specified, SSL mode is forced. The OpenLDAP documentation notes that SSL (ldaps://) support has been deprecated to be replaced with TLS, although the SSL functionality still works.

```
# Specify two CA certificate files
LDAPTrustedGlobalCert CA_DER "/certs/cacert1.der"
LDAPTrustedGlobalCert CA_BASE64 "/certs/cacert2.pem"
<Location "/ldap-status">
    SetHandler ldap-status

    Require host yourdomain.example.com

    LDAPTrustedClientCert CERT_BASE64 "/certs/cert1.pem"
    LDAPTrustedClientCert KEY_BASE64 "/certs/key1.pem"
    # CA certs respecified due to per-directory client certs
    LDAPTrustedClientCert CA_DER "/certs/cacert1.der"
    LDAPTrustedClientCert CA_BASE64 "/certs/cacert2.pem"
    Satisfy any
    AuthType Basic
    AuthName "LDAP Protected"
    AuthBasicProvider ldap
    AuthLDAPURL "ldaps://127.0.0.1/dc=example,dc=com?uid?one"
    Require valid-user
</Location>
```

Solaris SDK

SSL/TLS for the native Solaris LDAP libraries is not yet supported. If required, install and use the OpenLDAP libraries instead.

Microsoft SDK

SSL/TLS certificate configuration for the native Microsoft LDAP libraries is done inside the system registry, and no configuration directives are required.

Both SSL and TLS are supported by using the ldaps:// URL format, or by using the LDAPTrustedMode directive accordingly.

Note: The status of support for client certificates is not yet known for this toolkit.

LDAPCacheEntries Directive

Description:	Maximum number of entries in the primary LDAP cache
Syntax:	`LDAPCacheEntries number`
Default:	`LDAPCacheEntries 1024`
Context:	server config
Status:	Extension
Module:	mod_ldap

Specifies the maximum size of the primary LDAP cache. This cache contains successful search/binds. Set it to 0 to turn off search/bind caching. The default size is 1024 cached searches.

LDAPCacheTTL Directive

Description:	Time that cached items remain valid
Syntax:	`LDAPCacheTTL seconds`
Default:	`LDAPCacheTTL 600`
Context:	server config
Status:	Extension
Module:	mod_ldap

Specifies the time (in seconds) that an item in the search/bind cache remains valid. The default is 600 seconds (10 minutes).

LDAPConnectionPoolTTL Directive

Description:	Discard backend connections that have been sitting in the connection pool too long
Syntax:	`LDAPConnectionPoolTTL n`
Default:	`LDAPConnectionPoolTTL -1`
Context:	server config, virtual host
Status:	Extension
Module:	mod_ldap
Compatibility:	Apache HTTP Server 2.3.12 and later

Specifies the maximum age, in seconds, that a pooled LDAP connection can remain idle and still be available for use. Connections are cleaned up when they are next needed, not asynchronously.

A setting of 0 causes connections to never be saved in the backend connection pool. The default value of -1, and any other negative value, allows connections of any age to be reused.

For performance reasons, the reference time used by this directive is based on when the LDAP connection is returned to the pool, not the time of the last successful I/O with the LDAP server.

Since 2.4.10, new measures are in place to avoid the reference time from being inflated by cache hits or slow requests. First, the reference time is not updated if no backend LDAP conncetions were needed. Second, the reference time uses the time the HTTP request was received instead of the time the request is completed.

⟹ This timeout defaults to units of seconds, but accepts suffixes for milliseconds (ms), minutes (min), and hours (h).

LDAPConnectionTimeout Directive

Description:	Specifies the socket connection timeout in seconds
Syntax:	`LDAPConnectionTimeout seconds`
Context:	server config
Status:	Extension
Module:	mod_ldap

This directive configures the LDAP_OPT_NETWORK_TIMEOUT (or LDAP_OPT_CONNECT_TIMEOUT) option in the underlying LDAP client library, when available. This value typically controls how long the LDAP client library will wait for the TCP connection to the LDAP server to complete.

If a connection is not successful with the timeout period, either an error will be returned or the LDAP client library will attempt to connect to a secondary LDAP server if one is specified (via a space-separated list of hostnames in the AUTHLDAPURL).

The default is 10 seconds, if the LDAP client library linked with the server supports the LDAP_OPT_NETWORK_TIMEOUT option.

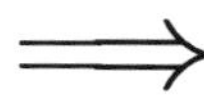LDAPConnectionTimeout is only available when the LDAP client library linked with the server supports the LDAP_OPT_NETWORK_TIMEOUT (or LDAP_OPT_CONNECT_TIMEOUT) option, and the ultimate behavior is dictated entirely by the LDAP client library.

LDAPLibraryDebug Directive

Description:	Enable debugging in the LDAP SDK
Syntax:	`LDAPLibraryDebug 7`
Default:	`disabled`
Context:	server config
Status:	Extension
Module:	mod_ldap

Turns on SDK-specific LDAP debug options that generally cause the LDAP SDK to log verbose trace information to the main Apache error log. The trace messages from the LDAP SDK provide gory details that can be useful during debugging of connectivity problems with backend LDAP servers

This option is only configurable when Apache HTTP Server is linked with an LDAP SDK that implements `LDAP_OPT_DEBUG` or `LDAP_OPT_DEBUG_LEVEL`, such as OpenLDAP (a value of 7 is verbose) or Tivoli Directory Server (a value of 65535 is verbose).

The logged information will likely contain plaintext credentials being used or validated by LDAP authentication, so care should be taken in protecting and purging the error log when this directive is used.

LDAPOpCacheEntries Directive

Description:	Number of entries used to cache LDAP compare operations
Syntax:	`LDAPOpCacheEntries number`
Default:	`LDAPOpCacheEntries 1024`
Context:	server config
Status:	Extension
Module:	mod_ldap

This specifies the number of entries MOD_LDAP will use to cache LDAP compare operations. The default is 1024 entries. Setting it to 0 disables operation caching.

LDAPOpCacheTTL Directive

Description:	Time that entries in the operation cache remain valid
Syntax:	`LDAPOpCacheTTL seconds`
Default:	`LDAPOpCacheTTL 600`
Context:	server config
Status:	Extension
Module:	mod_ldap

Specifies the time (in seconds) that entries in the operation cache remain valid. The default is 600 seconds.

LDAPReferralHopLimit Directive

Description:	The maximum number of referral hops to chase before terminating an LDAP query.
Syntax:	`LDAPReferralHopLimit number`
Default:	`SDK dependent, typically between 5 and 10`
Context:	directory, .htaccess
Override:	AuthConfig
Status:	Extension
Module:	mod_ldap

This directive, if enabled by the LDAPREFERRALS directive, limits the number of referral hops that are followed before terminating an LDAP query.

 Support for this tunable is uncommon in LDAP SDKs.

LDAPReferrals Directive

Description:	Enable referral chasing during queries to the LDAP server.
Syntax:	`LDAPReferrals On|Off|default`
Default:	`LDAPReferrals On`
Context:	directory, .htaccess
Override:	AuthConfig
Status:	Extension
Module:	mod_ldap
Compatibility:	The *default* parameter is available in Apache 2.4.7 and later

Some LDAP servers divide their directory among multiple domains and use referrals to direct a client when a domain boundary is crossed. This is similar to a HTTP redirect. LDAP client libraries may or may not chase referrals by default. This directive explicitly configures the referral chasing in the underlying SDK.

LDAPREFERRALS takes the following values:

"on" When set to "on", the underlying SDK's referral chasing state is enabled, LDAPREFERRALHOPLIMIT is used to override the SDK's hop limit, and an LDAP rebind callback is registered.

"off" When set to "off", the underlying SDK's referral chasing state is disabled completely.

"default" When set to "default", the underlying SDK's referral chasing state is not changed, LDAPREFERRALHOPLIMIT is not used to overide the SDK's hop limit, and no LDAP rebind callback is registered.

The directive LDAPREFERRALHOPLIMIT works in conjunction with this directive to limit the number of referral hops to follow before terminating the LDAP query. When referral processing is enabled by a value of "On", client credentials will be provided, via a rebind callback, for any LDAP server requiring them.

LDAPRetries Directive

Description:	Configures the number of LDAP server retries.
Syntax:	`LDAPRetries number-of-retries`
Default:	`LDAPRetries 3`
Context:	server config
Status:	Extension
Module:	mod_ldap

The server will retry failed LDAP requests up to LDAPRETRIES times. Setting this directive to 0 disables retries.

LDAP errors such as timeouts and refused connections are retryable.

LDAPRetryDelay Directive

Description:	Configures the delay between LDAP server retries.
Syntax:	`LDAPRetryDelay seconds`
Default:	`LDAPRetryDelay 0`
Context:	server config
Status:	Extension
Module:	mod_ldap

If LDAPRETRYDELAY is set to a non-zero value, the server will delay retrying an LDAP request for the specified amount of time. Setting this directive to 0 will result in any retry to occur without delay.

LDAP errors such as timeouts and refused connections are retryable.

LDAPSharedCacheFile Directive

Description:	Sets the shared memory cache file
Syntax:	`LDAPSharedCacheFile directory-path/filename`
Context:	server config
Status:	Extension
Module:	mod_ldap

Specifies the directory path and file name of the shared memory cache file. If not set, anonymous shared memory will be used if the platform supports it.

LDAPSharedCacheSize Directive

Description:	Size in bytes of the shared-memory cache
Syntax:	`LDAPSharedCacheSize bytes`
Default:	`LDAPSharedCacheSize 500000`
Context:	server config
Status:	Extension
Module:	mod_ldap

Specifies the number of bytes to allocate for the shared memory cache. The default is 500kb. If set to 0, shared memory caching will not be used and every HTTPD process will create its own cache.

LDAPTimeout Directive

Description:	Specifies the timeout for LDAP search and bind operations, in seconds
Syntax:	`LDAPTimeout seconds`
Default:	`LDAPTimeout 60`
Context:	server config
Status:	Extension
Module:	mod_ldap
Compatibility:	Apache HTTP Server 2.3.5 and later

This directive configures the timeout for bind and search operations, as well as the LDAP_OPT_TIMEOUT option in the underlying LDAP client library, when available.

If the timeout expires, httpd will retry in case an existing connection has been silently dropped by a firewall. However, performance will be much better if the firewall is configured to send TCP RST packets instead of silently dropping packets.

⟹ Timeouts for ldap compare operations requires an SDK with LDAP_OPT_TIMEOUT, such as OpenLDAP >= 2.4.4.

LDAPTrustedClientCert Directive

Description:	Sets the file containing or nickname referring to a per connection client certificate. Not all LDAP toolkits support per connection client certificates.
Syntax:	`LDAPTrustedClientCert type directory-path/filename/nickname [password]`
Context:	directory, .htaccess
Status:	Extension
Module:	mod_ldap

It specifies the directory path, file name or nickname of a per connection client certificate used when establishing an SSL or TLS connection to an LDAP server. Different locations or directories may have their own independent client certificate settings. Some LDAP toolkits (notably Novell) do not support per connection client certificates, and will throw an error on LDAP server connection if you try to use this directive (Use the LDAPTrustedGlobalCert directive instead for Novell client certificates - See the SSL/TLS certificate guide above for details). The type specifies the kind of certificate parameter being set, depending on the LDAP toolkit being used. Supported types are:

- CA_DER - binary DER encoded CA certificate
- CA_BASE64 - PEM encoded CA certificate
- CERT_DER - binary DER encoded client certificate
- CERT_BASE64 - PEM encoded client certificate
- CERT_NICKNAME - Client certificate "nickname" (Netscape SDK)
- KEY_DER - binary DER encoded private key
- KEY_BASE64 - PEM encoded private key

LDAPTrustedGlobalCert Directive

Description:	Sets the file or database containing global trusted Certificate Authority or global client certificates
Syntax:	`LDAPTrustedGlobalCert type directory-path/filename [password]`
Context:	server config
Status:	Extension
Module:	mod_ldap

It specifies the directory path and file name of the trusted CA certificates and/or system wide client certificates MOD_LDAP should use when establishing an SSL or TLS connection to an LDAP server. Note that all certificate information specified using this directive is applied globally to the entire server installation. Some LDAP toolkits (notably Novell) require all client certificates to be set globally using this directive. Most other toolkits require clients certificates to be set per Directory or per Location using LDAPTrustedClientCert. If you get this wrong, an error may be logged when an attempt is made to contact the LDAP server, or the connection may silently fail (See the SSL/TLS certificate guide above for details). The type specifies the kind of certificate parameter being set, depending on the LDAP toolkit being used. Supported types are:

- CA_DER - binary DER encoded CA certificate
- CA_BASE64 - PEM encoded CA certificate
- CA_CERT7_DB - Netscape cert7.db CA certificate database file
- CA_SECMOD - Netscape secmod database file
- CERT_DER - binary DER encoded client certificate
- CERT_BASE64 - PEM encoded client certificate
- CERT_KEY3_DB - Netscape key3.db client certificate database file

- CERT_NICKNAME - Client certificate "nickname" (Netscape SDK)
- CERT_PFX - PKCS#12 encoded client certificate (Novell SDK)
- KEY_DER - binary DER encoded private key
- KEY_BASE64 - PEM encoded private key
- KEY_PFX - PKCS#12 encoded private key (Novell SDK)

LDAPTrustedMode Directive

Description:	Specifies the SSL/TLS mode to be used when connecting to an LDAP server.
Syntax:	`LDAPTrustedMode type`
Context:	server config, virtual host
Status:	Extension
Module:	mod_ldap

The following modes are supported:

- NONE - no encryption
- SSL - ldaps:// encryption on default port 636
- TLS - STARTTLS encryption on default port 389

Not all LDAP toolkits support all the above modes. An error message will be logged at runtime if a mode is not supported, and the connection to the LDAP server will fail.

If an ldaps:// URL is specified, the mode becomes SSL and the setting of LDAPTrustedMode is ignored.

LDAPVerifyServerCert Directive

Description:	Force server certificate verification
Syntax:	`LDAPVerifyServerCert On|Off`
Default:	`LDAPVerifyServerCert On`
Context:	server config
Status:	Extension
Module:	mod_ldap

Specifies whether to force the verification of a server certificate when establishing an SSL connection to the LDAP server.

10.66 Apache Module mod_log_config

Description:	Logging of the requests made to the server
Status:	Base
ModuleIdentifier:	log_config_module
SourceFile:	mod_log_config.c

Summary

This module provides for flexible logging of client requests. Logs are written in a customizable format, and may be written directly to a file, or to an external program. Conditional logging is provided so that individual requests may be included or excluded from the logs based on characteristics of the request.

Three directives are provided by this module: TRANSFERLOG to create a log file, LOGFORMAT to set a custom format, and CUSTOMLOG to define a log file and format in one step. The TRANSFERLOG and CUSTOMLOG directives can be used multiple times in each server to cause each request to be logged to multiple files.

Directives

- BufferedLogs
- CustomLog
- LogFormat
- TransferLog

See also

- Apache Log Files (p. 53)

Custom Log Formats

The format argument to the LOGFORMAT and CUSTOMLOGdirectives is a string. This string is used to log each request to the log file. It can contain literal characters copied into the log files and the C-style control characters "\n" and "\t" to represent new-lines and tabs. Literal quotes and backslashes should be escaped with backslashes.

The characteristics of the request itself are logged by placing "%" directives in the format string, which are replaced in the log file by the values as follows:

FormatString	Description
`%%`	The percent sign.
`%a`	Client IP address of the request (see the MOD_REMOTEIP module).
`%{c}a`	Underlying peer IP address of the connection (see the MOD_REMOTEIP module).
`%A`	Local IP-address.
`%B`	Size of response in bytes, excluding HTTP headers.
`%b`	Size of response in bytes, excluding HTTP headers. In CLF format, *i.e.* a '–' rather than a 0 wher bytes are sent.
`%{`*VARNAME*`}C`	The contents of cookie *VARNAME* in the request sent to the server. Only version 0 cookies are f supported.
`%D`	The time taken to serve the request, in microseconds.
`%{`*VARNAME*`}e`	The contents of the environment variable *VARNAME*.
`%f`	Filename.
`%h`	Remote hostname. Will log the IP address if HOSTNAMELOOKUPS is set to `Off`, which is the defaul it logs the hostname for only a few hosts, you probably have access control directives mentioning tl by name. See the Require host documentation (p. 505) .

%H	The request protocol.
%{*VARNAME*}i	The contents of *VARNAME*: header line(s) in the request sent to the server. Changes made by o modules (e.g. MOD_HEADERS) affect this. If you're interested in what the request header was prio when most modules would have modified it, use MOD_SETENVIF to copy the header into an inte environment variable and log that value with the %{*VARNAME*}e described above.
%k	Number of keepalive requests handled on this connection. Interesting if KEEPALIVE is being u so that, for example, a '1' means the first keepalive request after the initial one, '2' the second, et otherwise this is always 0 (indicating the initial request).
%l	Remote logname (from identd, if supplied). This will return a dash unless MOD_IDENT is present IDENTITYCHECK is set On.
%L	The request log ID from the error log (or '-' if nothing has been logged to the error log for this reque Look for the matching error log line to see what request caused what error.
%m	The request method.
%{*VARNAME*}n	The contents of note *VARNAME* from another module.
%{*VARNAME*}o	The contents of *VARNAME*: header line(s) in the reply.
%p	The canonical port of the server serving the request.
%{*format*}p	The canonical port of the server serving the request, or the server's actual port, or the client's actual p Valid formats are canonical, local, or remote.
%P	The process ID of the child that serviced the request.
%{*format*}P	The process ID or thread ID of the child that serviced the request. Valid formats are pid, tid, hextid. hextid requires APR 1.2.0 or higher.
%q	The query string (prepended with a ? if a query string exists, otherwise an empty string).
%r	First line of request.
%R	The handler generating the response (if any).
%s	Status. For requests that have been internally redirected, this is the status of the *original* request. %>s for the final status.
%t	Time the request was received, in the format [18/Sep/2011:19:18:28 -0400]. The last num indicates the timezone offset from GMT
%{*format*}t	The time, in the form given by format, which should be in an extended strftime format (potentially localized). If the format starts with begin: (default) the time taken at the beginning of the request processing. If it starts with end: it is the t when the log entry gets written, close to the end of the request processing. In addi to the formats supported by strftime(3), the following format tokens are suppor sec — number of seconds since the Epoch msec — number of milliseconds since the Epoch usec — number of microseconds since the Epoch msec_frac — millisecond fraction usec_frac — microsecond fraction These tokens can not be combined with each other or strftime(3) formatting in the same for string. You can use multiple %{*format*}t tokens instead.
%T	The time taken to serve the request, in seconds.
%{*UNIT*}T	The time taken to serve the request, in a time unit given by UNIT. Valid units are ms for millisecon us for microseconds, and s for seconds. Using s gives the same result as %T without any format; u us gives the same result as %D. Combining %T with a unit is available in 2.4.13 and later.
%u	Remote user if the request was authenticated. May be bogus if return status (%s) is 401 (unauthorize
%U	The URL path requested, not including any query string.
%v	The canonical SERVERNAME of the server serving the request.
%V	The server name according to the USECANONICALNAME setting.
%X	Connection status when response is completed: X = Connection aborted before the response completed. + = Connection may be kept alive after the response is sent. − = Connection will be closed after the response is sent.
%I	Bytes received, including request and headers. Cannot be zero. You need to enable MOD_LOGIO to this.
%O	Bytes sent, including headers. May be zero in rare cases such as when a request is aborted befo response is sent. You need to enable MOD_LOGIO to use this.

`%S`	Bytes transferred (received and sent), including request and headers, cannot be zero. This is the con nation of %I and %O. You need to enable MOD_LOGIO to use this.
`%{`*VARNAME*`}^ti`	The contents of *VARNAME*: trailer line(s) in the request sent to the server.
`%{`*VARNAME*`}^to`	The contents of *VARNAME*: trailer line(s) in the response sent from the server.

Modifiers

Particular items can be restricted to print only for responses with specific HTTP status codes by placing a comma-separated list of status codes immediately following the `"%"`. The status code list may be preceded by a `"!"` to indicate negation.

Format String	Meaning
`%400,501{User-agent}`	Logs `User-agent` on 400 errors and 501 errors only. For other status codes, the literal string `"-"` be logged.
`%!200,304,302{Refer`	Logs `Referer` on all requests that do *not* return one of the three specified codes, `"-"` otherwise.

The modifiers `"<"` and `">"` can be used for requests that have been internally redirected to choose whether the original or final (respectively) request should be consulted. By default, the `%` directives `%s, %U, %T, %D,` and `%r` look at the original request while all others look at the final request. So for example, `%>s` can be used to record the final status of the request and `%<u` can be used to record the original authenticated user on a request that is internally redirected to an unauthenticated resource.

Format Notes

For security reasons, starting with version 2.0.46, non-printable and other special characters in `%r`, `%i` and `%o` are escaped using `\x`*hh* sequences, where *hh* stands for the hexadecimal representation of the raw byte. Exceptions from this rule are `"` and `\`, which are escaped by prepending a backslash, and all whitespace characters, which are written in their C-style notation (`\n`, `\t`, etc). In versions prior to 2.0.46, no escaping was performed on these strings so you had to be quite careful when dealing with raw log files.

Since httpd 2.0, unlike 1.3, the `%b` and `%B` format strings do not represent the number of bytes sent to the client, but simply the size in bytes of the HTTP response (which will differ, for instance, if the connection is aborted, or if SSL is used). The `%O` format provided by MOD_LOGIO will log the actual number of bytes sent over the network.

⟹ Note: MOD_CACHE is implemented as a quick-handler and not as a standard handler. Therefore, the `%R` format string will not return any handler information when content caching is involved.

Examples

Some commonly used log format strings are:

Common Log Format (CLF) `"%h %l %u %t \"%r\" %>s %b"`

Common Log Format with Virtual Host `"%v %h %l %u %t \"%r\" %>s %b"`

NCSA extended/combined log format `"%h %l %u %t \"%r\" %>s %b \"%{Referer}i\" \"%{User-agent}i\""`

Referer log format `"%{Referer}i -> %U"`

Agent (Browser) log format `"%{User-agent}i"`

You can use the `%{format}t` directive multiple times to build up a time format using the extended format tokens like `msec_frac`:

Timestamp including milliseconds `"%{%d/%b/%Y %T}t.%{msec_frac}t %{%z}t"`

Security Considerations

See the security tips (p. 338) document for details on why your security could be compromised if the directory where logfiles are stored is writable by anyone other than the user that starts the server.

BufferedLogs Directive

Description:	Buffer log entries in memory before writing to disk
Syntax:	`BufferedLogs On|Off`
Default:	`BufferedLogs Off`
Context:	server config
Status:	Base
Module:	mod_log_config

The BUFFEREDLOGS directive causes MOD_LOG_CONFIG to store several log entries in memory and write them together to disk, rather than writing them after each request. On some systems, this may result in more efficient disk access and hence higher performance. It may be set only once for the entire server; it cannot be configured per virtual-host.

⟹ This directive should be used with caution as a crash might cause loss of logging data.

CustomLog Directive

Description:	Sets filename and format of log file
Syntax:	`CustomLog file|pipe format|nickname [env=[!]environment-variable| expr=expression]`
Context:	server config, virtual host
Status:	Base
Module:	mod_log_config

The CUSTOMLOG directive is used to log requests to the server. A log format is specified, and the logging can optionally be made conditional on request characteristics using environment variables.

The first argument, which specifies the location to which the logs will be written, can take one of the following two types of values:

file A filename, relative to the SERVERROOT.

pipe The pipe character `"|"`, followed by the path to a program to receive the log information on its standard input. See the notes on piped logs (p. 53) for more information.

> **Security:**
> If a program is used, then it will be run as the user who started `httpd`. This will be root if the server was started by root; be sure that the program is secure.

> **Note**
> When entering a file path on non-Unix platforms, care should be taken to make sure that only forward slashed are used even though the platform may allow the use of back slashes. In general it is a good idea to always use forward slashes throughout the configuration files.

The second argument specifies what will be written to the log file. It can specify either a *nickname* defined by a previous LOGFORMAT directive, or it can be an explicit *format* string as described in the log formats section.

For example, the following two sets of directives have exactly the same effect:

```
# CustomLog with format nickname
LogFormat "%h %l %u %t \"%r\" %>s %b" common
CustomLog "logs/access_log" common

# CustomLog with explicit format string
CustomLog "logs/access_log" "%h %l %u %t \"%r\" %>s %b"
```

The third argument is optional and controls whether or not to log a particular request. The condition can be the presence or absence (in the case of a 'env=!*name*' clause) of a particular variable in the server environment (p. 82) . Alternatively, the condition can be expressed as arbitrary boolean expression (p. 89) . If the condition is not satisfied, the request will not be logged. References to HTTP headers in the expression will not cause the header names to be added to the Vary header.

Environment variables can be set on a per-request basis using the MOD_SETENVIF and/or MOD_REWRITE modules. For example, if you want to record requests for all GIF images on your server in a separate logfile but not in your main log, you can use:

```
SetEnvIf Request_URI \.gif$ gif-image
CustomLog "gif-requests.log" common env=gif-image
CustomLog "nongif-requests.log" common env=!gif-image
```

Or, to reproduce the behavior of the old RefererIgnore directive, you might use the following:

```
SetEnvIf Referer example\.com localreferer
CustomLog "referer.log" referer env=!localreferer
```

LogFormat Directive

Description:	Describes a format for use in a log file
Syntax:	`LogFormat format|nickname [nickname]`
Default:	`LogFormat "%h %l %u %t \"%r\" %>s %b"`
Context:	server config, virtual host
Status:	Base
Module:	mod_log_config

This directive specifies the format of the access log file.

The LOGFORMAT directive can take one of two forms. In the first form, where only one argument is specified, this directive sets the log format which will be used by logs specified in subsequent TRANSFERLOG directives. The single argument can specify an explicit *format* as discussed in the custom log formats section above. Alternatively, it can use a *nickname* to refer to a log format defined in a previous LOGFORMAT directive as described below.

The second form of the LOGFORMAT directive associates an explicit *format* with a *nickname*. This *nickname* can then be used in subsequent LOGFORMAT or CUSTOMLOG directives rather than repeating the entire format string. A LOGFORMAT directive that defines a nickname **does nothing else** – that is, it *only* defines the nickname, it doesn't actually apply the format and make it the default. Therefore, it will not affect subsequent TRANSFERLOG directives. In addition, LOGFORMAT cannot use one nickname to define another nickname. Note that the nickname should not contain percent signs (`%`).

Example

```
LogFormat "%v %h %l %u %t \"%r\" %>s %b" vhost_common
```

TransferLog Directive

Description:	Specify location of a log file
Syntax:	`TransferLog file|pipe`
Context:	server config, virtual host
Status:	Base
Module:	mod_log_config

This directive has exactly the same arguments and effect as the CUSTOMLOG directive, with the exception that it does not allow the log format to be specified explicitly or for conditional logging of requests. Instead, the log format is determined by the most recently specified LOGFORMAT directive which does not define a nickname. Common Log Format is used if no other format has been specified.

Example

```
LogFormat "%h %l %u %t \"%r\" %>s %b \"%{Referer}i\" \"%{User-agent}i\""
TransferLog logs/access_log
```

10.67 Apache Module mod_log_debug

Description:	Additional configurable debug logging
Status:	Experimental
ModuleIdentifier:	log_debug_module
SourceFile:	mod_log_debug.c
Compatibility:	Available in Apache 2.3.14 and later

Directives

- LogMessage

Examples

1. Log message after request to /foo/* is processed:

```
<Location "/foo/">
LogMessage "/foo/ has been requested"
</Location>
```

2. Log message if request to /foo/* is processed in a sub-request:

```
<Location "/foo/">
LogMessage "subrequest to /foo/" hook=type_checker expr=%{IS_SUBREQ}
</Location>
```

The default log_transaction hook is not executed for sub-requests, therefore we have to use a different hook.

3. Log message if an IPv6 client causes a request timeout:

```
LogMessage "IPv6 timeout from %{REMOTE_ADDR}" "expr=-T %{IPV6} && %{REQUEST
```

Note the placing of the double quotes for the `expr=` argument.

4. Log the value of the "X-Foo" request environment variable in each stage of the request:

```
<Location "/">
LogMessage "%{reqenv:X-Foo}" hook=all
</Location>
```

Together with microsecond time stamps in the error log, `hook=all` also lets you determine the times spent in the different parts of the request processing.

LogMessage Directive

Description:	Log user-defined message to error log
Syntax:	`LogMessage message [hook=hook] [expr=expression]`
Default:	`Unset`
Context:	directory
Status:	Experimental
Module:	mod_log_debug

This directive causes a user defined message to be logged to the error log. The message can use variables and functions from the ap_expr syntax (p. 89) . References to HTTP headers will not cause header names to be added to the Vary header. The messages are logged at loglevel info.

The hook specifies before which phase of request processing the message will be logged. The following hooks are supported:

Name
`translate_name`
`type_checker`
`quick_handler`
`map_to_storage`
`check_access`
`check_access_ex`
`insert_filter`
`check_authn`
`check_authz`
`fixups`
`handler`
`log_transaction`

The default is `log_transaction`. The special value `all` is also supported, causing a message to be logged at each phase. Not all hooks are executed for every request.

The optional expression allows to restrict the message if a condition is met. The details of the expression syntax are described in the ap_expr documentation (p. 89) . References to HTTP headers will not cause the header names to be added to the Vary header.

10.68 Apache Module mod_log_forensic

Description:	Forensic Logging of the requests made to the server
Status:	Extension
ModuleIdentifier:	log_forensic_module
SourceFile:	mod_log_forensic.c
Compatibility:	MOD_UNIQUE_ID is no longer required since version 2.1

Summary

This module provides for forensic logging of client requests. Logging is done before and after processing a request, so the forensic log contains two log lines for each request. The forensic logger is very strict, which means:

- The format is fixed. You cannot modify the logging format at runtime.
- If it cannot write its data, the child process exits immediately and may dump core (depending on your COREDUMPDIRECTORY configuration).

The `check_forensic` script, which can be found in the distribution's support directory, may be helpful in evaluating the forensic log output.

Directives

- ForensicLog

See also

- Apache Log Files (p. 53)
- MOD_LOG_CONFIG

Forensic Log Format

Each request is logged two times. The first time is *before* it's processed further (that is, after receiving the headers). The second log entry is written *after* the request processing at the same time where normal logging occurs.

In order to identify each request, a unique request ID is assigned. This forensic ID can be cross logged in the normal transfer log using the `%{forensic-id}n` format string. If you're using MOD_UNIQUE_ID, its generated ID will be used.

The first line logs the forensic ID, the request line and all received headers, separated by pipe characters (|). A sample line looks like the following (all on one line):

```
+yQtJf8CoAB4AAFNXBIEAAAAA|GET /manual/de/images/down.gif
HTTP/1.1|Host:localhost%3a8080|User-Agent:Mozilla/5.0 (X11; U; Linux
i686; en-US; rv%3a1.6) Gecko/20040216 Firefox/0.8|Accept:image/png,
etc...
```

The plus character at the beginning indicates that this is the first log line of this request. The second line just contains a minus character and the ID again:

```
-yQtJf8CoAB4AAFNXBIEAAAAA
```

The `check_forensic` script takes as its argument the name of the logfile. It looks for those +/- ID pairs and complains if a request was not completed.

Security Considerations

See the security tips (p. 338) document for details on why your security could be compromised if the directory where logfiles are stored is writable by anyone other than the user that starts the server.

The log files may contain sensitive data such as the contents of `Authorization:` headers (which can contain passwords), so they should not be readable by anyone except the user that starts the server.

ForensicLog Directive

Description:	Sets filename of the forensic log
Syntax:	`ForensicLog filename|pipe`
Context:	server config, virtual host
Status:	Extension
Module:	mod_log_forensic

The FORENSICLOG directive is used to log requests to the server for forensic analysis. Each log entry is assigned a unique ID which can be associated with the request using the normal CUSTOMLOG directive. MOD_LOG_FORENSIC creates a token called `forensic-id`, which can be added to the transfer log using the `%{forensic-id}n` format string.

The argument, which specifies the location to which the logs will be written, can take one of the following two types of values:

filename A filename, relative to the SERVERROOT.

pipe The pipe character "`|`", followed by the path to a program to receive the log information on its standard input. The program name can be specified relative to the SERVERROOT directive.

Security:
If a program is used, then it will be run as the user who started `httpd`. This will be root if the server was started by root; be sure that the program is secure or switches to a less privileged user.

Note
When entering a file path on non-Unix platforms, care should be taken to make sure that only forward slashes are used even though the platform may allow the use of back slashes. In general it is a good idea to always use forward slashes throughout the configuration files.

10.69 Apache Module mod_logio

Description:	Logging of input and output bytes per request
Status:	Extension
ModuleIdentifier:	logio_module
SourceFile:	mod_logio.c

Summary

This module provides the logging of input and output number of bytes received/sent per request. The numbers reflect the actual bytes as received on the network, which then takes into account the headers and bodies of requests and responses. The counting is done before SSL/TLS on input and after SSL/TLS on output, so the numbers will correctly reflect any changes made by encryption.

This module requires MOD_LOG_CONFIG.

⟹ When KeepAlive connections are used with SSL, the overhead of the SSL handshake is reflected in the byte count of the first request on the connection. When per-directory SSL renegotiation occurs, the bytes are associated with the request that triggered the renegotiation.

Directives

- LogIOTrackTTFB

See also

- MOD_LOG_CONFIG
- Apache Log Files (p. 53)

Custom Log Formats

This module adds three new logging directives. The characteristics of the request itself are logged by placing "%" directives in the format string, which are replaced in the log file by the values as follows:

FormatString	Description
`%I`	Bytes received, including request and headers, cannot be zero.
`%O`	Bytes sent, including headers, cannot be zero.
`%S`	Bytes transferred (received and sent), including request and headers, cannot be zero. This is the combination of %I and %O. Available in Apache 2.4.7 and later
`%^FB`	Delay in microseconds between when the request arrived and the first byte of the response headers are written. Only available if LOGIOTRACKTTFB is set to ON. Available in Apache 2.4.13 and later

Usually, the functionality is used like this:

Combined I/O log format: `"%h %l %u %t \"%r\" %>s %b \"%{Referer}i\" \"%{User-agent}i\" %I %O"`

LogIOTrackTTFB Directive

Description:	Enable tracking of time to first byte (TTFB)
Syntax:	`LogIOTrackTTFB ON|OFF`
Default:	`LogIOTrackTTFB OFF`
Context:	server config, virtual host, directory, .htaccess
Override:	none
Status:	Extension
Module:	mod_logio
Compatibility:	Apache HTTP Server 2.4.13 and later

This directive configures whether this module tracks the delay between the request being read and the first byte of the response headers being written. The resulting value may be logged with the `%^FB` format.

10.70 Apache Module mod_lua

Description:	Provides Lua hooks into various portions of the httpd request processing
Status:	Experimental
ModuleIdentifier:	lua_module
SourceFile:	mod_lua.c
Compatibility:	2.3 and later

Summary

This module allows the server to be extended with scripts written in the Lua programming language. The extension points (hooks) available with MOD_LUA include many of the hooks available to natively compiled Apache HTTP Server modules, such as mapping requests to files, generating dynamic responses, access control, authentication, and authorization

More information on the Lua programming language can be found at the the Lua website[46].

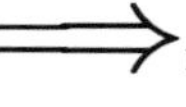`mod_lua` is still in experimental state. Until it is declared stable, usage and behavior may change at any time, even between stable releases of the 2.4.x series. Be sure to check the CHANGES file before upgrading.

Warning
This module holds a great deal of power over httpd, which is both a strength and a potential security risk. It is **not** recommended that you use this module on a server that is shared with users you do not trust, as it can be abused to change the internal workings of httpd.

Directives

- LuaAuthzProvider
- LuaCodeCache
- LuaHookAccessChecker
- LuaHookAuthChecker
- LuaHookCheckUserID
- LuaHookFixups
- LuaHookInsertFilter
- LuaHookLog
- LuaHookMapToStorage
- LuaHookTranslateName
- LuaHookTypeChecker
- LuaInherit
- LuaInputFilter
- LuaMapHandler
- LuaOutputFilter
- LuaPackageCPath
- LuaPackagePath
- LuaQuickHandler

[46]http://www.lua.org/

- LuaRoot
- LuaScope

Basic Configuration

The basic module loading directive is

```
LoadModule lua_module modules/mod_lua.so
```

mod_lua provides a handler named lua-script, which can be used with a SETHANDLER or ADDHANDLER directive:

```
<Files "*.lua">
    SetHandler lua-script
</Files>
```

This will cause mod_lua to handle requests for files ending in .lua by invoking that file's handle function.

For more flexibility, see LUAMAPHANDLER.

Writing Handlers

In the Apache HTTP Server API, the handler is a specific kind of hook responsible for generating the response. Examples of modules that include a handler are MOD_PROXY, MOD_CGI, and MOD_STATUS.

mod_lua always looks to invoke a Lua function for the handler, rather than just evaluating a script body CGI style. A handler function looks something like this:

```
example.lua
-- example handler

require "string"

--[[
     This is the default method name for Lua handlers, see the optional
     function-name in the LuaMapHandler directive to choose a different
     entry point.
--]]
function handle(r)
    r.content_type = "text/plain"

    if r.method == 'GET' then
        r:puts("Hello Lua World!\n")
        for k, v in pairs( r:parseargs() ) do
            r:puts( string.format("%s: %s\n", k, v) )
        end
    elseif r.method == 'POST' then
        r:puts("Hello Lua World!\n")
        for k, v in pairs( r:parsebody() ) do
            r:puts( string.format("%s: %s\n", k, v) )
        end
    elseif r.method == 'PUT' then
```

```
-- use our own Error contents
        r:puts("Unsupported HTTP method " .. r.method)
        r.status = 405
        return apache2.OK
    else
-- use the ErrorDocument
        return 501
    end
    return apache2.OK
end
```

This handler function just prints out the uri or form encoded arguments to a plaintext page.

This means (and in fact encourages) that you can have multiple handlers (or hooks, or filters) in the same script.

Writing Authorization Providers

MOD_AUTHZ_CORE provides a high-level interface to authorization that is much easier to use than using into the relevant hooks directly. The first argument to the REQUIRE directive gives the name of the responsible authorization provider. For any REQUIRE line, MOD_AUTHZ_CORE will call the authorization provider of the given name, passing the rest of the line as parameters. The provider will then check authorization and pass the result as return value.

The authz provider is normally called before authentication. If it needs to know the authenticated user name (or if the user will be authenticated at all), the provider must return `apache2.AUTHZ_DENIED_NO_USER`. This will cause authentication to proceed and the authz provider to be called a second time.

The following authz provider function takes two arguments, one ip address and one user name. It will allow access from the given ip address without authentication, or if the authenticated user matches the second argument:

```
authz_provider.lua

require 'apache2'

function authz_check_foo(r, ip, user)
    if r.useragent_ip == ip then
        return apache2.AUTHZ_GRANTED
    elseif r.user == nil then
        return apache2.AUTHZ_DENIED_NO_USER
    elseif r.user == user then
        return apache2.AUTHZ_GRANTED
    else
        return apache2.AUTHZ_DENIED
    end
end
```

The following configuration registers this function as provider `foo` and configures it for URL /:

```
LuaAuthzProvider foo authz_provider.lua authz_check_foo
<Location "/">
  Require foo 10.1.2.3 john_doe
</Location>
```

Writing Hooks

Hook functions are how modules (and Lua scripts) participate in the processing of requests. Each type of hook exposed by the server exists for a specific purpose, such as mapping requests to the file system, performing access control, or setting mime types:

Hook phase	mod_lua directive	Description
Quick handler	LUAQUICKHANDLER	This is the first hook that will be callec after a request has been mapped to a hosı or virtual host
Translate name	LUAHOOKTRANSLATENAME	This phase translates the requested URI into a filename on the system. Module: such as MOD_ALIAS and MOD_REWRITE operate in this phase.
Map to storage	LUAHOOKMAPTOSTORAGE	This phase maps files to their physical cached or external/proxied storage. It car be used by proxy or caching modules
Check Access	LUAHOOKACCESSCHECKER	This phase checks whether a client ha: access to a resource. This phase is run before the user is authenticated, so beware.
Check User ID	LUAHOOKCHECKUSERID	This phase it used to check the negotiatec user ID
Check Authorization	LUAHOOKAUTHCHECKER or LUAAUTHZPROVIDER	This phase authorizes a user based on the negotiated credentials, such as user ID client certificate etc.
Check Type	LUAHOOKTYPECHECKER	This phase checks the requested file anc assigns a content type and a handler to it
Fixups	LUAHOOKFIXUPS	This is the final "fix anything" phase before the content handlers are run. Any last-minute changes to the request shoulc be made here.
Content handler	fx. `.lua` files or through LUAMAPHANDLER	This is where the content is handled. File: are read, parsed, some are run, and the result is sent to the client
Logging	LUAHOOKLOG	Once a request has been handled, it enters several logging phases, which log: the request in either the error or access log. Mod_lua is able to hook into the start of this and control logging output.

Hook functions are passed the request object as their only argument (except for LuaAuthzProvider, which also gets passed the arguments from the Require directive). They can return any value, depending on the hook, but most commonly they'll return OK, DONE, or DECLINED, which you can write in Lua as `apache2.OK`, `apache2.DONE`, or `apache2.DECLINED`, or else an HTTP status code.

```
translate_name.lua
-- example hook that rewrites the URI to a filesystem path.

require 'apache2'

function translate_name(r)
    if r.uri == "/translate-name" then
        r.filename = r.document_root .. "/find_me.txt"
        return apache2.OK
    end
    -- we don't care about this URL, give another module a chance
    return apache2.DECLINED
end
```

```
translate_name2.lua
--[[ example hook that rewrites one URI to another URI. It returns a
     apache2.DECLINED to give other URL mappers a chance to work on the
     substitution, including the core translate_name hook which maps based
     on the DocumentRoot.

     Note: Use the early/late flags in the directive to make it run before
           or after mod_alias.
--]]

require 'apache2'

function translate_name(r)
    if r.uri == "/translate-name" then
        r.uri = "/find_me.txt"
        return apache2.DECLINED
    end
    return apache2.DECLINED
end
```

Data Structures

request_rec The request_rec is mapped in as a userdata. It has a metatable which lets you do useful things with it. For the most part it has the same fields as the request_rec struct, many of which are writable as well as readable. (The table fields' content can be changed, but the fields themselves cannot be set to different tables.)

Name	Lua type	Writable	Description
`allowoverrides`	string	no	The AllowOverride options plied to the current request.
`ap_auth_type`	string	no	If an authentication check made, this is set to the typ authentication (f.x. `basic`
`args`	string	yes	The query string argum extracted from the request (`foo=bar&name=johns`
`assbackwards`	boolean	no	Set to true if this is HTTP/0.9 style request (`GET /foo` (with no head)
`auth_name`	string	no	The realm name used for thorization (if applicable).
`banner`	string	no	The server ban f.x. `Apache H` `Server/2.4.3` `openssl/0.9.8c`
`basic_auth_pw`	string	no	The basic auth password with this request, if any
`canonical_filename`	string	no	The canonical filename of request
`content_encoding`	string	no	The content encoding of current request
`content_type`	string	yes	The content type of the rent request, as determi in the type_check phase (`image/gif` or `text/ht`

context_prefix	string	no	
context_document_root	string	no	
document_root	string	no	The document root of the h
err_headers_out	table	no	MIME header environment the response, printed even errors and persist across ir nal redirects
filename	string	yes	The file name that request maps to, /www/example.com/foo.txt This can be changed in translate-name or map storage phases of a req to allow the default han (or script handlers) to serv different file than what requested.
handler	string	yes	The name of the handler (p. that should serve this requ f.x. `lua-script` if it i be served by mod_lua. Thi typically set by the ADDH DLER or SETHANDLER di tives, but could also be set mod_lua to allow another h dler to serve up a specific quest that would otherwise be served by it.
headers_in	table	yes	MIME header environm from the request. This c tains headers such as `Hos` `User-Agent, Refere` and so on.
headers_out	table	yes	MIME header environment the response.
hostname	string	no	The host name, as set by `Host:` header or by a URI.
is_https	boolean	no	Whether or not this reques done via HTTPS
is_initial_req	boolean	no	Whether this request is the tial request or a sub-request
limit_req_body	number	no	The size limit of the req body for this request, or 0 i limit.
log_id	string	no	The ID to identify reques access and error log.
method	string	no	The request method, f.x. (or `POST`.
notes	table	yes	A list of notes that can passed on from one modul another.
options	string	no	The Options directive app to the current request.
path_info	string	no	The PATH_INFO extrac from this request.
port	number	no	The server port used by the quest.

protocol	string	no	The protocol used, HTTP/1.1
proxyreq	string	yes	Denotes whether this i: proxy request or not. value is generally set in post_read_request/translate_ phase of a request.
range	string	no	The contents of the Ranc header.
remaining	number	no	The number of bytes rem ing to be read from the req body.
server_built	string	no	The time the server executa was built.
server_name	string	no	The server name for this quest.
some_auth_required	boolean	no	Whether some authoriza is/was required for this requ
subprocess_env	table	yes	The environment variables for this request.
started	number	no	The time the server (re)started, in seconds si the epoch (Jan 1st, 1970)
status	number	yes	The (current) HTTP re code for this request, f.x. 2 or 404.
the_request	string	no	The request string as : by the client, f.x. (/foo/bar HTTP/1.1.
unparsed_uri	string	no	The unparsed URI of the quest
uri	string	yes	The URI after it has b parsed by httpd
user	string	yes	If an authentication check been made, this is set to name of the authenticated u
useragent_ip	string	no	The IP of the user agent m ing the request

Built in functions

The request_rec object has (at least) the following methods:

```
r:flush()    -- flushes the output buffer.
             -- Returns true if the flush was successful, false otherwise.

while we_have_stuff_to_send do
    r:puts("Bla bla bla\n") -- print something to client
    r:flush() -- flush the buffer (send to client)
    r.usleep(500000) -- fake processing time for 0.5 sec. and repeat
end

r:addoutputfilter(name|function) -- add an output filter:

r:addoutputfilter("fooFilter") -- add the fooFilter to the output stream
```

```
r:sendfile(filename) -- sends an entire file to the client, using sendfile if s

if use_sendfile_thing then
    r:sendfile("/var/www/large_file.img")
end

r:parseargs() -- returns two tables; one standard key/value table for regular G
              -- and one for multi-value data (fx. foo=1&foo=2&foo=3):

local GET, GETMULTI = r:parseargs()
r:puts("Your name is: " .. GET['name'] or "Unknown")

r:parsebody([sizeLimit]) -- parse the request body as a POST and return two lua
                         -- just like r:parseargs().
                         -- An optional number may be passed to specify the max
                         -- of bytes to parse. Default is 8192 bytes:

local POST, POSTMULTI = r:parsebody(1024*1024)
r:puts("Your name is: " .. POST['name'] or "Unknown")

r:puts("hello", " world", "!") -- print to response body, self explanatory

r:write("a single string") -- print to response body, self explanatory

r:escape_html("<html>test</html>") -- Escapes HTML code and returns the escaped

r:base64_encode(string) -- Encodes a string using the Base64 encoding standard:

local encoded = r:base64_encode("This is a test") -- returns VGhpcyBpcyBhIHRlc3

r:base64_decode(string) -- Decodes a Base64-encoded string:

local decoded = r:base64_decode("VGhpcyBpcyBhIHRlc3Q=") -- returns 'This is a t

r:md5(string) -- Calculates and returns the MD5 digest of a string (binary safe

local hash = r:md5("This is a test") -- returns ce114e4501d2f4e2dcea3e17b546f33

r:sha1(string) -- Calculates and returns the SHA1 digest of a string (binary sa

local hash = r:sha1("This is a test") -- returns a54d88e06612d820bc3be72877c74f

r:escape(string) -- URL-Escapes a string:

local url = "http://foo.bar/1 2 3 & 4 + 5"
local escaped = r:escape(url) -- returns 'http%3a%2f%2ffoo.bar%2f1+2+3+%26+4+%2

r:unescape(string) -- Unescapes an URL-escaped string:

local url = "http%3a%2f%2ffoo.bar%2f1+2+3+%26+4+%2b+5"
local unescaped = r:unescape(url) -- returns 'http://foo.bar/1 2 3 & 4 + 5'
```

```
r:construct_url(string) -- Constructs an URL from an URI

local url = r:construct_url(r.uri)

r.mpm_query(number) -- Queries the server for MPM information using ap_mpm_quer

local mpm = r.mpm_query(14)
if mpm == 1 then
    r:puts("This server uses the Event MPM")
end

r:expr(string) -- Evaluates an expr string.

if r:expr("%{HTTP_HOST} =~ /^www/") then
    r:puts("This host name starts with www")
end

r:scoreboard_process(a) -- Queries the server for information about the process

local process = r:scoreboard_process(1)
r:puts("Server 1 has PID " .. process.pid)

r:scoreboard_worker(a, b) -- Queries for information about the worker thread, b

local thread = r:scoreboard_worker(1, 1)
r:puts("Server 1's thread 1 has thread ID " .. thread.tid .. " and is in " .. t

r:clock() -- Returns the current time with microsecond precision

r:requestbody(filename) -- Reads and returns the request body of a request.
                -- If 'filename' is specified, it instead saves the
                -- contents to that file:

local input = r:requestbody()
r:puts("You sent the following request body to me:\n")
r:puts(input)

r:add_input_filter(filter_name) -- Adds 'filter_name' as an input filter

r.module_info(module_name) -- Queries the server for information about a module

local mod = r.module_info("mod_lua.c")
if mod then
    for k, v in pairs(mod.commands) do
       r:puts( ("%s: %s\n"):format(k,v)) -- print out all directives accepted b
    end
end

r:loaded_modules() -- Returns a list of modules loaded by httpd:

for k, module in pairs(r:loaded_modules()) do
    r:puts("I have loaded module " .. module .. "\n")
end
```

```
r:runtime_dir_relative(filename) -- Compute the name of a run-time file (e.g.,
                          -- relative to the appropriate run-time directory.


r:server_info() -- Returns a table containing server information, such as
                -- the name of the httpd executable file, mpm used etc.


r:set_document_root(file_path) -- Sets the document root for the request to fil


r:set_context_info(prefix, docroot) -- Sets the context prefix and context docu


r:os_escape_path(file_path) -- Converts an OS path to a URL in an OS dependent


r:escape_logitem(string) -- Escapes a string for logging


r.strcmp_match(string, pattern) -- Checks if 'string' matches 'pattern' using s
                        -- fx. whether 'www.example.com' matches '*.example.com

local match = r.strcmp_match("foobar.com", "foo*.com")
if match then
    r:puts("foobar.com matches foo*.com")
end


r:set_keepalive() -- Sets the keepalive status for a request. Returns true if p


r:make_etag() -- Constructs and returns the etag for the current request.


r:send_interim_response(clear) -- Sends an interim (1xx) response to the client
                       -- if 'clear' is true, available headers will be sent an


r:custom_response(status_code, string) -- Construct and set a custom response f
                              -- This works much like the ErrorDocument direct

r:custom_response(404, "Baleted!")


r.exists_config_define(string) -- Checks whether a configuration definition exi

if r.exists_config_define("FOO") then
    r:puts("httpd was probably run with -DFOO, or it was defined in the configu
end


r:state_query(string) -- Queries the server for state information


r:stat(filename [,wanted]) -- Runs stat() on a file, and returns a table with f

local info = r:stat("/var/www/foo.txt")
if info then
    r:puts("This file exists and was last modified at: " .. info.modified)
end
```

```
r:regex(string, pattern [,flags]) -- Runs a regular expression match on a strin

local matches = r:regex("foo bar baz", [[foo (\w+) (\S*)]])
if matches then
    r:puts("The regex matched, and the last word captured ($2) was: " .. matche
end

-- Example ignoring case sensitivity:
local matches = r:regex("FOO bar BAz", [[(foo) bar]], 1)

-- Flags can be a bitwise combination of:
-- 0x01: Ignore case
-- 0x02: Multiline search


r.usleep(number_of_microseconds) -- Puts the script to sleep for a given number


r:dbacquire(dbType[, dbParams]) -- Acquires a connection to a database and retu
                                -- See 'Database connectivity' for details.


r:ivm_set("key", value) -- Set an Inter-VM variable to hold a specific value.
                        -- These values persist even though the VM is gone or n
                        -- and so should only be used if MaxConnectionsPerChild
                        -- Values can be numbers, strings and booleans, and are
                        -- per process basis (so they won't do much good with a

r:ivm_get("key")        -- Fetches a variable set by ivm_set. Returns the conte
                        -- if it exists or nil if no such variable exists.

-- An example getter/setter that saves a global variable outside the VM:
function handle(r)
    -- First VM to call this will get no value, and will have to create it
    local foo = r:ivm_get("cached_data")
    if not foo then
        foo = do_some_calcs() -- fake some return value
        r:ivm_set("cached_data", foo) -- set it globally
    end
    r:puts("Cached data is: ", foo)
end

r:htpassword(string [,algorithm [,cost]]) -- Creates a password hash from a str
                                          -- algorithm: 0 = APMD5 (default), 1
                                          -- cost: only valid with BCRYPT algor


r:mkdir(dir [,mode]) -- Creates a directory and sets mode to optional mode para


r:mkrdir(dir [,mode]) -- Creates directories recursive and sets mode to optiona


r:rmdir(dir) -- Removes a directory.


r:touch(file [,mtime]) -- Sets the file modification time to current time or to
```

```
r:get_direntries(dir) -- Returns a table with all directory entries.

function handle(r)
  local dir = r.context_document_root
  for _, f in ipairs(r:get_direntries(dir)) do
    local info = r:stat(dir .. "/" .. f)
    if info then
      local mtime = os.date(fmt, info.mtime / 1000000)
      local ftype = (info.filetype == 2) and "[dir] " or "[file]"
      r:puts( ("%s %s %10i %s\n"):format(ftype, mtime, info.size, f) )
    end
  end
end

r.date_parse_rfc(string) -- Parses a date/time string and returns seconds since

r:getcookie(key) -- Gets a HTTP cookie

r:setcookie{
  key = [key],
  value = [value],
  expires = [expiry],
  secure = [boolean],
  httponly = [boolean],
  path = [path],
  domain = [domain]
} -- Sets a HTTP cookie, for instance:

r:setcookie{
  key = "cookie1",
  value = "HDHfa9eyffh396rt",
  expires = os.time() + 86400,
  secure = true
}

r:wsupgrade() -- Upgrades a connection to WebSockets if possible (and requested
if r:wsupgrade() then -- if we can upgrade:
    r:wswrite("Welcome to websockets!") -- write something to the client
    r:wsclose()  -- goodbye!
end

r:wsread() -- Reads a WebSocket frame from a WebSocket upgraded connection (see

local line, isFinal = r:wsread() -- isFinal denotes whether this is the final f
                                 -- If it isn't, then more frames can be read
r:wswrite("You wrote: " .. line)

r:wswrite(line) -- Writes a frame to a WebSocket client:
r:wswrite("Hello, world!")

r:wsclose() -- Closes a WebSocket request and terminates it for httpd:
```

```
if r:wsupgrade() then
    r:wswrite("Write something: ")
    local line = r:wsread() or "nothing"
    r:wswrite("You wrote: " .. line);
    r:wswrite("Goodbye!")
    r:wsclose()
end
```

Logging Functions

```
-- examples of logging messages
r:trace1("This is a trace log message") -- trace1 through trace8 can be
r:debug("This is a debug log message")
r:info("This is an info log message")
r:notice("This is a notice log message")
r:warn("This is a warn log message")
r:err("This is an err log message")
r:alert("This is an alert log message")
r:crit("This is a crit log message")
r:emerg("This is an emerg log message")
```

apache2 Package

A package named `apache2` is available with (at least) the following contents.

apache2.OK internal constant OK. Handlers should return this if they've handled the request.

apache2.DECLINED internal constant DECLINED. Handlers should return this if they are not going to handle the request.

apache2.DONE internal constant DONE.

apache2.version Apache HTTP server version string

apache2.HTTP_MOVED_TEMPORARILY HTTP status code

apache2.PROXYREQ_NONE, apache2.PROXYREQ_PROXY, apache2.PROXYREQ_REVERSE, apache2.PRO
internal constants used by MOD_PROXY

apache2.AUTHZ_DENIED, apache2.AUTHZ_GRANTED, apache2.AUTHZ_NEUTRAL, apache2.AUTHZ_GE
internal constants used by MOD_AUTHZ_CORE

(Other HTTP status codes are not yet implemented.)

Modifying contents with Lua filters

Filter functions implemented via LUAINPUTFILTER or LUAOUTPUTFILTER are designed as three-stage non-blocking functions using coroutines to suspend and resume a function as buckets are sent down the filter chain. The core structure of such a function is:

```
function filter(r)
    -- Our first yield is to signal that we are ready to receive buckets.
```

```
    -- Before this yield, we can set up our environment, check for conditions,
    -- and, if we deem it necessary, decline filtering a request alltogether:
    if something_bad then
        return -- This would skip this filter.
    end
    -- Regardless of whether we have data to prepend, a yield MUST be called he
    -- Note that only output filters can prepend data. Input filters must use t
    -- final stage to append data to the content.
    coroutine.yield([optional header to be prepended to the content])

    -- After we have yielded, buckets will be sent to us, one by one, and we ca
    -- do whatever we want with them and then pass on the result.
    -- Buckets are stored in the global variable 'bucket', so we create a loop
    -- that checks if 'bucket' is not nil:
    while bucket ~= nil do
        local output = mangle(bucket) -- Do some stuff to the content
        coroutine.yield(output) -- Return our new content to the filter chain
    end

    -- Once the buckets are gone, 'bucket' is set to nil, which will exit the
    -- loop and land us here. Anything extra we want to append to the content
    -- can be done by doing a final yield here. Both input and output filters
    -- can append data to the content in this phase.
    coroutine.yield([optional footer to be appended to the content])
end
```

Database connectivity

Mod_lua implements a simple database feature for querying and running commands on the most popular database engines (mySQL, PostgreSQL, FreeTDS, ODBC, SQLite, Oracle) as well as mod_dbd.

The example below shows how to acquire a database handle and return information from a table:

```
function handle(r)
    -- Acquire a database handle
    local database, err = r:dbacquire("mysql", "server=localhost,user=someuser,
    if not err then
        -- Select some information from it
        local results, err = database:select(r, "SELECT `name`, `age` FROM `peo
        if not err then
            local rows = results(0) -- fetch all rows synchronously
            for k, row in pairs(rows) do
                r:puts( string.format("Name: %s, Age: %s<br/>", row[1], row[2])
            end
        else
            r:puts("Database query error: " .. err)
        end
        database:close()
    else
        r:puts("Could not connect to the database: " .. err)
    end
end
```

To utilize MOD_DBD, specify mod_dbd as the database type, or leave the field blank:

```
local database = r:dbacquire("mod_dbd")
```

Database object and contained functions

The database object returned by dbacquire has the following methods:

Normal select and query from a database:

```
-- Run a statement and return the number of rows affected:
local affected, errmsg = database:query(r, "DELETE FROM 'tbl' WHERE 1")

-- Run a statement and return a result set that can be used synchronously or as
local result, errmsg = database:select(r, "SELECT * FROM 'people' WHERE 1")
```

Using prepared statements (recommended):

```
-- Create and run a prepared statement:
local statement, errmsg = database:prepare(r, "DELETE FROM 'tbl' WHERE 'age' >
if not errmsg then
    local result, errmsg = statement:query(20) -- run the statement with age >
end

-- Fetch a prepared statement from a DBDPrepareSQL directive:
local statement, errmsg = database:prepared(r, "someTag")
if not errmsg then
    local result, errmsg = statement:select("John Doe", 123) -- inject the valu
end
```

Escaping values, closing databases etc:

```
-- Escape a value for use in a statement:
local escaped = database:escape(r, [["'|blabla]])

-- Close a database connection and free up handles:
database:close()

-- Check whether a database connection is up and running:
local connected = database:active()
```

Working with result sets

The result set returned by db:select or by the prepared statement functions created through db:prepare can be used to fetch rows synchronously or asynchronously, depending on the row number specified:
result(0) fetches all rows in a synchronous manner, returning a table of rows.
result(-1) fetches the next available row in the set, asynchronously.
result(N) fetches row number N, asynchronously:

```
-- fetch a result set using a regular query:
local result, err = db:select(r, "SELECT * FROM 'tbl' WHERE 1")
```

```
local rows = result(0) -- Fetch ALL rows synchronously
local row = result(-1) -- Fetch the next available row, asynchronously
local row = result(1234) -- Fetch row number 1234, asynchronously
local row = result(-1, true) -- Fetch the next available row, using row names a
```

One can construct a function that returns an iterative function to iterate over all rows in a synchronous or asynchronous way, depending on the async argument:

```
function rows(resultset, async)
    local a = 0
    local function getnext()
        a = a + 1
        local row = resultset(-1)
        return row and a or nil, row
    end
    if not async then
        return pairs(resultset(0))
    else
        return getnext, self
    end
end

local statement, err = db:prepare(r, "SELECT * FROM `tbl` WHERE `age` > %u")
if not err then
     -- fetch rows asynchronously:
    local result, err = statement:select(20)
    if not err then
        for index, row in rows(result, true) do
            ....
        end
    end

     -- fetch rows synchronously:
    local result, err = statement:select(20)
    if not err then
        for index, row in rows(result, false) do
            ....
        end
    end
end
```

Closing a database connection

Database handles should be closed using `database:close()` when they are no longer needed. If you do not close them manually, they will eventually be garbage collected and closed by mod_lua, but you may end up having too many unused connections to the database if you leave the closing up to mod_lua. Essentially, the following two measures are the same:

```
-- Method 1: Manually close a handle
local database = r:dbacquire("mod_dbd")
database:close() -- All done
```

```
-- Method 2: Letting the garbage collector close it
local database = r:dbacquire("mod_dbd")
database = nil -- throw away the reference
collectgarbage() -- close the handle via GC
```

Precautions when working with databases

Although the standard `query` and `run` functions are freely available, it is recommended that you use prepared statements whenever possible, to both optimize performance (if your db handle lives on for a long time) and to minimize the risk of SQL injection attacks. `run` and `query` should only be used when there are no variables inserted into a statement (a static statement). When using dynamic statements, use `db:prepare` or `db:prepared`.

LuaAuthzProvider Directive

Description:	Plug an authorization provider function into MOD_AUTHZ_CORE
Syntax:	`LuaAuthzProvider provider_name /path/to/lua/script.lua function_name`
Context:	server config
Status:	Experimental
Module:	mod_lua
Compatibility:	2.4.3 and later

After a lua function has been registered as authorization provider, it can be used with the REQUIRE directive:

```
LuaRoot "/usr/local/apache2/lua"
LuaAuthzProvider foo authz.lua authz_check_foo
<Location "/">
  Require foo johndoe
</Location>
```

```
require "apache2"
function authz_check_foo(r, who)
    if r.user ~= who then return apache2.AUTHZ_DENIED
    return apache2.AUTHZ_GRANTED
end
```

LuaCodeCache Directive

Description:	Configure the compiled code cache.
Syntax:	`LuaCodeCache stat|forever|never`
Default:	`LuaCodeCache stat`
Context:	server config, virtual host, directory, .htaccess
Override:	All
Status:	Experimental
Module:	mod_lua

Specify the behavior of the in-memory code cache. The default is stat, which stats the top level script (not any included ones) each time that file is needed, and reloads it if the modified time indicates it is newer than the one it has already loaded. The other values cause it to keep the file cached forever (don't stat and replace) or to never cache the file.

In general stat or forever is good for production, and stat or never for development.

Examples:

```
LuaCodeCache stat
LuaCodeCache forever
LuaCodeCache never
```

LuaHookAccessChecker Directive

Description:	Provide a hook for the access_checker phase of request processing
Syntax:	`LuaHookAccessChecker /path/to/lua/script.lua hook_function_name [early|late]`
Context:	server config, virtual host, directory, .htaccess
Override:	All
Status:	Experimental
Module:	mod_lua
Compatibility:	The optional third argument is supported in 2.3.15 and later

Add your hook to the access_checker phase. An access checker hook function usually returns OK, DECLINED, or HTTP_FORBIDDEN.

**Ordering**

The optional arguments "early" or "late" control when this script runs relative to other modules.

LuaHookAuthChecker Directive

Description:	Provide a hook for the auth_checker phase of request processing
Syntax:	`LuaHookAuthChecker /path/to/lua/script.lua hook_function_name [early|late]`
Context:	server config, virtual host, directory, .htaccess
Override:	All
Status:	Experimental
Module:	mod_lua
Compatibility:	The optional third argument is supported in 2.3.15 and later

Invoke a lua function in the auth_checker phase of processing a request. This can be used to implement arbitrary authentication and authorization checking. A very simple example:

```
require 'apache2'

-- fake authcheck hook
-- If request has no auth info, set the response header and
-- return a 401 to ask the browser for basic auth info.
-- If request has auth info, don't actually look at it, just
-- pretend we got userid 'foo' and validated it.
-- Then check if the userid is 'foo' and accept the request.
function authcheck_hook(r)

   -- look for auth info
   auth = r.headers_in['Authorization']
   if auth ~= nil then
     -- fake the user
     r.user = 'foo'
   end
```

```
    if r.user == nil then
        r:debug("authcheck: user is nil, returning 401")
        r.err_headers_out['WWW-Authenticate'] = 'Basic realm="WallyWorld"'
        return 401
    elseif r.user == "foo" then
        r:debug('user foo: OK')
    else
        r:debug("authcheck: user='" .. r.user .. "'")
        r.err_headers_out['WWW-Authenticate'] = 'Basic realm="WallyWorld"'
        return 401
    end
    return apache2.OK
end
```

**Ordering**

The optional arguments "early" or "late" control when this script runs relative to other modules.

LuaHookCheckUserID Directive

Description:	Provide a hook for the check_user_id phase of request processing
Syntax:	`LuaHookCheckUserID /path/to/lua/script.lua hook_function_name [early|late]`
Context:	server config, virtual host, directory, .htaccess
Override:	All
Status:	Experimental
Module:	mod_lua
Compatibility:	The optional third argument is supported in 2.3.15 and later

...

**Ordering**

The optional arguments "early" or "late" control when this script runs relative to other modules.

LuaHookFixups Directive

Description:	Provide a hook for the fixups phase of a request processing
Syntax:	`LuaHookFixups /path/to/lua/script.lua hook_function_name`
Context:	server config, virtual host, directory, .htaccess
Override:	All
Status:	Experimental
Module:	mod_lua

Just like LuaHookTranslateName, but executed at the fixups phase

LuaHookInsertFilter Directive

Description:	Provide a hook for the insert_filter phase of request processing
Syntax:	`LuaHookInsertFilter /path/to/lua/script.lua hook_function_name`
Context:	server config, virtual host, directory, .htaccess
Override:	All
Status:	Experimental
Module:	mod_lua

Not Yet Implemented

LuaHookLog Directive

Description:	Provide a hook for the access log phase of a request processing
Syntax:	`LuaHookLog /path/to/lua/script.lua log_function_name`
Context:	server config, virtual host, directory, .htaccess
Override:	All
Status:	Experimental
Module:	mod_lua

This simple logging hook allows you to run a function when httpd enters the logging phase of a request. With it, you can append data to your own logs, manipulate data before the regular log is written, or prevent a log entry from being created. To prevent the usual logging from happening, simply return `apache2.DONE` in your logging handler, otherwise return `apache2.OK` to tell httpd to log as normal.

Example:

```
LuaHookLog "/path/to/script.lua" logger
```

```
-- /path/to/script.lua --
function logger(r)
    -- flip a coin:
    -- If 1, then we write to our own Lua log and tell httpd not to log
    -- in the main log.
    -- If 2, then we just sanitize the output a bit and tell httpd to
    -- log the sanitized bits.

    if math.random(1,2) == 1 then
        -- Log stuff ourselves and don't log in the regular log
        local f = io.open("/foo/secret.log", "a")
        if f then
            f:write("Something secret happened at " .. r.uri .. "\n")
            f:close()
        end
        return apache2.DONE -- Tell httpd not to use the regular logging functi
    else
        r.uri = r.uri:gsub("somesecretstuff", "") -- sanitize the URI
        return apache2.OK -- tell httpd to log it.
    end
end
```

LuaHookMapToStorage Directive

Description:	Provide a hook for the map_to_storage phase of request processing
Syntax:	`LuaHookMapToStorage /path/to/lua/script.lua hook_function_name`
Context:	server config, virtual host, directory, .htaccess
Override:	All
Status:	Experimental
Module:	mod_lua

Like LUAHOOKTRANSLATENAME but executed at the map-to-storage phase of a request. Modules like mod_cache run at this phase, which makes for an interesting example on what to do here:

```
LuaHookMapToStorage "/path/to/lua/script.lua" check_cache

require"apache2"
cached_files = {}

function read_file(filename)
    local input = io.open(filename, "r")
    if input then
        local data = input:read("*a")
        cached_files[filename] = data
        file = cached_files[filename]
        input:close()
    end
    return cached_files[filename]
end

function check_cache(r)
    if r.filename:match("%.png$") then -- Only match PNG files
        local file = cached_files[r.filename] -- Check cache entries
        if not file then
            file = read_file(r.filename)  -- Read file into cache
        end
        if file then -- If file exists, write it out
            r.status = 200
            r:write(file)
            r:info(("Sent %s to client from cache"):format(r.filename))
            return apache2.DONE -- skip default handler for PNG files
        end
    end
    return apache2.DECLINED -- If we had nothing to do, let others serve this.
end
```

LuaHookTranslateName Directive

Description:	Provide a hook for the translate name phase of request processing
Syntax:	`LuaHookTranslateName /path/to/lua/script.lua hook_function_name [early|late]`
Context:	server config, virtual host
Override:	All
Status:	Experimental
Module:	mod_lua
Compatibility:	The optional third argument is supported in 2.3.15 and later

Add a hook (at APR_HOOK_MIDDLE) to the translate name phase of request processing. The hook function receives a single argument, the request_rec, and should return a status code, which is either an HTTP error code, or the constants defined in the apache2 module: apache2.OK, apache2.DECLINED, or apache2.DONE.

For those new to hooks, basically each hook will be invoked until one of them returns apache2.OK. If your hook doesn't want to do the translation it should just return apache2.DECLINED. If the request should stop processing, then return apache2.DONE.

Example:

```
# httpd.conf
LuaHookTranslateName "/scripts/conf/hooks.lua" silly_mapper

-- /scripts/conf/hooks.lua --
require "apache2"
function silly_mapper(r)
    if r.uri == "/" then
        r.filename = "/var/www/home.lua"
        return apache2.OK
    else
        return apache2.DECLINED
    end
end
```

⟹ **Context**
This directive is not valid in <DIRECTORY>, <FILES>, or htaccess context.

⟹ **Ordering**
The optional arguments "early" or "late" control when this script runs relative to other modules.

LuaHookTypeChecker Directive

Description:	Provide a hook for the type_checker phase of request processing
Syntax:	`LuaHookTypeChecker /path/to/lua/script.lua hook_function_name`
Context:	server config, virtual host, directory, .htaccess
Override:	All
Status:	Experimental
Module:	mod_lua

This directive provides a hook for the type_checker phase of the request processing. This phase is where requests are assigned a content type and a handler, and thus can be used to modify the type and handler based on input:

```
LuaHookTypeChecker "/path/to/lua/script.lua" type_checker

    function type_checker(r)
        if r.uri:match("%.to_gif$") then -- match foo.png.to_gif
            r.content_type = "image/gif" -- assign it the image/gif type
            r.handler = "gifWizard"      -- tell the gifWizard module to handle
            r.filename = r.uri:gsub("%.to_gif$", "") -- fix the filename reques
            return apache2.OK
        end

        return apache2.DECLINED
    end
```

LuaInherit Directive

Description:	Controls how parent configuration sections are merged into children
Syntax:	`LuaInherit none|parent-first|parent-last`
Default:	`LuaInherit parent-first`
Context:	server config, virtual host, directory, .htaccess
Override:	All
Status:	Experimental
Module:	mod_lua
Compatibility:	2.4.0 and later

By default, if LuaHook* directives are used in overlapping Directory or Location configuration sections, the scripts defined in the more specific section are run *after* those defined in the more generic section (LuaInherit parent-first). You can reverse this order, or make the parent context not apply at all.

In previous 2.3.x releases, the default was effectively to ignore LuaHook* directives from parent configuration sections.

LuaInputFilter Directive

Description:	Provide a Lua function for content input filtering
Syntax:	`LuaInputFilter filter_name /path/to/lua/script.lua function_name`
Context:	server config
Status:	Experimental
Module:	mod_lua
Compatibility:	2.4.5 and later

Provides a means of adding a Lua function as an input filter. As with output filters, input filters work as coroutines, first yielding before buffers are sent, then yielding whenever a bucket needs to be passed down the chain, and finally (optionally) yielding anything that needs to be appended to the input data. The global variable `bucket` holds the buckets as they are passed onto the Lua script:

```
LuaInputFilter myInputFilter "/www/filter.lua" input_filter
<Files "*.lua">
  SetInputFilter myInputFilter
</Files>
```

```
--[[
    Example input filter that converts all POST data to uppercase.
]]--
function input_filter(r)
    print("luaInputFilter called") -- debug print
    coroutine.yield() -- Yield and wait for buckets
    while bucket do -- For each bucket, do...
        local output = string.upper(bucket) -- Convert all POST data to upperca
        coroutine.yield(output) -- Send converted data down the chain
    end
    -- No more buckets available.
    coroutine.yield("&filterSignature=1234") -- Append signature at the end
end
```

The input filter supports denying/skipping a filter if it is deemed unwanted:

```
function input_filter(r)
    if not good then
        return -- Simply deny filtering, passing on the original content instea
    end
    coroutine.yield() -- wait for buckets
    ... -- insert filter stuff here
end
```

See "Modifying contents with Lua filters" for more information.

LuaMapHandler Directive

Description:	Map a path to a lua handler
Syntax:	`LuaMapHandler uri-pattern /path/to/lua/script.lua [function-name]`
Context:	server config, virtual host, directory, .htaccess
Override:	All
Status:	Experimental
Module:	mod_lua

This directive matches a uri pattern to invoke a specific handler function in a specific file. It uses PCRE regular expressions to match the uri, and supports interpolating match groups into both the file path and the function name. Be careful writing your regular expressions to avoid security issues.

Examples:

```
LuaMapHandler "/(\w+)/(\w+)" "/scripts/$1.lua" "handle_$2"
```

This would match uri's such as /photos/show?id=9 to the file /scripts/photos.lua and invoke the handler function handle_show on the lua vm after loading that file.

```
LuaMapHandler "/bingo" "/scripts/wombat.lua"
```

This would invoke the "handle" function, which is the default if no specific function name is provided.

LuaOutputFilter Directive

Description:	Provide a Lua function for content output filtering
Syntax:	`LuaOutputFilter filter_name /path/to/lua/script.lua function_name`
Context:	server config
Status:	Experimental
Module:	mod_lua
Compatibility:	2.4.5 and later

Provides a means of adding a Lua function as an output filter. As with input filters, output filters work as coroutines, first yielding before buffers are sent, then yielding whenever a bucket needs to be passed down the chain, and finally (optionally) yielding anything that needs to be appended to the input data. The global variable `bucket` holds the buckets as they are passed onto the Lua script:

```
LuaOutputFilter myOutputFilter "/www/filter.lua" output_filter
<Files "*.lua">
  SetOutputFilter myOutputFilter
</Files>
```

```
--[[
    Example output filter that escapes all HTML entities in the output
]]--
function output_filter(r)
    coroutine.yield("(Handled by myOutputFilter)<br/>\n") -- Prepend some data
                                                          -- yield and wait for
    while bucket do -- For each bucket, do...
        local output = r:escape_html(bucket) -- Escape all output
        coroutine.yield(output) -- Send converted data down the chain
    end
    -- No more buckets available.
end
```

As with the input filter, the output filter supports denying/skipping a filter if it is deemed unwanted:

```
function output_filter(r)
    if not r.content_type:match("text/html") then
        return -- Simply deny filtering, passing on the original content instea
    end
    coroutine.yield() -- wait for buckets
    ... -- insert filter stuff here
end
```

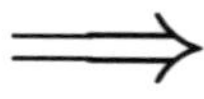**Lua filters with MOD_FILTER**

When a Lua filter is used as the underlying provider via the FILTERPROVIDER directive, filtering will only work when the *filter-name* is identical to the *provider-name*.

See "Modifying contents with Lua filters" for more information.

LuaPackageCPath Directive

Description:	Add a directory to lua's package.cpath
Syntax:	`LuaPackageCPath /path/to/include/?.soa`
Context:	server config, virtual host, directory, .htaccess
Override:	All
Status:	Experimental
Module:	mod_lua

Add a path to lua's shared library search path. Follows the same conventions as lua. This just munges the package.cpath in the lua vms.

LuaPackagePath Directive

Description:	Add a directory to lua's package.path
Syntax:	`LuaPackagePath /path/to/include/?.lua`
Context:	server config, virtual host, directory, .htaccess
Override:	All
Status:	Experimental
Module:	mod_lua

Add a path to lua's module search path. Follows the same conventions as lua. This just munges the package.path in the lua vms.

Examples:

```
LuaPackagePath "/scripts/lib/?.lua"
LuaPackagePath "/scripts/lib/?/init.lua"
```

LuaQuickHandler Directive

Description:	Provide a hook for the quick handler of request processing
Syntax:	`LuaQuickHandler /path/to/script.lua hook_function_name`
Context:	server config, virtual host
Override:	All
Status:	Experimental
Module:	mod_lua

This phase is run immediately after the request has been mapped to a virtal host, and can be used to either do some request processing before the other phases kick in, or to serve a request without the need to translate, map to storage et cetera. As this phase is run before anything else, directives such as <LOCATION> or <DIRECTORY> are void in this phase, just as URIs have not been properly parsed yet.

**Context**

This directive is not valid in <DIRECTORY>, <FILES>, or htaccess context.

LuaRoot Directive

Description:	Specify the base path for resolving relative paths for mod_lua directives
Syntax:	`LuaRoot /path/to/a/directory`
Context:	server config, virtual host, directory, .htaccess
Override:	All
Status:	Experimental
Module:	mod_lua

Specify the base path which will be used to evaluate all relative paths within mod_lua. If not specified they will be resolved relative to the current working directory, which may not always work well for a server.

LuaScope Directive

Description:	One of once, request, conn, thread – default is once
Syntax:	`LuaScope once|request|conn|thread|server [min] [max]`
Default:	`LuaScope once`
Context:	server config, virtual host, directory, .htaccess
Override:	All
Status:	Experimental
Module:	mod_lua

Specify the life cycle scope of the Lua interpreter which will be used by handlers in this "Directory." The default is "once"

once: use the interpreter once and throw it away.

request: use the interpreter to handle anything based on the same file within this request, which is also request scoped.

conn: Same as request but attached to the connection_rec

thread: Use the interpreter for the lifetime of the thread handling the request (only available with threaded MPMs).

server: This one is different than others because the server scope is quite long lived, and multiple threads will have the same server_rec. To accommodate this, server scoped Lua states are stored in an apr resource list. The `min` and `max` arguments specify the minimum and maximum number of Lua states to keep in the pool.

Generally speaking, the `thread` and `server` scopes execute roughly 2-3 times faster than the rest, because they don't have to spawn new Lua states on every request (especially with the event MPM, as even keepalive requests will use a new thread for each request). If you are satisfied that your scripts will not have problems reusing a state, then the `thread` or `server` scopes should be used for maximum performance. While the `thread` scope will provide the fastest responses, the `server` scope will use less memory, as states are pooled, allowing f.x. 1000 threads to share only 100 Lua states, thus using only 10% of the memory required by the `thread` scope.

46025812R00202

Made in the USA
San Bernardino, CA
23 February 2017